STRATEGIC ASIA 2012–13

STRATEGIC ASIA 2012–13

CHINA'S MILITARY CHALLENGE

Edited by

Ashley J. Tellis and Travis Tanner

With contributions from

Dan Blumenthal, Andrew S. Erickson, Thomas Fingar,
Christopher W. Hughes, Roy Kamphausen, Kevin Pollpeter,
Arun Sahgal, Andrew Shearer, Mark A. Stokes, and Ashley J. Tellis

 THE NATIONAL BUREAU *of* **ASIAN RESEARCH**
Seattle and Washington, D.C.

THE NATIONAL BUREAU *of* ASIAN RESEARCH

Published in the United States of America by
The National Bureau of Asian Research, Seattle, WA, and Washington, D.C.
www.nbr.org

ISBN (print): 978-0-9818904-3-2
ISBN (electronic): 978-1-939131-10-2

This material is based upon work supported in part by the Department of Energy (National Nuclear
Security Administration).

This report was prepared as an account of work sponsored by an agency of the United States
Government. Neither the United States Government nor any agency thereof, nor any of their
employees, makes any warranty, express or implied, or assumes any legal liability or responsibility
for the accuracy, completeness, or usefulness of any information, apparatus, product, or process
disclosed, or represents that its use would not infringe privately owned rights. Reference herein to
any specific commercial product, process, or service by trade name, trademark, manufacturer, or
otherwise does not constitute or imply its endorsement, recommendation, or favoring by the United
States Government or any agency thereof. The views and opinions of authors expressed herein do
not necessarily state or reflect those of the United States Government or any agency thereof.

NBR makes no warranties or representations regarding the accuracy of any map in this volume.
Depicted boundaries are meant as guidelines only and do not represent the views of NBR or
NBR's funders.

Design and publishing services by The National Bureau of Asian Research

Cover design by Stefanie Choi

Publisher's Cataloging-In-Publication Data
(Prepared by The Donohue Group, Inc.)

China's military challenge / edited by Ashley J. Tellis and Travis Tanner ; with contributions
from Dan Blumenthal ... [et al.].

   p. : ill., maps ; cm. -- (Strategic Asia 1933-6462 ; 2012-13)

   Based upon work supported in part by the Department of Energy (National Nuclear Security
Administration).

   Includes bibliographical references and index.

   ISBN: 978-0-9818904-3-2

   1. China--Military policy--21st century. 2. China--History, Military--21st century. 3. Asia-
-Military relations. 4. China--Military relations--United States. 5. United States--Military
relations--China. I. Tellis, Ashley J. II. Tanner, Travis. III. Blumenthal, Dan. IV. National
Bureau of Asian Research (U.S.) V. Series: Strategic Asia ; 2012-13.

UA835 .C55 2012

355.3/0951

Printed in Canada

The paper used in this publication meets the minimum requirement of the American National
Standard for Information Sciences—Permanence of Paper for Printed Library Materials, ANSI
Z39.48-1992.

Praise for NBR's Strategic Asia *Series*

"As America bolsters its engagement with Asia, there has never been a more pressing need for careful and thorough analysis of the world's rising military power, China. The National Bureau of Asian Research has answered that call with its latest volume, building on the excellence of previous volumes. *Strategic Asia 2012–13: China's Military Challenge* is absolutely essential reading for policymakers, government officials, and military officers alike who seek a greater understanding of what China's expanding military capabilities mean for the United States and our relationships throughout the region."

> ——DENNIS C. BLAIR, Former Director of National Intelligence and Former Commander, U.S. Pacific Command

"This is an especially important time in America's security relationships in the Asia-Pacific. NBR's Strategic Asia Program provides the vital expert insights necessary to understand new policies, new positions, and the strategic dynamic challenges emerging in the region."

> ——THOMAS B. FARGO, Former Commander, U.S. Pacific Command, and John M. Shalikashvili Chair in National Security Studies, The National Bureau of Asian Research

"NBR's *Strategic Asia* series is an unparalleled resource for the classroom, the boardroom, and the situation room. My staff used it at the NSC, and it serves as a core text for courses I now teach at Georgetown."

> ——MICHAEL J. GREEN, Former Senior Director for Asian Affairs, National Security Council, and Professor, Georgetown University

"For those interested in Asia, NBR's *Strategic Asia* series is invaluable in identifying and clarifying the strategic imperatives that our nation must confront in dealing with the most vibrant region of the world."

> ——CARLA A. HILLS, Chair and CEO, Hills and Company International Consultants, and Chair, National Committee on United States–China Relations

Contents

U.S. Responses

Special Study

Indicators

Preface

Richard J. Ellings

The Strategic Asia Program chronicles, explains, and forecasts the critical international developments in what is today the core of world power and influence. As the program has made clear for many years, according to nearly every meaningful measure—from economic and military to political—usable national power is concentrating in the Asia-Pacific, and extraordinarily so. In this new volume, *Strategic Asia 2012–13: China's Military Challenge*, we return to Strategic Asia's central concern and the theme of the highly popular 2005–06 book. We focus again on China's People's Liberation Army (PLA) because its development is shifting the balance of power in the Asia-Pacific and beyond. China's strategic posture is improving rapidly relative to that of all of its major regional competitors, including the United States, and recent Chinese assertiveness reflects this trend. Fully appreciating the range of developments that could slow or reverse China's ascent, our new volume seeks to provide an up-to-date and forward-looking analysis of (1) China's increasingly capable military and Beijing's use of it, (2) the responses of the principal states whose interests are affected, including their responses to America's rebalancing policy, (3) the rising risks to peace that are associated with these developments, and (4) the responsibilities and options now facing the United States.

The challenges of China's growing military capacity and more aggressive foreign policy come at a difficult time. The United States sustained its commitments and engagement in the Asia-Pacific through the post–Cold War period, and indeed, reflecting the growth of China and Asia more broadly, sought strategic rebalancing even before the events of September 11, 2001. That first effort to bolster attention to the region lost momentum for a decade due to the immediate requirement and subsequent decisions to fight the global war on terrorism. Though the Obama administration now seeks to refocus America's strategic attention on the Asia-Pacific and reinvigorate our alliances and partnerships in the region, such plans seem to be "colliding with the realities of the defense budget," as Dan Blumenthal argues cogently in this volume.

There is no question that the U.S. government faces exceedingly difficult economic choices. The issues at stake involve, however, nothing less than the future of U.S. influence and capacity in the world's most critical region—and probably nothing less than peace in the region. Budget decisions must therefore be made with long-term strategic interests in mind. These decisions will send loud messages about the level of our commitment and reverberate among our allies and partners and in China itself, because in these decisions we will, or will not, fund the systems, people, operations, and training upon which our capability, credibility, and leadership rest.

For three decades, the People's Republic of China (PRC) stuck mostly to a route toward self-strengthening and domestic restructuring—an apt itinerary for a country in a weaker geopolitical position—but it seems to have reached a turning point. Three decades of relative quiescence, punctuated occasionally by modest demonstrations of military power, masked an extension of economic interests and ambitions around the globe. For the past two years especially, however, the PRC has acted more in accord with much of its military history and the rising power it is. China has sent a drumbeat of increasingly aggressive signals through military and paramilitary activities from the North Pacific to the South China Sea, by a host of diplomatic initiatives and stands, and through propaganda. Two of these policies are particularly striking: an uncompromising baseline of support for the Democratic People's Republic of Korea (DPRK) despite military threats and actions by the North Koreans against their non-Communist neighbors, and the drive to absorb nearly the entirety of the South China Sea as a sovereign part of China.

The latter is informative because of China's direct confrontations and clashes with its neighbors. Over the past several decades, with an opportunistic and evolving set of diplomatic, fishing, energy development, and paramilitary and military actions, China has sought in piecemeal fashion, and by dividing ASEAN members diplomatically whenever it can, to achieve sovereignty over most of the South China Sea in spite of possessing no internationally recognized legal basis. It began with mostly nonmilitary efforts led by announcing claims; it established an administrative office with supposed jurisdiction over the area and conducted fishing and energy-related activity; it occupied islets, more intensely harassed boats from other littoral nations, and built an ever-stronger military capacity to fill the relative vacuum of the South China Sea. As next logical steps, perhaps spurred by the new U.S. policy of rebalancing and to reveal weaknesses in U.S. policy, on July 23, 2012, the

Chinese Central Military Commission announced that the PLA's Guangzhou Military Command would field a garrison in Sansha in the Paracel Islands. Then, on July 24, in spite of constituting an outpost of just hundreds of stationed Chinese, Sansha was upgraded by the PRC to a prefecture-level city with claimed jurisdiction over the major disputed island groups and undersea atolls, including the Spratlys, Paracels, and Macclesfield Bank. What all this means is that China is on a collision course with reinvigorated U.S. policy in the region, which is grounded in international law, claimants resolving their disputes through negotiations, and commitment to freedom of the seas backed up by the U.S. Navy.

Unlike the rise of Japan in the 1970s and 1980s, the rise of China is the reascent of a nation unburdened by the psychological legacies of utterly failed imperialism and horrifying experiences with nuclear weapons. Like many leaders of rising powers of the past, Chinese strategists and policymakers possess a high degree of dissatisfaction with the current international system, believing it to be tilted in favor of the United States and the other advanced democracies, all of which are perceived as working to prevent China from achieving its rightful place. The nineteenth and early and middle twentieth-century impulses of state-centric nationalism, which have moderated in developed countries, appear to remain potent in today's China. And China's leaders draw lessons from the PRC's successful military campaigns between 1949 and 1979 that achieved important strategic objectives.

In fact, since the Opium Wars, when the inadequacies of the Qing dynasty's Eight Banner armies became apparent, Chinese nationalists and political elites have understandably sought a modern fighting force capable of re-establishing Chinese sovereignty and prestige, defending Chinese interests, and maintaining domestic stability. The PRC was founded through revolution and military conquest, with the Chinese Red Army—later christened as the PLA—at the forefront and using a variety of doctrines and tactics borrowed from Soviet, European, U.S., and classical Chinese sources, as well as from Mao Zedong's own theories of "people's war." Following its defeat of the Kuomintang in 1949, the PLA continued to fight, first to solidify control of interior provinces and eventually Tibet, and second at great cost in the Korean War to prevent the United States, many nations under the United Nations banner, and the Republic of Korea from turning the tables on North Korean aggression. During the 1950s, in the aftermath of the Korean War, the PLA was greatly modernized with Soviet assistance.

In 1962, strategically coinciding with the Cuban Missile Crisis, China attacked India in the Himalayas. China's goals were multiple. The first was to punish India for granting asylum to the Dalai Lama several years earlier and for perceived meddling in Tibetan affairs, ultimately humiliating Nehru while reasserting Chinese control over disputed border areas in the Himalayas. The second was to punish Khrushchev for supporting Nehru against China on key issues, and the third was to let the United States know that China would not allow any encroachment anywhere on its territory. During the Great Proletarian Cultural Revolution of the late 1960s through mid-1970s, the PLA served simultaneously in a policing, system-stabilizing role and, ironically, as Mao's model for "continuing revolution" for new generations of Chinese who had not experienced Korea or the civil war. Most importantly in this period, the PLA fought deadly border skirmishes against Soviet troops and literally dug in to prepare for waging a war of attrition against the Soviet Union, which seemed poised to invade with a million soldiers positioned in Siberia and Mongolia. In 1979, China attacked Vietnam to "punish" it for invading and occupying Cambodia in 1978 and in the process defeating the PRC-supported Khmer Rouge. This attack, preceded by Deng Xiaoping's strategic, historic visit to the United States, served another purpose. It laid bare the incapacity of the Soviets to protect their Vietnamese allies.

Nonetheless, limited resources and Maoist doctrine left the country at the end of the 1970s with an immense and unwieldy ground force inappropriate to extraordinary international developments and new generations of weapons. Chinese leaders came to appreciate the need for major changes as the war against Vietnam was more difficult than they anticipated, the threat of a Soviet invasion dissipated in subsequent years, and they watched foreign news coverage of high-tech U.S. military actions in the first Gulf War of 1990–91. During the 1996 Taiwan Strait crisis, President Clinton ordered the *Independence* and *Nimitz* aircraft carrier battle groups to the area, demonstrating U.S. military superiority. Consequently, the PRC redoubled its effort to build the industrial and knowledge bases needed to train and equip an advanced fighting force of its own.

Even before, beginning under the leadership of Deng Xiaoping, national defense was specifically championed as one of the "four modernizations," alongside industry, agriculture, and science and technology, areas where China sought to learn from foreign advances in order to improve its own lagging competence. As China's economic base and military budgets grew, the PLA sought to move beyond defensive doctrines and plan for the challenges of the 21st century and beyond. The modernization of the Chinese military was initially dependent on foreign arms and expertise. However, along with industrial and technological gains China demonstrated greater capacity to produce and field components of a modern military, although its ability to innovate and produce new capabilities remains uncertain.

New capabilities have brought new doctrine and "new historic missions" for the PLA, which include protecting China's foreign economic interests and expansive definitions of Chinese territorial seas, particularly the South China Sea. The Chinese military now aspires to greater things than simply protecting the homeland and sustaining domestic stability.

While the PLA remains significantly less capable than the U.S. military and lacks recent combat experience, the PLA's ambitions, advancing capabilities, increasing confidence, and growing assertiveness raise questions about the ability of the United States to project power in the region—as our alliance responsibilities require—and preserve open access to the global commons necessary for international trade and prosperity. China's increasing military strength and assertiveness are inspiring a variety of responses from its neighbors, many of whom seek to maintain good relations with Beijing while cultivating strategic partnerships and new military capabilities to counter China's growing might—all the while wondering when "bandwagoning" might be the wiser choice.

History reminds us that serious tensions are inevitable when neighboring states grow at uneven rates, and particularly between a major rising power and the existing world power. Political systems matter enormously too. While China should have the opportunity to grow into an appropriately weighty role in world affairs, its authoritarian government, lack of transparency, potential instability, demonstrated dissatisfaction with international arrangements and national borders on land and at sea, and rising nationalism create legitimate concerns internationally about how it will use its growing power. The PRC's robust military history, including using military force for strategic purposes, should not be lost on any strategic analyst. Added together, these factors require that the fundamental changes that are underway in the balance of power must be managed no less than brilliantly. While the bulk of responsibility for this job falls on China moderating its policies and not underestimating its competitors, and on the United States maintaining a steady, but calibrated, policy and revitalizing its economy at home, judicious contributions will need to be made by the other regional players. Frankly, in my lifetime I can recall no international challenges greater in complexity or gravity than today's challenges in Asia.

Acknowledgments

The National Bureau of Asian Research (NBR) has a long and proud history of involvement in the study of the Chinese military, centered for the past six years on the annual PLA Conference, which is the premier conference on China's armed forces held in the United States. NBR co-hosts the program with the Strategic Studies Institute of the U.S. Army War College and U.S. Pacific Command. The results of the PLA Conference are released each year in an edited volume. This year's *Strategic Asia* volume complements this tradition of advanced research and rigorous discussion on the Chinese military.

Over the past year, as the U.S. government has announced and begun implementing plans for strategic rebalancing toward the Asia-Pacific, NBR has responded with renewed focus on the strategic dynamics in the region. This fall, the Kenneth B. and Anne H.H. Pyle Center will organize an international conference examining recent and upcoming elections and other leadership changes taking place throughout Northeast Asia, in part to memorialize the late Senator Henry M. Jackson in the one-hundredth year since his birth.

This year NBR welcomed Abraham Denmark as a senior project director. His expertise extends from political and security issues involving the Asia-Pacific to U.S. strategy toward the region. In addition to serving as an advisor to the Strategic Asia Program, he manages several NBR programs, including the John M. Shalikashvili Chair in National Security Studies, now held by Admiral Thomas B. Fargo (retired).

The Strategic Asia database, redesigned last year to include a cutting-edge geospatial mapping tool incorporating satellite imagery, was further enhanced in 2012. In addition to the mapping feature, which displays current and historical Asian military developments, including international military exercises, we have updated the database to include data for 70 indicators across 37 countries from 1990 to 2011. Under the guidance of NBR senior vice president Karolos Karnikis and senior project director Travis Tanner, interns Nicholas Steiner, Naomi McMillen, and Gregory Chaffin worked extensively to ensure the timely addition of current data.

This year's volume would not have been possible without the hard work and dedication of many individuals. The program's senior advisor—founding research director Aaron Friedberg, professor of politics at Princeton University and former deputy national security advisor to the vice president—provided invaluable guidance and support. Dr. Friedberg served as the first research director for the Strategic Asia Program. His scholarship and support are directly responsible for the success of many programs at NBR, including Strategic Asia.

For nine consecutive years, Ashley Tellis has served as research director of the Strategic Asia Program. As always, the volume's pertinent focus and the high quality of the authors are testaments to his essential leadership and expertise. Travis Tanner continues to manage the Strategic Asia Program as part of his extensive portfolio at NBR, which includes directing the Kenneth B. and Anne H.H. Pyle Center for Northeast Asian Studies. As senior program director, Travis made important contributions at every stage of the book production process and worked to build cohesiveness across the program.

Erin Fried and Gregory Chaffin provided logistical support for the production of this year's book and the planning of launch events surrounding its release. NBR's editorial team—Joshua Ziemkowski, publications director; Jessica Keough, managing editor of *Asia Policy*; Jonathan Walton, former Next Generation Fellow and newly appointed project manager; copyeditors Marites Mendoza and Rebecca Kennedy; and publications intern Noelle Jung—was responsible for the technical editing, layout, and proofreading of the entire volume. Behind the scenes, the program has relied on NBR fellows and interns heavily to bring this volume to publication. Former Next Generation Fellows Anton Wishik and Jonathan Walton, along with intern Brianna Jordan, provided thorough research assistance to scholars and contributed in many other essential ways, notably by producing a high quality "Strategic Asia by the Numbers" section.

Since the inception of Strategic Asia in 2000, NBR vice president Michael Wills has worked to ensure its continued success. His efforts have contributed tremendously to sustaining the program's institutional support. In 2012, he directed an innovative outreach effort that drew on the resources of the Strategic Asia Program's extensive network in order to publish nearly a dozen online interviews with scholars and practitioners. In March, the program released the first edition of its monthly electronic newsletter, the Strategic Asia Update, featuring NBR activities, the publications of nearly 120 contributing *Strategic Asia* authors, and a graphic referencing data from the database. We look forward to publishing this newsletter on a monthly basis.

Our scholars did an extraordinary job in assessing the capabilities and implications of China's military modernization. This year, authors offered unique regional perspectives and technical insights. For our singular special study, Thomas Fingar, a distinguished fellow in the Freeman Spogli Institute for International Studies at Stanford University, wrote an exceptional chapter on the Chinese political order. Special thanks to each of our authors for their diligence in adhering to a very tight production schedule and yet producing such excellent work. These authors join a community of nearly 120 leading specialists who have written for the series. In addition, the anonymous reviewers, both scholars and government experts, also deserve acknowledgement for their substantive evaluations of the draft chapters, which were essential to developing the final product.

Finally, I would like to express my deep gratitude to the Strategic Asia Program's core sponsors—the Lynde and Harry Bradley Foundation, the National Nuclear Security Administration (NNSA) at the U.S. Department of Energy, the Smith Richardson Foundation, the Chevron Corporation, and the General Electric Company. Their support of the Strategic Asia Program is a testament to its necessity. The Bradley Foundation has generously supported the Strategic Asia Program since the beginning and continues to be a critical partner. Likewise, NNSA at the U.S. Department of Energy was early to recognize and appreciate the vision of the Strategic Asia Program, supporting it since 2002 and becoming a partner and participant in our many activities and events. I am endlessly grateful to our colleagues at these organizations for their commitment to NBR's values and mission in strengthening and informing policy toward the Asia-Pacific region.

Richard J. Ellings
President
The National Bureau of Asian Research

STRATEGIC ASIA 2012–13

OVERVIEW

EXECUTIVE SUMMARY

This chapter provides an overview of the dramatic shifts in the Asian balance of power as a result of China's military modernization over the last two decades and assesses the U.S. response.

MAIN ARGUMENT:

The military advantages that previously allowed the U.S. to deny its great-power rivals hegemony over Asia also enabled Washington to dampen regional security competition and create a liberal economic order. This order was grounded in U.S. military superiority, economic power, and willingness to bear the costs of global leadership, as well as the inability of any Asian power to prevent the U.S. from operating along the Asian littorals in defense of its allies. China's current military modernization, however, challenges the U.S. military's ability to operate in proximity to the Asian land mass, thereby threatening the larger structure of regional stability built on American hegemony.

POLICY IMPLICATIONS:

- If unarrested, the erosion of U.S. preeminence portends the rise of new hegemonies that will come to dominate Asia in time, creating a far more pernicious strategic environment.

- The increased geopolitical competition resulting from decaying U.S. hegemony will undermine regional and global economic growth.

- The U.S. needs rational policies to protect its primacy that include preserving its critical military advantages during the current budgetary crisis and rebuilding its financial and economic foundations.

Uphill Challenges: China's Military Modernization and Asian Security

Ashley J. Tellis

Although the United States was engaged in Asian geopolitics long before World War II, the decisive U.S. victory in that conflict marked a turning point in U.S.-Asian relations. The demise of Japan as a major challenger paved the way for the inauguration of a new regional order underwritten by the military power of the United States. Although a transformed order of some kind would have inevitably materialized as a result of the U.S. triumph over Japan, the Cold War that followed—involving the struggle with the Soviet Union, and with global Communism more generally—defined the specific character of the "hegemonic stability" that came to prevail in maritime Asia. It is one that survives, even if increasingly challenged, to this day.

The success of this hegemonic stability, as manifested in the postwar Asian political order, was wrought through a bitter struggle with a powerful, but ultimately weaker, coalition of Communist states. This U.S.-led system itself evolved slowly, beginning first in Northeast Asia and then extending over time to Southeast Asia in both its continental and maritime configurations. Throughout this process, it was shaped by actual or threatened conflicts with the Communist powers, who at various points threatened the local states that were U.S. allies. The military protection offered to these states against the Communist threat created the nucleus of a pacified Asian order, which survived ultimately because of the U.S. capacity to bring considerable military power to bear in its defense at different points along the Asian littoral.

Ashley J. Tellis is a Senior Associate at the Carnegie Endowment for International Peace and Research Director of the Strategic Asia Program at the National Bureau of Asian Research. He can be reached at <atellis@carnegieendowment.org>.

This ability to muster concentrated force when required along the Asian periphery was contested by Soviet power for most of the Cold War, but Moscow's challenge here was consistently overcome thanks to the United States' technological superiority, better internal balancing, and sturdy regional coalition. Furthermore, even during the height of the Cold War, when its military capabilities were at their most potent, the Soviet Union was severely handicapped in its capacity to definitively deny the United States access to maritime Asia for several reasons: the core of Soviet national power was based in the European half of its Eurasian territory rather than in its Asiatic fringes; the air and land lines of communication between European and Asiatic Russia were long, tenuous, and relatively underdeveloped, making the sustainability of Soviet military forces in the Far East a challenging proposition; and, finally, Soviet combat power adjacent to the Pacific, however significant in absolute terms, was considerably weaker than its equivalent in Europe.

These realities all combined to bequeath the United States with functional access to the Asian land mass even during the Cold War. Although the gradient imposed by distance inevitably eroded the ease with which military power could be brought to bear, these limitations were substantially circumvented by the U.S. ability to deploy powerful forward-based and forward-operating forces either in or in close proximity to Asia.[1] This extended reach was reinforced by the traditional U.S. command of the commons, especially its mastery over the open oceans, which in effect made them a "great highway" through which massive reserves of military power could be ferried from the continental United States to any trouble spots along the Asian periphery.[2] Thanks to these umbilicals, the United States became, in effect, an Asian power geopolitically, even if it was physically far removed from the continent.

The Legacy of U.S. Military Dominance in Asia

Despite the contest with the Soviet Union, U.S. military dominance laid the foundations for making East Asia one of the critical successes enjoyed by American grand strategy in the postwar era. It did so in three ways.

First, the preeminence of U.S. warfighting capabilities ensured that attempts at seeking hegemonic domination in Asia by any regional or extra-regional state would end up being both costly and ultimately unsuccessful. By

---

[1] For more on the "loss of strength gradient" (the inverse relationship between geographic distance and the amount of military power that can be brought to bear), see Kenneth E. Boulding, *Conflict and Defense: A General Theory* (New York: Harper, 1962), 262.

[2] Alfred T. Mahan, *The Influence of Sea Power upon History, 1660–1783* (1890; repr., New York: Barnes & Noble Books, 2004), 26. On the importance of access to the global commons for the U.S. military, see Barry R. Posen, "Command of the Commons: The Military Foundation of U.S. Hegemony," *International Security* 28, no. 1 (2003): 5–46.

so shaping the calculus of all potential competitors, Washington ensured—through almost half a century of containment—that the concentration of resources present in this continent, as in Europe, would not come under the control of any single competitor or a consortium of rivals who might exploit them to sustain a larger threat directed at the United States. The success of this strategy also ensured simultaneously that the United States would enjoy continued economic, political, and strategic access to this critical area of the globe, thereby cementing the still-critical role of the United States as the guarantor of regional security.

While U.S. military capabilities at both the global and the regional levels were indispensable for countering the rise of competing local hegemonies, their effectiveness was mediated through a unique and asymmetrical alliance system—often dubbed "hub and spokes" to describe the centrality of the United States in the arrangement. This system called on Washington to guarantee the security of multiple allies without requiring the protected partners to make any reciprocal commitments to U.S. safety in return. The effectiveness of such an alliance system, which was designed to contain the Soviet Union (and, initially, China as well), hinged fundamentally on the United States' ability to maintain military superiority vis-à-vis its adversaries and on its capacity to bring such superiority to bear whenever required at any specific locale along the Asian periphery.

Second, the very military advantages that permitted the United States to ultimately deny its great-power rivals hegemony over the Asian land mass also enabled Washington to dampen local security competition between the regional states, including among its own protectees. Power political rivalries among the Asian states have been among the chief causes of continental instability for centuries.[3] Although historically these competitions had generally been bounded by geography and the limitations of national military capabilities—making the struggles within local "security complexes" more significant than the rivalries across them—both these restraints appeared fragile in the postwar period. World War II had demonstrated new technologies that permitted states to apply power beyond their immediate frontiers; hence the fear that key dyadic rivalries within Northeast, Southeast, and South Asia could spill over beyond their traditional confines acquired special significance in the era of tight bipolarity, where larger confrontations escalating beyond their original precipitants were an ever-present possibility.

Where local security competitions were concerned, therefore, the interests of the two superpowers in avoiding an unwanted major war combined with the security guarantees offered by the United States to its own

---

[3] For more on the rivalrous nature of Asian politics, see Aaron L. Friedberg, "Ripe for Rivalry: Prospects for Peace in a Multipolar Asia," *International Security* 18, no. 3 (1993/1994): 5–33.

allies to tamp down many of the historical rivalries that previously marred relations between key Asian states. Although intense conflicts did occur occasionally, these were relatively limited in scope; none at any rate succeeded in either crippling the pacified enclaves populated by the United States' core allies or fundamentally transforming the Asian subsystem in a way that undermined U.S. power in the long run. Many of the biggest convulsions in Asia during this period, in fact, involved conflicts that implicated the United States and were linked to bipolar struggles for advantage, but they did not lead to unwanted systemic conflicts. Further, large local wars that took place outside the interests of the superpowers were relatively rare, and when they did occur, failed to conclusively threaten those zones of stability inhabited by the United States' principal allies.

While tight bipolarity and U.S. power thus combined to produce a remarkable pacification of Asian politics, they did something more as well, at least within the extended U.S. alliance system to begin with: they enabled the smaller allies to concentrate their energies on economic pursuits rather than dissipating their resources excessively on national defense. This investment in "butter" over "guns," then, laid the foundation for the rapid national reconstruction that occurred in the aftermath of World War II and the reinvigoration of the alliance system that proved able to successfully contain Soviet expansionism even as it laid the foundations for a future era of intra-Asian stability.[4]

Third, the net military superiority of the United States permitted Washington to create a liberal international economic order that would have had little chance of success in the absence of overwhelming U.S. power. The economic strategy pursued by the United States during the postwar period had multiple components. It included a major aid program to the United States' war-torn allies, which was implemented with the intention of raising their economic strength in order to resist Soviet pressure. It also involved providing the allied states with asymmetric access to the U.S. market for the export of their goods and services, again without any expectation of equal U.S. access (at least during the early years). Finally, this strategy involved the creation of a global trading order that included not only the formation of new international institutions to manage global exchange, financial stability, and growth and development but also supernormal U.S. contributions to the public goods required to sustain such an order—everything from offering the dollar as the new international reserve currency to utilizing the U.S. military

---

[4] Ashley J. Tellis et al., "Sources of Conflict in Asia," in *Sources of Conflict in the 21st Century: Regional Futures and U.S. Strategy*, ed. Zalmay Khalilzad and Ian O. Lesser (Santa Monica: RAND, 1998), 46–52.

for ensuring the security of the global commons through which all trade would be conducted.[5]

The foundation of this liberal trading system would lead in time to a tighter integration of Europe and Pacific Asia with the United States. With the eventual inclusion of China, it would lead to deepened trans-Pacific and Asian-European connections as well as a wider integration of both continental and maritime Asia itself. Altogether, the system would eventually propel the phenomenon of globalization wherein both friends and rivals would, in one more rare episode, find themselves enmeshed in economic ties of unbelievable density and diversity. While the success of globalization—and the "Asian miracle" that both preceded and continues to sustain it—is usually explained largely on the basis of comparative advantage, the fact of the matter is that it could not have materialized without the reassuring presence of U.S. military power.

Absent the strong guarantees of security arising from the presence of U.S. power, it is highly unlikely that national rivals would engage in sustained international trade because of their fears that the gains from trade would be asymmetrically distributed and, even worse, often applied by their competitors to the production of military instruments that could undermine their security. To the degree that the Asian states have continued to trade with their neighbors (who often are either larger powers or political rivals), this commerce has survived not only because the absolute gains are indeed valuable but also, and more importantly, because superior U.S. military power has provided the assurance that no trading partner would be able to use the fruits of trade to threaten the security of the others without running afoul of the United States.

The legacy of U.S. military dominance born out of World War II thus came to have significant salutary benefits for stability in Asia. It served as a robust defense for the protection of the United States' treaty allies against both Communist and internal threats. And it served to dampen the traditional security competition that would have materialized thanks to the historical rivalries among local Asian states. U.S. power, consequently, became the instrument for the relative pacification of Asia, pacification understood not as the eradication of war but as the mitigation of threats faced by key U.S. allies and the prevention of any radical disruptions to the continental balance of power. The presence of this new order—which hinged on the military capabilities of the United States—would progressively nurture a new economic order as well, one that began through deepened trading relationships between

---

[5] For a discussion of the contribution of the U.S.-created economic order to the growth of states, see Michael Mastanduno, "System Maker and Privilege Taker: U.S. Power and the International Political Economy," *World Politics* 61, no. 1 (2009): 121–22, 124, 147–48.

the United States and its allies but slowly extended to incorporate neutrals and even erstwhile and potential rivals—to the degree that they chose to participate in this order.

In retrospect, then, the structural conditions that permitted the creation and maintenance of this order can be readily discerned. They include the following factors:

- The economic hegemony of the United States globally, which was amplified by the use of the dollar as the international reserve currency, fiscal stability at home, and a highly effective national innovation system that underwrote repeated cycles of transformative growth

- The political willingness within the United States to bear the costs of global leadership as evinced through the bipartisan consensus on protecting American hegemony, which in turn spawned diverse domestic policies oriented toward expanding the nation's power

- The irreducible military superiority of the United States, encompassing both the nuclear and conventional realms and extending to at least functional mastery over the global commons in the face of serious challenges from the Soviet Union and sometimes lesser states

- The inability of any of the Asian powers to decisively threaten the security of key neighbors in a system-transforming manner, as well as their incapacity to undermine the U.S. ability to defend its regional allies or to impede the United States from either operating freely in the continent or bringing force to bear at any point along the Asian littorals

The concatenation of these variables paved the way for the U.S. victory during the Cold War. In fact, this victory was finally procured because Washington succeeded in enjoying the best of both worlds: it maintained a remarkable degree of military advantage despite Soviet opposition, while at the same time sustaining an open economic system at home and an open trading system abroad, both of which interacted to permit the United States and its close allies to grow at a rate much faster than the autarkic economies of its opponents. The fact that the United States' allies were able to regenerate their national power so quickly after the devastation of World War II was also a testament to the enlightened elites in these countries: they consciously pursued economic strategies that enabled their nations to make the best of the open economic order that the United States maintained in its interest but which provided collective benefits. The rise of these allies, such as Japan, South Korea, Taiwan, and eventually the smaller Southeast Asian "tigers," undoubtedly portended the relative decline of the United States. But such a decline was judged acceptable because these were friendly states threatened by common enemies, and their revival was judged—correctly—to be essential for the larger success of containment.[6]

Yet the ascendancy of these allies signaled a serious problem that marks all imperial orders, namely, that success produces transformations that can lead to their undoing. This phenomenon would be manifested even more clearly in the second iteration of the Asian miracle when the United States finally consented to admit its one-time Cold War foe, China, into the global trading system.

Asia's Looming Challenge: Chinese Military Modernization

China's own domestic reforms, which liberated the Chinese economy from centralized control without, however, replacing it entirely with a market economy, produced explosive effects when the country came to be embedded in the larger liberal trading system. As the historical record now demonstrates, it led to the single most dramatic episode of sustained growth in modern times, with China chalking upward of, or close to, double-digit growth rates for some 30 years. Within a generation, this transformation made China the world's second-largest economy, a dynamic participant in global trade, the new center for global manufacturing, and the largest creditor in the global economy.[7]

In the wake of China's economic success, however, serious challenges have developed for the United States. The rise of China has generated three specific and simultaneous problems.

At the economic level, for all the benefits that interdependence with China has brought the United States in terms of consumer welfare, capital flows, and corporate competitiveness, China's ascendancy has accelerated what globalization had already set in motion: deindustrialization at home and a contraction in the size of the U.S. middle class, especially those blue-collar segments that depended on manufacturing for their livelihood. The shift of manufacturing abroad has also resulted in the greater diffusion of technology, including high technology, and has spawned new sources of innovation in China thanks to the technology and skill shifts arising from U.S. joint

---

[6] For an elaboration of this argument, see Ashley J. Tellis, "Power Shift: How the West Can Adapt and Thrive in an Asian Century," German Marshall Fund of the United States, Asia Paper Series, January 2010, http://www.gmfus.org/galleries/ct_publication_attachments/AsiaPowerShiftGMFPaper.pdf.

[7] For more on China's explosive growth and what the country will need to do to sustain it, see World Bank and Development Research Center of the State Council for the People's Republic of China, *China 2030: Building a Modern, Harmonious, and Creative High-Income Society* (Washington, D.C.: World Bank, 2012).

ventures. Finally, the "codependency" that has developed between the United States and China has transformed Washington into an inveterate debtor. The United States is increasingly reliant on foreign borrowings (including from China) to sustain its large budgetary and current account deficits at a time when the paralysis in domestic politics prevents Washington from pursuing economic policies that might advance its ambitions at rebalancing.

At the geopolitical level, the United States is confronted with a challenge that it never faced in its rivalry with the Soviet Union: the growing dependence of its own allies and key neutrals in Asia on China for markets, capital, goods, and in many cases even technology. China's enormous size and its huge economy have made it the center of a highly integrated Asian economic system, where the growth of every country on its periphery increasingly depends on the extent and density of the linkages enjoyed with China. Such intermeshing inevitably produces geopolitical effects insofar as it makes the littoral nations, even when formally allied with the United States, more sensitive to Chinese interests than they would otherwise be in the absence of regional integration. Even if this process does not lead eventually to the creation of a hermetic trading bloc that excludes the United States—an unlikely prospect for now—it creates an expanded Chinese sphere of influence that, enveloping the United States' allies and important neutrals, complicates their decision-making as they attempt to juggle competing demands pertaining to security and prosperity.

At the military level, the challenges posed by growing Chinese power to the U.S. order in Asia are perhaps the most acute and immediate. At the simplest level, three decades of relentless Chinese economic growth have provided the country's leaders with the resources required to transform what was a relatively obsolete military force throughout the Cold War into a modern, and dramatically improving, instrument of coercive power.

If the progressive modernization of the Chinese military were to be merely an ordinary extension of China's economic growth, it might have produced less reason for concern, though even that is debatable. The persistence of the "security dilemma" in competitive international politics generally ensures that any improvements in military capacity, even if unaccompanied by questionable intentions, invariably create anxiety and suspicion in neighboring states because of the increased possibility of harm. In the case of China, the security dilemmas associated with its military modernization become even more acute for other reasons. For starters, China's great size and the sheer resources allocated by Beijing to its military exacerbates regional concerns because most of its neighbors, with a few exceptions like Russia, Japan, and India, have defense budgets that are dwarfed by China's. Even for these more capable states, China's defense expenditure gives pause because it is already between twice and thrice as large as their own. Further, China's central location makes it the geostrategic heartland of Asia: because all the regional states are located along either its continental or maritime periphery, the growth of Chinese military power affects almost every Asian state. The intensity of this impact obviously varies depending on whether the country in question has political or border disputes with China or is enmeshed in larger explicit or latent rivalries. But even countries that are at some remove from China physically are still affected by its growing military capabilities, either because they are implicated in Beijing's expansive maritime claims or because they find themselves potentially the targets of its evolving stand-off attack capabilities.

Finally, and certainly most problematically from the viewpoint of preserving American hegemonic stability in Asia, the core of Chinese military capabilities, unlike those of the erstwhile Soviet Union, are based along China's eastern seaboard, directly abutting Pacific Asia. These forces have been consciously directed, at least since 1996, at interdicting the geostrategic umbilicals that connect the United States to its Asian allies and have been responsible for preserving the regional stability witnessed in the postwar era. The impetus for creating instruments that would undermine U.S. extended deterrence in Asia derived initially from the Sino-American wrangling over Taiwan: Beijing fears that the island will one day assert *de jure* independence under the political cover offered by U.S. military protection. Ever since such a development appeared as a realistic possibility in the mid-1990s, China reoriented its armed forces toward servicing two critical warfighting missions: overwhelming the island's defenses by force, if necessary, in order to preclude a conclusive break with the mainland, while at the same time preventing its U.S. ally from bringing rearward reinforcements to bear in support of Taiwan and operating in its defense.

This investment in anti-access/area-denial (A2/AD) capabilities is manifested in the formidable land-based "reconnaissance-strike complex" that China has assiduously built during the last two decades. This capability is anchored in an extensive intelligence, surveillance, and reconnaissance (ISR) system that includes terrestrial and space-based sensors to detect, track, and target mobile U.S. military systems operating at great distances from Chinese territory, as well as activities at fixed U.S. bases throughout the Pacific. This information, supplemented by other intelligence collected by Chinese naval and air elements, is then disseminated to various Chinese offensive forces through a national command-and-control grid.[8]

---

[8] For a useful survey of China's A2/AD capabilities, see Roger Cliff, Mark Burles, Michael S. Chase, Derek Eaton, and Kevin L. Pollpeter, *Entering the Dragon's Lair: Chinese Antiaccess Strategies and Their Implications for the United States* (Santa Monica: RAND, 2007).

Thanks to the problems provoked by Taiwan, China's current military modernization has thus been explicitly designed to keep the United States entirely out of its "near seas" by controlling access to their farther approaches through a variety of stand-off attacks that, if successful, would transform the western Pacific into a contained enclosure where Chinese dominance is assured because of China's ability to neutralize U.S. military power. Even as Beijing has steadily improved its capacity to meet this goal, however, it has also sustained a wider military modernization aimed at improving its larger warfighting capabilities across all combat arms—land, air, and sea—and in every dimension: manpower, technology, training, doctrine, organization, logistics, and command and control. China has also demonstrated dramatic improvements where the utilization of critical enablers is concerned: space, electronic warfare, cyberwarfare, and nuclear weaponry and their associated delivery systems.

As these capabilities have been steadily integrated into its arsenal, China—unsurprisingly—has begun to move gingerly in the direction of conceptualizing how its military forces might secure its wider interests as a great power. This shift beyond merely controlling the country's periphery was signaled in 2004 when Hu Jintao committed the People's Liberation Army (PLA) to "new historic missions" that went beyond the previous focus on safeguarding China's territory, sovereignty, unity, and security.[9] The new missions emphasized instead the importance of protecting the Chinese Communist Party (CCP), safeguarding China's expanding national interests, and contributing to the preservation of world peace. The promulgation of these new tasks clearly indicated that China's growing power and expanding interests demanded that its military forces expand, as Hu phrased it, "our field of vision for security strategy and military strategy." As China's 2006 white paper would subsequently elaborate, implementing these new historic missions would require expanded military capabilities and a new Chinese proficiency in diverse spatial and functional areas, including information warfare, trans- and extra-regional mobility, long-distance maneuverability, effective counterterrorism, extended maritime depth, strategic air projection, and robust strategic nuclear deterrence.[10]

---

[9] For more on the PLA's new historic missions, see James Mulvenon, "Chairman Hu and the PLA's 'New Historic Missions,'" *China Leadership Monitor*, no. 27 (2009), http://media.hoover.org/sites/default/files/documents/CLM27JM.pdf.

[10] Information Office of the State Council of the People's Republic of China, *China's National Defense in 2006* (Beijing, December 2006), http://www.china.org.cn/english/features/book/194421.htm.

With such aspirations, China has embarked on a road that all other great powers have traversed before.[11] Increasing economic growth has produced material success that must be protected by ever more capable military instruments, and national interests, too, have expanded as national wealth continues to accumulate. The military investments currently pursued by China, therefore, reflect its interests in larger goals beyond simply territorial integrity, although the still significant challenges associated with this objective ensure that China's continuing military buildup will never be permitted to detract from satisfying this core goal. This fact notwithstanding, China's geopolitical "field of regard" currently is larger than it has ever been in the reform era: today it is essentially global in nature, even if China's "field of view" remains focused on Asia in some concentrated way. The profound geopolitical significance of this latter fact cannot be underestimated. Because Asia remains today the material core of the evolving international order, any Chinese hegemony over even this delimited space would decisively advantage it in any future struggle for control of the global system. The distension in China's military capabilities during the last two decades has already precipitated enormous increases in its political confidence. It is again not surprising that China's behavior toward its Asian neighbors has in recent years been marked by a striking assertiveness that is rooted both in its expanding capabilities and interests and in growing Chinese perceptions of a global balance that appears to be shifting in its favor.[12]

Confronting the Challenge: America and Asia Respond

While managing the everyday consequences of such assertiveness remains the bread-and-butter task of U.S. and Asian diplomacy, what cannot be lost sight of is the fact that China's military modernization has now reached a level of maturation that portends a consequential disequilibration in the continental balance of power. As the U.S. Department of Defense had warned as early as 2005, China's ongoing military modernization "provide[s] [it] with a force capable of prosecuting a range of military operations in Asia—well beyond Taiwan—potentially posing a credible threat to modern militaries operating in the region."[13] Thanks to the fruits of improvements accruing over

---

[11] For an analysis that juxtaposes China's rise with previous power transitions, see the discussion in Michael D. Swaine and Ashley J. Tellis, *Interpreting China's Grand Strategy: Past, Present, and Future* (Santa Monica: RAND, 2000), 218–29.

[12] Suisheng Zhao, "China's New Foreign Policy 'Assertiveness': Motivations and Implications," *ISPI Analysis*, no. 54 (2011), http://www.ispionline.it/it/documents/Analysis_54_2011.pdf.

[13] Office of the U.S. Secretary of Defense, *Annual Report to Congress: The Military Power of the People's Republic of China 2005* (Washington, D.C., 2005), http://www.defense.gov/news/Jul2005/d20050719china.pdf, 13.

the last several years, China's military modernization can currently not only "put regional military balances at risk," but just as problematically threaten the U.S. military's ability to operate in proximity to the Asian land mass, thereby holding at risk the larger structure of regional stability that since World War II has been built on American hegemony.[14]

This volume of *Strategic Asia*, the twelfth in the series, focuses systematically on understanding the contours of China's ongoing military modernization and the challenges posed to different parts of the Asian land mass and to U.S. extended deterrence in Asia. Consistent with the analysis earlier in this overview, the studies in this volume take as their point of departure the fact that Asian success in the postwar period owes greatly to the hegemonic stability provided by the United States. Although this hegemonic power found manifestation in many dimensions—economic, political, ideological, and military—the larger impact of China's new military capabilities on the effectiveness of the United States as a regional security guarantor remains a special focus of this volume.

Jonathan Pollack once summarized the unique role of the United States in Asia through a metaphor, "holding the ring." The metaphor describes a situation where none of the major Asian powers had the capacity to seriously harm their rivals or prevent the United States from being able to come to an ally's aid, while the only external entity possessing puissant capabilities— the United States—lacks the incentives to use them abusively, because its power better serves larger political and economic interests.[15] Because—for the first time since the fall of the Soviet Union—China's ongoing military improvements might be on the cusp of undermining these factors that traditionally made for stability, this volume of *Strategic Asia* concentrates its gaze on this issue.

The timing of this study is appropriate for at least three reasons. First, most of the critical programs centered on developing disruptive military technologies in China in the aftermath of the 1995–96 Taiwan Strait crisis have now reached maturity and are yielding systems that are presently entering operational employment within the PLA. Second, China itself is undergoing yet another major leadership transition with new leader Xi Jinping poised to become party secretary and president. Xi's close ties with the PLA, and his ascendancy at a time when China's central presence in global politics is secure, suggest that this is an appropriate moment to take stock of what

---

[14] Office of the U.S. Secretary of Defense, *Annual Report to Congress: The Military Power of the People's Republic of China 2005.*

[15] Jonathan D. Pollack, "The United States in East Asia: Holding the Ring," in *Asia's International Role in the Post–Cold War Era: Part I Papers from the IISS 34th Annual Conference,* Adelphi Paper 275 (London: International Institute for Strategic Studies, 1993), 69–82.

the PLA's new capabilities imply for Asian security before the next iteration of technological innovations in the wings begins to materialize. Third, and finally, the *Strategic Asia* series last reviewed China's military modernization in 2005–6. The assessment at this point was still relatively optimistic in regard to the impact of China's military growth on regional stability. Much has changed during these intervening years, and even the U.S. intelligence community now admits that although there have been few surprises where the detection of new Chinese programs is concerned, the United States often has been taken aback by the pace of these programs and their speed in reaching maturity. A contemporary reassessment of China's new military capabilities and their impact on stability is therefore necessary.

Given these interests, the first part of this volume summarizes the major improvements that China has made during the last two decades in restructuring the land, air, naval, missile, space, cyber, and electronic warfare capabilities that have bestowed substantial increases in Beijing's warfighting capability. The four chapters that examine Chinese progress in these areas aim to provide a baseline of current Chinese capabilities in each arena as well as a projection of how these are slated to evolve up to circa 2025. Beyond describing technological improvements, they specifically analyze what new operational capabilities result from these programs of modernization. In other words, these chapters inform the reader about what various PLA components can do now and prospectively at the strategic, operational, and tactical levels in the relevant combat realm that they could not do before. Further, they attempt, to the degree possible, to discern the PLA's intentions in developing these capabilities and to understand—based on the PLA's own writings and commentary (as well as the assessments of others)—what the PLA specifically seeks to achieve at the various levels of combat. And, finally, each of these chapters addresses what these achievements, if realized, will enable Beijing to do in the Asian political arena, especially vis-à-vis key Asian competitors and the United States (and its forces in Asia).

Roy Kamphausen's chapter on land forces modernization serves as a penetrating reminder that for all the dramatic innovations witnessed in the PLA's arsenal recently—stealth fighters, the antiship ballistic missile, and counter-space capabilities—the core of China's combat power continues to reside in its still substantial land forces. Although the ground force components have contracted substantially since their numerical apotheosis in the mid-1980s, Kamphausen demonstrates that the PLA has moved decisively away from its traditional orientation as a static force intended mainly for internal defense *in situ* and for frontier defense along the areas it was bivouacked in during peacetime. Because China's land frontiers are relatively secure—with a few exceptions to its south and southwest—the PLA has divested its internal security responsibilities to the People's Armed Police (PAP), while remaining the safeguard of last resort available to the CCP, in order to focus on becoming a more flexible force capable of operating wherever required along China's borders. The new emphases on joint logistics, increased tactical mobility, enhanced organic firepower, and better command and control all now permit the major ground armies to deploy and operate across the military regions in which they are ordinarily based. The increased investments in training and digitization have improved the capabilities of the combat arms even further. These improvements, Kamphausen concludes, will be increasingly manifested in tailored approaches for dealing with specific foreign threats and will propel further organizational changes to permit the PLA to carry out the new historic missions that may require the force to be able to project land power around China's periphery.

Given the emphasis that China has placed on defeating the U.S. ability to reinforce its forward-operating military forces in Asia in a crisis, Andrew Erickson's chapter on the transformation of Chinese naval and air power demonstrates that Beijing takes the threats emerging off its seaboard all too seriously. Since the most important military constraints on China today are levied by maritime and aerospace powers, it is not surprising to find China focused on integrating combat aviation (across the PLA Air Force and the PLA Navy), advanced tactical missilery (of different kinds), modern surface and subsurface combatants, and unmanned aerial vehicles—all supported by various combat support aircraft and advanced air defenses—to create a barrier that limits both its regional competitors and the United States from operating freely in its vicinity. Erickson emphasizes that although these capabilities are still uneven and subject to various limitations, they are constantly improving and now bestow on China the ability to control the air and sea spaces proximate to its mainland, with decreasing control as a function of distance from its coastline. Because China's ability to dominate the water and air space of its near seas automatically impacts the security of key U.S. allies such as Japan, South Korea, and Taiwan, the stage is set for a vigorous offense-defense contest throughout the East Asian littoral. This competition in fact threatens to expand to Southeast Asia and possibly over time to the Indian Ocean as well, depending both on how China reorients its current "reconnaissance-strike complex" and on its evolving ambitions in more distant seas. Erickson's chapter serves as a critical reminder that naval and air power not only constitute key warfighting instruments for China but will increasingly be its principal tools of influence in an area that will witness greater competition because of Beijing's desire for preclusive control.

Mark Stokes's chapter focuses on the most critical instruments of Chinese power projection and ones that represent a long history of technological excellence: ballistic and cruise missiles. For various historical and institutional reasons, China developed proficiency in missile technology, especially ballistic systems, that permitted it to apply force at great distances from its homeland even when its other, more traditional instruments of power projection were either immature or ineffective. Stokes's detailed analysis of current Chinese ballistic and cruise missiles—and its institutional guardian, the Second Artillery Force—demonstrates that both nuclear and conventional precision-strike capabilities retain pride of place in China's offensive arsenal. Their diversification to new roles such as counter-carrier and counter-space operations only makes them all the more valuable, either because they can interdict key adversary assets at great distance or because their all-but-certain penetrability bequeaths them with an operational effectiveness unmatched by other systems. Stokes carefully demonstrates that China's offensive missile forces remain the cornerstone of its warfighting capabilities vis-à-vis every major regional adversary, including the United States. The continuing increase in the number of missile systems deployed, along with their supporting sensors and command-and-control capabilities, thus embodies the potential of providing the PLA with a decisive military edge in the event of conflict over territorial or sovereignty claims.

The fourth chapter in the survey of China's emerging military capabilities focuses on the vital but more intangible realms of space, cyber, and electronic warfare. These arenas of activity were traditionally conceived largely as means of shaping outcomes in other more conventional battlespaces where the interaction of firepower and maneuver provided the victory that advanced a state's political aims. Because modern warfare, however, incorporates extraordinary degrees of digitization across vast distances, dominating the three arenas has virtually become an end in itself. Kevin Pollpeter's chapter, which rounds out the volume's survey of China's military modernization, scrutinizes Beijing's approach, investments, capabilities, and impact in each of these three realms. He stresses that their importance rests on the PLA's view that these are distinct domains that must be seized and defended in order to achieve the information superiority that produces "kinetic" victories on the battlefield. On reviewing Chinese capabilities, Pollpeter concludes that the PLA has made dramatic gains and has reached advanced technology levels in at least two areas, space and cyber. It is likely that a comparable conclusion cannot be reached in the realm of electronic warfare only because there is less information publicly available about various Chinese capabilities that have been designed to control or interfere with specific segments of the electromagnetic spectrum. All the same, the evidence adduced in Pollpeter's chapter demonstrates that China has embarked on a concerted effort to exploit the benefits of integrated attacks across all three domains, to deny both its regional adversaries and the United States the freedom to operate in these realms unhindered, and, increasingly, to dominate these arenas in order to secure its own operational and strategic aims. China's activities in space, cyber, and electronic warfare, therefore, have moved beyond asymmetric strategies to reflect larger ambitions, including the need to project power globally in defense of its national interests.

Taking these assessments of new Chinese military capabilities as a backdrop, the second section of the volume seeks to understand how their impact on the existing military balances between Beijing and China's key neighbors in Northeast, Southeast, and South Asia are viewed from within these regions, as well as what the important states located there are doing in response. These chapters focus especially on how the various dimensions of Chinese military modernization detailed in the first part of the book specifically affect the security of key Chinese neighbors: how they impinge on the current military balances, or undermine some current defense plans and postures, or complicate the geopolitical challenges facing key countries or regions. Further, the chapters detail the strategies and programs adopted by these neighboring states to protect their core defense interests. And finally, they assess how these counter-responses at the levels of acquisition, doctrine, organization, and force posture fit into the larger political strategies of these nations for coping with China. In particular, they examine how these countries juggle between internal and external balancing (in the widest sense) and, equally importantly, how the United States fits into their broadest political and military strategies for managing China.

Christopher Hughes's chapter focuses on the critical northeast quadrant of Asia, which not only hosts the United States' oldest Asian allies—Japan, South Korea, and Taiwan—but also remains, in many ways, the cockpit of continental geopolitics. His conclusions are entirely sobering. In contrast to the judgments aired just a few years ago, Hughes finds that all three countries now share great concern about both the symmetric and asymmetric threats embedded in China's military modernization. China's ballistic and cruise missiles, its naval and air power systems, and its advanced air defenses are viewed as posing especially significant threats not only to these individual states but, equally importantly, to their external protector, the United States. As a result, all three regional powers—including South Korea, despite the dangers emerging from its northern neighbor—are focused on major counter-modernizations of their own. These responses, centered for the most part on the integration of advanced weapon systems as countermeasures to emerging Chinese capabilities, are intended to mitigate the symmetric threats, while buying time to cope with asymmetric challenges—even as all three states hope that continued economic engagement with China might help defuse the otherwise strong security dilemmas present in the region. The increased threat posed by new Chinese offensive capabilities, however, has had the salutary effect of dampening the frictions between these allies, particularly between Japan and South Korea, and again in a further evolution has deepened the reliance of all three countries on the United States ever more intensely. Strong external balancing against China thus appears to be the new norm in Northeast Asia, despite the politeness with which such activities are packaged and despite the fact that bilateral disputes among U.S. protectees continue to persist.

Reflecting the incipient regional disequilibrium threatened by the growth of China's military power, Hughes's central finding is reflected in Andrew Shearer's analysis of the greater Southeast Asian region as well. Because of the diversity and complexity of this quadrant, Shearer focuses his analysis on three exemplars: Vietnam, a continental power on the edge of the Southeast Asian promontory; Indonesia, a maritime state that hosts the critical chokepoints connecting the Pacific and the Indian oceans; and Australia, the huge island continent lying off Southeast Asia but with a long history of regional engagement and an ally of the United States. Despite the diversity of these cases, Shearer concludes that China's transition to exercising influence now as a sea power—without forgoing its traditional influence as a land power—has provoked region-wide balancing behaviors that nevertheless reflect the area's diversity in their style and presentation. The ongoing crisis in the South China Sea, the growing awareness among the regional states of their own weakness vis-à-vis China, the new challenges posed by China's concerted "turn to the sea," and the old anxieties about each other's neighbors, have all precipitated a push toward new air and maritime acquisitions, a mix of soft and hard balancing, and renewed reliance on the United States for protection—as manifested through the quiet but clear welcome for the rebalancing initiative announced by the Obama administration. As Shearer concludes plainly, despite the region's long-standing efforts to deal with China with a light touch that emphasizes geopolitical subtlety, Beijing's emergence as a new maritime power has propelled a shift from softer to harder forms of balancing. This shift is likely to be sustained long after the current contretemps evoked by China's muscle-flexing disappear, even as the region waits with bated breath for conclusive reassurance from the United States about the durability of its protective role.

Arun Sahgal's chapter on India's reading of, and response to, China's emerging military capabilities concludes the roundup of surveys involving the indigenous Asian powers in this volume. Although the South Asian region is populated by several states, none is affected by the growth of Chinese power as much as India. India is the other rising power in Asia. It has a major territorial dispute with China, is threatened by Chinese nuclear proliferation to Pakistan, and now finds itself confronted by a new Chinese naval presence in the Indian Ocean. Sahgal's conclusions about the impact of China's growing military capabilities on India are stark and direct. He notes that India will face a major window of vulnerability until 2025 for many reasons: China's infrastructure modernization in Tibet undermines the current military balance along the Sino-Indian border; India's nuclear deterrence will not reach full maturity for at least another decade; Indian naval and air power are in dire need for major recapitalization, if their extant advantages are to be preserved; and India's defense procurement system, defense industrial base, and higher national security decision-making system need to be revamped to deal with the Chinese threat effectively. Even as New Delhi faces up to these challenges, Sahgal leaves no doubt that India is already engaged in a deliberate internal balancing against China. New Delhi's geopolitical diffidence about entering into formal alliances with others, including the United States, however, leaves India with serious challenges if its domestic efforts do not turn out to be as successful as is necessary. This problem is only exacerbated by the country's ambivalent political discourse, which trumpets cooperation with China and plays down the rivalry.

The three regional assessments in *Strategic Asia 2012–13* demonstrate clearly that irrespective of how China's new military power affects the local Asian states, these states are all equally concerned about its impact on U.S. military power in Asia because U.S. security guarantees remain their last line of protection—either directly or through their implicit benefits. The thematic analysis in this volume, consequently, concludes with a chapter on the United States, since it is not only an Asian power effectively but also a direct target of many, if not most, of the Chinese modernization efforts. Because the United States' extended security guarantees remain critical both for regional stability and for its own security, the chapter on the United States scrutinizes in some detail the viability of Washington's current response to China's comprehensively expanding military power. It specifically asks whether the U.S. efforts underway to cope with rising Chinese challenges will suffice to defeat the threats posed by China's improving offensive capabilities and thereby rejuvenate the American hegemonic order in Asia.

This chapter, authored by Dan Blumenthal, reaches pessimistic conclusions. It clearly affirms the vital importance of restoring U.S. military superiority in Asia as a precondition for sustaining the success of the Asian system. But Blumenthal argues with great persuasion that the current U.S. response to the problem of eroding supremacy is inadequate for multiple reasons: the present state of U.S. public finances simply does not permit the military to capitalize its forces at the levels and quality necessary to defeat the Chinese threat; the solutions adduced by the United States focus predominantly on the operational level of war to the neglect of the larger strategy required for success; and U.S. political and military planners have failed to connect the necessities of conventional military operations to the requirements for escalation dominance at the nuclear level, given that China remains a major and growing nuclear power. The net result, Blumenthal fears, might be a U.S. response that is far less effective than is necessary to restore the primacy essential to produce regional stability.

As has been the tradition for *Strategic Asia* since its inception, this volume includes a special study, and the one in this year's collection involves a particularly challenging topic: China's vision of world order and how that might apply to Asia. The analysis is fraught with difficulty because the subject is at once abstract and involves interpretation; it must capture the essentialist core (if one exists), yet appreciate how that might be molded by time, successes, and new circumstances; and finally, it must explain how the vision will impact China's behavior in shaping the world as Beijing grows in power and becomes a new entity at the core of the global system.

Thomas Fingar's chapter, "China's Vision of World Order," represents a creative exploration of this difficult subject. Starting from the premise that China is still a weak state despite its many achievements—but desirous of continued growth through the processes that have served it well—Fingar speculates that China would seek to preserve much of the international order it has inherited precisely because that system has served its interests well. Thus, although China is shaped by strong ideals of hierarchic order with itself at the apex, the impulses flowing from that tradition do not—at least for now—push it in the direction of seeking a wholesale renovation of the existing system but rather of improving its own position within. The fact that China's own rise has been enabled by interdependence with others limits its freedom to revamp the existing order without suffering high costs, a burden that China would prefer to avoid so long as its rise to greatness is not entirely complete. When pressed by the question of what China seeks, Fingar's conclusions are thus largely optimistic. But precisely because such an answer is tinged by uncertainty, he argues that the United States and its partners must continue to maintain the regional frameworks in Asia that have underwritten postwar stability, even if sustaining these investments continues to stoke Chinese suspicions of U.S. and allied intentions.

A Burdensome, Yet Necessary, Task: Maintaining American Hegemony

The rise of China as a new great power raises the old and uncomfortable question of hegemonic order even more tellingly: how can the prevailing hegemon continue to maintain a global system, which it constructed primarily for advancing its own self-interest, if that achievement begets new competitors who threaten to displace it in the international hierarchy of power? In the competitive world of international politics, all states—but especially great powers—are particularly sensitive to the relative costs and benefits of their strategic choices. Not surprisingly, then, Washington remains haunted by its open-ended commitment to sustaining a global order that breeds new challengers and new security threats, and is struggling to develop an appropriate response.

The chapters in this volume collectively point to the painful reality to which the United States must respond: China's military modernization over the last two decades has succeeded in forcing dramatic shifts in the Asian balance of power. From deploying a conventional capability that was largely sufficient mainly for its own defense, China has now moved toward fielding offensive conventional components that can seriously put at risk the security of its major peers in Asia. Equally of consequence, China has already integrated within its force structure diverse weapon systems that are aimed at—and capable of—undermining the U.S. ability both to defend its threatened allies in Asia and to reach, and operate freely along, the littorals in support of their security. These transformations signal the atrophy of the most important operational preconditions for maintaining the American hegemonic order in Asia—an order that has been responsible thus far for preventing the rise of any major continental challengers, dampening intra-regional competition, and sustaining a robust economic transformation that has come to serve as the motor of global growth.

The growing constraints on U.S. power projection in Asia as a result of the maturation of China's warfighting capabilities are unfortunately further accompanied by the serious challenge that China has come to embody in the nuclear realm and in the global commons. Today, thanks to the continuing Chinese investments in new robust and survivable nuclear weapon systems, the United States has lost the easy escalation dominance that it enjoyed over China's nuclear forces as recently as a decade ago. The U.S. command of the commons has also eroded in varying degrees depending on the arena and the location in question: China's counter-space investments are both extensive and impressive; its efforts in the cyberwarfare realm are intense and are already at play in pressing the United States through constant probing; Beijing's focus on contesting the U.S. ability to operate in every class of the electromagnetic spectrum implies that the traditional American superiority at seeing first and farther is at risk; and even the customary American dominance at air and sea has weakened the closer the United States operates to the Asian littoral.

Redressing these disadvantages is essential if the United States is to recover its regional military superiority. That is no longer an optional task, not simply for operational but also for fundamentally political reasons. If the United States cannot assuredly come to the defense of its allies in the face of local adversaries, no matter how powerful—and, equally, be seen as capable of providing effective protection despite the severity of the threat—the entire edifice of Asian stability that the United States assiduously constructed on the foundations of its hegemonic power set at the end of World War II stands at risk. Its erosion portends the rise of new hegemonies that not only will come to dominate Asia in time but may also eventually challenge the United States globally as well. The resulting upsurge in power political rivalries both at the core of the international system and regionally, complemented by the serious threats that will materialize to the liberal international trading order, will undermine both the security and the prosperity of the United States, engulfing it in a far more pernicious strategic environment than if this dissolution had been arrested in time.

The imperatives of restoring the United States' military superiority and its freedom of maneuver in Asia are, therefore, absolute. The task is not beyond the technological capacity of the United States or the innovative capacity of its armed forces. But it will be resource intensive, and it appears at exactly the time when the United States is still reeling from the consequences of the excesses that created the global financial crises and deeply wounded the U.S. economy. Yet the United States still has untapped depths of resilience and strength. The U.S. economy is still the world's largest, whether measured by GDP or by levels of inclusive wealth. Further, this economy is deleveraging at a much faster rate than had been expected; U.S. exports and energy production have made dramatic comebacks; the dollar remains a robust store of value and is still the world's only meaningful reserve currency; the nation's innovation system shows no signs of slowing; and, finally, as Australia's foreign minister Robert Carr recently put it, "The United States is one budget deal away from restoring its global preeminence."[16]

What is needed more than ever in the first instance, therefore, are not technological antidotes to China's new military capabilities; those will materialize gracefully once the United States puts its mind to it. Rather, what

---

[16] Quoted in "World Bank Head Robert Zoellick Offers Broad View of Global Issues" (speech at the Economic Club of Washington, D.C., Washington, D.C., May 16, 2012), http://www.economicclub. org/doc_repo/Final%20Transcript%20of%20Robert%20Zoellick%20Event%20May%2016.pdf.

is most essential is an awareness of the stakes—and the risks involved should the United States fail to regain the capacity to operate at will in and around the Asian land mass. From there on, it is imperative that Washington recover the political willingness to bear the costs necessary to sustain American hegemony over the long run. This must be done not through cheap slogans but through rational policies that will effectively protect the United States' critical military capabilities during the coming fiscal cliff and through the larger, yet harder, decisions that will rebuild the nation's public finances and refurbish its economic foundations to permit continued technological innovation, consistent productivity increases, and sustained GDP growth. To the degree that the United States masters these challenges at home, it will have paved the way for defeating the emerging Chinese military threats to its hegemony in Asia far more resolutely than any superficial fixes might in the interim.

STRATEGIC ASIA 2012–13

EMERGING CHINESE MILITARY CAPABILITIES

EXECUTIVE SUMMARY

This chapter examines the missions, force structure, and capabilities of the PLA ground forces and assesses their relative importance and future roles in China's accomplishment of its security goals.

MAIN ARGUMENT:
China's national security goals have grown in scale and geographical scope with the increase in its overall comprehensive national power. The once-central role for the ground forces in defending China's national sovereignty is diminishing as China's regional neighborhood poses fewer direct threats that would require a large standing army. Meanwhile, China's increasing overseas interests are largely secured by the other services, especially the navy. The PLA ground forces nonetheless retain a critical role as the force of last resort in defending the Chinese Communist Party, especially against internal challenges, and are modernizing, albeit at a modest and somewhat uneven pace. The result is a force structure and set of capabilities that are tailored to the challenges and opportunities found in each of the subregions that border China.

POLICY IMPLICATIONS:
- The current structure and capabilities of the PLA land forces allow for only limited power projection, largely because of mobility shortfalls. Improvements and increases in the helicopter force would enable the PLA to more rapidly project land power throughout China and potentially into border regions.

- Changes to the structure of military regions would signal changes in the operational orientation of the PLA, including likely greater priority for the other services.

- That the PLA land forces apparently have little operational interaction with the Korean People's Army suggests that the PLA is not preparing to assist the North Korean leadership in the event of a crisis but would respond to crises unilaterally.

China's Land Forces: New Priorities and Capabilities

Roy Kamphausen

China's place as the preeminent continental power of Asia is well established. The historical "middle kingdom" has been master of the eastern half of the Eurasian land mass since antiquity. Integral to China's historical supremacy in the region were the fundamental advantages its military forces enjoyed by means of interior lines—China is in the center of Asia—and the continental depth afforded by being Asia's largest country.

With the arrival of the Chinese Communist Party (CCP), and later the establishment of the People's Republic of China (PRC) in 1949, China's People's Liberation Army (PLA) under Mao Zedong appropriated these advantages into the CCP's "people's war" doctrine. Indeed, Mao's famous dictum to "draw the enemy in deep" was simply the mid–twentieth century adaptation of the established military advantage available to a big country surrounded by other potentially competing states with long, and at times difficult to defend, borders.

People's war also essentially reflected the inherently defensive approach to China's national security, in which the central task after the formation of the PRC in 1949 was seen to be the consolidation and defense of what then constituted China. In the process, national defense became intertwined with national psychology, such that people's war was also understood as a popular

Roy Kamphausen is a Senior Associate for Political and Security Affairs at the National Bureau of Asian Research. He can be reached at <rkamphausen@nbr.org>.

and necessary response to China's "century of humiliation" suffered when a weak China was unable to defend its borders.[1]

This defensive approach and orientation gave rise to a set of missions for the PLA that reflected a ground force–intensive approach to national defense. These missions were hardly unique for a post-revolutionary state consolidating power and, moreover, could be accomplished with available resources (particularly once China became a nuclear power and established its own limited nuclear deterrent in 1964). The missions of the PLA for the first 40 years of the PRC were the following:

- Maintain the leadership of the CCP, in the process providing for domestic stability and the deterrence of political chaos, and suppress large-scale political action against the party
- Defend at or near China's north and northwest frontiers against continental invasion from the Soviet Union and its satellite states
- Defend the northeastern border against invasion into China from the Korean Peninsula
- Defeat invasion from the coast by preparing to conduct strategic withdrawals until an invading enemy is stretched out and is vulnerable to counterattack
- Contribute to national construction, primarily through infrastructure development

By the mid-1980s, the PLA was an army-centric force nearly four-million strong, whose large infantry-based formations were essentially static, geographically based forces with limited organic transportation. Great emphasis was placed on the garrison functions of the ground forces that played an important role in national construction. Emblematic of this mindset was the mission of the Xinjiang Production and Construction Corps. The corps was essentially an organization of demobilized PLA units that remained in China's northwest after the incorporation of the Xinjiang Autonomous Region into the PRC in 1949 in order to contribute to economic development, build up agricultural production, maintain stability in this potentially restive minority region, and enhance border defense.[2]

---

[1] That the strategic orientation of China's ground forces is primarily defensive should not be construed to mean that the PLA eschews offensive action. Quite the contrary, the doctrine of "active defense" mandates offensive action as a means of seizing the initiative even within the context of an overall defensive action. See Dennis Blasko, *The Chinese Army Today: Tradition and Transformation for the 21st Century*, 2nd ed. (New York: Routledge, 2012).

[2] Information Office of the State Council of the People's Republic of China, *History and Development of Xinjiang* (Beijing, May 2003), section 9, http://www.china.org.cn/e-white/20030526/9.htm.

While particularly in the 1960s the PRC was associated with international liberation movements, for the most part military support to those movements was limited. Moreover, while in the first four decades of the PRC there were several notable instances in which PLA land forces were used to project power against neighboring countries—including the Chinese People's Volunteers in the Korean War, the Sino-Indian conflict in 1962, the Sino-Russian border conflict of 1969, and the 1979 "counter-attack in self-defense" against Vietnam)—by the late 1980s the vast majority of PLA land forces were static, inwardly focused, and defensive-minded.

This chapter assesses what has changed in the last two decades for PLA land forces,[3] what the drivers for that change have been, what key developments have emerged, and how the PLA now presents itself to bordering countries. The chapter first identifies the key events during 1989–91 that helped shock China's land force from its inward and defensive orientation into becoming a more outward-looking organization. The next section identifies the key developments of land-force modernization over the last twenty years and performs a limited net assessment of the capabilities that PLA land forces currently employ. The chapter then assesses these forces' capabilities in the context of how the PLA presents itself to regional neighbors. The chapter concludes with assessments of the trajectory of PLA land forces over the next decade both in terms of functional capabilities and in interactions with regional neighbors.

The chapter finds that Chinese national security interests have moved beyond limited continental defensive objectives. Consequently, the relevance of PLA land forces to accomplishing new, higher-priority missions in the air and at sea farther from China has diminished, and bureaucratic power and budget resources have devolved to some degree to the PLA Navy, Air Force, and Second Artillery Corps. Meanwhile, the land forces (primarily the army) have retained the traditional missions for territorial integrity and defense of sovereignty, which have somewhat diminished in importance as China has become more powerful (and less threatened) and as PRC diplomatic efforts have reduced China's land-border disputes and improved

---

[3] This chapter considers PLA ground forces to comprise the group army structure; provincial military districts and their subordinate entities, including military districts, military subdistricts, and garrison commands; and the army reserves and militia. The People's Armed Police (PAP) is not considered part of the PLA ground forces, despite a secondary mission to serve as light infantry under the command and control of the Central Military Commission in a military crisis, because the PAP's primary mission—population control writ large but especially to quell large-scale domestic unrest— relieves the general PLA land forces of this mission. Despite having ground-force missions, neither the PLA Airborne Corps nor the two brigades of PLA Marines are included. This is primarily because they are assigned to separate services and too little is understood about joint command and control to make judgments about whether they would be controlled by land force commanders or employed as a separate force in a joint command-and-control structure. The helicopter force (army aviation), however, is included in the discussion of PLA land forces, because it is subordinate to the army.

regional bilateral relations. The land forces are also largely responsible for keeping the CCP in power, a mission that for the most part has been handed off to the People's Armed Police (PAP), but for which the PLA retains ultimate responsibility.

The PLA has much-improved capabilities in numerous dimensions, including tactical mobility, secure command and control, and supporting personnel and structural dimensions that serve as force multipliers for its various capabilities. Although China's borders are essentially secure, the PLA land forces still plan for contingencies with neighboring states. Consequently, the PLA land forces have developed specialized capabilities and structures for addressing each border contingency in which they might be engaged.

The chapter also finds that the PLA land forces have tailored their approach to each of the subregions. On China's northern border with Russia, two decades of operational-level confidence-building efforts have reduced China's strategic risk and enhanced bilateral military ties to the degree that the two countries now display limited interoperability, at least of the sort that might complicate U.S. contingency planning for Northeast Asia. With China's Central Asian partners in the Shanghai Cooperation Organisation (SCO), the more mobile PLA land forces are accomplishing national imperatives—suppressing dissent cloaked as separatism, terrorism, and extremism—while appearing to support broader international goals regarding nonstate terrorism. Moreover, Central Asia and the counterterrorism exercise regime of which the PLA is a part have become a test case for how Chinese land forces might be employed in foreign crises. With respect to India, the PLA is benefiting from infrastructure development in Tibet that is improving the mobility of military forces in ways designed to achieve a strategic deterrent effect and help ensure access to water resources. In Southeast Asia, the PLA's chief concerns appear to be limited, but are modestly focused on cross-border ethnic issues. Finally, on China's northeast border with North Korea, land force efforts appear to be weighted toward mitigating Chinese risk in the event that the North Korean regime collapses.

Changes Afoot

In 1989 a new era for China's national defense was ushered in, with dramatic impacts on the conservative PLA of the PRC's early period, which was ground-force heavy and not apt to engage in long-range power projection. Central to this development were three events and one ongoing trend. The three important events were the Tiananmen Square massacre of June 1989, the fall of the Berlin Wall and dissolution of the Soviet Union from 1989 to 1991, and the U.S.-led coalition operation to expel Iraqi forces from Kuwait in 1991,

Operation Desert Storm. The key trend was the continuation and acceleration of the growth of the Chinese economy, which has both created wealth at unprecedented rates and made great contributions to the development of Chinese comprehensive national power (*zonghe guoli*). Each factor in turn has helped transition the PLA away from its traditional approach to a more outward-looking defense structure.

Tiananmen Square

The first event—the Tiananmen Square massacre of June 1989—was a violent response on the part of the central leadership to a complicated combination of Chinese domestic political factors, including elite competition about China's future development path. The mass mobilization of student and labor movements made the events much more incendiary and added to the lethality of the response in ways that had important impacts on the future trajectory of the PLA. In the end, the PLA did follow orders to enter and use deadly force to clear Tiananmen Square of those students and others who had occupied it for weeks. In the process, the PLA reaffirmed to the central leadership its role as the force of final resort for the CCP. But this was not without costs and complications for the party center. Some military leaders strongly opposed the orders; for instance, the commander of the elite 38th Group Army refused to command his troops into the square on both legal and moral grounds.[4] Reflecting a more widely held sentiment along these lines than is usually acknowledged, the PLA has vowed never again to undertake combat operations against its own people. China's minister of national defense, General Chi Haotian, even asserted as much in a speech at the U.S. National Defense University in December 1996 when he said that actions such as those taken at Tiananmen Square "would not happen again."[5]

In terms of impact on the PLA, some analysts have suggested that the army's top leadership was able to leverage its adherence to orders at Tiananmen for financial advantage. They point to the dramatic increases in defense spending since 1990 as evidence of a quid pro quo arrangement between the PLA and the Politburo—an assertion that is difficult to dismiss out of hand given the spectacular growth in Chinese defense spending over that period.[6]

---

[4] General Xu Qinxian is reported to have sensed that the absence of written orders cast doubt on their legitimacy and thus introduced great risk of historical "scapegoating" if he obeyed. Verna Yu, "No Regrets for Defiant Tiananmen General," *South China Morning Post*, February 25, 2011, http://topics.scmp.com/news/china-news-watch/article/No-regrets-for-defiant-Tiananmen-general.

[5] Dennis J. Blasko and John F. Corbett, Jr., "No More Tiananmens: The People's Armed Police and Stability in China, 1997,"*China Strategic Review* 3, no. 1 (1998): 88–89.

[6] Robert L. Suettinger, *Beyond Tiananmen: The Politics of U.S.-China Relations, 1989–2000* (Brookings Institution, 2003), 223.

Others cite the dramatic increase in PLA-related business activities over the ensuing decade after Tiananmen as another example of a deal made for the PLA following orders.[7]

Another immediate impact of the Tiananmen incident on PLA land forces was the growth in capabilities and resources of the People's Armed Police , a paramilitary force with dual lines of command to both the Central Military Commission and the Ministry of Public Security. First established in 1982, the PAP received greater emphasis and resources after the Tiananmen crackdown, including the transfer in the mid-1990s of fourteen PLA divisions to the PAP. The PAP plays many roles—including forest, mine, and hydropower security; firefighting; and counterterrorism and border security—but arguably its central and most important mission is to respond to large-scale domestic unrest. This role and the enhanced authorities that accompany it were finally put into law in August 2009.[8] While the PLA retains a supporting role to the PAP in specific cases of large-scale unrest— for example, transportation, logistics, and intelligence[9]—the PLA leadership is intentionally unclear about the circumstances that might see PLA ground forces directly involved against Chinese citizens. The continued development of the PAP has allowed the PLA to work on improving its public image and remain distant from most internal disturbances,[10] while also freeing up some capacity to respond to new challenges and opportunities. The PAP's improved capabilities notwithstanding, the top PLA leadership still understands and accepts that the PLA, especially its land forces, represents the last line of the CCP's defense.[11]

---

[7] Ultimately, in July 1998 the PLA was ordered to "get out of business" by the end of 1998, owing to a range of concerns about the negative impacts of the business activities related to PLA military capabilities. (The author participated in a series of briefings given by PLA deputy chief of general staff, General Xiong Guangkai, while assigned as a military attaché at the U.S. Embassy in China during 1998–2001.)

[8] "Top Legislature Passes Armed Police Law," Xinhua, August 27, 2009, http://www.chinadaily.com.cn/china/2009-08/27/content_8625494.htm.

[9] Murray Scot Tanner, "How China Manages Internal Security Challenges and Its Impact on PLA Missions," in Beyond the Strait: PLA Missions Other Than Taiwan, ed. Roy Kamphausen, David Lai, and Andrew Scobell (Carlisle: Strategic Studies Institute, 2009), 39–98.

[10] The author attended a briefing given by then deputy chief of general staff General Xiong Guangkai in fall 1998, at which General Xiong asserted to his Western listeners that the PLA's active response to the ongoing floods had helped repair the civil-military bond that had been ruptured by the Tiananmen Square incident.

[11] PAP-PLA interaction in response to the large-scale unrest in Tibet in March 2008 provides an important case study. Despite widespread rumors of significant PLA involvement, the most credible analysis of the situation depicts the PAP in the lead and the PLA in a supporting role, providing intelligence, logistical support, and security. Dennis Blasko in The Chinese Army Today noted that a PLA motorized infantry regiment, already stationed in Lhasa, provided transportation and security support (pp. 100, 217–18). But the position of PLA troops, whether in a leading or support role, does not change the fundamental reality of the PLA's ultimate responsibility to sustain CCP power.

Dissolution of the Soviet Union

The end of the Cold War was a second important event that helped shape the PLA of today, starting in 1989 with the fall of the Berlin Wall and culminating with the dissolution of the Soviet Union in December 1991. China and the Soviet Union already had begun a process to resolve border disputes and demarcate boundaries and thus avoid the sort of conflict that occurred at Damansky Island in 1969. With the disappearance of the Soviet threat in 1991, the process gained new impetus and the opportunity emerged to reduce the risk for strategic miscalculation along China's northern and western borders via confidence-building and threat-reduction measures with the new Russian Federation. The work was finally concluded in 2005.[12] In a parallel effort, the original "Shanghai Five"—China, Kazakhstan, Kyrgyzstan, Russia, and Tajikistan—signed the Treaty on Deepening Military Trust in Border Regions in 1996, which, along with later treaties, included goals for border demarcation, military confidence-building, and risk reduction.

The end of the Soviet strategic challenge and diminution of the historic military threat from China's northwest frontier also created the conditions for a strategic reorientation of the PLA. First, the same northwest frontier that in the past had represented an overland invasion route had become, within a decade of the Soviet Union's demise, home to a nascent regional security structure—the Shanghai Cooperation Organisation. The SCO helped the PLA discover a new land force mission—counterterrorism—while at the same time creating a regional security forum in which China might eventually play an occasional leadership role. Two decades after the end of the Soviet Union and the resolution of contentious border issues, multilateral cooperation with the states of Central Asia and Russia has enabled China both to address the regional security challenges of terrorism with domestic implications and to contribute to the fight against global terrorism.

Second, the end of the Soviet Union provided an opportunity for a reassessment of China's strategic environment. This process resulted in new military strategic guidelines that reoriented China's main strategic direction from the now-stable north and northwest to China's eastern coast, so as to increase security in coastal regions, focus on securing China's new wealth centers, and prevent moves toward independence by Taiwan.[13] The new military strategic guidelines also had the necessary effect of shifting more

---

[12] "China, Russia Solve All Border Disputes," Xinhua, June 2, 2005, http://news.xinhuanet.com/english/2005-06/02/content_3037975.htm.

[13] David M. Finkelstein, "China's National Military Strategy: An Overview of the 'Military Strategic Guidelines,'" in *Right Sizing the People's Liberation Army: Exploring the Contours of China's Military*, ed. Roy Kamphausen and Andrew Scobell (Carlisle: Strategic Studies Institute, 2007), 69–140.

budgetary and operational priorities to the PLA Navy and Air Force, reflecting important priority shifts to the air and maritime domains.

U.S. Success in the First Persian Gulf War

The third major development prompting shifts in the PLA was China's observation of the nonpareil performance of the U.S.-led coalition in the first Persian Gulf War. Operation Desert Storm demonstrated a spectacular, synergistic approach to modern warfare, with such drastic improvements in combined arms (multiple ground-force arms, such as tanks and infantry), joint services (integration of two or more services, especially ground and air forces), and combined forces (integration of two or more nations' armed forces) that PLA leaders experienced true "shock and awe." The war was an eye-opener for China's military and demonstrated firsthand that a revolution in military affairs had occurred within the U.S. armed forces. For a PLA that was itself just a few years removed from a defense relationship with the U.S. military and an overall Chinese-U.S. entente in the 1980s,[14] the smashing success of the U.S. Army demonstrated how risky an adversarial relationship with the United States could become.

Chinese Economic Development

The fourth development has been the spectacular growth of the Chinese economy since 1990, resulting in China now having the world's largest trading economy and overall second-largest economy in the world. The growth in China's economy has provided the means for the PLA's total defense spending to increase more than sevenfold over the period from 1990 to 2011—from $17.9 billion to $129.3 billion based on constant 2010 dollars—even as Chinese overall defense spending as a percentage of GDP has experienced a modest decline.[15] The massive military modernization campaign undertaken by the PLA in the post-Tiananmen era simply would not have been possible without the investments in defense made possible by a flourishing economy. Although the publicly declared Chinese defense budgets do not break down spending by service, if the amount of the PLA budget that is spent on land

[14] The U.S. Department of Defense had four foreign military sales programs with the PLA in the 1980s, including a large-caliber ammunition program, a torpedo program, an artillery-locating radar program, and an avionics upgrade to the Chinese F-8 fighter, as well as a direct commercial sales program for the civilian S-70 version of the Sikorsky Black Hawk helicopter. President George H.W. Bush canceled the programs in the wake of the Tiananmen Square massacre, and the sanctions against technical defense cooperation between the United States and China remain in place.

[15] "The 15 Countries with the Highest Military Expenditure in 2011 (table)," Stockholm International Peace Research Institute (SIPRI), http://www.sipri.org/research/armaments/milex/resultoutput/milex_15.

forces even roughly approximates the 60% of the PLA that these forces constitute, then the PLA land forces alone still would have the world's third-largest defense budget, just ahead of Russia, but behind the United States and China's overall defense budget.

The PLA Land Forces of 2012

The following section examines how the PLA land forces of today are different in function and capabilities from the ground forces that were in place two decades ago.

International and Regional Security Environments

The PLA land forces face a regional strategic environment markedly different from 1989. China does not face fundamental state-led challenges in the region, and all but one of China's land border disputes—the exception being the Sino-Indian border—have been resolved. Thus, China does not face the sort of external regime challenge that so worried Mao Zedong and Zhou Enlai in the early years of the PRC.

However, the linkages of external nonstate regional threats to domestic security challenges are stronger than ever, particularly with respect to terrorist groups and separatist movements. Especially in China's northwest Xinjiang region, linkages of Uighur nationalist movements with separatist elements outside China (e.g., the East Turkestan independence movement, for instance) are alarming to state security officials in Beijing and the restive provinces.

China also finds itself as the national power closest in capabilities to the United States in a still nearly unipolar world. The growth in overall Chinese comprehensive national power, especially in its economic dimension, has put China in an ever-stronger position to potentially "stand up" to the United States. This development has had dramatic consequences for China's own sense of place on international security matters, including contributing to periodic rash or assertive behavior as Chinese security entities attempt to adjust to new realities that have thrust China into positions of leadership perhaps sooner than expected.[16] For their part, Chinese military leaders continue to emphasize the (perhaps still-growing) difference between the United States and China in defense capabilities, with assertions that the "gap between us and that of advanced countries is still at least two to three

---

[16] David M. Lampton, "Power Constrained: Sources of Mutual Strategic Suspicion in U.S.-China Relations," National Bureau of Asian Research, NBR Analysis, June 2010.

decades."[17] Chinese assertions to the contrary notwithstanding, the PRC's behavior and capabilities suggest an increasing willingness to challenge long-standing U.S. military operations near China.

New Historic Missions

The PLA of 2012 operates within the context of the era of the "new historic missions," as gleaned from a speech by Hu Jintao in December 2004, just three months after he rose to the chairmanship of the Central Military Commission (CMC). The missions cited in that speech are:

- to consolidate the ruling status of the Communist Party
- to help ensure China's sovereignty, territorial integrity, and domestic security in order to continue national development
- to safeguard China's expanding national interests
- to help maintain world peace[18]

The new historic missions (officially titled the "Historic Missions of the Armed Forces in the New Period of the New Century," or *xin shiji xin jieduan wojun lishi shiming*) maintain the PLA's focus on providing military support to the CCP and conducting traditional defense functions and at the same time undertake a more internationalist outlook. In the latter two missions—safeguarding China's expanding national interests and helping maintain world peace—the PLA has involved itself in entirely new activities such as naval escort and antipiracy operations in the Gulf of Aden, as well as new and deeper commitments to UN international peacekeeping missions. The new dimensions have also been described as diversified military tasks that encompass the many new operational activities that the PLA is intended to be able to accomplish, including military operations other than war. The new historic missions push the PLA writ large to be more international, and this too has set the scene for the ground forces of the PLA to become more outwardly focused.

In particular, PLA land forces have markedly increased their support for UN peacekeeping operations since 2000, with a twentyfold increase in participants over the course of that decade. As of June 30, 2012, China has

---

[17] See, for instance, comments by the Chinese minister of national defense, General Liang Guanglie, in a joint press conference with the U.S. secretary of defense Robert Gates during General Liang's visit to the Pentagon. "Joint Press Conference with Secretary Gates and General Liang from Beijing, China," U.S. Department of Defense, News Transcript, January 10, 2011, http://www.defense.gov/transcripts/transcript.aspx?transcriptid=4750.

[18] Daniel Hartnett, "Towards a Globally Focused Chinese Military: The Historic Missions of the Chinese Armed Forces," Center for Naval Analyses, June 2008.

contributed 1,928 troops, police, and military observers to support twelve of sixteen UN peacekeeping missions, ranking the PRC sixteenth out of all contributing countries and first among the permanent members of the UN Security Council.[19] Chinese peacekeepers have not yet included combat forces; rather, military participants to date have been engineers, logistics personnel, or medical support. More than three-fourths of China's contributions have been to Africa, reflecting both opportunity (more missions) and a potential to achieve strategic effect.[20]

New Capabilities

The PLA land force now finds itself with both new modernized traditional capabilities as well as enabling "force multipliers." China's 2010 defense white paper (published in March 2011) highlights the most salient developments:

> The PLAA [PLA Army] has *emphasized the development of new types of combat forces, optimized its organization* and structure, *strengthened military training* in conditions of *informationization,* accelerated the digitized upgrading and retrofitting of main battle weaponry, organically deployed new types of weapon platforms, and significantly *boosted its capabilities in long-distance* maneuvers and integrated assaults.[21]

The PLA asserts that the accomplishments to date are part of a measured, step-by-step process, which will result in completely mechanized land forces by 2020, with informationization of the force to be complete by 2049.

Traditional Capabilities

The defense white paper goes on to describe the singular improvements in each arm of the ground forces. The armored arm has sought higher degrees of mechanization of most units while also supporting the digitization of advanced units and experimenting with flexible task force organizations using a variety of nonorganic systems assembled for specific missions. The artillery arm is working on both informationization as well as a much more advanced Chinese-style "reconnaissance strike complex" that pursues the ability to carry out precision operations by means of "integrated reconnaissance, control, strike and assessment capabilities." The air-defense arm is combining

---

[19] "Troop and Police Contributors," United Nations Peacekeeping, June 2012, http://www.un.org/en/peacekeeping/resources/statistics/contributors.shtml.

[20] Bates Gill and Chin-hao Huang, "China's Expanding Role in Peacekeeping: Prospects and Policy Implications," SIPRI, Policy Paper, no. 25, November 2009, http://books.sipri.org/files/PP/SIPRIPP25.pdf.

[21] Information Office of the State Council of the PRC, *China's National Defense in 2010* (Beijing, March 2011), http://news.xinhuanet.com/english2010/china/2011-03/31/c_13806851.htm (emphasis added).

new radar types with advanced missiles and has stepped up the development of new types of radar and command-and-control information systems, with artillery and surface-to-air missiles of various ranges. The aviation wing of the PLA land forces has worked to move from being a "support force" to being a "main-battle assault force" by employing innovative "modular grouping" and upgraded armored transport and assault helicopters in an effort to enhance mobility and improve short-range power projection. According to the 2010 defense white paper, "the engineering arm has accelerated its transformation into a new model of integrated and multi-functional support force, which is rapid in response and can be used in both peacetime and war" to accomplish the diversified military tasks the PLA might be charged with. The chemical defense arm has worked to develop an integrated force for nuclear, biological, and chemical defense, "which operates both in peacetime and in war, combines civilian and military efforts, and integrates systems from various arms and services." It has developed enhanced permanent, multidimensional, and multi-terrain defense capabilities against nuclear, biological, and chemical threats.[22]

These subjective claims have been supported by real improvements to military equipment. Over the last two decades, the total number of ground force warfighting systems has markedly declined, even as the quality has improved. Today, approximately one-third of China's systems are considered modern.[23] The key development here includes an obvious enhancement of mobility for the land forces—less than five divisions are now considered to be without motorized or mechanized capability. However, procurement and deployment of helicopters, a principal means for enhancing land force mobility, still lag behind expectations, as the total number of helicopters is still only around five hundred. **Table 1** summarizes the important developments in China's key land force warfighting systems.

Perhaps the most important development over the last two decades has been the quest of the PLA land forces to build "informationized armed forces"—that is, forces that leverage advanced information and communication technologies to gain increased battlefield awareness of both enemy and friendly locations, to communicate securely, to conduct a variety of lethal and nonlethal warfighting actions as part of an information operations approach, to build a "system of systems" approach in which advanced systems talk with each other using computer technology, and to use simulators to train more effectively. Space technologies also play an increasingly important role.[24]

---

[22] Information Office of the State Council of the PRC, *China's National Defense in 2010*, 9.

[23] Blasko, *The Chinese Army Today*, 172.

[24] Ibid., 16–17.

TABLE 1   Modernization of key warfighting systems, 1991–2011

	1990 total	2011 total	Modern	Recent models
Transport helicopters	250	500	200	Russian MI-17 and indigenous Z-9
Attack helicopters	60	110	~10	Z-10 indigenous attack helicopter
Tanks	7,750	7,050	~2,000	Type 96 and Type 98/99
Infantry fighting vehicles (IFV) and armored personnel carriers (APC)	2,800*	5,090	~2,250	Type 97 IFV and WZ 551 series
Artillery	18,300	8,000	~1,710	120-mm mortar-howitzer and a variety of 122-mm, 152-mm, and 155-mm self-propelled howitzers

SOURCE: International Institute of Strategic Studies, *The Military Balance 2012* (London: Routledge, 2012); U.S. Department of Defense, "Annual Report on the Military Power of the People's Republic of China," July 2002, http://www.defense.gov/news/Jul2002/d20020712china.pdf; Office of the Secretary of Defense, "Annual Report to Congress: Military and Security Developments Involving the People's Republic of China," May 2012, http://www.defense.gov/pubs/pdfs/2012_CMPR_Final.pdf; and Dennis J. Blasko, *The Chinese Army Today: Tradition and Transformation for the 21st Century*, 2nd ed. (New York: Routledge, 2012).

NOTE: "Modern" implies developed and delivered to the force within the last fifteen years. Asterisk indicates that the total is for APCs. Additionally, there were a small number of IFVs, but these had not entered the force in large numbers.

As these capabilities are difficult to observe with the eyes, they are best seen when applied in real-world operations or in military exercises. In its exercises, the PLA regularly emphasizes the importance of digitized warfare.

Functional Enablers

Joint logistics. The PLA has also undertaken important strides in joint logistical operations. Logistics are integral to successful operations, and the PLA has long recognized the backward state of its capabilities. An integrated (national to regional level) joint (multi-service) approach to logistical support places emphasis on mobility, digitization (both of location and identification of resupply materials), civil-military support, and consideration of various methods for supporting forces operating outside China. Writing in 2010, Susan Puska, the foremost American scholar of PLA logistical capabilities, still finds a high tolerance for the inefficiencies of experimentation and innovation, suggesting a lack of urgency for best practices to be rapidly disseminated throughout the force. This obviously affects operational capabilities. Looking forward, Puska notes numerous challenges that the PLA must overcome in order to adequately support forces operating far from China, in power projection or other missions. These challenges include intra-staff role delineation, removal of excess layers of staffing, and improved resourcing for logistics activities. Overall, despite dramatic improvements in the last 30 years, Puska still finds PLA logistical support to be an inhibitor to more ambitious operational plans.[25]

Personnel. The last twenty years have seen remarkable development of the PLA's personnel systems, much of which took place in the late 1990s. At the level of officer accession and initial education, the PLA's top leadership determined that the Soviet-style academy structure—in 1998 the PLA had more than one hundred military academies—was too inefficient and thus incapable of teaching officers the skills necessary to operate in the sorts of modern, high-intensity conflicts that the 21st century was expected to feature.

As a result, China's CMC instituted two changes. First, it downsized and consolidated China's bloated military academy system, with one-third of the institutions shuttered or consolidated within a few years. Second, in March 1999, it instituted a program to commission PLA officers from civilian universities in China.[26] Starting with fourteen universities and slightly over one hundred cadets in 1999, by 2011 more than ten thousand cadets were expected to be commissioned from civilian universities on an annual basis, or about half of the PLA's new lieutenants each year.[27] In 1999 the PLA also instituted a noncommissioned officer program to provide a career path for experienced conscripts to remain in the PLA and thus provide specialized expertise as well as continuity for a PLA that turns over one-half of its conscripts every year.[28]

---

[25] Susan M. Puska, "Taming the Hydra: Trends in China's Military Logistics Since 2000," in *The PLA at Home and Abroad: Assessing the Operational Capabilities of China's Military*, ed. Roy Kamphausen, David Lai, and Andrew Scobell (Carlisle: Strategic Studies Institute, 2010), 553–636.

[26] "All-PLA Cadre Training Work Meeting," *Liberation Army Daily*, April 2, 1999.

[27] John F. Corbett, Jr., Edward C. O'Dowd, and David D. Chen, "Building the Fighting Strength: PLA Officer Accession, Education, Training, and Utilization," in *The "People" in the PLA: Recruitment, Training, and Education in China's Military*, ed. Roy Kamphausen, Andrew Scobell, and Travis Tanner (Carlisle: Strategic Studies Institute, 2008), 139–90.

[28] Dennis Blasko, "PLA Conscript and Noncommissioned Officer Individual Training," in Kamphausen, Scobell, and Tanner, *The "People" in the PLA*, 99–138.

The net effect of these changes to officer accession and the development of a noncommissioned officer program is a more professionalized force—that is, one with higher individual capabilities in the profession of arms, even as the force remains an inherently political one, as the coercive arm of the CCP.

Organization. Beginning in the mid-1990s, the PLA land forces undertook several changes (see **Table 2**). First, the PLA has downsized, with a disproportionate share of the overall 1.7 million reduction in personnel felt by the land forces.[29] The PLA land forces currently consist of roughly 1.25–1.50 million soldiers, of which 12% are in border-defense units. The downsizing of the last two decades resulted in the elimination of six group army headquarters and more than a dozen divisions. Additionally, fourteen PLA divisions were transferred to newly formed PAP divisions, thus dramatically improving the mobility of China's leading counter-separatist and counterterrorism force. Additionally, an infantry division was transferred to form a marine brigade in the South Sea Fleet. Newer capabilities have also been introduced, such as the special operations forces that are now in each military region and the modestly increased army aviation.[30] See the Appendix for an overview of the order of battle for PLA land forces.

TABLE 2   Changes in army maneuver units (infantry, armored, helicopter, and special operations) since 1997

	1997	2012
Group armies	24	18
Infantry divisions	90	26
Armored divisions	12	7–9
Infantry brigades	7	28–31
Armored brigades	13	9–11
Helicopter regiments/brigades	7/0	9/4
Special operations groups/regiments	7/0	8/1

SOURCE: Office of the Secretary of Defense, "Annual Report to Congress," May 2012; and Blasko, *The Chinese Army Today,* 87–102.

---

[29] For instance, China's 1998 defense white paper reported that the reduction of 500,000 personnel from 1997 to 2000 saw more than 400,000 of the 500,000 troops demobilized come from the army. If the percentage of army soldiers demobilized in the follow-on downsizing efforts is consistent, this suggests that around 1.2–1.4 million of the overall 1.7 million reduction from 1985 to 2002 came from the land forces.

[30] Blasko, *The Chinese Army Today,* 25–26.

Second, PLA land forces have been restructured. The PLA began experimenting with the conversion of infantry divisions to infantry-heavy combined arms brigades in the late 1990s. The new brigades would include three to four battalions of infantry, a battalion of tanks, a battalion of artillery, and other combat support capabilities, including logistics, communications, and radar. These smaller and more capable units began to look like hybrid tailored-force packages designed for specific missions.[31] It is now estimated that nearly all PLA infantry divisions have been restructured into infantry brigades and that a good portion of armored (tank) divisions have undergone a similar restructuring into brigades. The implications of this restructuring are many, including some cost savings, an expectation for revised training regimes and operational command-and-control relationships, and the potential to structure force packages for specific missions.[32]

Military Exercise Regimes

Multilateral exercises. Multilateral exercises by PLA land forces have increased in number and complexity in the last decade, and almost all of these have taken place under the rubric of the SCO. Units from throughout China have participated in the exercises, with usually one exercise held per year in the period 2002–6, after which the number of annual exercises increased to two or more a year. Most exercises were on a smaller scale and almost all involved Chinese special operations forces. Adversaries are generally nonstate actors with limited high-tech equipment. Military benefits to the PLA in these multilateral exercises include experience with foreign forces, command-and-control training, long-distance mobility, logistics, and to a lesser extent operational tactics.

Important examples include the largest exercise, the joint Sino-Russian Peace Mission 2005 exercise, which featured nearly 10,000 participants; Coalition 2003, which included 1,300 soldiers from five SCO states (new member Uzbekistan did not participate) and interestingly included militia personnel from the Xinjiang Production and Construction Corps; and Coordination 2006, which saw Chinese and Tajik participation in an exercise that included the first deployment of Chinese air forces outside China to deliver PLA troops to rescue Chinese citizens captured (in the exercise scenario) by terrorists in Tajikistan. The joint exercise with Tajikistan was also noteworthy in that an army aviation regiment from the Xinjiang

---

[31] Cortez Cooper III, "'Preserving the State': Modernizing and Task-Organizing a 'Hybrid' Ground Force," in Kamphausen and Scobell, *Right Sizing the People's Liberation Army*, 237–79.

[32] Of course, this too speaks of a PLA high command that can make significant structural changes of this sort in a relatively low-risk and static environment, that is, an environment without a direct military threat that either demands such a response or puts at risk its accomplishment.

Military District self-deployed to support the Chinese special forces in Tajikistan. In August 2007, all six SCO states sent troops to Peace Mission 2007 in Chelyabinsk, Russia, the PLA's first major land-air joint exercise outside China.[33]

All in all, these multilateral exercises suggest that the PLA has become more comfortable operating with foreign forces, albeit those of countries within Asia with which the PRC has agreeable political relationships and which are not part of U.S. alliance relationships.

Domestic exercises. In a new study, Dennis Blasko argues that intra-PLA exercises that feature land forces moving from one military region to another have been a priority for the PLA land forces since 2006. In exercises that have demonstrated ever-increasing complexity, participating units have been compelled to emphasize mobility, flexible command-and-control procedures, and employment of innovative and tailored command-and-control structures. In 2011 the scope of exercises was somewhat downsized, even as more stringent mobility requirements were introduced, including "no notice" movements of one-thousand kilometers (km) or longer, integration with air assets for transportation, and other elements. Blasko's chief finding is that exercises in the 2008–11 period seemed designed to rapidly project military power within China in response to contingencies, whether known or not yet anticipated, and were almost explicitly not directed at a single contingency, such as a Taiwan scenario.[34]

Blasko does not find evidence of advanced preparation to deploy land-force power abroad. Indeed, he finds that much of the mobility priority is placed on rail movement, suggesting that the limits of forward movement by land forces terminate at China's borders with neighboring countries. Airlift is still only used in limited cases, even in airborne exercises in which only a small portion of troopers and equipment are actually airdropped. Helicopter lift is employed in similarly sparse ways. It may be that given current levels of military air- and helicopter-lift support, civilian rail transport remains the most efficient means of moving large numbers of troops and equipment to China's border regions. Air and helicopter support could be employed to lift limited numbers of Chinese forces into neighboring countries once they arrive in border regions. Nonetheless, the relative dearth of air and helicopter lift appears to be an enduring challenge for the power projection of PLA ground forces. Finally, in terms of providing strategic warning, Blasko suggests that

---

[33] Dennis Blasko, "People's Liberation Army and People's Armed Police Ground Exercises with Foreign Forces, 2002–2009" in Kamphausen, Lai, and Scobell, *PLA at Home and Abroad*, 377–428.

[34] Dennis Blasko, "Clarity of Intentions: PLA Trans-regional Exercises to Defend China's Borders," in *Learning By Doing: The PLA Trains at Home and Abroad*, ed. Roy Kamphausen, David Lai, and Travis Tanner (Carlisle: Strategic Studies Institute, forthcoming, 2012).

increased attention be paid to the role of forces in the Jinan Military Region, whose ground forces are assessed to constitute China's strategic reserve.

An important implication of the foregoing is that the land forces' top two missions—protection of CCP power and defense of China's land territory—may together be merged in the now more rapid capability to deploy military power anywhere within China. These responses might be to quell large-scale armed unrest to which the PAP gives an inadequate response, or potentially respond to a situation in which transnational forces interact with Chinese domestic insurgencies at levels that require a PLA land-force response. In some respects, this is a both new and old *raison d'être* for the PLA, not as the overmatched defender that "lures the enemy in deep" but rather as a semi-modern force that seeks to act decisively at and within China's borders in response to any threat of reduced sovereignty or domestic disturbance that threatens the CCP.

Twenty-Year Retrospective: Net Assessment of Changes in the PLA

As noted, China's 2010 defense white paper asserts that PLA ground forces have experienced significant changes in recent years. The PLA has emphasized the development of new types of combat forces, optimized organizational structure, strengthened military training with particular emphasis on mobility and informationization, fielded new systems, and significantly boosted its capabilities in long-distance maneuvers and integrated assaults.[35] But taken together, what is the PLA capable of today that it could not do in 1990? This section will examine two generalized capabilities the PLA has acquired over the last twenty years, and then it will examine each of them within the context of challenges in China's border regions.

The first important change is that the PLA can now rapidly deploy brigade-sized elements throughout China on very short notice by employing PLA Air Force (PLAAF) airlift and PLA Army helicopter lift. For larger-scale movements, rail remains the preferred mode of transport, with trucks and air and helicopter lift providing specialized support for specific capabilities. The PLA has marginally better lift, including helicopters, than it had twenty years ago, but still has limitations (as was seen most poignantly in the limited helicopter-lift support the PLA was able to muster in response to the 2008

---

[35] Information Office of the State Council of the PRC, *China's National Defense in 2010.*

Sichuan earthquake).[36] The PLA does not have the quantities of medium-lift aircraft needed to move large-scale forces at the pace and volume that would support combat operations above the brigade level, suggesting that helicopters would be employed in more specialized air-assault missions and not for general purpose missions that require higher numbers of aircraft.

Second, the PLA is increasingly comfortable conducting more sophisticated trans-regional combined arms exercises, which suggests both the possibility of an emerging trans-regional command-and-control structure and a growing potential to amass forces in response to regional challenges. What might be looming is a change in the current peacetime command-and-control arrangement reducing the seven military regions to five or fewer, or even a more radical restructuring away from the dual-chain military-region structure (with paired military district administrative functions) to a completely operational approach. But to move away from the existing structure would likely result in tremendous opposition from entrenched interests that have grown up around the military district system.

Third, the PLA is comfortable participating in (and sometimes leading) bilateral and multilateral exercises with neighbors, especially the countries of the SCO. This suggests that strategic realities are likely putting pressure on China's long-held adherence to a policy of noninterference in the internal affairs of other states, especially where China's direct interests are at stake. What is not suggested is that the PLA is interested in the near term in military coalition-building or that the SCO is a nascent collective security organization that China might leverage solely toward its own purposes.

Fourth, the PLA is making investments in, and is increasingly comfortable employing, the force multiplier components of advanced personnel training, joint logistics, and innovative structures to respond to national security challenges.

Yet there is much that makes a net assessment a challenging proposition. The PLA self-reports the employment of all means of transportation to deploy within China, but a quick review of available assets shows that land forces are incapable of self-deploying and so must extensively rely on civilian transportation to "get to the fight."[37] While it reports an increasing effort to

---

[36] Chinese media reported the deployment of up to 150 helicopters to support the relief effort, of which the majority were from the PLA. However, there were numerous reports of an inadequate number of the airframes. Blasko's analysis is that the total number of PLA helicopters is about five hundred, of which approximately three-quarters are of the transport variety. The number of helicopters of all types is less than one-tenth of the total inventory of all types in the U.S. armed forces. Blasko, *The Chinese Army Today*, 164.

[37] If all the approximately 200 MI-17 helicopters (each of which can carry about 30 troops) and the 200 Z-9 helicopters (each of which can carry 10 troops) in the PLA aviation units operated simultaneously in a specific region, the PLA could lift a maximum of the equivalent of two brigades of infantry at once.

engage in free-play force-on-force exercises at the division and brigade levels and regularly recounts its shortcomings from those exercises, one wonders about the basis on which top military leaders can assess combat readiness, especially without the real-world gauge of combat operations. It is unknown to what degree PLA exercise and peacetime activity is synched with national security posture and foreign policy objectives in areas where the PLA is seen to play important roles. The next section will analyze this last point—that is, the ways in which the PLA land force presents itself to neighboring countries.

How the PLA Army of 2012 Presents Itself to Regional Neighbors

Force posture and military activities in China's border regions are relatively easy to determine. Assessing what these deployments and other activities actually mean is a much more difficult task, largely because the intent of military leaders is almost entirely opaque. Contingency plans—the means by which a variety of options are explored—prove especially challenging to ferret out.[38] Whereas Western (especially U.S.) strategic culture sees the selective leaking of contingency plans as an occasional tool of deterrence, Chinese obsession with security and secrecy almost completely rules out the possibility that plans might leak. Moreover, even if Beijing-based units—either in the General Staff Department's Operations Department or the Academy of Military Sciences' departments of strategy, operations, and tactics—were to play important roles, it cannot be ruled out that planning cells in specific military-region headquarters are engaged in parallel efforts. Western observers, however, have virtually no insights into these structures or the ways in which they interact with the center.

The best one can do is to piece together a picture from what is observable (exercises, deployments, and statements), what can be inferred (how counterpart nations are reacting, presumably as a function of the intelligence they have gathered on issues of grave national security concern to them), and what is implied by China's long-standing national security goals.

This section examines Chinese interactions with Russia to China's north and northwest; the countries of Central Asia to China's west; India, to China's southwest; continental Southeast Asia and Taiwan, to China's south and east; and North Korea on China's northeast border.

---

[38] All militaries engage in one form of contingency planning or another. Planning for contingencies is not, however, the same as preparing for military operations, although it is often a necessary preparatory phase.

Russia

As a result of the confidence-building measures and steps toward risk reduction previously undertaken under the rubric of the SCO, the nature of the Sino-Russian defense relationship has changed markedly. PLA ground forces present themselves to Russia on China's northern and northeast borders as a cooperative force for regional stability and a willing partner in bilateral and multilateral exercises. PLA ground forces have moved their bases back from the borders and do not conduct exercises within a 100-km belt along the 4,300-km-long Sino-Russian border in accordance with the confidence-building measures begun in the 1990s. The PLA also sees Russian ground forces as an important partner in broader national security objectives. Emblematic of this cooperation is the emergence of the Peace Mission series of annual bilateral and multilateral exercises in which the PLA land forces and Russian armed forces are central participants.

Parts of three military regions—Shenyang, Beijing, and Lanzhou—border Russia, but the ground operational forces are well removed from the border areas. An estimated twelve border-defense regiments help secure the Sino-Russian border. What are judged to be the PLA's best group armies—the 38th Group Army near Beijing and the 39th Group Army near Changchun[39]— still receive newer equipment before other units. Additionally, both have subordinate aviation regiments. While occasionally the 38th Group Army is called a "showcase" unit because it is most frequently visited by foreign guests, in fact it has long played a critical role in defense of the capital. The 38th Group Army retains its historical priority despite a dramatic reduction in the threat of land invasion from China's north and northwest.

Central Asia

China presents itself to the Central Asian states—Kazakhstan, Kyrgyzstan, Tajikistan, Turkmenistan, and Uzbekistan—as a partner in responding to terrorist groups and as a powerful neighbor whose opinions carry considerable weight in the capitals of the region. The PLA occasionally takes a leadership role in SCO security activities in Central Asia.

The Lanzhou Military Region has more than a dozen border-defense regiments poised to help secure China's borders with the Central Asian states, with four mobile divisions within close proximity to the border region. Additionally, the PAP forces in the area constitute an additional mobile force. Together, these land forces are focused on responding to internal uprisings

---

[39] Blasko, *The Chinese Army Today*, 87.

of disaffected minority peoples and preventing the incursion of international terrorist and separatist groups into China.

Joint counterterrorism military exercises within the SCO framework provide the context for this military activity, and these exercises are being institutionalized. In 2002, China ran a joint counterterrorism military exercise with Kyrgyzstan, its first ever with a foreign country. In 2003, it ran a multilateral joint counterterrorism military exercise with other SCO members, again the PLA's first ever with foreign countries. In 2006, China and Tajikistan ran a joint counterterrorism military exercise, which saw Chinese forces operationally deploy into another country within the context of the exercise scenario. China and Russia, as well as other SCO members, likewise ran a series of Peace Mission joint counterterrorism military exercises in 2005, 2007, 2009, and 2010.[40] The June 2012 Peace Mission exercise was the ninth one organized by the SCO.

The SCO counterterrorism exercise regime is also an incubator for policy and operational innovations of the sort that saw PLA forces self-deploy into a foreign country to conduct military activities. This suggests that future SCO multilateral exercises bear watching for innovations that the PLA might undertake first in that context before employing them elsewhere.

South Asia

China's only unresolved land border dispute is with India, and this has provided the strategic backdrop for the infrastructure improvements within the Tibet Autonomous Region that can be construed as efforts to shape the thinking of Indian planners and decision-makers with regard to Chinese contingency planning. PLA combat forces stationed in Tibet include two mountain infantry brigades in Nyingchi (three hundred kilometers east of Lhasa) and a motorized infantry brigade in Lhasa.[41] The completion of the Golmud-Lhasa rail line in October 2005, the first of four anticipated rail lines into Tibet,[42] provides for reliable support, resupply, and potentially reinforcement, but it limits the speed with which reinforcements can deploy into the region. Moreover, the high altitudes of Tibet make widespread employment of helicopter lift problematic, given the ceiling limitations of the Chinese helicopter force. The closest army aviation regiment is in Chengdu, more than two thousand kilometers away.

[40] Information Office of the State Council of the PRC, *China's National Defense in 2010.*

[41] Blasko, *The Chinese Army Today*, 100–101.

[42] Raviprasad Narayanan, "Railway to Lhasa: An Assessment," *Strategic Analysis* 29, no. 4 (2005): 739–45, http://www.idsa.in/strategicanalysis/RailwaytoLhasaAnAssessment_rnarayanan_1008.

In addition to seeking to shape Indian thinking on the border resolution issues, the increase of infrastructure development in Tibet may serve at least two other purposes from a Chinese perspective. The first, domestic in origin, is to respond to demands from Beijing for infrastructure development in poorer regions. Tibet has proved a likely destination for the relatively free-flowing investment capital in infrastructure development in recent years.

The second is that infrastructure development in Tibet may serve Chinese strategic purposes by helping secure access to resources, especially the waters of the Himalayas from which glacier melt flows into eight of Asia's major rivers and supports the irrigation, drinking, and power-generation needs of nearly one-third of the world's population.[43] By facilitating the means for the rapid movement of reinforcing PLA land forces into the border regions, Chinese strategists complicate the planning of other water claimants downstream, in much the same way as more robust PLA presence in disputed areas of the East and South China seas raise concerns by other disputants. While cross-border raids to seize and divert riverine resources is a highly unlikely course of action for the PLA, an integrated Chinese security policy approach usually entails an important role for the PLA, especially if the stakes can be raised for other nations in ways that tilt the balance toward China.

Southeast Asia

China's interests concerning the countries of continental Southeast Asia with which it shares borders center on water usage and management issues, as well as on managing insurgent minority rights issues that have cross-border implications. The PLA plays very limited roles in these contexts. Myanmar is a case in which PLA roles, especially in arms sales and training, may have been more significant and potentially oriented toward a strategic effort to gain overland access to the Bay of Bengal and wider Indian Ocean. But here too Myanmar's rebuff of a Chinese plan for a hydroelectric dam demonstrates the importance of water issues and points out the limits to cooperation between the two militaries.[44]

Elsewhere in Southeast Asia, the PLA has previously sought an opportunity to provide leadership to the nations of the Association of Southeast Asian Nations (ASEAN) in a military context but was rebuffed. Chinese efforts to initiate an ASEAN +3 structure with initial meetings

---

[43] This is a conservative estimate of the population supported by these rivers. Kenneth Pomeranz broadly suggests that half of the world's population is affected by Himalayan waters. See Kenneth Pomeranz, "The Great Himalayan Watershed: Agrarian Crisis, Mega-Dams and the Environment," *New Left Review* 58 (2009): 5–39.

[44] Bertil Lintner, "Burma Delivers Its First Rebuff to China" *YaleGlobal Online*, October 3, 2011, http://yaleglobal.yale.edu/content/burma-delivers-its-first-rebuff-china.

at the vice-ministerial level were met with disinterest by the countries of Southeast Asia, not least because the Chinese plan would have excluded observers (including the United States). More recently, the PLA has appeared much more willing to participate in the new ASEAN Defence Ministers' Meeting-Plus (ADMM-Plus) and be supportive without seeking disproportionate leadership.[45]

PLA forces in the Nanjing and Guangzhou military regions include the only two amphibious mechanized infantry divisions, as well as an amphibious armored brigade.[46] While historically associated with potential operations against Taiwan, these forces are also postured to undertake missions in the disputed regions of the East and South China seas. Their amphibious orientation suggests that contingency planning for missions in continental Southeast Asia is a lower priority; transnational crime poses greater security challenges for China in these areas than traditional military threats. Even the border region between China and Vietnam—the scene of fierce fighting in 1979—remains relatively quiescent, even as two countries pursue conflicting maritime claims in the South China Sea.

Northeast Asia

Whereas Chinese military planning with other bordering regions appears to center on either bringing about changes in the other country or accomplishing goals collectively, China's military contingency planning for North Korea appears to focus on the ways in which China will need to secure its own interests in the event of a North Korean collapse. These include securing China's border with North Korea in anticipation of a large-scale cross-border movement of refugees, deployment of small-scale units within North Korea to secure strategic sites (namely, nuclear facilities), and movement into North Korea to secure economic interests such as those in Rajin-Sonbong.[47] The PLA land forces in the Shenyang Military Region bordering North Korea include some of the most capable units in the PLA, especially in the 39th Group Army, which is one of the few group armies with an organic helicopter regiment. Coupled with robust border-defense regiments, the PLA in the Shenyang Military Region is poised to respond to a range of contingencies in North Korea.[48]

[45] "ASEAN Defence Ministers' Meeting-Plus (ADMM-Plus)" (concept paper prepared for the inaugural ADMM-Plus meeting in Hanoi, October 2010), http://www.aseansec.org/21216.pdf.

[46] Blasko, *The Chinese Army Today*, 97–99.

[47] Rowan Callick, "Beijing 'Sends Troop Contingent' into North Korea," *Australian*, January 18, 2011, http://www.theaustralian.com.au/news/world/beijing-sends-troop-contingent-into-north-korea/story-e6frg6so-1225989815007.

[48] Blasko, *The Chinese Army Today*, 87–88.

That there is little evidence of interaction between the PLA ground forces of the Shenyang Military Region and the Korean People's Army (KPA) suggests that the PLA is mostly undertaking unilateral planning preparation, perhaps hedging against the possibility of regime collapse in North Korea. The interaction that does exist between the two militaries is mostly of the political commissar type or involves military foreign affairs exchanges. For example, head of the PLA General Political Department and CMC member General Li Jinai visited the Democratic People's Republic of Korea in November 2011, continuing the practice of PLA political department interactions with KPA political counterparts; and Major General Qian Lihua, chief of the Foreign Affairs Office of the Ministry of National Defense, led a delegation to North Korea in April 2012.

Trajectories for PLA Ground Forces in the Coming Decade

Looking ahead to 2025, one can anticipate some important changes for the PLA. There are four likely changes that are important to understand for their potential impact on the PLA's ability to conduct power projection of its land forces to China's periphery.

First, one can expect the debate to intensify over when or how the PLA might reform the current structure of seven military regions. The outcome of the debate will have important ramifications for the degree to which the PLA land forces become more expeditionary. The current structure of the military regions evokes the pre-modernization period in which PLA ground forces were essentially static garrison forces whose chief role was to help defend Chinese territory. An updated capabilities-based structure would appear to be better suited to carry out the new historic missions and could more easily accomplish a variety of tasks, including to array forces for border contingencies and project land power at China's periphery. A capabilities-based structure also presents opportunities to reduce needless force structure, allowing for resource reallocation or savings. Recent ground-force exercise patterns provide support for all these possibilities.[49]

However, the military-region structure serves more than simply to prepare for operational contingencies. Indeed, the provincial military districts and their subordinate military districts and subdistricts both perform critical civil-military roles related to mobilization and demobilization and represent entrenched bureaucracies that might prove difficult to dislodge. Thus, any

---

[49] Blasko, "Clarity of Intentions."

significant changes to the military-region structure are likely to be contentious events observable by outsiders.

Second, one can also expect PLA land forces to continue to play an active, if distant, role in internal security, the mission that "dare not speak its name."[50] While it is true the PLA learned the lesson after Tiananmen Square in June 1989 that it never wants to be called on again to use deadly force against Chinese citizens, it does serve the PLA's interests for the central leadership to be reminded on occasion that only the PLA ground forces can be completely counted on to perform this mission in a crunch. The immense problems posed to the public security apparatus in 2012 only serve to highlight this point. In an era in which the air and maritime forces will see an ever-greater emphasis based on new external mission requirements, it will be important for the central leadership to remember that PLA ground forces are the force of last resort to guarantee domestic security.

Third, we may also see an intensified set of intra-PLA struggles between land forces and the surging navy, Second Artillery, and air force over resources and priorities. The land forces still comprise the bulk of the PLA, are the linkage between the CCP and its revolutionary past, and are charged with the fundamental national security missions of defending China's sovereignty and the rule of the Communist Party. Yet, as we have seen, the number of ground forces in place to carry out these missions is outsized for the task, suggesting that more realignment of forces is necessary.[51] This realignment, or "rebalancing" between the army, navy, air forces, and Second Artillery, becomes more necessary as the PLA looks to secure China's global national security interests. In many respects, the struggles for resources between the services will provide insight into how expeditionary China's CMC hopes the PLA will become. One can conjure up a variety of scenarios for how a future PLA might seek to project power—for instance, from a modest regional power-projection posture in which land forces would still play a significant role, all the way to a full-scale global capability in which a blue water navy and robust air force and Second Artillery would be more prominent. The new slate of PLA leaders, who will assume their positions after the 18th Party Congress in fall 2012, may well include a doubled representation of senior officers from the PLA Air Force and Navy, perhaps lending strength to a move

---

[50] Tanner, "How China Manages Internal Security," 39–40.

[51] There are other explanations beyond historical links and bureaucratic inertia for why the PLA maintains such a large ground force. Chief among them may well be the neuralgia the central leadership feels about its internal security challenges.

toward a globally expeditionary PLA and thus necessarily more powerful and capable air and naval forces.[52]

Fourth, one will likely continue to see evolutions in land force structure and capabilities mix. Bearing in mind the sort of hybrid force structure discussed earlier that the PLA ground forces are evolving into, it becomes important to understand the tailored approaches for different regions that the PLA is likely pursuing. How the PLA sees its preparations for contingencies in bordering regions appears to be a function of at least several factors, notably the pattern of exercises undertaken by the PLA in those regions within the context of overall strategic relations. The next section analyzes these individual subregions and the likely roles the PLA will take in them in coming years.

Russia: Confidence-Building Bilaterally with a Strategic Hedge

Some Russian strategic thinkers remain wary of potential Chinese designs on the wide-open spaces in the Russian Far East,[53] and strategic cooperation between the two on issues such as a joint missile-defense response to U.S. nuclear hegemony and new space and cyber capabilities is uneven and tenuous, suggesting strategic disconnects.[54] However, at the operational level the Sino-Russian defense and security partnerships have implemented the confidence-building and risk-reduction measures envisioned in the early 1990s, and these are unlikely to change in significant ways or be reversed. Clearly demarcated borders, troop reductions in the border regions, and advance notification of domestic military exercises have raised the level of mutual confidence and reduced the risk of accidental conflict that had marked the bilateral relationship since the Sino-Soviet split of the early 1960s. These bilateral steps have provided important context for the SCO military exercise series that falls under the "Peace Mission" moniker. The Peace Mission exercises serve to address counterterrorism missions in partnership with the SCO's Central Asian members. The exercises also serve more strategic purposes for China and Russia, inasmuch as they can help convey strategic deterrent messages to each country's regional and global strategic challengers.

---

[52] PLA Navy commander Wu Shengli and PLA Air Force commander Xu Qiliang, neither of whom has yet reached retirement age, are likely candidates to be promoted within the CMC to either of the commission's vice-chairman positions or to the minister of national defense. If this were to happen, and if their successors as service commanders were likewise made CMC members, the number of non-army CMC members would double. In some scenarios, PLA Navy and Air Force officers might occupy up to two other CMC positions, further strengthening the naval and air arms' positions.

[53] Rajan Menon, "The China-Russia Relationship: What It Involves, Where It Is Headed, and How It Matters for the United States," Century Foundation, Report, 2009, http://tcf.org/publications/pdfs/pb690/Menon.pdf.

[54] Richard Weitz, *China-Russia Security Relations: Strategic Parallelism without Partnership or Passion?* (Carlisle: Strategic Studies Institute, 2008).

For China, this means that although the Peace Mission exercises might superficially have the mission to respond to terrorist challenges, the format and structure of the exercises suggest that Taiwan, Japan, and even the United States are intended recipients of the deterrent messages.

This approach is likely to continue. Recently the ninth exercise organized by the SCO was held in Tajikistan, with all but Uzbekistan participating. In coming years, we might well anticipate increasing numbers of observers from neighboring countries, in a format not dissimilar to that employed by Cobra Gold, the annual U.S.-led multilateral exercise in Thailand.

Central Asia: Enhanced Counterterrorism with Overtones of a More Active PLA Abroad

China long had an aversion to the stationing of troops abroad and vowed never to intervene in the internal affairs of another state.[55] This was a rigid position that denied relevance and responsibilities to a China that was becoming a global power. In the context of jointly responding to shared risks, the PLA has recently seemed to be willing to move beyond this position. As described above, when in September 2006 the PLA and Tajik armed forces participated in a joint exercise that featured the PLA deploying troops across the border into neighboring Tajikistan to help rescue Chinese engineers who had been kidnapped by terrorists while working on a road project, the veil on the self-prohibition against deployment of forces into other countries was partially lifted. This sort of operational and policy innovation, carried out in a multilateral context, may well be a template for future reforms. Indeed, one can expect to see continuing innovations of operations and policy for the PLA ground forces within the context of the SCO, in particular given these forces' relationships with the countries of Central Asia.

South Asia: Pressure with Little Likelihood of Conflict

China will likely retain its desire for the PLA's activities in Tibet to complicate the strategic thinking of Indian administrations by combining an intimidating presence and enhanced logistical support in the region. The degree to which China has attracted the attention of Indian strategic planners suggests that the Chinese approach has been successful, at least on its face, and may well continue.

PLA planners might also foresee a role for its land forces in Tibet as a player in the resolution of water rights issues. Highly mobile special

---

[55] This has been a central tenet of China's noninterference approach to national security policy since the beginnings of the Non-Aligned Movement at the 1954 Bandung Conference in Indonesia.

operations forces supported by much more capable helicopter assault might serve this role well.

Northeast Asia: Maintaining Options

Beijing's clear desire is that North Korea reform—perhaps following the Chinese model—ostensibly for the benefit of the Korean people but especially so that the North Korean regime retains its unique buffer-state status. Yet the PLA appears to be playing little role in support of the Kim family regime, despite the PLA's historic closeness to the KPA and the capabilities that the PLA might bring to bear, suggesting a level of mistrust. That the PLA is not seen as meddling in North Korean domestic political affairs, as was sometimes purported in the past, may be desirable from Pyongyang's perspective, but the absence of any observable interaction between the operational forces of the PLA and North Korea's KPA suggests there are limits to Beijing's support. Indeed, the absence of contact may well mean that the PLA is unilaterally preparing for contingencies that respond to developments in the DPRK rather than shape outcomes there.

Potential PLA contingency plans likely include the employment of forces resident in the Shenyang Military Region to perform a range of missions that deal with the fallout from a collapse of the North Korean regime. Refugees are a big concern, and so one can anticipate a range of contingencies, including a strict closure of the border to prevent refugee flow and more aggressive cross-border operations to establish a screen within North Korea and limit refugee movement up to the border. Beijing would also be concerned with North Korean nuclear sites and facilities, and the contingencies for dealing with these challenges likely involve the special operations forces in the Shenyang Military Region. But the absence of coordination and contact with U.S. and South Korean special forces concerned with these same nuclear sites makes for a potentially risky and volatile situation. One can also imagine a more extreme contingency in which PLA forces enter North Korea in large numbers to restore order and maintain a buffer region. While much lower in probability—and the evidence for such planning is scanty, if it exists at all—PLA forces in the Shenyang Military Region would almost certainly be insufficient for the task. One could anticipate the strategic reserve forces from Jinan Military Region moving into the Shenyang Region, and the movement of these forces would also increase the chances of observation by outsiders.

Conclusion

The chapter finds that Chinese national security interests have moved beyond limited continental defensive goals, leading to a somewhat diminished importance for PLA land forces. As China's interests increasingly require the ability to project power globally in scope, if still limited in the means and methods of doing so, the PLA Navy, Air Force, and Second Artillery are now much more consequential in the accomplishment of broader goals. The army finds itself left with the traditional territorial integrity and defense of sovereignty missions. Meanwhile, the PLA has continued to modernize and now has much-improved capabilities in numerous dimensions, including tactical mobility, secure command and control, and supporting personnel and structural dimensions that serve as force multipliers.

Despite reasonably secure borders, China still faces security challenges, and the PLA land forces have developing specialized capabilities and structures for dealing with each of the regions bordering China. Indeed, the chapter finds that the PLA land forces have tailored their approach to each of the regions. On China's northern border with Russia, two decades of operational-level confidence-building efforts have reduced China's strategic risk and enhanced bilateral military ties to the degree that the two sides now display limited interoperability, at least of the sort that could complicate U.S. contingency planning for Northeast Asia. With China's Central Asian co-partners in the SCO, the PLA is accomplishing national goals—suppressing dissent cloaked as separatism, terrorism, and extremism—while appearing to support broader international goals regarding nonstate terrorism in ways that support leadership opportunities for China's defense establishment. Moreover, Central Asia and the counterterrorism exercise regime to which the PLA belongs have become test cases for how Chinese land forces might be employed in foreign crises. In South Asia, the PLA appears to be enjoying the results of infrastructure improvement in Tibet that will increase the mobility of forces in that remote region and thus position the PLA to be a player in multilateral deliberations on natural resources, including water. In Southeast Asia, the PLA's chief defense goals appear to be limited but are modestly concerned with cross-border ethnic issues and a vague, far-off hope for multilateral leadership opportunities. Finally, on China's northeast border with North Korea, PLA land force efforts appear to be weighted toward mitigating Chinese risk from refugees and other challenges that might emanate from a collapsing North Korean regime.

Appendix: PLA Land Forces

PLA land forces consist of approximately 1.25–1.50 million soldiers in 18 group armies, approximately 18 motorized infantry divisions, 8 mechanized infantry divisions, 9 armor divisions, 22 motorized infantry brigades, 6 mechanized infantry brigades, and 9 armored brigades.

Shenyang Military Region

- 16th Group Army (Changchun, Jilin): two motorized divisions and two motorized brigades
- 39th Group Army (Liaoyang, Liaoning): two mechanized infantry divisions and an armored division, and one helicopter regiment
- 40th Group Army (Jinzhou, Liaoning): three brigades, two motorized and one armored

Beijing Military Region

- 27th Group Army (Shijiazhuang, Hebei): two motorized brigades, two mechanized infantry brigades, and one armored brigade
- 38th Group Army (Baoding, Hebei): two mechanized infantry divisions, one armored brigade, and one helicopter regiment
- 65th Group Army (Zhangjiakou, Hebei): one infantry division, one armored division, and one motorized infantry brigade

Lanzhou Military Region

- 21st Group Army (Baoji, Shaanxi): one infantry division and one armored division
- 47th Group Army (Lintong, Shaanxi): two motorized infantry brigades, one mechanized infantry brigade, and one armored brigade

Jinan Military Region

- 20th Group Army (Kaifeng, Henan): one motorized brigade, one mechanized infantry brigade, and one armored brigade
- 26th Group Army (Weifang, Shandong): three motorized infantry brigades, one armored division, and one helicopter regiment

- 54th Group Army (Xinxiang, Henan): one motorized division, one mechanized infantry division, one armored division, and one helicopter regiment

Nanjing Military Region

- 1st Group Army (Huzhou, Zhejiang): one amphibious division, one motorized infantry division, one armored division, and one helicopter regiment
- 12th Group Army (Xuzhou, Jiangsu): three motorized infantry brigades and one armored division
- 31st Group Army (Xiamen, Fujian): two motorized infantry divisions, one motorized infantry brigade, one amphibious armored brigade, and one helicopter regiment

Guangzhou Military Region

- 41st Group Army (Liuzhou, Guangxi): one infantry division, one motorized infantry division, and one armored brigade
- 42nd Group Army (Huizhou, Guangdong): one amphibious mechanized infantry division, one infantry division, one armored brigade, and one helicopter regiment

Chengdu Military Region

- 13th Group Army (Chongqing): two infantry divisions, one armored brigade, and one helicopter regiment
- 14th Group Army (Kunming, Yunnan): two infantry divisions and one armored brigade
- Other (Tibet): two motorized infantry brigades and one mechanized infantry brigade

SOURCE: Office of the Secretary of Defense, "Annual Report to Congress: Military and Security Developments Involving the People's Republic of China," May 2012, http://www.defense.gov/pubs/pdfs/2012_CMPR_Final.pdf; and Dennis J. Blasko, *The Chinese Army Today: Tradition and Transformation for the 21st Century*, 2nd ed. (New York: Routledge, 2012), 87–102.

EXECUTIVE SUMMARY

This chapter assesses China's modernization of its naval and air power capabilities and draws implications for U.S. interests in the Asia-Pacific.

MAIN ARGUMENT:
At the strategic and tactical levels, China's naval and air forces can now achieve a variety of effects unattainable a decade or two ago. Although these capabilities are concentrated on operations in the near seas close to mainland China, with layers radiating outward, the PLA is also conducting increasing, albeit nonlethal, activities farther from China's periphery, including in the Indian Ocean. Over the next decade and beyond, China's naval and air power forces could assume a range of postures and trajectories. At a minimum, a greater diversity of out-of-area missions will depend on strengthening and broadening anti-access/area-denial (A2/AD) capabilities. While China is likely to develop and acquire the necessary hardware should it elect to expend sufficient resources, "software" will be harder to accrue.

POLICY IMPLICATIONS:
- The PLA will continue to focus on high-end A2/AD capabilities to secure China's maritime periphery, along with its growing but low-intensity capabilities farther abroad.

- U.S. policymakers should seek ways to resist Chinese pressure in the near seas and cooperate with China in areas of mutual interest farther afield.

- The U.S. must demonstrate the ability to persist amid A2/AD threats in a manner that is convincing to China, allies, and the general public.

- The U.S. must demonstrate a commitment to sustaining a properly resourced and continually effective presence in the Asia-Pacific. Rebalancing by redirecting resources from elsewhere will be essential and determine the success of these initiatives.

China's Modernization of Its Naval and Air Power Capabilities

Andrew S. Erickson

The People's Republic of China (PRC) entered the second decade of the 21st century as a global economic and political power. The country is now in its third decade of rapid military modernization and boasts growing regional capabilities. Poverty in its vast interior, ethnic unrest in its western regions, and ongoing territorial and maritime disputes continue to necessitate that China prioritize military development and focus high-end military capabilities on its homeland and immediate periphery. Specifically, China's naval and air power modernization has been concerned largely with developing a variant of regional anti-access/area-denial (A2/AD)—or "active defense" and "counter-intervention" from Beijing's perspective—to deter Taiwan from declaring independence. An important part of this strategy is to demonstrate China's ability to hold U.S. forces at risk should Washington elect to intervene in a cross-strait crisis or other disputes in the near seas.

Operationally, asymmetric capabilities represent the core of the high-end development of the People's Liberation Army (PLA). Based partially on "nonlinear, noncontact, and asymmetric" (*sanfei*) operations, they match key Chinese strengths against U.S. weaknesses. China systematically targets physics-based limitations in U.S., allied, and friendly military platforms, thereby seeking to place them on the wrong end of physics. By developing the world's foremost sub-strategic missile force, for instance, the PLA

Andrew S. Erickson is an Associate Professor in the Strategic Research Department at the U.S. Naval War College. He can be reached at <andrew.erickson@usnwc.edu>.

The author thanks Ken Allen, Roger Cliff, Richard Fisher, Alison Kaufman, Nan Li, Oriana Mastro, William Murray, Ben Purser, and four anonymous reviewers for helpful suggestions and Jonathan Walton for invaluable research assistance.

exploits the fact that it is generally easier to attack with missiles than to defend against them. This affords China a defensive posture along interior lines and renders U.S. forces inherently vulnerable.

At the tactical level, China's actual approach of employing "active strategic counterattacks on exterior lines" may be more nuanced and change more with specific circumstances than Western depictions of A2/AD imply.[1] For example, compared with the U.S. and some allied militaries, the PLA continues to face weaknesses in command, control, communications, computers, intelligence, surveillance, and reconnaissance (C4ISR). For high-priority missions on China's periphery, however, the PLA can compensate for these limitations in complex real-time monitoring and coordination capability by massing forces selectively, maneuvering them specifically, and separating them in time and space. In peacetime, services may not be in perfect alignment and may have other tasks to perform.

With cross-strait relations stabilizing and China continuing to grow as a global stakeholder, the PLA Navy (PLAN) is likely to supplement this A2/AD strategy centered on Taiwan and the South China Sea, which China's current naval platforms and weaponry largely support, with "new but limited requirements for protection of the sea lines of communication (SLOC) beyond China's own waters, humanitarian assistance/disaster relief (HADR), and expanded naval diplomacy."[2] As the world's second-largest economy, China's interests increasingly extend beyond its shores to resource-rich areas of the developing world and the trade- and energy-choked SLOCs of the Indian Ocean. The country's manufacturing industries consume a tremendously high volume of imported resources, with 40% of oil arriving by sea.

By 2020, the PLA seeks a "regional [blue water] defensive and offensive-type" navy with extended A2/AD capabilities, limited expeditionary capabilities, and corresponding defensive and offensive air power.[3] Such a force would be able to deny access by holding opposing forces at risk throughout China's periphery and the approaches to it (out to and beyond the second island chain and the full extent of the South China Sea). In addition, this force could conduct marine interception operations and high-level noncombatant evacuation operations (NEO), when necessary, in the western Pacific and Indian Ocean.

---

[1] Anton Lee Wishik II, "An Anti-Access Approximation," *China Security* 19 (2011): 37–48.

[2] Office of Naval Intelligence, *The People's Liberation Army Navy: A Modern Navy with Chinese Characteristics* (Suitland, August 2009), 45.

[3] Nan Li, "The Evolution of China's Naval Strategy and Capabilities: From 'Near Coast' and 'Near Seas' to 'Far Seas,'" *Asian Security* 5, no. 2 (2009): 168.

Achieving this goal, however, will require significant improvements in China's defense industry, military organizational structure, and Second Artillery and space forces—all of which are beyond the scope of this chapter—as well as in personnel, training, and software integration. China is not making the necessary preparations to achieve a military with U.S.-style global power projection within the next ten to twenty years and apparently does not currently aspire to such a capability. While it is possible that changes or opportunities could alter Beijing's approach, at present, quality is being emphasized over quantity in many respects, to the point that the PLA of 2020–25—in terms of platforms, in particular, like all major modern navies—is likely to be far more capable, but limited in size. Indicators of dramatic deviations from this course would be visible well in advance, and the majority have not yet manifested themselves. This is hardly surprising, as many near-seas territorial and maritime claims remain unresolved, whereas the far seas (e.g., the western Pacific and Indian Ocean) lack such disputes and hence an obvious basis for strategic focus. Regardless, as China's naval and air forces continue rising, while its neighbors worry and the United States remains determined to advance U.S. interests in the strategic Asia-Pacific region, it is highly likely that the near seas, and possibly adjacent areas, will represent an important zone of strategic competition. China has fundamentally different strategic interests in the near and far seas, so one cannot take Chinese behavior in one area as indicative of the other.

This chapter begins by outlining China's national interests, the PLA's "new historic missions," and current naval and air power forces. It then identifies these forces' integration, limitations, and prospects for improvement before offering near-term strategic implications, with a focus on new strategic, operational, and tactical capabilities produced by the PLA's two decades of military modernization. The next section examines alternative naval and air power force postures and trajectories through 2025, while highlighting PLA goals, the new historic missions to date, necessary hardware and software, and visible indicators, including the possible establishment of overseas access points. The chapter then analyzes possible new effects, including enhanced Chinese leverage vis-à-vis the United States and its Asian allies and the PLA's ability to establish suzerainty in the near seas, before concluding with a discussion of larger strategic implications.

China's National Interests

Throughout its history, China has pursued three core grand strategic goals: "first and foremost, the preservation of domestic order and well-being in the face of different forms of social strife; second, the defense against persistent external threats to national sovereignty and territory; and third, the attainment and maintenance of geopolitical influence as a major, and perhaps primary, state."[4] According to its 2010 defense white paper, China today pursues five major national interests, which build on the earlier foundation:[5]

- Safeguarding national sovereignty and security
- Promoting national development
- Maintaining domestic social stability
- Modernizing military forces
- Maintaining world peace and stability

In focusing on maintaining national sovereignty and furthering reunification, China devotes attention to border issues and territorial and maritime claims, which the United States has not had to confront for over a century. Based on these larger national interests, China's main military priorities, in descending order, include:[6]

- Addressing Taiwan's status, still the "main strategic direction" (*zhuyao zhanlüe fangxiang*)
- Fortifying and increasing China's maritime and aerial buffer zones
- Addressing territorial and maritime claims in the near seas
- Enhancing China's great-power status
- Achieving and maintaining a secure second-strike nuclear deterrent (with a sea-based component)

To pursue these priorities, China's leaders must direct the PLA's development. Building on Jiang Zemin's doctrinal foundation, Chairman Hu Jintao introduced a new military policy that defined the four new historic missions of the PLA at an expanded Central Military Commission (CMC) conference on December 24, 2004:

---

[4] Michael D. Swaine and Ashley J. Tellis, *Interpreting China's Grand Strategy: Past, Present, and Future* (Santa Monica: RAND, 2000), x.

[5] Information Office of the State Council of the People's Republic of China, *China's National Defense in 2010* (Beijing, March 2011), http://news.xinhuanet.com/english2010/china/2011-03/31/c_13806851.htm.

[6] U.S. Department of Defense, *Military and Security Developments Involving the People's Republic of China 2011*, annual report prepared for Congress (Washington, D.C., August 24, 2011), 59, http://www.defense.gov/pubs/pdfs/2011_CMPR_Final.pdf.

- Ensuring military support for continued Chinese Communist Party (CCP) rule
- Defending China's sovereignty, territorial integrity, and national security
- Protecting China's expanding national interests
- Ensuring a peaceful global environment and promoting mutual development[7]

The last two missions reflected new emphases for the PLA, and the fourth was unprecedented. Hu required the PLA "to not only pay close attention to the interests of national survival, but also to national development interests; and not only to safeguard the security of national territory, territorial waters, and airspace, but also to safeguard electromagnetic space, outer space, the ocean, and other aspects of national security."[8]

In 2007, Hu elaborated on this shift: "As we strengthen our ability to fight and win limited wars under informationized conditions, we have to pay even more attention to improving noncombat military operations capabilities."[9] In an attempt to transform Hu's general guidance into more specific policy, articles in state and military media have argued that the PLA must go beyond its previous mission of safeguarding national "survival interests" (*shengcun liyi*) to protecting national "development interests" (*fazhan liyi*)—that is, economic growth.[10] That same year, a CCP constitutional amendment codified these missions further.[11] In March 2009, Hu exhorted military delegates to the National People's Congress to emphasize not only "building core military capabilities" but also "the ability to carry out military operations other than war [*feizhanzheng junshi huodong*]."[12] High-level PLA officers are now conducting sophisticated analysis of the noncombat military operations needed to promote these interests.

---

[7] "Qieshi jiaqiang jundui dang zuzhi nengli jianshe" [Earnestly Step Up Ability-Building within CPC Organizations of Armed Forces], *Jiefangjun bao*, December 13, 2004.

[8] Liu Mingfu, Cheng Gang, and Sun Xuefu, "Renmin jundui lishi shiming de youyici yushi jujin" [The Historical Mission of the People's Army Once Again Advances with the Times], *Jiefangjun bao*, December 8, 2005.

[9] Shen Jinlong, "Haijun fei zhanzheng junshi xingdong: Mianlin de tiaozhan ji duice" [Naval Noncombat Military Operations: Challenges Faced and Countermeasures], *Renmin haijun*, December 1, 2008.

[10] Tian Bingren, "Xin shiji jieduan wo jun lishi shiming de kexue fazhan" [The Scientific Development of the Historical Mission of Our Army in the New Phase of the New Century], *Zhongguo junshi kexue* (2007): 21–27.

[11] U.S. Department of Defense, *Military and Security Developments Involving the People's Republic of China 2011*, 16.

[12] Ibid., 17.

China's 2010 defense white paper explains that "the PLAAF [PLA Air Force] is working to ensure the development of a combat force structure that focuses on air strikes, air and missile defense, and strategic projection, to improve its leadership and command system and build up an [informationized], networked base support system."[13] According to the U.S. Department of Defense, the PLA's new missions are "driving discussions about the future of the PLAAF, where a general consensus has emerged that protecting China's global interests requires an increase in the PLAAF's long-range transportation and logistics capabilities." Nevertheless, the report concludes that "it is likely that the Air Force's primary focus for the coming decade will remain on building the capabilities required to pose a credible military threat to Taiwan and U.S. forces in East Asia, deter Taiwan independence, or influence Taiwan to settle the dispute on Beijing's terms."[14]

PLA naval and aviation forces must thus prepare for the traditional missions of coercing Taiwan and furthering China's other territorial and maritime claims in the near seas, while also supporting increasing nontraditional operations. Indeed, aside from operations in the East and South China seas since 2002, China's major uses of naval and air power under Hu's tenure have been in the latter category. PLA out-of-area operations have taken the form of well-publicized peacetime missions that do not themselves demonstrate high-intensity military capabilities. The guided-missile destroyer *Qingdao* and supply ship *Taicang* visited ten countries in 132 days during 2002 in the PLAN's first global circumnavigation. Under the aegis of the fourth new historic mission, the PLAN has begun initial forays into HADR. Likewise, eleven counterpiracy task forces have deterred pirates in the Gulf of Aden since December 2008. China's first purpose-built (vice converted) hospital ship, the 10,000-ton Type 920 Daishandao-class (called *Heping Fangzhou*, or "Peace Ark"), was sent on an 88-day mission in August–October 2010 (Harmonious Mission 2010) to treat PLAN personnel in the Gulf of Aden and 15,500 people in Djibouti, Kenya, Tanzania, Seychelles, and Bangladesh. In October 2011 the *Peace Ark* began the PLAN's first operational naval deployment to the Caribbean, with port calls in Cuba, Jamaica, Trinidad and Tobago, and Costa Rica over three months as part of Harmonious Mission 2011.

The PLAN's nontraditional security contributions are likely to grow and could ultimately include direct support to UN operations. In September 2010 the training vessel *Zheng He* and guided-missile frigate *Mianyang*

[13] Information Office of the State Council of the PRC, *China's National Defense in 2010.*

[14] U.S. Department of Defense, *Military and Security Developments Involving the People's Republic of China 2010*, annual report prepared for Congress (Washington, D.C., August 16, 2010), 25, http://www.defense.gov/pubs/pdfs/2010_cmpr_final.pdf.

called on Papua New Guinea, Tonga, New Zealand, and Australia. In February 2011, in its first operational Mediterranean deployment, the PLAN diverted the Jiangkai II–class frigate *Xuzhou* with an embarked Z-9C helicopter to escort a ship evacuating Chinese nationals from Libya. Simultaneously, the PLAAF sent four IL-76 transport aircraft to Libya via Khartoum, Sudan, to evacuate over 1,700 Chinese. Most recently, in April 2012, the *Zheng He* departed Dalian on the first single-ship global circumnavigation by a Chinese training vessel.

The Baseline of Current Capabilities

China is achieving rapid but uneven maritime and air power development. These capabilities, which are divided among PLA service arms, will be addressed in the following two sections.

Current Naval Power Capabilities

The PLAN has five service arms: submarine, surface, naval aviation, coastal defense, and marine corps. It has three fleets (North Sea, East Sea, and South Sea), as well as naval airbases and testing ranges, and controls 25 coastal defense districts with roughly 35 artillery and missile units (see **Tables A1** and **A2** in the Appendix).[15] The PLAN's greatest strengths include conventional submarines, offensive mines, and missiles. Since the early 2000s, the PLAN has made organizational changes to facilitate the mixing, matching, and supporting of vessels to enable their more complex and effective use operationally, both farther from their home ports and under different weather conditions.[16] It currently focuses on improving "combat force integration" and "strategic deterrence and counterattack" in the near seas and the ability to operate and counter nontraditional security threats in the far seas.[17]

Submarines. Arguably the true capital ship in the post–Cold War era, submarines are being prioritized by China as missile-delivery platforms. China is currently developing and producing as many as six different classes of submarines: two classes of indigenously designed diesel vessels, including the Yuan-class (Type 041), and four of nuclear vessels. The latter include the Shang-class (Type 093) and Jin-class (Type 094) nuclear-powered ballistic

---

[15] *Directory of People's Republic of China Military Personalities* (Honolulu: Serold Hawaii, 2011).

[16] U.S. Office of Naval Intelligence, *China's Navy 2007* (Washington, D.C., 2007), 39–40.

[17] Information Office of the State Council of the PRC, *China's National Defense in 2010*.

missile submarines (SSBN) and the follow-on Type 095 nuclear-powered attack submarine (SSN) and Tang-class (Type 096) SSBN.

PLAN organizational interests, long-term force development, and prospects for stressing missile-defense systems at vulnerable azimuths likely propel SSBN development in the direction of constant deterrent patrols. China's first Type 094 SSBN was launched in July 2004, its second was launched in 2006, and its third in 2009; additionally, as many as three hulls remain under construction.[18] However, the JL-2 submarine-launched ballistic missile (SLBM) has not reached initial operational capability. Moreover, China's nuclear-powered submarines remain relatively noisy, suggesting that Types 095 and 096, or other variants, could be the first truly capable vessels, although that remains to be seen.[19] China's conventional submarines, by contrast, are already relatively quiet,[20] and in this area the PLAN boasts the world's premier force (see **Table A3** in the Appendix).

Surface combatants. Since the early 1990s, China has deployed four Russian-purchased Sovremenny-class destroyers and nine classes of indigenous surface vessels: five new incrementally improved classes of destroyers and four new classes of indigenously constructed frigates (the latter two classes are based on the earlier two). Though still one of the world's largest, China's fleet has decreased in number but increased rapidly in quality, value (due to platforms fielding such weapons as antiship missiles), the sophistication and range of its air-defense systems, and the diversity of possible missions.[21] The PLAN's emphasis on smaller frigates over larger destroyers further represents a transition from quantity to quality. This parallels other navies' shift to assigning missions to smaller classes of ships because of the increasing cost of larger platforms. As part of an overall focus on missiles, many surface vessels and conventionally powered submarines are apparently prioritized as delivery platforms for antiship cruise missiles (ASCM).[22]

China's fast-attack craft include over 60 stealthy Houbei-class (Type 022) wave-piercing missile catamarans. The high-speed, low-observability catamaran, which is based on an Australian ferry design, has become a key component of the new PLAN. This impressive

---

[18] "Jin Class (Type 094)," *Jane's Fighting Ships*, July 30, 2012.

[19] Ronald O'Rourke, "China Naval Modernization: Implications for U.S. Navy Capabilities—Background and Issues for Congress," Congressional Research Service, CRS Report, August 10, 2012, 13, http://www.fas.org/sgp/crs/row/RL33153.pdf.

[20] Ibid., 14.

[21] Zhang Ju and A Wen, "Quanfu wuzhuang de xin shiji huweijian" [The Complete Armaments of the New Century's Frigate], *Feihang daodan*, no. 5 (2008): 23.

[22] William Murray, "China's Undersea Warfare: A USN Perspective" (paper presented at China Maritime Studies Institute Annual Conference, U.S. Naval War College, May 11, 2011).

antisurface weapon system—armed with eight YJ-83 ASCMs, each with a range of approximately 50 nautical miles[23]—might be given a mission to quickly destroy Taiwan's surface force, in the event of hostilities, if that fleet survived earlier attacks. However, the 022's limited endurance would not allow it to operate for extended periods at much greater distances, and its operational capability in heavy seas remains unclear. The 022's minimal in-water profile and high speeds could make it very difficult to hit with torpedoes or ASCMs. The use of such small, fast craft to attack carrier strike groups would represent a modern, cruise missile–focused realization of swarming tactics, a traditional PLAN concept.[24]

As limitations in air- and sea-lift are overcome, PLA amphibious forces, supplemented by large civilian vessels (e.g., roll-on/roll-off ferries), might support operations against Taiwan and perform diversified tasks such as NEOs and HADR in increasingly strategic littoral areas and beyond. China is also building additional hulls of the 17,600-ton Yuzhao-class (Type 071) landing platform dock, a large flush-deck amphibious ship. Cheaper and quicker to build than a big-deck flattop, 071s are limited in their quantity and quality of firepower but are truly modern amphibious assault vessels.[25] For an overview of PLAN capabilities, please see **Tables A4**, **A5**, and **A6** in the Appendix.

Current Air Power Capabilities

The PLAAF is divided into seven military-region air forces, thirteen deputy corps–level and division leader–level command posts, and three airborne divisions assigned to the 15th Airborne Corps. PLAAF and PLAN aviation forces currently possess 2,300 operational combat aircraft, of which 490 are currently capable of conducting operations against Taiwan without refueling.[26] Their range is limited severely by China's lack of multiple operational carriers, substantial aerial refueling capabilities, and overseas bases. Still hampered to some extent by bottlenecks in China's domestic aviation industry, the PLAAF continues to import large numbers of advanced aircraft, components, and aero-engines from Russia and has

---

[23] U.S. Department of Defense, *Military and Security Developments Involving the People's Republic of China 2012,* annual report prepared for Congress (May 18, 2012), 23, http://www.defense.gov/pubs/pdfs/2012_CMPR_Final.pdf.

[24] Nan Li, "All at Sea: China's Navy Develops Fast Attack Craft," *Jane's Intelligence Review,* September 2009, 3.

[25] Ye Qi, "Yaowang 'xiaoping ding': Qian tan Zhongguo daxing liangqi zuozhan jianting de weilai" [The Long View on the "Flattop": An Overview of the Future of Chinese Large Amphibious Vessels], *Dangdai haijun* (2011): 42–44.

[26] U.S. Department of Defense, *Military and Security Developments Involving the People's Republic of China 2012,* 24, 29.

"encountered some difficulty in expanding its fleet of long-range heavy transport aircraft" and tankers.[27] Still primarily focused on fighters and fighter-bombers, China's air forces have very little aerial refueling capability and hence only several hundred miles of reach.

The PLAAF is finally making varying degrees of progress, however, in a wide range of areas. China has produced its own fourth-generation fighters, the J-10 and J-11B (an all-Chinese variant of the Russian Flanker Su-27) and is developing the J-15 carrier-based fighter and the J-20 low-observability aircraft. PLA aircraft are also outfitted with a variety of increasingly advanced weapon systems. In some cases, particularly involving cruise missiles, these systems have extended the operational utility of otherwise obsolescent platforms. For an overview of China's air power order of battle, see **Table A7** in the Appendix.

The PLAAF also controls the majority of ground-based air defenses, which operate under the 1999 concept of the new "three attacks" (against stealth aircraft, cruise missiles, and armed helicopters) and "three defenses" (against precision strikes, electronic jamming, and electronic reconnaissance and surveillance).[28] According to a U.S. Department of Defense report, the PLAAF "has continued expanding its inventory of long-range, advanced SAM [surface-to-air missile] systems and now possesses one of the largest such forces in the world."[29] The PLAAF has also received multiple battalions of upgraded Russian S-300/SA-20 PMU-2 long-range (200 kilometers) SAM systems since 2006. Russia's most modern SAM system available for export, the SA-20 PMU-2, offers Taiwan Strait coverage and reportedly provides limited ballistic- and cruise-missile defense capabilities.[30] China has also introduced the indigenously deweloped HQ-9 (see **Table A8** in the Appendix).

PLAAF aviation. The PLAAF is transitioning from a past mission of territorial air defense to both offensive and defensive operations. Over the past two decades, it has shifted from playing a supporting role in offense-capable missions to assuming a more active role. According to China's latest defense white paper, the PLAAF is currently developing "a combat force structure that focuses on air strikes, air and missile defense, and strategic projection, to improve its leadership and command system and build up

---

[27] U.S. Department of Defense, *Military and Security Developments Involving the People's Republic of China 2012*, 33–34.

[28] Han Tingjin and Qi Zeqing, eds., *Fangkongbing xin "san da san fang"* [The Air Defense Forces' New "Three Attacks and Three Defenses"] (Beijing: PLA Press, 2001).

[29] U.S. Department of Defense, *Military and Security Developments Involving the People's Republic of China 2012*, 24.

[30] U.S. Department of Defense, *Military and Security Developments Involving the People's Republic of China 2011*, 32.

an informationized, networked base support system."[31] To this end, it has pursued an aggressive procurement program and reformed its defense industry to produce a new generation of fighter aircraft and refit and modernize its bomber fleet (see **Table A9** in the Appendix). Specifically, the PLAAF has acquired fourth-generation (third-generation, in Chinese terminology) Russian fighters (Su-27 and Su-30MKK) and transports (Il-76), air-defense systems, and domestically produced bombers (H-6) and fighter aircraft (J-10, J-11B, and JH-7A), as well as upgrades to older fighters such as the J-7 and J-8II. PLAAF aircraft are now equipped with Russian and domestic missiles and precision-guided munitions.

PLAN aviation. Chinese naval aviation has traditionally lagged behind even the PLAAF, probably in part because during the Cold War Beijing had no hope of controlling the airspace on its maritime periphery. In contrast, the PLAAF played a useful, if very limited, role in safeguarding China's airspace and contesting the airspace over North Korea in conjunction with major Soviet assistance during the Korean War. Although inter- and intra-service PLAAF-PLAN coordination still needs improvement, recent equipment upgrades and enhanced doctrine and training will increase China's prospects of conducting effective joint operations in the future. Already, the PLAN controls a formidable land-based air force (see **Table A10** in the Appendix).

Airborne intelligence, surveillance, and reconnaissance (ISR). Aircraft play an essential role in maritime reconnaissance because they can be rapidly redirected in a fluid tactical environment. China's fixed- and rotary-wing aircraft and unmanned aerial vehicles (UAV) are playing a significant role in peacetime signals intelligence (SIGINT) and communications intelligence (COMINT). In wartime, they would contribute to air defense and antisubmarine warfare (ASW).

China employs a growing variety of fixed-wing aircraft as dedicated ISR platforms offering an important airborne capacity for managing military operations. To enhance PLAAF and PLAN effectiveness, China is improving its airborne ISR capabilities by developing several variants of airborne early warning aircraft. These include two major indigenous platforms that improve on previous efforts based on modified Ilyushin Il-76 and Tupolev Tu-154 variants. In addition, China is developing the KJ-2000 indigenous airborne warning and control system (AWACS) aircraft based on the Russian Il-76 to conduct surveillance, perform long-range air patrol,

---

[31] Information Office of the State Council of the PRC, *China's National Defense in 2010.*

and thereby coordinate naval air operations.[32] For example, a November 2007 exercise held jointly by the South Sea Fleet and East Sea Fleet in the South China Sea included employment of one or more KJ-2000s.

China's smaller KJ-200/Y-8 "balance beam" airborne early warning and control (AEW&C) aircraft complements the KJ-2000 by performing tactical electronic warfare more economically. Most of China's more than one hundred Y-8s are divided among transports, but there are also seven "Gaoxin" variants that perform such missions as electronic intelligence (ELINT), SIGINT, communications relay, electronic warfare and countermeasures, AEW, and ASW.[33] Tupolev Tu-154 variants perform similar roles. On March 12, 2010, a PLAAF KJ-200 may have been spotted by the Japan Maritime Self-Defense Force near the Miyako Strait.[34]

In addition to dedicated AEW&C platforms, the PLAAF and PLAN possess reconnaissance regiments with a wide range of other specialized aircraft. Relevant fixed-wing aircraft, including a number of H-6s (derivatives of Russia's Tu-16), also conduct reconnaissance and ELINT. In late 2003, a Su-30MKK fighter used synthetic aperture radar to surveil the length of Taiwan electronically.[35]

Helicopters. In contrast to recent improvements in fixed-wing aviation, helicopters remain limited—perhaps because the PLA is wary of acquiring a large number of helicopters until improved models are available. Most helicopters in the PLA's disproportionately small fleet, totaling 700–800 airframes, are either imports or copies of foreign models (see **Tables A11** and **A12** in the Appendix).[36] This weakness was exposed most directly following the tragic Sichuan earthquake of May 12, 2008, when relief

---

[32] At present, China has AEW&C rather than true AWACS. In a Western AWACS system, the operator of the aircraft communicates directly with the operators of affiliated aircraft to update them regarding information gathered. Service newspaper accounts suggest that flight officers on Chinese AEW&C aircraft, by contrast, are merely airborne radio operators who relay information through a PLA commander in a ground control tower. They are not yet part of a culture of aircraft controlling aircraft. PLAAF and PLAN control of aircraft is conducted on a unit basis, in which the commander, a deputy commander, or the chief of staff is either in the control tower or the division/regiment's command post and talks to aircraft only in their own units. This raises the question of who in a KJ-200, KJ-2000, or Y-8 aircraft would control pilots from multiple units. Moreover, it remains uncertain where the information goes, where it is fused, how and when it is disseminated, and how far down the chain of command it goes.

[33] "Yun-8 Turboprop Transport Aircraft," SinoDefence website, http://www.sinodefence.com/airforce/airlift/y8.asp.

[34] Torbjørg Hemmingsen, "Enter the Dragon: Inside China's New Model Navy," *Jane's Navy International*, April 20, 2011.

[35] "Air Force, China," *Jane's World Air Forces*, June 10, 2012.

[36] This total includes roughly one hundred PLAAF and one hundred PLAN helicopters. See Dennis J. Blasko, "Chinese Helicopter Development: Missions, Roles, and Maritime Implications," in *Chinese Aerospace Power: Evolving Maritime Roles*, ed. Andrew S. Erickson and Lyle J. Goldstein (Annapolis: Naval Institute Press, 2011), 154.

operations were limited significantly by the lack of helicopters, particularly those with heavy-lift capacity. China is attempting to remedy its helicopter deficiency further by developing joint ventures with foreign manufacturers. For example, Eurocopter has begun assembly and production of medium-sized helicopters in China. Likewise, helicopter-delivered submarine-detecting sonar buoys will help the PLAN address one aspect of its serious long-term weakness in ASW.

Deck aviation. PLAAF and PLAN aviation already have a wide variety of bases from which to operate on China's immediate maritime periphery. A new dimension of Chinese air power is emerging, however, in the form of deck aviation. The most comprehensive and far-reaching question concerning PLAN modernization is the extent to which Beijing will supplement its navy (now based fundamentally on submarines and surface ships) with large-deck aviation, likely needed for the PLAN to move beyond Taiwan to genuine blue water power projection. In the order in which they are likely to be considered, Chinese carrier missions will probably include training, naval diplomacy, NEOs, HADR, the assertion of claims in the South China Sea, and support for SLOC operations against low-intensity threats.

Having begun sea trials in August 2011, the rebuilt Soviet carrier ex-*Varyag* will become operational in 2012. However, according to the U.S. Department of Defense, "it will take several years for an operationally viable air group of fixed and rotary wing aircraft to achieve even a minimal level of combat capability." To achieve this objective, the PLAN "has initiated a land-based program to begin training navy pilots to operate fixed-wing aircraft from an aircraft carrier."[37] In addition, the Defense Department states that "this program will probably be followed in about three years by full-scale ship-borne training aboard" the ex-*Varyag* and that "China likely will build multiple aircraft carriers with support ships over the next decade."[38] China's first indigenously constructed carrier, which would likely be based on the ex-*Varyag*, could achieve operational capability as early as 2015.[39]

China is developing the J-15 shipborne fighter based on the Russian Su-33—albeit with more advanced, indigenously made avionics, including a wide-angle holographic head-up display, as well as more complex trailing-edge double-slotted flaps. J-15 prototypes reportedly made their maiden

---

[37] U.S. Department of Defense, *Military and Security Developments Involving the People's Republic of China 2011*, 46.

[38] U.S. Department of Defense, *Military and Security Developments Involving the People's Republic of China 2012,* 22.

[39] U.S. Department of Defense, *Military and Security Developments Involving the People's Republic of China 2011,* 46.

flight on August 31, 2009, and their first takeoff from a land-based simulated ski jump on May 6, 2010.[40] Google Earth and Internet photos suggest that the cities of Huludao and Xian have pilot training facilities, and substantial footage is available of land-based J-15 flight testing.[41] In addition, as of the end of July 2012, Internet photos showed the ex-*Varyag* in port in Dalian with J-15 fighter and Z-8 AEW helicopter mock-ups on the deck.[42]

Developing and training the necessary forces for long-range combat capabilities is extremely difficult, however. Building an aircraft carrier is one thing; mastering the complex "system of systems" that enables air power projection requires years of time and typically entails the loss of expensive aircraft and hard-to-replace pilots.

UAVs. Inspired by the global buildup of UAVs and drones by the United States and others, China is purchasing foreign models, transforming piloted aircraft into unmanned aerial combat vehicles, and developing indigenous variants. This is an area of particular emphasis and investment; more than 25 UAV prototypes or models were on display at the 2010 Zhuhai Air Show, up from 12 in 2008. According to the U.S. Office of Naval Intelligence, "China is developing UAVs that have the potential to bring multimission capabilities to the maritime environment. In recent years, Chinese officials have openly touted the benefits of UAVs, such as low manufacturing costs, lack of personnel casualties, and inherent 'stealth-like' characteristics."[43] In fact, a UAV has already been spotted deployed from a PLAN vessel.[44] China's growing UAV arsenal offers improved reconnaissance and strike capabilities, including the ability to penetrate Taiwan's defenses by disabling early warning and missile-defense radars. Nevertheless, China may face significant challenges in developing, sustaining, and protecting the electronic tethers of its UAVs. For an overview of China's capabilities concerning UAVs, see **Table A13** in the Appendix.

---

[40] Daniel J. Kostecka, "From the Sea: PLA Doctrine and the Employment of Sea-Based Airpower," *Naval War College Review* 64, no. 3 (2011): 13, http://www.usnwc.edu/getattachment/61dc4903-260f-4158-947c-d40fd2f708c5/From-the-Sea--PLA-Doctrine-and-the-Employment-of-S.

[41] See "J-15 Test-Flight Compilation," YouTube video, posted by IvanXylakantsky, May 6, 2011, http://www.youtube.com/watch?v=G6AcVQmk8Eg.

[42] See, for example, "Jian 15 zai shang hangmu, kefu dianci jianrong" [Jian-15 Fighter Jet Is Again Moved on Board the Aircraft Carrier, the Problem of Electromagnetic Compatibility Has Been Overcome], *Ta Kung Pao*, July 18, 2012, http://paper.takung.cn/html/2012-07/18/content_4_4.htm.

[43] Office of Naval Intelligence, *Modern Navy with Chinese Characteristics*, 28–29.

[44] "China Increases Naval UAV Use," United Press International, April 9, 2012, http://www.upi.com/Top_News/Special/2012/04/09/China-increases-naval-UAV-use/UPI-87321333977162/.

Capability Realization, Integration, and Limitations

Notwithstanding its growing strengths, particularly in hardware, the PLA suffers from manifold weaknesses and limitations in software development and capabilities integration. Despite progress, achievements remain uneven, and actual combat capabilities are uncertain. Most importantly, while the current generation of U.S. Navy officers lack combat experience against a major military and have always been essentially unopposed at sea, their PLA counterparts lack combat experience entirely. The most recent PLAN combat was a skirmish with Vietnam over disputed islands in 1988. China's air forces have not fought combat engagements since the late Vietnam War, when a small number of U.S. Navy and U.S. Air Force aircraft were shot down by Chinese fighters off the southern China mainland and Hainan Island. Some Chinese analysts argue that current nontraditional security missions offer the equivalent of combat experience, and hence represent a partial exception. For example, Major General Jin Yinan of China's National Defense University has written: "For a military, the results of participating in this kind of action are not just about gaining experience at combating pirates. It is even more about raising the ability to perform missions on seas far away."[45] Another source states that "non-war military operations have a very important practical significance for improving the ability of the armed forces to counter security threats of many kinds and accomplish a diverse array of military tasks."[46] High-level exercises with advanced militaries such as the Russian Air Force, to the extent that they are actually substantive, may help as well.

In analyzing PLA progress, then, hardware determinism must be avoided. Doctrine, human capital, and training—particularly the complexity and realism of joint operations—represent three other significant limitations. The PLAAF and PLAN forces lack experienced pilots but are gradually expanding their corps and increasing flying hours—though it remains less clear what they are accomplishing specifically. Fighter and bomber pilots average 100–150 flight hours per year, while transport pilots average more than 200.[47] China's maritime and air forces appear to suffer from three main training shortfalls. First, the state of education, training, and jointness in China's maritime and air

---

[45] Ben Blanchard, "Chinese Naval Ships to Head for Somali Waters," Reuters, December 26, 2008, http://uk.reuters.com/article/2008/12/26/uk-somalia-piracy-china-idUKPEK29613620081226.

[46] Guo Yan, "Jiefangjun duoyanghua junshi renwu tisheng zhandouli" [The PLA's Diversified Military Tasks Enhance Combat Effectiveness], *Zhongguo guofang bao,* August 26, 2008, http://mil.sinoth.com/Doc/web/2008/8/26/14045.htm.

[47] Institute for International Strategic Studies (IISS), *The Military Balance 2012* (London: Routledge, 2012), 237.

forces, including professional military education for its leaders, remains unclear. In particular, the education, skill, and overall quality of the enlisted forces remain critical unknowns.[48]

Second, although markedly improved in recent years, the realism of training conducted remains limited. For China's air forces, this appears particularly true vis-à-vis jamming, minimum altitude, and night flight operations. Chinese military publications emphasize the importance of flying in a "complex electromagnetic environment" but fail to clarify whether China's air forces actually train under conditions of their own jamming and understand fully the practical ramifications. If jamming is merely simulated, how will they know what would happen under real conditions?

Yet major improvement efforts are underway, despite the impediments of the organizational culture. The PLAAF is in the process of creating air brigades, and PLAAF and PLAN pilots are being given autonomy to develop their own flight plans instead of simply following instructions from the control tower. Likewise, the sophistication and range of exercises are rapidly improving, albeit from a low baseline. China did not send combat aircraft abroad until August 2007, when the PLAAF deployed eight JH-7As and six Il-76 transports to Russia for the Peace Mission 2007 exercise. Then in September 2010 the PLAAF sent four H-6Hs and two J-10s into Kazakh airspace for a day of modest participation in the Peace Mission 2010 exercise.[49] The following month, in its longest exercise deployment to date, the PLAAF sent four J-11s for its Anatolian Eagle 2010 exercise with Turkey, China's first with a NATO military. In June–July 2010, the PLAN executed surface-vessel attack exercises that included ASCM-firing Houbei-class catamarans from the East Sea Fleet's 16th Fast Attack Flotilla. In recent years, amphibious forces have conducted assault and island-seizure exercises in the South China Sea, including an exercise in July 2012 with over twelve warships, drawing

---

[48] U.S. National Air and Space Intelligence Center, *People's Liberation Army Air Force 2010* (Wright-Patterson Air Force Base, August 1, 2010).

[49] The exercise was scripted, unrealistic, and minimally coordinated. The aircraft flew out of a base near Ürümqi. Two J-10s escorted two H-6s into Kazakhstan. The J-10s refueled inside China. A KJ-2000 escorted them to the border and likely simply relayed commands. In Kazakh airspace, the bombers dropped bombs, and the J-10s conducted jamming. Two more H-6s were escorted by Kazakh pilots, but they had difficulty communicating. Upon completion of the exercise, the aircraft returned to Ürümqi. Thus, two army aviation Z-9 attack helicopters were the only Chinese aircraft actually based in Kazakhstan for the exercise. See Daniel M. Hartnett, "Looking Good on Paper: PLA Participation in the Peace Mission-2010 Multilateral Military Exercise" (forthcoming).

from all three fleets.[50] The PLAN has conducted few high-level exercises outside the near seas, but in April 2010, June 2011, and May 2012 dispatched exercise-engaging flotillas comprising some of its most advanced platforms through the East China Sea and the Miyako Strait. Joint and combined arms exercises are also increasingly prevalent.

Finally, a third critical shortfall concerns the integration of operational capabilities. For example, it is unclear how China is able to deconflict the aircraft and SAMs working in the same airspace—still a difficult problem for U.S. forces in actual battle conditions. PLAAF writings suggest that SAMs and aircraft conduct "combined-arms training," but by U.S. standards this would be considered "opposition-force training," with the aircraft attacking areas the SAMs are covering. Documentation of SAMs and aircraft working together against attacking aircraft and naval aviation aircraft flying combat air patrols to protect PLAN ships against attacking aircraft remains elusive. Can PLAAF and naval aviation aircraft actually fly in the same airspace covered by the various services' SAMs? How do they coordinate to ensure the SAMs do not shoot down friendly aircraft? Will the fighters fly out and meet enemy aircraft with SAMs covering them, or will the aircraft be the last line of defense in case the SAMs do not shoot down the enemy?

Other challenges also remain. Organizational rigidity and "stove-piping" will likely remain problems, rooted as they are in political structures that the CCP refuses to change significantly. The attendant challenges of real-time coordination among sensors and systems owned by different services will also likely continue to hamper C4ISR and target deconfliction. The PLA likewise faces considerable challenges in integrating existing platforms and weapon systems. More positively, China's overall industrial capabilities and comprehensive approach to technological acquisition should help it surmount the vast majority of technological bottlenecks (including high-level military aero-engine production). But in terms of hardware and the ability to use it, the PLA remains particularly weak in ASW, mine countermeasures, anti-air warfare, and C4ISR.

Strategic Implications

As the above analysis of capabilities suggests, China is already a world-class, if uneven, military power—but one with a regional, not global,

---

[50] Pan Xiaomin and Wu Chao, "'Luzhan menghu qiaoran jinji wuming jiao" [Fierce Tigers of Land Warfare Quietly Invade Unnamed Reef], *Renmin haijun*, December 17, 2008; Wei Gang, Li Yanlin, and Wu Chao, "Haijun jianting biandui shouci huan Nan Zhongguo Hai yuanhang xunlian" [A Chinese Naval Ship Formation Conducts the First Long-Voyage Training Sail around the South China Sea], *Renmin haijun*, December 2, 2008, 1; and Yang Bai, "Shuaxin 3 xiang jianting buji jilu" [Three Underway Replenishment Records Have Been Reset], *People's Navy*, June 22, 2009.

focus. The most common source of error in Chinese and U.S. analyses of Chinese naval and air power development is the conflation of two factors: scope and intensity. Chinese naval and air power development should be observed through the lens of distance and can best be understood in terms of radiating range rings or ripples of capability. Like water displaced by a stone, waves of capability radiate outward, dissipating progressively.

Geographic Context

Close to home, China's military capabilities designed to control near-seas water and airspace are escalating rapidly. Four of the PLAN's five campaigns appear to apply there specifically: naval base defense, antiship, anti-SLOC, and blockade. According to three professors at China's Naval Command College, "At present and for a long time to come, safeguarding near-seas security should be the primary goal of China's maritime security strategy."[51] All four of the PLAAF's focus areas—strike, air and missile defense, early warning and reconnaissance, and strategic mobility—as well as the PLAAF's leading role in A2/AD operations, apply to the near seas. Likewise, all four of the PLAAF's campaigns—offensive, air defense, air blockade, and airborne—and its joint role in anti–air strike campaigns apply there primarily. Additionally, both services play key roles, along with the Second Artillery, in the joint blockade campaign. The PLA thus has many ways to mitigate the limitations to its Taiwan and near-seas operations.

Secondary capabilities are allocated for the border area with India, where China enjoys force and geographic advantages. Given the PLAAF's lack of transports and difficulties in operating fixed-wing aircraft in the Himalayas' thin air and extreme weather, land-based air power lags behind ground forces. The latter can exploit China's Qinghai-Tibet railway and superior road network to move forces rapidly—as seen in the PLA's effective road-building operations leading up to the 1962 Sino-Indian War. Because snow covers airfields through most of the year, save for July–September, army aviation helicopters provide the primary air support to ground troops. There is a token presence of J-10s and J-11s, but the logistics remain challenging and their air-air role is unclear, other than perhaps conducting combat air patrol for ground forces.

Last, nontraditional security forces are allocated to unstable areas of southwest China, and now slightly beyond. For example, a border defense

---

[51] Feng Liang, Gao Zichuan, and Duan Tingzhi, *Zhongguo de heping fazhan yu haishang anquan huanjing* [China's Peaceful Development and Maritime Security Environment] (Beijing: World Knowledge Press, 2010), 300–301; and Nan Li, "The People's Liberation Army Navy as an Evolving Organization" (paper presented at Center for Intelligence Research and Analysis Conference, June 2012), 26. The author is indebted to Professor Li for permission to cite.

unit of the People's Armed Police (PAP) began patrolling the Mekong River alongside neighboring nations' forces in December 2011.

By contrast, PLA capabilities designed to influence conditions farther afield are making much slower progress, starting from a much lower baseline. Two of the PLAN's campaigns, anti-SLOC and maritime transportation protection, might apply beyond the near seas, but this remains unclear, particularly in high-end warfare conditions. The PLAAF might contribute long-range transportation and logistics, but it currently lacks platforms and experience. Conducting combat operations in contested environments at this range is, and is likely to remain, much harder for China. Chinese efforts in this environment are intended primarily to shape peacetime conditions, address nontraditional security threats, and support low-end deterrence rather than to prepare for warfare with other great powers far from China.

Regional Impact

Securing China's homeland and continental periphery remains Beijing's central military imperative. In this respect, the PLA and the PAP are already well equipped to defend the status quo. Efforts to influence territorial claims are supported by military strength but informed by concerns about domestic stability in China's restive border regions populated by ethnic and religious minorities. China's leaders believe that they cannot be seen by their domestic Han audience as being too soft on territorial claims and that such softness would encourage separatism in Xinjiang and Tibet. Protection for trade- and resource-focused efforts to integrate economic activities and infrastructure with bordering nations is also a growing concern.

Beijing has settled its territorial disputes with all land neighbors except India and Bhutan, and these are unlikely to be resolved militarily given the population of non-Chinese citizens in those areas. In October 2011, Indian defense minister A.K. Antony stated that India and China would "establish a 'mechanism' to better handle 'intrusions into each other's territory'" as part of a larger effort to contain their border dispute.[52] Maritime claims and influence thus constitute China's principal area of presence-expansion and hence the primary variable in China's territorial defense and reunification policies.

At the strategic level, China's maritime and air power capabilities are already creating a potential window of vulnerability for U.S. forces. Beijing enjoys a sweet spot of stability, comparatively rapid development, and the tail end of a demographic dividend. In contrast, Washington, still burdened by the costs of the conflicts in Iraq and Afghanistan, and possibly distracted

---

[52] IISS, *The Military Balance 2012*, 216.

by Iran, confronts fiscal and policy adjustments. With around 30% of Asia's defense spending, not including U.S. expenditures in the region, China is poised to consolidate power regionally.[53] The focus of strategic friction is the near seas and the airspace above them, where China seeks to carve out a zone where it is exempt from the international legal norms of the global commons in order to redress perceived historical injustices and return to great-power status.[54]

The East China Sea: Most dangerous and volatile. Because of Taiwan's and Japan's claims and strength of forces, as well as the likelihood of U.S. involvement in any crisis or conflict, this sea has the greatest possibility for high-end warfare and hence the most dangerous force-on-force engagements. Central to these unresolved conflicts is Taiwan's status. Despite ongoing bottlenecks in several areas, the PLA's acquisition of large amounts of sophisticated equipment in important categories is shifting the balance of military power to China, probably permanently. The resulting inventory of modern aircraft and associated weapons is increasing the PLA's ability to achieve sea and air superiority in the Taiwan Strait and even over the island itself. If unopposed by U.S. or Japanese forces, the PLA could today conduct an intensive air, missile, and naval firepower strike and blockade campaign against Taiwan. In that sense, there simply is no longer a cross-strait balance between Taiwan's military and the PLA. However, according to *Jane's*, "the navy is not ready to [defeat] combined American and Japanese naval operations to thwart an attack on Taiwan and formal PLAN amphibious forces are insufficient to enable a Taiwan invasion of necessary scale to achieve victory."[55] The disputes with Japan over the Senkaku/Diaoyu Islands and the exclusive economic zone (EEZ) represent a second area of possible conflict. *Jane's* assesses that "the PLAN is on the verge of obtaining a credible sea denial capability against the U.S. Navy in the western Pacific and an ability to undertake offensive operations against Japan and Taiwan, absent U.S. military support."[56]

The South China Sea: Less dangerous, more active. Though less likely to see high-intensity conflict, the South China Sea is the most likely to witness friction and unexpected encounters between Chinese and foreign military platforms. China has shown willingness to use force in the sea, which is the

---

[53] IISS, *The Military Balance 2012*, 216.

[54] Peter A. Dutton, "Cracks in the Global Foundation: International Law and Instability in the South China Sea," in *Cooperation from Strength: The United States, China and the South China Sea*, ed. Patrick M. Cronin (Washington, D.C.: Center for a New American Security, 2012), http://www.cnas.org/files/documents/publications/CNAS_CooperationFromStrength_Cronin_1.pdf.

[55] "China," *Jane's World Navies*, August 6, 2012.

[56] Ibid.

only site of PLAN conflict over the past four decades, and Chinese interests are increasing there. Following counterproductive overreach in 2010, since June 2011 Beijing has been taking a more measured approach to sovereignty claims. PLA-affiliated individuals continue to advocate preemptive strikes against Vietnam and the Philippines, however, and Chinese civil maritime forces engaged in a stand-off with a Philippine naval vessel in April 2012 near the contested Scarborough Reef. Beijing appears open to resource-sharing, but not claim resolution, and may yet reassert itself.

The Yellow Sea: Indirect risks. Despite the threat of North Korean destabilization, which places the Yellow Sea within the most likely zone of conflict—albeit not with China per se—this sea remains the calmest. To be sure, China is extremely sensitive about the Yellow Sea for historical reasons, as it has seen invasions come through that area, and there are continued concerns that China's capital is vulnerable to attack from this direction. In addition, the Yellow Sea contains important Chinese coastal areas and shipping lanes. In part because of such sensitivities, Beijing has expressed opposition to the United States holding exercises in the Yellow Sea.[57] Nevertheless, Chinese disagreements with both Koreas are ongoing but limited. Beijing's primary goal is to restrict outside military influence so as to control both the adjacent sea areas and the Korean Peninsula's future.

The Projected Evolution to 2025

The PLA's modernization is driven by China's national interests at home and abroad. While the PLA might prefer to focus on honing its regional A2/AD capabilities, events abroad and out of China's control will ultimately determine where the PRC and PLA leadership decides to invest in the future. In particular, access to energy and natural resources is one of China's critical national interests and will drive some of the decisions on how much and what type of expeditionary capabilities the PLA needs to develop.

At Jiang Zemin's behest, China's military developed a "three-step action plan" for the PLA in 2002: "lay a solid foundation for force informationization and mechanization by 2010, complete force mechanization and the initial stage of informationization by 2020, and complete informationization for all the services and national defense modernization by 2050."[58]

---

[57] "Why China Opposes U.S.–South Korean Military Exercises in the Yellow Sea," *People's Daily*, July 16, 2010, http://english.peopledaily.com.cn/90001/90780/91342/7069743.html.

[58] David Lai, "Introduction" in *The PLA at Home and Abroad: Assessing the Operational Capabilities of China's Military*, ed. Roy Kamphausen, David Lai, and Andrew Scobell (Carlisle: Strategic Studies Institute, 2010), 15, http://www.strategicstudiesinstitute.army.mil/pdffiles/pub995.pdf.

Completely unchallenged for more than half a century after the PLA's overarching "active defense" strategy was implemented in the 1930s, the relative dominance of China's ground forces is finally decreasing, though at uncertain speed. The PRC's defense white papers consistently refer to the PLAN, PLAAF, and Second Artillery as "strategic services," whereas the ground forces have no out-of-area missions save peacekeeping and are not afforded this distinction. There are mounting indications that the PLA may replace the current military regions with a streamlined, outward-looking organizational posture.[59] These emerging developments suggest that the ground forces are becoming less dominant within the military and that the other services may grow correspondingly over time in funding and mission scope. This perception is only reinforced by the gradually increasing, though still disproportionately low, representation of PLAN, PLAAF, and Second Artillery representatives on the CMC,[60] on the CCP Central Committee, and at the helm of PLA institutions.

The PLAAF strategy—"integrated air and space, [preparation for] simultaneous offensive and defensive operations" (*kong-tian yiti, gong-fang jianbei*)—was approved in 2004.[61] The PLAAF is upgrading its inventory and competing with the General Armaments Department and Second Artillery to control military space assets. But the PLAN is even further ahead in terms of new mission areas and its relevance to China's growing global interests. The PLAN was granted its near-seas defense strategy around 1985, making it an independent service with an independent mission for the first time. Proposed by Deng Xiaoping in 1979 and endorsed by PLAN commander Admiral Liu Huaqing in 1987, the concept of "active defense, near-seas operations" (*jiji fangyu, jinhai zuozhan*) was subsequently operationalized.[62] As the most comprehensive,

---

[59] In an interview, Major General Peng Guangqian, Academy of Military Science, and Zhang Zhaozhong, National Defense University, state that in the future China's ground forces will be downsized, the PLAN will be enhanced and become the second-largest service, the PLAAF and Second Artillery will stay the same, and new services such as space and cyber forces will be established. Senior Captain Li Jie says that China's approach to carriers will be incremental and that, once acquired, they will be deployed to important sea lanes and strategic sea locations for conventional deterrence and also deployed for nontraditional security missions. See Ma Zhengang, "'Zhongguo moshi' hui qudai 'Meiguo moshi' ma?" [Can the "Chinese Model" Replace the "American Model"?], *Renmin wang*, October 22, 2009, http://cn.chinareviewnews.com/doc/5 0_1074_101111301_2_1022081349.html; and Wu Ming and Qiu Lifang, "Qi da junqu de huafen" [The Division of the Seven Military Regions], Xinhua, April 8, 2008.

[60] Due to time-in-grade requirements, service chiefs are not always appointed immediately to the CMC. See Kenneth Allen, "Assessing the PLA's Promotion Ladder to CMC Member Based on Grades vs. Ranks—Part 1," Jamestown Foundation, China Brief, July 22, 2010, http://www.jamestown.org/single/?no_cache=1&tx_ttnews%5Btt_news%5D=36660.

[61] Yao Wei, ed., *Zhongguo kongjun baike quanshu* [Chinese Air Force Encyclopedia, vol. 1] (Beijing: Hangkong gongye chuban she, 2005), 57.

[62] Li, "The Evolution of China's Naval Strategy and Capabilities," 150, 156.

strategic, multirole, multidimensional, diplomatically relevant, and internationally oriented of the services, the PLAN may benefit most from the PLA's increasingly outward orientation.[63] Specifically, its goal of becoming a regional blue water navy by 2020 would appear to correspond to the PLA's three-step plan.

Potential Force Postures

China's Naval Future

What are the PLA's prospects for developing power-projection capabilities by 2020, the projected end of Beijing's "strategic window of opportunity," and beyond? What are its prospects for consolidating great-power autonomy while the United States remains preoccupied in Afghanistan, with Iran, and with counterterrorism more generally? Broadly speaking, China's future naval and air posture may progress along a continuum defined by the ability to sustain high-intensity combat under contested conditions at progressively greater distances from China, as shown in **Table 1**.

The first three benchmarks fall under the rubric of "sea denial," which is the ability of a country to prevent opponents from using a given sea area without controlling it. The next four benchmarks are variants of "sea control," which is a country's ability to allow its own vessels to operate freely in a given sea area by preventing direct attacks from opponents. Most naval theorists would differentiate between these two approaches, the latter of which is far more demanding than the former and requires a much broader range of capabilities, even for operations within the same geographic area. It is not simply a question of being able to do more from farther away. A robust version of the first benchmark thus lies within China's grasp today; however, there is no guarantee that the last will ever be pursued fully.

Experts at China's Naval Military Studies Research Institute envision that by 2020 China will have a "regional [blue water] defensive and offensive-type" navy.[64] This, in turn, will hinge on compatible air power capabilities. U.S. government projections echo Chinese aspirations. According to the Department of Defense, between now and 2020 "the PLA is likely to steadily expand its military options for Taiwan, including those to

---

[63] The author thanks Nan Li for these points. This process is being facilitated by gradual development and potential consolidation of China's civil maritime forces, which are assuming missions within China's coastal waters and EEZ that previously occupied the navy.

[64] Li, "The Evolution of China's Naval Strategy and Capabilities," 161, 168.

TABLE 1 Previous and potential naval and air force postures

Posture	Sea/air denial	Sea/air control	Scope	Nature
Near-coast defense	X	–	Delay enemy invasion of waters/airspace up to ~12 nm from China's coastline and ~300 miles inland.	Lasted from 1949 to the 1980s. The PLAN defended strategic straits: Bohai, Taiwan, and Qiongzhou. Air forces defended territorial airspace. Both supported ground forces.
Near-seas active defense	X	–	Achieve sea or air control for a certain time in certain areas of the near seas, the first island chain, and its inner and outer rims.	Designed to deter enemy interference by nuclear and conventional means, safeguard resources, defend major wartime SLOCs, and recover Taiwan and other territories. Defensive and offensive missions for naval and air forces.
Regional anti-access	X	–	Ability to deny access by holding opposing forces at risk throughout China's periphery (sea and air within and on either side of the first island chain).	Similar in scope to present efforts but far more robust in realization.
Extended blue water anti-access	X	–	Ability to deny access by holding opposing forces at risk throughout China's periphery and all approaches thereto (out to and east of the second island chain, throughout the South China Sea, and to its southwest) to a distance of 1,000+ nm from territorial waters or airspace.	Represent the low-end and high-end versions of a regional (blue water) defensive and offensive navy. Related air force capabilities include aerial refueling, antiship missiles, overwater flight operations, long-duration maritime patrol and intelligence collection, and strategic bombing.
Limited expeditionary	–	X	All the above, and the ability to conduct MIO and high-level NEO when necessary in and above the far seas (western Pacific and Indian Ocean).	

Table 1 continued.

Posture	Sea/air denial	Sea/air control	Scope	Nature
Blue water expeditionary	–	X	All the above, some form of limited-intensity global presence, and the ability to surge combat-ready forces in and above core strategic far-ocean areas (e.g., Persian Gulf).	Represent the low-end and high-end versions of a "global, far oceans, blue water" navy, as PLAN planners categorize today's U.S. Navy. China does not aspire to such a navy in the medium term, although some interpret Liu Huaqing's writings as calling for such a navy by 2050.
Global expeditionary	–	X	All the above and the robust presence of combat-ready naval and air forces in all major strategic regions of the world.	

SOURCE: Nan Li, "The Evolution of China's Naval Strategy and Capabilities: From 'Near Coast' and 'Near Seas' to 'Far Seas,'" *Asian Security* 5, no. 2 (2009): 150, 156, 160, 168; and Phillip C. Saunders and Erik Quam, "Future Force Structure of the Chinese Air Force," in *Right-Sizing the People's Liberation Army*, ed. Roy Kamphausen and Andrew Scobell (Carlisle: Strategic Studies Institute, 2007), 381.

deter, delay, or deny third party intervention."[65] Additionally, "by the latter half of the current decade, China will likely be able to project and sustain a modest-sized force, perhaps several battalions of ground forces or a naval flotilla of up to a dozen ships in low-intensity operations far from China."[66] As Nan Li explains, "This type of navy can compete effectively for control of the seas within its own region. In the meantime, it also possesses the capability to project power beyond its own region and compete effectively for sea-control and impose sea-denial in the seas of the other oceans, as did the British Navy during the Falklands War."[67]

China's Future Air Power

Air power will help determine how far China's military will operate intensively out-of-area in conjunction with its sea power. Whereas naval capabilities interact strongly with geography, air power provides surveillance and protection for sea power and is largely a product of range and technical parameters. Chinese air power development should thus be understood in the context of the aforementioned naval-force postures. To support power projection overseas, both for national prestige and for limited missions beyond Taiwan, Beijing must extend air power range and lethality. This requires strategic airlift, aerial refueling, enhanced deck-aviation capability, and long-range strike capabilities, as well as modest access rights to overseas military facilities. With respect to precision-strike capabilities beyond the near seas, Guam likely represents an initial target. Allocation of missions and operating areas among PLAAF and PLAN forces will present challenges, particularly once the latter contains carrier-based aircraft. Regardless, the China issue manager at the U.S. National Air and Space Intelligence Center projects that "China will have one of the world's foremost air forces by 2020."[68]

Barometers for Naval and Air Buildup

The biggest uncertainty for the PLA over the next two decades is the extent to which China will develop capabilities supporting major combat force-projection beyond Taiwan and the near seas. Specifically, can the PLA do more than simply sharpen sea-denial (submarine-centric) capabilities

---

[65] U.S. Department of Defense, *Military and Security Developments Involving the People's Republic of China 2011*, 2.

[66] Ibid., 27.

[67] Li, "The Evolution of China's Naval Strategy and Capabilities," 161, 168.

[68] Wayne A. Ulman, "China's Military Aviation Forces," in Erickson and Goldstein, *Chinese Aerospace Power*, 38.

and instead achieve blue water sea-control, which would require air dominance as well? Here, hardware acquisition and deployment are straightforward to monitor and thus offer a useful indicator. For example, a significant increase in constructing replenishment-at-sea ships and Type 056 escort ships would signal a serious plan to increase naval power-projection capabilities. On the other hand, PLAAF power projection might be facilitated by procurement of additional transports, such as the Y-20 four-engine aircraft based on the Il-76. However, the PLA already enjoys access to commercial airlines, whose B-747 freighter variants can carry roughly twice the cargo of an Il-76.

Although the PLA's assets, trained personnel, and experience are currently insufficient to support long-range missions to defend SLOCs, it is conceivable that the PLA could gradually acquire the necessary funding and mission scope. Certainly, modern multi-mission warships enjoy the flexibility to perform operations in a wide range of circumstances and locations. But fully pursuing robust long-range capabilities demands larger, more numerous platforms. With respect to force structure, indicators of a more ambitious Chinese naval presence, particularly one concerned with SLOC protection, are presented in **Table 2**.

Perhaps the strongest indicator of Chinese intentions to develop blue water power-projection capabilities would be the PLA's pursuit of reliable access to overseas shore supplies and air- and naval-basing infrastructure to improve transit and on-station time. China remains far from having overseas bases. But recent debate among PLA scholars and other analysts suggests that China may be actively reconsidering its traditional approach of avoiding "hegemonism" and "power politics" by eschewing such facilities wholesale.[69] While there are indications of growing Chinese influence in the South Pacific for commercial and perhaps even monitoring purposes, the Indian Ocean—with its rich littoral resources, busy energy SLOCs, and diverse access options—seems the most likely Chinese beachhead location. There Beijing will probably pursue access incrementally in countries such as Pakistan and Burma that are politically insulated from Indian and U.S. pressure, as well as in nonaligned countries like Oman that enjoy well-balanced relations internationally and hence cannot easily be pressured to eschew closer cooperation with China. Facilities will probably be exposed and challenging to defend, however, and the host nations may destabilize (see **Table 3**).

---

[69] Li Peng, "Main Characteristics of China's Foreign Policy" (excerpts from speech at the 96th Inter-Parliamentary Conference, Beijing, September 19, 1996), http://www.china-embassy.org/eng/zmgx/zgwjzc/t35077.htm.

TABLE 2 Indicators of emerging blue water/air capabilities

Capability	Approach
PNT	Beidou/Compass system transitions from regional to global coverage.
C4ISR	Increasingly integrated global network.
ASW	More, and increasingly quiet, nuclear-powered submarines. Regular deployments of SSNs, and surface warships, and the demonstrated ability to provide deployed air superiority for ship- and land-based aircraft with significant ASW prowess.
Area air defense	More advanced surface vessels with long-range area air defense systems and aircraft to support radar. Increased Soviet-style adoption of long-range antiship cruise missiles in surface fleet to compensate for lack of proximity to land-based missile forces on extended missions. Introduction of improved hardware variants, increasing practice of their utilization.
Long-range air power	Development/procurement of strike and long-range transport aircraft, possibly long-range stealthy bombers, helicopters to operate off carriers and land bases overseas; aerial refueling capabilities; related doctrine and training programs.
Military production	Establishment of new, modern shipyards dedicated to military ship production or expansion of areas in coproduction yards that are dedicated to military ship production. Improved facilities and practices for manufacturing aircraft and aero-engines. Increased production in extant facilities.
At-sea replenishment	Expansion of the PLAN auxiliary fleet, particularly long-range, high-speed oilers and replenishment ships.
Remote repair	Development of ability to conduct sophisticated ship and aircraft repairs overseas, either through tenders or land-based repair facilities.
Operational readiness	More complex, joint exercises. Coordinated multi-axis antiship/carrier operations. Steady deployment to vulnerable SLOCs to increase presence, familiarity, and readiness. More long-range training missions.
Overall capacity	Maturation of advanced levels of increasingly joint PLA doctrine, training, and human capital. More all-weather, overwater, attack training for pilots.
Overseas facilities	Acquisition of "places," if not "bases," to support the above capabilities, e.g., in the Indian Ocean. The cultivation of true "allies" in a Western/U.S. sense as opposed to "friends and acquaintances."

TABLE 3 PLAN ports of call and possible naval and air access points

Port (country)	Chinese investment (reported)	Type	Development status	Draft limits (m)
Salalah (Oman)	None	Deepwater; major container transshipment port for the Persian Gulf	Already well-established; construction of new port-side fuel bunkering facility underway; massive container terminal expansion plan contracted out	17.5
Aden (Yemen)	None	Container/bulk cargo	Modest port; berth extension planned	15.8
Djibouti (Djibouti)	None	Principal port for Ethiopian cargo transshipment; containers, bulk cargo	Container terminal phase 1 construction completed; can berth 2 large container vessels together	12
Gwadar (Pakistan)	$198 million; funded 80% of the initial $248 million city construction; provided technicians, skilled workers	Commercial port receiving break bulk cargos, with capacity to handle containers	Significant infrastructure foundation; further development to include 15 berths, ship cargo handling equipment, port machinery, and warehouses; not commercially viable at present	14
Karachi (Pakistan)	None	Pakistan's largest, busiest port	Already well-established; development of bulk cargo, deepwater container terminals, and other expansion underway, including 18-m container terminal	9.8 upper harbor; 12.2 approach channel (13.5 in future)
Hambantota (Sri Lanka)	$360-million export buyer's credit from China's EXIM Bank; Chinese contractors constructing	Large deepwater port under development	To be constructed in 4 stages over 15 years. Phase 1 accommodated first vessel in 2010; general cargo berth of 610 m; handles vessels up to 100,000 DWT; phase 2 initiated	16 (17 in future)

Table 3 continued.

Port (country)	Chinese investment (reported)	Type	Development status	Draft limits (m)
Colombo (Sri Lanka)	$1.5 billion Chinese-built port completed 2012; agreement to build second port; Chinese firms pledged ≥ $500 million over the next 10–15 years	Currently Sri Lanka's main port; South Asia's largest, busiest port	Deepwater port opened in 2012; Colombo South Harbor Development project will increase depth to 18 m, then 23 m; phased development of 4 new terminals with 3–4 berths each	15
Trincomalee (Sri Lanka)	Apparently none as of June 2012, but future investment likely	Large natural harbor; South Asia's only completely sheltered harbor	Under development	13
Chittagong (Bangladesh)	Agreement to finance collocated deep sea port, help establish rail/road links in $8.7 billion package	Bangladesh's main sea port; 6 general cargo berths and 11 container berths (3 dedicated with gantry crane)	New collocated port to be completed in three phases by 2015; will increase capacity from current 1.1-million to 3-million TEU for container traffic, and 30.5-million to 100-million tons for bulk cargo	7.5–9.15
Sittwe/ Kyaukpyu (Burma)	Chinese funding development of two deep sea ports, special economic zone near Sittwe in Kyaukpyu; connecting infrastructure	Natural harbor near large rice-exporting port of Sittwe (being developed with Indian assistance); terminus of oil pipeline from Kunming, China	Kyaukpyu deep sea port on Maday Island by Than Zit river mouth; initiated in 2009, project will produce 91 berths, accommodate 300,000-ton oil tankers; May 2010 MOU between China and Burma to develop land route Kunming-Mandalay-Kyaukpyu (which will connect to Sittwe)	8.2

Table 3 continued.

Port (country)	Chinese investment (reported)	Type	Development status	Draft limits (m)
Victoria (Seychelles)	Possible investment, nature unclear	Port with currently limited facilities	Restoration of east coast phase 3 underway, including development of new commercial/fishing harbor	11.5
Singapore (Singapore)	None	Large, sophisticated, commercial ports; busiest in world; 1 terminal, 9 sub-ports; military ports	Already well-established but potential for further development	22

SOURCE: *Ports & Terminals Guide 2011–12* (Redhill: IHS Fairplay, 2012); Port of Salalah, http://www.salalahport.com; Port of Aden, http://www.portofaden.net; "Useful Links," Djibouti Free Zone, http://www.djiboutifz.com/en/useful-links/useful-links.html; Gwadar Port, http://www.gwadarport.gov.pk; Karachi Port Trust, http://www.kpt.gov.pk/index.htm; Project Sri Lanka Ports Authority, http://www.slpa.lk/index.asp; "Sri Lanka's Chinese-Built Port Opens for Business," Agence France-Presse, June 5, 2012; Chittagong Port Authority, http://cpa.gov.bd/portal/; "China to Invest US$8.7 billion in Bangladesh," *Marine News China*, May 15, 2010; Myanmar Port Authority; Seychelles Port Authority, http://www.spa.sc/; and Maritime and Port Authority of Singapore, http://www.mpa.gov.sg/.

Hardware Trends

A wide variety of platforms and weapon systems are coming online or being integrated into the PLA force structure. Those that the PLA avoided or limited previously for lack of capability or need will likely now be developed as emerging capability and need converge. China will doubtless achieve and implement several potentially cutting-edge breakthroughs in military technology, which could improve its A2/AD capabilities radically. It will continue to favor missiles, particularly conventional variants, of increasing range, precision, and advanced characteristics. Maturing and diversifying anti-satellite (ASAT) capability will emphasize ground-based kinetic kill vehicles and lasers. The ability to launch saturation attacks with cruise missiles will come from air-, sea-, undersea-, and land-based platforms in multi-axis coordination. Antiship ballistic missile capability will likely include multiple operational variants of growing range. Beijing's Compass, or Beidou II, position, navigation, and timing system will be deployed globally by 2020. Land-based J-20 "stealth" aircraft, if operated and maintained to achieve minimal-signature capabilities despite their potentially problematic architecture and Chinese inexperience in maintaining their sensitive surface coatings, could have similar impact when they become operational around 2018, probably for strike missions against enemy early warning and tanker aircraft, as well as ships.

China's defense industry will likely be given the requisite resources and master the relevant technology. The key variable in determining the actual performance of these systems is the extent to which the PLA is capable of sufficient bureaucratic coordination and adaptation to exploit new technologies and operational concepts. The remaining uncertainties are largely organizational: Will the ground forces acquiesce to the PLAN and PLAAF becoming more important proportionally? To what extent will inter-service rivalry limit the development of long-distance capability? To what degree can joint wartime confidence be achieved? Although new long-range capabilities could provide potent command and control options, such developments would necessitate continued transformation of the PLA and stoke ongoing debates regarding decentralization.

During this time frame, other Chinese capabilities will develop less disruptively. Type 094 and 096 SSBNs with JL-2 and follow-on SLBMs will afford China's nuclear forces a sea leg, but will be more expensive than land-based mobile forces, as well as more vulnerable because of acoustic problems. China may develop significant amphibious forces with long-range expeditionary platforms, including perhaps six to eight Type 071 landing platform docks and three to eight Type 081 landing helicopter docks.[70] However, these will be vulnerable to submarine-launched torpedoes and antiship missiles and can only carry several hundred personnel each. Hence, no foreseeable number could have any impact on a Taiwan campaign, but they would be suitable for small-island landings (e.g., in the South China Sea), NEOs, and special operations.

Even PLA success in developing out-of-area capabilities, however, could have unintended consequences. Mastering long-range platforms and C4ISR would create extensive deployment, logistics, and communications chains out of area, or what geostrategists term "exterior lines."[71] The systems thus exposed could be jammed or geolocated, creating tremendous vulnerabilities. Key platforms would operate in international waters and airspace over which sovereignty cannot be claimed even with the most revisionist legal interpretation (in contrast to a country's own EEZ and the airspace above it).

Resulting Possibilities

At the strategic level, many uncertainties persist, including the trajectory of China's rise. Key internal and external challenges may slow Chinese growth and limit defense spending increases. Political instability could reprioritize government spending. For these reasons, and because of the diminishing returns on investment explained above, China's ability and willingness to develop robust capabilities beyond the near seas and their immediate approaches remains unclear.

Strategic Effects

Assuming China avoids major internal problems, the near seas will likely become more favorable to China's claims as the country's overall power and military capabilities increase. In the Yellow Sea, Beijing's influence over any major changes in the status quo of the Korean Peninsula is likely to mitigate Korean claim disputes with Beijing. Similarly, in the South China Sea, Beijing may be able to persuade some maritime neighbors to pursue joint resource development or even settle claims in exchange for resource ownership. In contrast, disputes in the East China Sea may see only partial resolution on Beijing's terms. The Taiwan issue could come much closer to settlement, with economic integration,

---

[70] Kostecka, "From the Sea," 20.

[71] Milan N. Vego, *Operational Warfare* (Newport: Naval War College Press, 2000), 172–75.

military imbalances, and possible mainland domestic reforms persuading islanders to embrace a loose symbolic confederation. However, cross-strait political agreements could also trigger internal instability and consequent strategic introversion. The disputes with Japan over the Senkaku/Diaoyu Islands and EEZ boundary, by contrast, are unlikely to be resolved. Even if demographic and other challenges continue to reduce Japan's power relative to China's, Tokyo's administration of the islands and bilateral acrimony will frustrate efforts at accommodation, and Beijing is unlikely to risk a Falklands scenario to seize them.

Farther afield, Beijing will probably continue to rely on the global system, from which it benefits as a free or minimum-payment rider. Containing no Chinese claims and serving as a major conduit for Chinese inputs, the far seas offer cooperative benefits and conflict deterrents. The Indian Ocean contains great-power navies that prioritize its security given their proximity and reliance on SLOCs for commerce and energy flows. The United States will continue to exploit strategically located Diego Garcia, provided that rising seas do not compromise its utility. India's navy will enjoy an increasingly strong presence in its own backyard and make considerable diplomatic efforts to thwart excessive Chinese influence in littoral nations. Likewise, the Japanese, Korean, and Australian navies will leverage their presence and partnerships to safeguard supply lines.

At the operational level, then, a more robust version of A2/AD in the near seas will likely remain the PLA's core focus because China appears unlikely to gain similarly strong, unilateral interests in the far seas. Uncertainties include how far and how comprehensively its "range rings" extend and how extensive combat capabilities become in the far seas. At the tactical level, the key question will be to what extent the PLA can mitigate vulnerabilities along new exterior lines. In terms of software, the key question will be how the PLA changes the overall organizational structure and the way that the PLAN and PLAAF train.

Political Implications

Size, geographic proximity, and economic integration make China likely to gain leverage vis-à-vis key Asian competitors. Less clear is whether China will challenge strategic stability, or the geostrategic status quo, in Asia. What seems certain is that the maritime and aerospace arenas will continue to witness great-power competition in East Asia, where Beijing desires preeminence. Given China's overall rise, however, there will be considerable spillover effects in the Asia-Pacific more broadly, particularly in the strategic Indian Ocean region. China's approach of "using the land to control the sea" exemplifies how technology and geography are often interlinked.[72] Furthermore, by harnessing capitalism's positive aspects, China has the potential for competitive dynamism far surpassing that of the Soviet Union.

The United States thus increasingly faces a strong competitor with the ability to contend in all aspects of national power. Key variables concerning the influence of U.S. forces in the near seas will be their size and ability to operate in an A2/AD environment through some combination of distributed, less-vulnerable architecture and active countermeasures. However, China's rise as a major regional maritime and aerospace power may mark the end of an era in which the U.S. military enjoyed unobstructed access to the entire global commons. The central question is whether Washington will need to accept a zone of Chinese suzerainty in East Asia, and whether such an exception can be accommodated without compromising core U.S. interests or establishing an unacceptable precedent.

Alternatively, can the United States affordably counter China's asymmetric military approaches and reclaim the technological advantage in a relatively comprehensive fashion? Approaches to relevant platform and weapon systems may include shifting to less-manned and unmanned systems; limiting reliance on manpower wherever feasible; shifting some operations to smaller, dispersed, and networked elements; moving from the sea surface to the harder-to-access undersea (and, in some cases, air) realms; substituting passive defenses for active ones; adopting new approaches to basing and presence; and targeting China's own physics-based limitations with improved and more extensively deployed missiles, mines, and submarines. Of course, as the United States develops such advanced systems as autonomous underwater vehicles, China may follow suit.

Conclusion

The Chinese naval and air forces' evolving role in defending China's expanding economic interests has broad significance. For now, China seems to be pursuing a multilayered approach to naval development. This approach is marked by a consistent focus on increasingly high-end A2/AD capabilities to support major combat operations on China's

---

[72] Wang Wei, "Zhanshu dandao daodan dui Zhongguo haiyang zhanlüe tixi de yingxiang" [The Effect of Tactical Ballistic Missiles on the Maritime Strategy System of China], *Jianzai wuqi* 84 (2006): 12–15.

maritime periphery and relatively low-intensity but gradually growing capabilities to influence strategic conditions in Beijing's favor farther afield.

While China will no doubt build several carriers over the next decade, its naval and air forces are likely to develop within today's multilayered rubric for the foreseeable future, with parallel implications for U.S. security interests. China's military has achieved rapid, potent development by maintaining an A2/AD posture along interior lines and exploiting the physics-based limitations inherent in the performance parameters of U.S. and allied platforms and C4ISR systems. This should be of tremendous concern to Washington. But dramatic breakthroughs here cannot easily be translated out of area.

Just as these limiting factors increasingly threaten U.S. platforms operating in or near China's maritime periphery, they likewise haunt China's forces, which still lag considerably behind the United States' in overall resources, technology, and experience, as they venture farther afield. Thus far, Chinese decision-makers, having carefully studied the lessons of the Soviet Union's overextension, seem unlikely to expend overwhelming national resources to fight these realities. Despite growing concerns abroad, they have too many imperatives closer to home demanding funding and focus. Ongoing requirements for China's naval and air forces to secure Chinese near-seas interests also make it highly unlikely that a force that is modest, or even smaller, in quantity will be able to sustain a robust top-end footprint in the far seas, no matter how much its capabilities improve.

Perhaps most sobering, naval influence and operations remain untested in the age of long-range, large-scale missile threats. The December 10, 1941, sinking of the battleship *Prince of Wales* and the battlecruiser *Repulse* by land-based bombers and torpedo bombers of the Imperial Japanese Navy in the Naval Battle off Malaya offers one of the better examples of the risk of disregarding A2/AD threats.[73] With ships viewed increasingly as targets, stressed U.S. taxpayers may ask increasingly what port calls and naval diplomacy actually accomplish. This is part of a larger pattern in which U.S. military influence and operations have not demonstrated the ability to persist amid A2/AD threats. They will need to do so increasingly, in a manner that is convincing to their Chinese counterparts, allies, and the general public.

While these overall dynamics seem readily apparent, the implications for U.S. policy and influence in the Asia-Pacific remain uncertain. As recent agreements to rotate U.S. Marines into Darwin, Australia, amid overall strengthening of U.S.-Australian security ties suggest, Washington

---

[73] Correlli Barnett, *Engage the Enemy More Closely: The Royal Navy in the Second World War* (New York: W.W. Norton and Company, 1991), 391–92.

is devoting a greater proportion of its forces to the region as part of a larger rebalancing strategy, while seeking to deploy them with a flexible, light footprint. In the region more broadly, it remains unclear what shape this policy will take and to what extent the five U.S. treaty allies (Japan, South Korea, Australia, the Philippines, and Thailand) and other security partners (such as Singapore) will be willing to grant access. This strategy will also be subject to domestic public opinion, the extent to which regional nations are willing to depend on the United States and each other, and perceptions concerning the United States' and China's relative power and intentions. Finally, there is the question of whether this renewed U.S. focus and prioritization, coupled with enhanced cooperation with other regional actors, will be sufficient to counter Beijing's growing capabilities and deter their operational employment. To address these challenges, Washington must demonstrate its commitment to a sustained, properly resourced, and continually effective presence in the Asia-Pacific. It must work constructively with a broad range of allies, friends, and partners—including China, in many respects—to achieve broader public goods. To do so in this time of austerity will require rebalancing by redirecting resources from elsewhere. Such prioritization is the essence of strategy.

Appendix: PLA Naval and Air Forces

Except where otherwise indicated in notes and citations, the following methodology was used to determine order-of-battle categories and numbers. Data from unclassified U.S. government reports, including the latest Department of Defense and Office of Naval Intelligence reports, was taken as authoritative, although limited in coverage. Beyond these, IISS's *The Military Balance* provided an overall baseline for the tables in this appendix, as it is the most demonstrably reliable comprehensive source available. The latest relevant *Jane's* reports were used to supplement this data. These reports are less demonstrably reliable, but no other open source save *The Military Balance* approaches their comprehensiveness. With regard to certain naval vessels, some calculations were made using Google Earth images. With regard to certain aircraft, some calculations were made using the latest *Directory of Military Personalities* and websites such as Chinese Military Aviation and China Defense Forum. Photographs and data from these websites were used to compile aircraft BORT and ship hull numbers, thereby enabling estimates to be made based on the assumption that there are approximately 24 aircraft per regiment (although that figure might vary).

The differing figures offered by IISS, *Jane's*, and the more specific methods were adjudicated in the following fashion:

- where a value appeared to be an overall figure as opposed to one for the respective variants into which a given platform was divided;

- when a value appeared to reflect recently higher numbers of a platform that was in the process of being reduced in number; or

- when the values of naval hulls were very close and the *Jane's* value of three correlated with a logical division among the PLAN's three fleets.

In most such exceptions, the *Jane's* figures were used. In the event of a large disparity between IISS and *Jane's* that did not stem from one of these three scenarios, the number not selected for the matrix is noted. In the rare event that the more specific methods approach yielded a higher figure, that figure was used instead on the assumption that such methods would often yield an incomplete figure (i.e., due to incomplete photographic coverage) but would be unlikely to yield an exaggerated one. Finally, all findings were vetted with experts on open source order-of-battle estimation. Subsequently, missing information was filled in using SinoDefense.com, which, though outdated regarding platform numbers, offers apparently reliable information concerning history and platform lineage. Given the difficulty in estimating PLA order-of-battle numbers, these findings must be treated with caution.

TABLE A1   China's naval order of battle

Platform	North Sea Fleet	East Sea Fleet	South Sea Fleet	Total in 2012	Total in 2015 (projected)	Total in 2020 (projected)
Nuclear-powered ballistic-missile submarines[a]	3	0	1	4	4–5?	5?
Attack submarines (total)	21		35	56	~70	~72
Nuclear-powered attack submarines (SSN)	3		2	5	?	?
Diesel-powered attack submarines (SS)	18		30	48	?	?
Aircraft carriers		1		1[b]	1?	2?
Destroyers	10	8	8	26	~26	~26
Frigates	9		44	53	~45	~42
Subtotal of above ships				137	~146–47?	~146–47?
Amphibious ships	2	26		28	?	?
Medium landing ships	5	18		23	?	?
Missile patrol craft	19		67	86	?	?
Mine warfare ships		40		40	?	?
Major auxiliaries		50 (5 are fleet AORs)		50	?	?
Minor auxiliaries and service/support craft		250+		250+	?	?

SOURCE: U.S. Department of Defense, *Military and Security Developments Involving the People's Republic of China 2012*, annual report prepared for Congress (May 18, 2012), 31; and Ronald O'Rourke, "China Naval Modernization: Implications for U.S. Navy Capabilities—Background and Issues for Congress," Congressional Research Service, CRS Report for Congress, RL33153, August 10, 2012, 38.

NOTE: *a* indicates "Jin class (Type 094)," *Jane's Fighting Ships*; and *b* indicates that aircraft carrier is undergoing sea trials and is projected to become operational in 2012.

TABLE A2 PLAN coastal defense forces (ground-launched)

Type	Role	Manufacturer	Launch platform	Range (km)	Payload (kg)	Speed (supersonic/ subsonic)	Guidance (initial/terminal)	Total in service
YJ-62C/C-602	Antiship cruise missile (ASCM)	CASIC Third Academy	Eight-by-eight wheeled TEL, 3 tubular ribbed missile canisters, 20-degree launch elevation. Typical battery: 4 TELs, C2 vehicle, support vehicle	280+	210	Subsonic	Inertial/active terminal guidance	120
HY-4/YJ-63/C-201/ CSSC-7 "Sadsack" (improved HY-4A version)	ASCM / turbojet	CASIC Third Academy	–	135/ 200–280	513; high explosive shaped charge warhead	–	Inertial with GPS updates for mid-course guidance/ multimode active-passive monopulse radar for terminal guidance	?
HY-3/C-301/ CSSC-6 "Sawhorse" (improved HY-3A version)	ASCM (dual ramjets)	CASIC Third Academy	Typical battery: 4 missiles on their launchers, 4 missile transport vehicles, radar and command vehicle, 3 power supply vehicles	35–140/ 180	513; fragmentation warhead	Supersonic (Mach 2.0)	Inertial mid-course guidance with radio altimeter controlling cruise altitude/active monopulse radar seeker, likely similar to YJ-16; delayed contact fuse, active laser proximity fuse	50–150

Table A2 continued.

Type	Role	Manufacturer	Launch platform	Range (km)	Payload (kg)	Speed (supersonic/ subsonic)	Guidance (initial/terminal)	Total in service
YJ-16/C-101/ CSSC-5 "Saples"	ASCM (dual ramjet)	CASIC Third Academy	–	–	300; high explosive semi-armor piercing	Supersonic	Inertial/active monopulse radar, 10–20 GHz (X-band) seeker	?
HY-2A/CSSC-3 "Seersucker"	ASCM	CASIC Third Academy	–	95	454; hollow-charge warhead	Subsonic (Mach 0.9)	Autopilot/active radar; alternative IR seeker	?
HY-1A/CSSC-2 "Silkworm"	ASCM	CASIC Third Academy	–	40	454; hollow-charge warhead	Subsonic (Mach 0.9)	Autopilot/active radar	?
130-mm	Coastal artillery		–	–	–	–	–	250
100-mm	Coastal artillery		–	–	–	–	–	500
85-mm	Coastal artillery		–	–	–	–	–	500

SOURCE: *Jane's Strategic Weapon Systems;* and *Jane's World Navies.*

TABLE A3   Submarines

Class	Manufacturer	Role	In service	First hull commissioned
Jin (Type 094)	Huludao Shipyard	Ballistic-missile, nuclear-powered	3[a]	2007
Xia (Type 092)	Huludao Shipyard	Ballistic-missile, nuclear-powered	1	1987
New "Qing (Type 043)" with large sail	Wuchang Shipyard	Ballistic-missile? (Test?) Other missions? Diesel-powered	1[b]	2010
Shang (Type 093)	Huludao Shipyard	Attack, nuclear-powered	2	2006
Han (Type 091/091G)	Huludao Shipyard	Attack, nuclear-powered	3	1980
Kilo (Project 877EKM/636)	Various Russian shipyards	Patrol, diesel-powered	12	1995
Yuan (Type 041)	Wuhan/ Changxing Island shipyards	Patrol, diesel-powered (likely air-independent-power)	8–9	2006
Song (Type 039/039G)	Wuhan/ Jiangnan shipyards	Patrol, diesel-powered	13	1999
Ming (Type 035)	Wuhan Shipyard	Patrol, diesel-powered	19	1971
Golf (Type 031)	Dalian Shipyard	Ballistic-missile (test), diesel-powered	1	1966
Romeo (Type 033 Wuhan SSG)	–	Test platform; 6 YJ-1 (CSS-N-4) Sardine AShM, 8 single 533-mm, diesel-powered	1	–
Romeo (Type 033 SS)	–	Diesel-powered	Numbers uncertain; being retired	~1962

SOURCE: IISS, *The Military Balance 2012*; *Jane's World Navies*; and, for *a*, "Jin class (Type 094)," *Jane's Fighting Ships*.

NOTE: *a* indicates operational as a submarine but not as a missile launcher until the JL-2 SLBM trials are complete; and *b* indicates launched but apparently not yet commissioned.

TABLE A4   PLAN surface fleet

Class	Manufacturer	Role	In service	First hull commissioned
Luyang II (Type 052C)	Jiangnan/ Changxing Island shipyards	Destroyer (area air-defense)	8	2004
Luyang I (Type 052B)	Jiangnan Shipyard	Destroyer (area air-defense)	2	2004
Luzhou (Type 051C)	Dalian Shipyard	Destroyer	2	2006
Sovremenny (Project 956E/956EM)	North Yard, Russia	Destroyer	4	1999
Luhu (Type 052A)	Jiangnan Shipyard	Destroyer	2	1994
Luda-class (Type 051DT/051G/051G II)	Dalian Shipyard	Destroyer	4[a]	1991
Luda (Types 051/051D/051Z)	Various	Destroyer	8[b]	1971
Luhai (Type 051B)	Dalian Shipyard	Destroyer	1	1999
Jiangkai II (Type 054A)	Huangpu/ Hudong-Zhonghua shipyards	Frigate (air defense)	16–19	2008
Jiangkai I (Type 054)	Hudong-Zhonghua/ Huangpu shipyards	Frigate	2	2005
Jiangwei II (Type 053H3)	Huangpu/ Hudong-Zhonghua shipyards	Frigate	10	1998
Jiangwei I (Type 053H2G)	Hudong-Zhonghua Shipyard	Frigate	4	1991
Jianghu I/II/V (Type 053H/053H1/053H1G)	Hudong-Zhonghua/ Jiangnan/ Huangpu shipyards	Frigate	22[c]	Mid-1970s
Jianghu IV (Type 053HTH)	Hudong-Zhonghua Shipyard	Frigate	1[d]	1986
Jianghu III (Type 053H2)	Hudong-Zhonghua Shipyard	Frigate	3	1986

Table A4 continued.

Class	Manufacturer	Role	In service	First hull commissioned
Houbei (Type 022)	Various	New-generation, fast-attack craft (missile)	60+	2004
Houjian/Huang (Type 037-II)	Huangpu Shipyard	Fast-attack craft (missile)	5–6	1991
Houxin (Type 037/IG)	Qiuxin/Huangpu shipyards	Fast-attack craft (missile)	16	1991
Huangfeng (Type 021) (Osa I Type)	?	Fast-attack craft (missile)	11	1985
Haiqing (Type 037-IIS)	Qiuxin/Qingdao/ Chongqing/ Huangpu shipyards	Fast-attack craft (patrol)	25	1992
Hainan (Type 037)	Chongqing/ Qingdao/ Qiuxin/Huangpu shipyards	Fast-attack craft (patrol)	50	1963
Shanghai II (Type 062C)	Shanghai/various shipyards	Fast-attack craft (gun)	35 (declining numbers)	1961
Haizhui/Shanghai III (Type 062/1)	?	Patrol craft (coastal)	25[e]	1992
Haijiu (Type 037-I)	?	Patrol craft (large)	3	1984
[Unknown]	?	Patrol craft (harbor)	3	1997
Wolei (Type 918)	Dalian Shipyard	Minelayer	1	1988
Wozang (Type 082-II?)	Qiuxin Shipyard	Minehunter/ minesweeper	2	2005
T-43 (Type 6610)	Wuhan/ Guangzhou shipyards	Minesweeper (ocean)	16	1966
Wochi (Type 081)	Qiuxin/Shanghai/ Wuhan shipyards	Minesweeper (coastal)	7	2007
Wosao (Type 082)	?	Minesweeper (coastal)	16	1988
Futi (Type 312)	?	Minesweeper (drone)	4	Early 1970s
Yuzhao (Type 071)	Hudong-Zhonghua Shipyard	Amphibious assault ship/ LHD	3	2008

Table A4 continued.

Class	Manufacturer	Role	In service	First hull commissioned
Yuting II (Type 072 III)	Various	Landing ship tank (LST)	10	2003
Yuting I (Type 072 II)	Hudong-Zhonghua Shipyard	LST	10	1992
Yukan (Type 072)	Wuhan Shipyard	LST	7	1980
Yushu	Hudong-Zhonghua/Wuhu/ Qingdao/Lüshun shipyards	Landing ship mechanized (LSM)	10	2004
Yuhai (Type 074) (Wuhu-A)	Wuhu/various shipyards	LSM	10	1995
Yuliang (Type 079)	Various	LSM	30	1980
Yudeng (Type 073)	Hudong-Zhonghua Shipyard	LSM	1	1994
Yudao (Type 073)	?	LSM	1	1980
Yubei (Type 074A)	Qingdao/ Zhanjiang/ Shanghai/ Dinghai shipyards	Landing craft utility (LCU)	10	2004
Yuqing (Type 068/069)	Hudong-Zhonghua/Dahe/ Guangzhou shipyards	LCU	20	Late 1960s
Yunan (Type 067)	Hudong-Zhonghua/ Hangzhou/ Qinhuangdao shipyards	LCU	120	1968
Type 271-II/III	Qingdao/ Changsha shipyards	LCU	25	1970
Jingsha II	Dagu	Hovercraft/landing craft air-cushion (LCAC)	10	1979
Yuyi	Qiuxin Shipyard	Hovercraft/LCAC	1	2008

SOURCE: IISS, *The Military Balance 2012*; and *Jane's World Navies*.

NOTE: *a* is from IISS and comprises 2 Luda mod (Type 051DT), 1 Luda II (Type 051G), 1 Luda III (Type 052G II). *b* is from *Jane's*; Type 051/Luda-class destroyer *Yinchuan* (107) was decommissioned on April 5, 2012. *c* is from IISS and comprises 9 Jianghu I (Type 053H), 8 Jianghu II (Type 053H1), and 6 Jianghu V (Type 053H1G). *d* is from IISS and indicates Type 053H1Q are in a training role. *e* indicates that IISS lists 34+ for this value.

TABLE A5   Selected PLAN amphibious vehicles and weapons

Type	Manufacturer	Role	In service	First delivery
Type 05/ZBD2000/ ZBD-05	China North Industries Corp (NORINCO)	Amphibious assault vehicle (AAV)/light tank	124[a, b]	2005
Type 63A/ZTZ-63A/ WZ213	NORINCO	Amphibious light tank	62[c, d]	?
Type 05/ZTD-05	NORINCO	AAV/armored personnel carrier (APC)	124	?
Type 63C/YW531C	NORINCO	Amphibious APC	62[c]	?
Type 77-I/77-II/WZ511	NORINCO	Amphibious APC	400[e]	?
ZBD-04	NORINCO	Amphibious IVF	?[f]	?
Type 86/WZ501/YW501	NORINCO	Amphibious infantry fighting vehicle	62	?
122-mm Type 54 (similar chassis to Type 63A)	NORINCO	Self-propelled field howitzer	40+[g]	?
122-mm Type 89	NORINCO	Self-propelled howitzer	20+[h]	?
Type 07	NORINCO	Artillery	20+	?
122-mm Type 83	NORINCO	Multiple rocket launcher (MRL)	83	?
107-mm Type 89 (improved variant of Type 63)	NORINCO	MRL	?	?
130-mm Type 63-1/70	NORINCO	MRL	?	Production complete, in service, no longer marketed.
Hongjian/Red Arrow 73 (HJ-73) (multiple variants)	NORINCO	Anti-tank guided missile (ATGM)	?	?
Hongjian/Red Arrow 8 (HJ-8) (multiple variants)	NORINCO	ATGM	?	?

Table A5 continued.

Type	Manufacturer	Role	In service	First delivery
120-mm Type 98 (PF-98)	NORINCO	Anti-tank rocket system	?	?
82-mm	NORINCO	Mortar	?	?
Hongnu/Red Cherry (HN-5)	NORINCO	Man-portable surface-to-air missile system	?	?

SOURCE: IISS, *The Military Balance 2012*; *Jane's World Navies*; *Jane's Armour and Artillery 2012*; and *Jane's Armour and Artillery Upgrades 2012*.

NOTE: *a* indicates that *Jane's World Navies* lists 400. *b* indicates that *Jane's Armour and Artillery 2012* estimates that approximately 600 ZBD2000s will be built in total. *c* indicates that *Jane's World Navies* lists 800. *d* indicates *Jane's Armour and Artillery 2012* estimates 150. *e* indicates that this system is not listed in IISS. *f* indicates *Jane's Armour and Artillery 2012* estimates 500 total in PLA service. *g* indicates *Jane's World Navies* lists 100. *h* indicates that *Jane's Armour and Artillery 2012* lists 500 total in PLA service. Numerical discrepancies may reflect numbers actually in PLAN service versus total numbers (including exports in some cases).

TABLE A6 Auxiliaries

Class	Manufacturer	Role	In service	Commissioned
Yuanwang 6	Jiangnan Shipyard	Space event support ship	1	2008
Yuanwang 5	Jiangnan Shipyard	Space event support ship	1	2007
Yuanwang 3	Jiangnan Shipyard	Space event support ship	1	1995
Type 851/851G/ NATO: Dongdiao 232	Qiuxin Shipyard	Intelligence ship	2	1999
Dadie (Type 814A)	Wuchang Shipyard	Intelligence ship	1	1986
Type 813/NATO: Xiangyanghong 21 (V350/ Nandiao 350)	Hudong-Zhonghua Shipyard	Intelligence ship	1	1983
[Unknown]	?	Survey ship	1	~2005
Haiyang 20	?	Research ship	1	~2005
Type 636A/ NATO: Kanjie/ Li Siguang 871	?	Research ship	1	1998
Dahua	Hudong-Zhonghua Shipyard	Survey and research ship	2–3	1997
Kan	Shanghai?	Survey and research ship	2	1985
Binhai	Niigata Engineering Company, Japan	Survey and research ship	1	1975
Ganzhu	Zhujiang	Survey and research ship	1	1975
Yenlai	Hudong-Zhonghua Shipyard	Survey and research ship	5	1970
Shuguang	?	Survey and research ship	1	?
Yanha	?	Icebreaker	3	1989
Yanbing (modified Yanha)	?	Icebreaker	1	1982

Table A6 continued.

Class	Manufacturer	Role	In service	Commissioned
Dachou	Wuzhou Shipyard	Torpedo recovery vessel	1	2006
Dongba	–	Twin-hull remote-controlled target barge (with cube reflectors to direct ASCMs)	2+	–
Daishandao (Type 920)	Guangzhou Shipyard International	Hospital ship	1	2008
Nankang	Guangzhou Shipyard International	Hospital/medical transport ship (small)	1–4[a]	1991
Dalao (Type 926)	Guangzhou Shipyard International	Submarine rescue ship	1–3	2010
Dadong (Type 946A)	Hudong-Zhonghua Shipyard	Submarine rescue ship	1	1982
Dazhou (Type 946)	Guangzhou Shipyard	Submarine rescue ship	2	1977
Type 648	?	Submarine tender	1	1985
Dalang (Type 922 II/III)	Guangzhou/Wuhan shipyards	Submarine salvage and rescue ship	4	1987
Dajiang (Type 925)	Jiangnan Shipyard	Submarine salvage and rescue ship	3	1976
Roslavl	China-built, Soviet design	Tug	19	Mid-1960s
Gromovoy	Luda Shipyard/Shanghai International	Tug	17	1958
Daozha	?	Tug	1	1993
Hujiu	Wuhu	Tug	10	1980s
Tuzhong	Hudong-Zhonghua Shipyard	Tug	3	1980
Yannan	?	Sea-going buoy tender	7	1980

Table A6 continued.

Class	Manufacturer	Role	In service	Commissioned
Yanbai	?	Degaussing	5	?
Qiongsha	Guangzhou Shipyard	Troop transport	6	1980
Fuchi (Type 903)	Hudong-Zhonghua/ Huangpu shipyards	Replenishment ship	2	2004
Nanyun/ NATO: Fusu Qinghaihu (885)	Kherson Shipyard, Ukraine; outfitted at Dalian Shipyard	Replenishment ship	1	1996
Fuqing (Type 905)	Dalian Shipyard	Replenishment ship	2	1979
Fulin	Hudong-Zhonghua Shipyard	Replenishment ship	15+	~1972
Jinyou	Kanashashi Shipyard, Japan	Coastal tanker	3	1989
Guangzhou	?	Coastal tanker	5–8	1970
Leizhou	Qingdao/ Wudong	Coastal tanker	9	Late 1960s
[Unknown]	?	Supply tanker	4	?
Danyao (Type 904A)/Fuxianhu 888	Guangzhou Shipyard International	Supply ship	1	2007
Dayun (Type 904)	Hudong-Zhonghua Shipyard	Supply ship	2	1992
Yantai	?	Supply ship	3	1992
Dandao	?	Supply ship	7[b]	Late 1970s
Fuzhou	?	Supply ship	26–27[c]	1970

Table A6 continued.

Class	Manufacturer	Role	In service	Commissioned
Danlin	?	Supply ship	13[d]	1962
Shengli	Hudong-Zhonghua Shipyard	Auxiliary	2	1980
Hongqi	?	Auxiliary	6	?
Hull 88	–	Crew quarters ship (with ex-*Varyag*, Dalian)	1	–
Shichang	Qiuxin	Training ship	1	1997
Daxin (Type 795)	Qiuxin	Training ship	1	1987

SOURCE: IISS, *The Military Balance 2012*; and *Jane's World Navies*.

NOTE: *a* indicates that Nankang ships are extremely limited in capacity; perhaps only 1 is currently operational. *b* indicates that *Jane's* gives this value as 13. *c* indicates transport ships for liquid, consisting of 18 oil and 8–9 water. *d* indicates 7 oil transport ships and 6 refrigerated container ships for the South Sea Fleet.

TABLE A7 China's air power order of battle

Platform	Total in 2012	Total in 2015 (projected)	Total in 2020 (projected)
PLAAF			
Bombers	80	?	?
Fighters	~1,363	?	?
AWACs/ reconnaissance/ ELINT/EW/C2	~98	?	?
Transport/combat support/utility	~355	?	?
Tankers	~10	?	?
Trainers	~590	?	?
Helicopters	20–100[a]	?	?
Subtotal above aircraft	*~2,516–2,596*	*?*	*?*
PLAN aviation			
Land-based maritime-strike aircraft	~145	~255	~258
Carrier-based fighters	0	~60	~90
Helicopters	~34–100+[b]	~153	~157
Subtotal above aircraft	*~179–245+*	*~468 (+helicopters)*	*~505 (+helicopters)*

SOURCE: "Air Force, China," *Jane's World Air Forces,* June 10, 2012; O'Rourke, "China Naval Modernization," 33; for *a,* low estimate is drawn from "Air Force, China," and high estimate is from Dennis J. Blasko, "Chinese Helicopter Development: Missions, Roles, and Maritime Implications," in *Chinese Aerospace Power: Evolving Maritime Roles*, ed. Andrew S. Erickson and Lyle J. Goldstein (Annapolis: Naval Institute Press, 2011), 154; and, for *b,* low estimate is drawn from O'Rourke, "China Naval Modernization," and high estimate is from Blasko, "Chinese Helicopter Development," 154.

TABLE A8 PLAAF air-defense systems

Type	Role	Manufacturer	Launch platform	Range (km)	Payload (kg)	Guidance
S-300 PMU (SA-10C "Grumble")/ PMU-1 (SA-10D) /PMU-2 Favorit (SA-20 "Gargoyle")[a]	Surface-to-air missile (SAM)	Russian; some licensed production	–	–	–	–
HQ-9/-9A (B?)/FT-2000/2000A[b]	SAM	CASIC	–	90-120 (HQ-9)/100 (FT-2000)	130; HE fragmentation	Inertial with updates, semi-active radar (HQ-9)/ inertial/GPS, passive radar (FT-2000)
HQ-12A (KS-1A/-2/FT-2100)	SAM	–	Battery has a phased-array radar guidance station, four twin-missile launch vehicles on a HY 2220 six-by-six truck chassis, a communications vehicle, a command and control vehicle, and associated support vehicles	40 (HQ-12), 50 (HQ-12A)	100; HE blast/ fragmentation	Command; phased-array radar

SOURCE: "Air Force, China"; and *Jane's Strategic Weapon Systems*.

NOTE: *a* indicates that there are approximately eight PLAAF S-300 regiments, which may increase to twenty, with 30–48 missiles each. *b* indicates this is the active-guided version, which has reportedly been in service in small numbers since 2003.

TABLE A9 PLAAF fixed-wing aircraft

Type	Manufacturer	Role	In service	First delivery
H-6 (including -G/-H/-K/-M missile variants)	XAC	Bomber	82	1968
JH-7A	XAC	Fighter (ground attack/strike)	83[a]	2004
Q-5 "Fantan"	HAIC	Fighter (ground attack/strike)	120	1970
J-8H	SAC Shenyang	Fighter (interceptor/ air defense)	144	2002
J-8F	SAC Shenyang	Fighter (interceptor/ air defense)	80	2003
J-8D	SAC Shenyang	Fighter (interceptor/ air defense)	80?[b]	1990
J-8B	SAC Shenyang	Fighter (interceptor/ air defense)	90[c]	1988
Su-30MKK "Flanker"	Sukhoi, Russia	Fighter (multirole)	73	2000
J-11B/BS1[e]	SAC Shenyang	Fighter (multirole)	96	2004
J-11A (Chinese kit-assembled Su-27SK)	SAC Shenyang	Fighter (multirole)	96	2001
Su-27SK "Flanker-B"	Sukhoi, Russia	Fighter (multirole)	43	1992
J-10B	CAC	Fighter (multirole)	10	2009
J-10A/S	CAC	Fighter (multirole)	216	2001
J-7G	CAC	Fighter (multirole)	50	2003
J-7E	CAC	Fighter (multirole)	144	1993
J-7C	CAC	Fighter (multirole)	48	1985
J-7B	CAC	Fighter (multirole)	183	1980
KJ-2000 (A-50 "Mainstay"/ Il-76MD)	Beriev, Russia/ XAC-modified	Airborne early warning and control	4[d]	2004
Y-8W/KJ-200	SAC Shaanxi	Airborne early warning and control	5	2007
Y-8G	SAC Shaanxi	Reconnaissance/ surveillance	7	2007
JZ-8F	SAC Shenyang	Reconnaissance/ surveillance	24	?
JZ-8	SAC Shenyang	Reconnaissance/ surveillance	24	?

Table A9 continued.

Type	Manufacturer	Role	In service	First delivery
JZ-6	SAC Shenyang	Reconnaissance/surveillance	48	1976
Y-8XZ	SAC Shaanxi	Electronic warfare	2	2007
Y-8CB	SAC Shaanxi	Electronic warfare	4	–
Tu-154M/D "Careless"	Tupolev, Russia	Electronic intelligence	4[g]	1998
Y-8T	SAC Shaanxi	Command/control	3	2007
737-300	Boeing, U.S.	C3I	2[f]	?
H-6U	XAC	Tanker	10[g, h]	1998
737-800	Boeing, U.S.	Transport	2[f]	2010
737-700	Boeing, U.S.	Transport	2[f]	2003
737-300	Boeing, U.S.	Transport	15[g, l]	1988
Il-76MD "Candid"	Ilyushin, Russia	Transport	14	1991
Tu-154M "Careless"	Tupolev, Russia	Transport	12[g, n]	1986
An-30 "Clank"	Antonov, Ukraine	Transport	8[j]	?
An-26 "Curl"	Antonov, Ukraine	Transport	12	?
An-24 "Coke"	Antonov, Ukraine	Transport	10	?
Y-7	XAC	Transport	41[h, o]	1984
Y-8	SAC Shaanxi	Transport (medium)	25[k, m]	1981
Y-12	HAI	Transport (light)	8	–
Y-11	HAI	Transport (light)	20	–
CRJ-700	Bombardier, Canada	Transport (passenger)	5	–
CRJ-200	Bombardier, Canada	Transport (passenger)	5	–
Challenger 870	Bombardier, Canada	Utility	5[f, g]	2005
Challenger 800	Bombardier, Canada	Utility	5[f, g]	1997
Y-5	SAIC	Utility	170[p]	1958
Su-27UB "Flanker-C"	Sukhoi, Russia	Trainer	32	1992
JL-9/FTC-2000	GAIC	Trainer	~12+?	–

Table A9 continued.

Type	Manufacturer	Role	In service	First delivery
JL-8 (Export designation: "Karakorum")	HAIC	Trainer	300	1998
An-30 "Clank"	Antonov, Ukraine	Trainer	6^j	1975
JJ-7	GAIC	Trainer	50^q	1985
JJ-6	SAC Shenyang	Trainer	100	1970
JJ-5	CAC	Trainer	?	1966
CJ-6/A	HAIC	Trainer	350^r	1963

SOURCE: IISS, *The Military Balance 2012*; "Air Force, China"; and "Picture Gallery: J-11/11B/11BS," Chinese Military Aviation, website, May 28, 2012, http://cnair.top81.cn/gallery.htm#J-11.

NOTE: *a* indicates that the Chinese Military Aviation website offers no photos with JH-7 aircraft PLAAF BORT numbers. *b* indicates that the Chinese Military Aviation website lists 4 regiments but all were later upgraded to J-8H. *c* indicates that *The Military Balance 2012* lists only 24. *d* indicates that according to *Jane's*, these are not yet fully operational and a further 2 are required. *e* indicates that this is an indigenized Su-27 variant and that the total includes 1 development aircraft used for system trials. *f* indicates these are not yet fully operational and a further 2 are required. *g* indicates civil-registered. *h* indicates an undisclosed number of additional aircraft awaiting modification. *i* indicates that value includes some modified to HYJ-7 configuration for use in navigation and bomber training tasks. *j* indicates that *Jane's* lists the An-30 "Clank" as transport/survey and lists 6 of those in total. *k* indicates *The Military Balance 2012* lists 40+ Y-8s, but this appears to include some subcategories that *Jane's* breaks out separately. *Jane's* lists 2 Y-8s devoted to "combat support," and it is unclear whether this represents 2 additional airframes or different roles from transport. *l* indicates that *The Military Balance 2012* lists 10. *m* indicates that *The Military Balance 2012* lists a total of 9 B-737s (VIP) for light transport. *n* indicates that *Jane's* lists 5. *o* indicates that *Jane's* lists 50. *p* indicates that *Jane's* lists 200. *q* indicates that *Jane's* lists 100. *r* indicates that *The Military Balance 2012* lists 400.

TABLE A10 PLAN fixed-wing aviation

Type	Manufacturer	Role	In service	First delivery
H-6G	XAC	Bomber (missile variant)	30[b]	2005?
H-6D	XAC	Bomber (missile variant)	?[b]	1985
JH-7A	XAC	Strike fighter/ bomber	75[a]	2004
JH-7	XAC	Strike fighter/ bomber	50–65[a]	1998
Su-30 MKK2 "Flanker"	Sukhoi, Russia	Fighter (interceptor/ air defense)	24	2004
J-8 IV "Finback D"	SAC Shenyang	Fighter (interceptor/ air defense)	20[c]	1990
J-8 II "Finback B"	SAC Shenyang	Fighter (interceptor/ air defense)	20[c]	1990
J-8 I "Finback A"	SAC Shenyang	Fighter (interceptor/ air defense)	70[e]	1990
J-7 IV (J-7E)	CAC	Fighter (multirole)	24	1992
J-7 II (J-7B)	CAC	Fighter (multirole)	40	1971
J-11BH/BSH	SAC	Fighter (surface attack)	4+	–
J-10A/S	CAC	Fighter (multirole)	24	–
Q-5 "Fantan-A"	HAIC	Fighter (surface attack/strike)	35	1970
SH-5	HAIC	Maritime patrol/ antisubmarine (flying boat)	4	1986
H-5 (Il-28 Beagle)	HAIC	Antisubmarine	20[f]	?
Y-8JB	SAC Shaanxi	Electronic intelligence	4–5	2004
Y-8J/W	SAC Shaanxi	Airborne early warning and control	4	1998
HZ-5	?	ISR	7	?
H-6U	XAC	Tanker	3	1998
Yak-42D	Yakovlev, Russia	Transport	2[d]	1990

Table A10 continued.

Type	Manufacturer	Role	In service	First delivery
Y-8X "Cub"	SAC Shaanxi	Transport (medium)	4	1985
Y-7H	XAC	Transport (light)	6	–
Y-7	XAC	Transport (light)	4	1984
Y-5	–	Transport (light)	50	–
JL-9/FTC-2000	GAIC	Trainer	12+	–
JL-8 (Export designation: "Karakorum")	HAIC	Trainer	12	1998
JJ-7	GAIC	Trainer	4	1985
HY-7	?	Trainer	21	?
HJ-5	?	Trainer	5	?
CJ-6/6A	HAIC	Trainer	38	1963

S O U R C E : IISS, *The Military Balance 2012*; and *Jane's World Navies*.

N O T E : *a* indicates deliveries ongoing. *b* indicates that the H-6D may be being replaced with the H-6G. *c* indicates that *The Military Balance 2012* lists 24 J-8F Finback and 24 J-8H Finback. *d* indicates civil-registered. *e* indicates that *Jane's* lists 29. *f* indicates that *Jane's* lists 30.

TABLE A11   PLAAF helicopters

Type	Manufacturer	Role	In service	First delivery
Zhi (Z)-9/SA-365 Dauphin (multiple variants)	HAI; French technology, licensed production	Light-utility twin-engine helicopter	20	1989
Z-8/SA-321 Super Frelon	CHAIG; French technology, licensed production	Multirole medium helicopter	10[a]	1977
AS-332 Super Puma	France (precursor to Z-8)	Multirole medium helicopter	6+	–
Mi-17V-5/7 "Hip"	Mil, Russia; Russian technology, limited local production	Multirole medium helicopter/ utility	20–50?	?
Mi-171	Mil, Russia	Transport (medium)	4+	–
Mi-8 Hip	Mil, Russia	Transport (medium)	50	–
Bell 214	Bell, U.S.	Transport (medium)	4	–

SOURCE: IISS, *The Military Balance 2012*; and *Jane's World Air Forces.*

NOTE: *a* indicates *The Military Balance 2012* lists 18+.

TABLE A12   PLAN helicopters

Type	Manufacturer	Role	In service	First delivery
Ka-31	Kamov, Russia	Airborne early warning	$2-8+^{d,e}$	–
Zhi (Z)-8/ SA-321 Super Frelon	CHAIG; French technology, licensed production	Airborne early warning	$1+^d$	–
Z-9/SA-365 Dauphin (multiple variants)	HAI; French technology, licensed production	Maritime/ antisubmarine	25^a	1989
Z-8/SA-321 Super Frelon	CHAIG; French technology, licensed production	Maritime/ antisubmarine	40^b	1977
Ka-28PL/PS "Helix-A"	Kamov, Russia	Maritime/ antisubmarine	15^c	1999
Mi-17V-5/7/ Mi-8 "Hip"	Mil, Russia; Russian technology, limited local production	Transport	8	?

SOURCE: IISS, *The Military Balance 2012*; *Jane's World Navies* (low estimate); Blasko, "Chinese Helicopter Development," 154 (high estimate); "Russia Starts Ka-28 ASW Helicopter Deliveries to Chinese Navy," *Defence Professionals News*, October 9, 2009, http://www.defpro.com/news/details/10411/; Internet photos; and "Kamov Ka-31 Helix B," *Jane's Fighting Ships*, March 2, 2012.

NOTE: *a* indicates data from *Jane's* that only 11 are still in service. *b* indicates that *The Military Balance 2012* breaks this value down as: search and rescue, 2 Z-8S; heavy transports, 15 SA321 Super Frelon, 20 Z-8/Z-8A, and 3 Z-8JH. *c* indicates that *The Military Balance 2012* breaks this down as antisubmarine warfare, 13 Ka-28 Helix A; and airborne early warning, 2 Ka-31. *Jane's* lists up to 12 more awaiting delivery. *d* indicates value drawn from Internet photos. *e* indicates that China has ordered a total of 9 according to *Defence Professionals News*. *Jane's* states that 8 were delivered by 2011 and are now in service.

TABLE A13   Selected unmanned aerial vehicles (UAV)

Designation	Type	Manufacturer	Range/ endurance	Comments
COMBAT/SURVEILLANCE				
Harpy	Unmanned combat aerial vehicle (UCAV)	Israeli Aircraft Industries	250-km/hr speed, 3-km service ceiling, 400–500-km mission radius, 2-hr endurance	Israel supplied 100 in 2001; China may have reverse-engineered and produced additional units. Propeller-driven, 120–135 kg. Loiters until detects pre-programmed radar emission, dives directly at emitting radar antenna, destroys it with 32-kg explosive warhead.
Winglong/ Pterodactyl 1	UAV/medium-altitude, long-endurance (MALE)	?	5-km service ceiling, 20-hr endurance	Perhaps China's most-established indigenous UAV. Project launched May 2005; prototype displayed at 2008 Zhuhai Airshow; tested in 2008, weapons trials beginning 2009; cleared for export June 2009; redesigned significantly by 2010. 1,150-kg maximum takeoff weight, 200-kg payload; Ku-band sitcom antenna, 2 HJ-10 (ADK-10) 50-kg laser-guided anti-tank missiles. 100-hp reciprocating engine.
CH-3/PW-3	UCAV	China Aerospace Science and Technology Corp (CASC)	5-km service ceiling, 2,398-km range, 12-hr endurance	In production. Approved for export; potential competitor of Winglong/ Pterodactyl 1. Unveiled at 2008 Zhuhai Airshow; foreign order reported October 2009. Optimized for low-to-medium close air support missions. S-band data link. 60-kg max payload; 2 AR-1 semi-active-laser-guided missiles. Propeller-driven, reciprocating piston engine.
WJ-600 (turbojet) /600A (turbofan)	UAV/MALE	China Aerospace Science and Industry Corp (CASIC)	600-km/hr max speed, 10-km service ceiling, 6-hr endurance	Delivered to PLAAF. First displayed at 2010 Zhuhai Airshow. High-speed ISR and strike missions: optical reconnaissance, SAR, electronic warfare, and target simulation payload options. 2 KD-2/TB1 air-to-surface missiles, ZD1 laser-guided bomb. Jet-engined, unlike most other Chinese UAVs.

Table A13 continued.

Designation	Type	Manufacturer	Range/endurance	Comments
COMBAT/SURVEILLANCE				
ASN-209 tactical UAV system	UAV/medium-altitude, medium-endurance (MAME)	Xian Northwest Polytechnic University ASN Technology Group Company (Xian ASN)	180-km/hr max speed, 5-km service ceiling, 10-hr endurance	Xian's leading tactical UAV, one of the few that is armed. ASN series includes more than a dozen designs, at least seven of which have been approved; some of these have been produced in small numbers. Marketed by China National Aero-Technology Import & Export Corp; civil and military applications. 320-kg military payloads (up to 50 kg): SAR, electrooptical (EO), multifunction, ground moving target indication (GMTI), electronic intelligence (ELINT), electronic warfare (EW), ground target designation (GTD), communications relay. Propeller-driven, piston engine. Guidance and control likely autonomous. Parachute recovery, skid landing.
ASN-229A reconnaissance and precise-attack UAV	UAV	Xian ASN	180-km/hr max speed, 8-km operating altitude, 10-km service ceiling, 1,998-km operational radius, 20-hr endurance	Possible service entry ~2011. Single piston-engine. Tactical, reconnaissance payload: combined EO/infrared (IR)/laser rangefinder/designator. SATCOM datalink. Mini precision-guided weapon.
"Luoyang UCAV"	UCAV	Guizhou Aircraft Corporation Industry (GAIC)/Luoyang Optoelectro Technology Development Center (LOEC)	?	Likely based on WZ-9/WZ-2000; turbofan powered; unveiled in 2008. Similar in size to U.S. Predator-2. Armed with TY-90 air-to-air missile (AAM) and AR-1 air-to-surface missile (ASM). LOEC developing wide range of UAV weapons. Home to LOEC and AVIC's 613 Research Institute, Luoyang is China's military electrooptical sensor payloads center.

Table A13 continued.

Designation	Type	Manufacturer	Range/endurance	Comments
COMBAT/SURVEILLANCE				
J-6	UCAV	Shenyang Aircraft Corp (SAC)	640-km radius with 2 drop tanks	Converted from J-6 fighters; about 200 reportedly in service in 2008.
SURVEILLANCE				
Changhong 1/ WZ-5/A	UAV/high-altitude, long-endurance (HALE)	Beijing University of Aeronautics & Astronautics (BUAA)	800-km/hr max speed, 17.5-km operating altitude, 2,500-km range, 3-hr endurance	Production finished; still in PLA, civil agency service. Offered for export from 2000 onward, no sales reported. Airframe based largely on Northrop Grumman BQM-34A Firebee aerial target, overall design based on Teledyne Ryan Model 147H (AQM-34N) shot down over China before 1972. Development began in 1969, entered service for training/tactical reconnaissance in 1981. Updated in the late 1990s with digital flight control/management system and an inertial navigation system with embedded GPS. 1,700-kg (65-kg payload). 8.35 kN BUAA WP11 turbojet. Launched by Y-8E aircraft, preprogrammed flight plan, recovered mid-air during parachute descent.
ASN-207	UAV/MAME	Xian ASN	Parameters similar to/ possibly greater than ASN-206	Improved version of ASN-206. Market-ready, possibly already in PLA service. Leads unarmed reconnaissance portion of Xian's extensive ASN series. 250–480 kg.
ASN-206	UAV/short-range, multirole	Xian ASN	209-km/hr max speed, 5-km service ceiling, 150-km range, 8-hr endurance	In PLA service. Capable of conducting ISR and EW and countermeasures with various optical/laser instruments, imagery downlink. 222 kg 7.3 kW SAEC (Zhuzhou) HS-700 four-cylinder two-stroke engine. Launched via booster rocket, parachute recovery. Operating in tandem with similar UAV performing relay function extends max speed to 180 km/hr, service ceiling to 8 km, range to 600 km, endurance to 16 hr.
ASN-104/ -105B	UAV (extended range) light		2-hr endurance	In PLA service. 2 hrs or more of real-time reconnaissance. Single Xian 4-cylinder 2-stroke engine.

Table A13 continued.

Designation	Type	Manufacturer	Range/endurance	Comments
			SURVEILLANCE	
W-30/50	UAV	Nanjing Research Institute on Simulation Technique	–	Reportedly in PLA service. Video camera with real-time telemetry/imagery downlink. 2-stroke engine.
PW-1/2	UAV	Nanjing Research Institute on Simulation Technique	–	PW-1 reportedly in PLA service; PW-2's status unknown. Video camera with real-time telemetry/imagery downlink. 2-stroke engine.
WZ-9 (WZ-2000)	UAV/MALE	GAIC	–	Unveiled at 2000 Zhuhai Airshow, updated version revealed 2002. Twin turbojet-powered. Visually similar to General Atomics' Predator. Possibly technology demonstrator, apparent flight testing.
BZK-005 Heavy UAV		BUAA	219-km/hr max speed, 8-km service ceiling, 40-hr endurance	Apparently began development in 2005, first seen in video at 2006 Zhuhai Airshow; present status uncertain. 1,250 kg; 150-kg payload includes EO/IR capabilities, with real-time data transmission, apparent SATCOM antenna. Piston engine, propeller-driven.

Table A13 continued.

Designation	Type	Manufacturer	Range/endurance	Comments
VERTICAL TAKEOFF AND LANDING UNMANNED AERIAL VEHICLE (VTUAV)				
Yotaisc X200	VTUAV/ rotary wing	–	150-km cruise speed, 220-km/hr max speed, 5-km service ceiling, 5-hr endurance	Undergoing flight tests, ready to field September 2012. Multiple units reportedly sold to military customer for land-based operations. Autonomous. Coaxial main rotor configuration, rotor diameter 3.2 m, 3.16-m height, and 1.76-m length. Standard aviation-fuel powerplant.
Yotaisc X200S	VTUAV/ rotary wing	–	–	Maritime variant of X200, more powerful diesel engine. May be fielded in 2013.

SOURCE: Data derived from *Jane's Unmanned Aerial Vehicles and Targets*; and Robert Hewson, "Unmanned Dragons: China's UAV Aims and Achievements," *International Defence Review, Jane's*, January 23, 2012.

NOTE: Given the recent profusion of display items and photos from multiple enterprises and universities, it is particularly difficult to determine the actual status and characteristics of specific systems. The data in this table is, therefore, notional and must be interpreted with caution. Unless otherwise specified, all figures represent maximum operational parameters.

EXECUTIVE SUMMARY

This chapter evaluates China's investment in long-range precision-strike capabilities and the impact on key areas of U.S. concern over the coming ten to fifteen years.

MAIN ARGUMENT:
The People's Liberation Army (PLA) relies on the Second Artillery Force for achieving strategic effects through direct targeting of enemy centers of gravity. The Second Artillery has a phased approach to fielding increasingly long-range conventional precision-strike systems that could have global reach by 2025. While the Second Artillery has not exercised a synchronized launch of more than a half dozen missiles, U.S. missile defenses would likely be unable to counter larger and more sophisticated Chinese missile raids. U.S. aircraft carriers and other ships could also be vulnerable. Addressing these challenges requires greater collaboration not only within the U.S. defense establishment but also between the U.S. and allies and partners in the region.

POLICY IMPLICATIONS:
- Emerging PLA anti-access/area-denial capabilities could not only complicate the U.S. ability to operate in the Asia-Pacific region but also give the PLA a decisive edge in securing control over the skies around its periphery should territorial disputes erupt into conflict.

- A conventional global-strike capability would allow the PLA to reach targets deep inside the continental U.S. without relying on forward bases.

- The PLA's growing capacity for long-range precision strike provides an incentive for China's neighbors to shore up their defenses and develop similar strike capabilities, given that the most effective and efficient means of defending against China's theater missiles would be neutralizing the missile infrastructure on the ground.

The Second Artillery Force and the Future of Long-Range Precision Strike

Mark A. Stokes

The emergence of the People's Republic of China (PRC) as a major economic, technological, military, and political power is changing the dynamics within the Asia-Pacific region and the world at large. Efforts by the People's Liberation Army (PLA) to acquire long-range precision-strike capabilities—ballistic missiles in particular—support the PRC's quest for domestic and international political legitimacy, and help render the PLA a military that is commensurate with China's rise as a major global power. The PLA is rapidly advancing its capacity to integrate sensors and long-range precision-strike assets in order to defend against perceived threats to national sovereignty and territorial integrity and thereby bolster the legitimacy of the Chinese Communist Party (CCP).

The Second Artillery Force is the PLA's strategic missile force, tasked with achieving strategic effects through direct targeting of enemy centers of gravity. Previously, the Second Artillery's mission was limited to deterrence and blunt instruments of mass destruction. However, since the fall of the Soviet Union in 1991, the Second Artillery has become central to PLA warfighting plans. Ballistic and extended-range cruise missiles are an attractive means of delivering lethal payloads due to the inherent difficulties in defending against them. Firepower delivered directly against critical nodes within an opponent's operational system allows conventional air, naval, and ground operations to be carried out at reduced risk and cost. Control of the skies

Mark A. Stokes is Executive Director of the Project 2049 Institute. He can be reached at <stokesm@project2049.net>.

enables dominance on the surface below. With Second Artillery firepower support, PLA Air Force (PLAAF) and PLA Navy (PLAN) assets may gain and maintain the air superiority needed to coerce political concessions or achieve a decisive edge on the surface.

The Second Artillery's conventional reach is gradually extending throughout the Asia-Pacific region as it expands its brigade infrastructure and introduces increasingly sophisticated missile systems. Its force modernization program encompasses the fielding of increasingly longer-range systems with improvements in accuracy and expanded infrastructure. At the same time, the Second Artillery is developing sophisticated warheads that could increase the destructiveness of China's ballistic-missile force.

Ballistic missiles capable of delivering conventional payloads with precision have a coercive effect on neighbors with limited countermeasures. Use of force against Taiwan has been the principal illustrative planning scenario guiding PLA and Second Artillery force modernization. Enjoying the broadest support within the CCP Central Committee and Central Military Commission (CMC), the focus on a Taiwan scenario allows the PLA to modernize its forces without precipitating neighbors to invest significant additional resources into deterrents and defenses. Over time and with an industrial surge in missile production, the same coercive military capabilities focused on Taiwan could be directed against South Korea, Japan, the Philippines, Vietnam, Singapore, Australia, Thailand, India, and other countries in the region.

Emerging PLA anti-access/area-denial (A2/AD) capabilities may complicate the ability of the United States to operate in the region. Anti-access threats, designed to prevent an opposing force from entering an operational area, include long-range precision-strike systems that could be employed against bases and moving targets at sea, such as aircraft carrier battle groups. Area-denial involves shorter-range engagements and capabilities designed to complicate an opposing force's freedom of action. Extended-range conventional precision-strike assets could suppress U.S. operations from forward bases in Japan, from U.S. aircraft carrier battle groups operating in the western Pacific, and perhaps—over the next five to ten years—from U.S. bases on Guam. The Second Artillery also appears to have developed and deployed an initial capability to strike moving targets at sea, such as aircraft carriers and destroyers.

A demonstrated ability to complicate U.S. operations within the region would reduce confidence in U.S. security assurances. Intended to counter lower-end threats, such as those of North Korea and Iran, U.S. missile defenses would likely be unable to counter larger and more sophisticated Chinese ballistic-missile raids. As a result, U.S. allies and *ad hoc* coalition partners in the region may eventually face a dilemma: invest significant resources into counterstrike systems or adopt conciliatory policies under increasingly coerced conditions.

This chapter addresses the emerging challenges that the Second Artillery poses to regional stability. The chapter's discussion centers on conventional long-range precision strike because such capabilities represent the most significant change over the last two decades. The chapter first describes the drivers behind China's missile force modernization. It then outlines the Second Artillery's role within the CCP and CMC as well as the force's command, control, and administrative organization. The following section outlines the defense industrial enterprise supplying the Second Artillery with increasingly advanced missile systems, as well as the emerging operational capabilities most relevant to balance and stability in the Asia-Pacific region. Finally, the chapter explains the regional implications of these developments and concludes with some thoughts on how the United States might respond.

Drivers of China's Missile Force Modernization

Over the last 50 years, the Second Artillery has emerged as the PLA's primary force for strategic strike missions. A number of political and military drivers explain this relative priority granted to the Second Artillery by the PLA. First, long-range precision-strike capabilities—ballistic missiles in particular—support the CCP's quest for domestic and international political legitimacy. The PLA is a party army, and the Second Artillery is the party's instrument for achieving strategic effects—such as manipulating the cost-benefit calculus of an opposing leadership—through direct targeting of enemy centers of gravity. The most immediate challenge to the CCP's domestic and international legitimacy is Taiwan. Because Taiwan's democratic system of government—an alternative to mainland China's authoritarian model—presents an existential challenge to the CCP, China continues to rely on military coercion to compel concessions on sovereignty. Since the official establishment of the PLA's first conventional short-range ballistic-missile (SRBM) brigade in 1993, ballistic missiles have been a primary instrument of psychological and political intimidation, as well as potentially devastating tools of military utility.

A second driver of the Second Artillery Force's importance is operational in nature. Constrained by a relatively underdeveloped aviation establishment, the PLA is investing in capabilities that may offset shortcomings in the face of a more technologically advanced adversary. Basic Chinese operational theory is founded on the notion that unimpeded access to the skies over a region not only enables operational success on the surface, but also has intrinsic value as an instrument of national power. Theater missiles, defined as conventional ballistic and land-attack cruise missiles (LACM) with ranges between 500 and 5,500 kilometers (km), create a more permissive environment for PLAAF and PLAN operations.

Among all PLA service branches, the Second Artillery best understands the art of nodal analysis, strategic targeting, and effects-based operations, competencies that are traditionally enjoyed by air forces. The PLAAF appears to be still in the early stages of transforming from a defensive counter-air mission to an offensive interdiction orientation. To date, PLA conventional air platforms have been insufficient to suppress air defenses, conduct strategic strike missions, or gain air superiority around the Chinese periphery, at least by themselves. Increasingly accurate conventional ballistic and land-attack cruise missiles are the optimal means for suppressing enemy air defense and creating a more permissive environment for subsequent conventional air operations due to their relative immunity to defense systems.

Conventional long-range precision-strike systems could also enable political leaders in Beijing to apply effective military measures to enforce territorial claims in the South China Sea and Senkaku/Diaoyu Islands. Theater missiles, including those tailored for the maritime environment, could enable precise targeting of Japanese or other naval combatants that would have no defenses. An extended-range strike capability would allow China to defend its interests in other parts of the world, including assured access to energy resources transiting through the Strait of Malacca and perhaps even the Indian Ocean.[1]

Missile strike operations also are viewed as a vital element of territorial air defense, in which missiles are intended to suppress adversary strike capabilities at their source. Along these lines, the Second Artillery is central to the PLA's strategy of complicating the ability of the United States to project global power and operate freely within the Asia-Pacific region. As analyst Andrew Krepinevich observes, "since the Taiwan Strait crisis of 1996…China has moved to shift the military balance in the Western Pacific in its favor by fielding systems capable of driving up the cost of U.S. military access to the region to prohibitive levels."[2] Theater missiles are essential for A2/AD capabilities. Over time, conventional strikes against critical infrastructure in the continental United States, such as space-related ground stations, could further complicate military operations.

---

[1] See, for example, National Air and Space Intelligence Center, "Ballistic and Cruise Missile Threat," April 2009, 14, http://www.fas.org/irp/threat/missile/naic/NASIC2009.pdf.

[2] Andrew F. Krepinevich, "Why AirSea Battle?" Center for Strategic and Budgetary Assessments (CSBA), February 19, 2010, http://www.csbaonline.org/wp-content/uploads/2010/02/2010.02.19-Why-AirSea-Battle.pdf.

A final driver for the Second Artillery is technological. China's ability to leverage and absorb a global diffusion of technology has grown over the years.[3] Under its fifteen-year "Medium- to Long-Term Plan for the Development of Science and Technology," China seeks to become an "innovation-oriented society" by the year 2020 and a technological leader by 2050. A conventional strategic-strike capability could be one step in a longer journey to attain technological parity with the United States and other developed nations.

Organizational Command and Control

Second Artillery Force Command

The commander of the Second Artillery Force directly reports to and is a member of the CMC. General policy development and major personnel decisions are the responsibility of the Second Artillery's party committee. The commander and political commissar oversee four first-level administrative departments—the Headquarters Department, the Political Department, the Logistics Department, and the Equipment Department. Each department oversees subordinate second-level staff departments, bureaus, and support regiments that report directly to department directors. In addition to managing current operations, the Second Artillery command is also responsible for planning and developing a future force capable of striking any target on earth with conventional precision-guided munitions.

The Second Artillery Headquarters Department oversees operational planning, operational support, and the force's command and control (C2) system. Its primary command center appears to be located in Beijing's Western Hills. A reserve command center may be collocated with the Second Artillery's central nuclear weapons storage base in the mountains west of Xian, and perhaps with the alternate command center of the PLA's General Staff Department (GSD). The Headquarters Department manages a C2 communications system separate from that of the GSD, linking command elements in Beijing with six operational bases. The department also oversees two engineering groups—the 308 Engineering Command and the Engineering

---

[3] For an overview of the technological imperative theory, see Barry Buzan and Eric Herring, *The Arms Dynamic in World Politics* (Boulder: Lynne Rienner, 1998). Also see Hasan Ozbekhan, "The Triumph Of Technology: 'Can Implies Ought,'" in *An Introduction to Technological Forecasting*, ed. Joseph P. Martino (New York: Gordon and Breach, 1972), 83–92.

Technology Group—responsible for the tunneling of underground facilities and civil engineering.[4]

The Political Department ensures the CCP remains firmly in control of the Second Artillery Force. In addition to administering the political commissar system, the Political Department oversees personnel issues, distributes propaganda, and ensures discipline in accordance with party edicts. The Logistics Department oversees a number of support functions, including budget and finance, materiel, medical, and transportation.[5] Lastly, the Second Artillery Equipment Department manages force-structure planning and the acquisition of warheads, delivery vehicles, critical components, and associated ground equipment.

These four departments of the Second Artillery general headquarters also oversee a number of direct reporting units that would provide support to an operational campaign. For example, a regiment-sized unit north of Beijing specializes in imagery and all-source intelligence, and would likely be deployed to a theater command center as the intelligence cell.[6] At least one and probably two electronic countermeasures (ECM) regiments would support the Second Artillery corps-level component commander within a joint theater command (JTC). The Second Artillery's Technical Reconnaissance Bureau is likely the service-level cryptologic authority and may engage in computer network operations.[7] The Second Artillery maintains separate systems for missile and nuclear warhead storage and handling. The force centrally stores most of the country's nuclear warheads in Taibai County, deep in the Qinling Mountains of Shaanxi Province.[8]

---

[4] Headquartered in Hanzhong, Shaanxi Province, the 308 Engineering Command is responsible for tunneling and launch-site construction. Headquartered in the Luoyang suburb of Xujiaying in Henan Province, the Engineering Technology Group is responsible for installation engineering, including ventilation for underground facilities and fixed communications. In addition to three installation regiments, the Engineering Technology Group commands a communications engineering regiment responsible for installing fiber-optic cable in support of a dedicated internal communications network for the Second Artillery.

[5] A central depot north of Beijing stores non–mission essential supplies for the entire force. See "Di Er Paobing houqinbu mou zonghe cangku yuren jingyan tan" [Experience in Personnel Education in the Second Artillery Logistics Department Integrated Depot], *Zhongguo qingnian bao*, November 30, 2000.

[6] See, for example, Liu Feng and Wang Bingjun, "Di Er Paobing 96637 budui yingzao 'shangwu' wenhua" [Second Artillery Unit 96637 Establishes 'Warrior' Culture], *Gongren ribao*, August 3, 2006.

[7] See Mark A. Stokes, Jenny Lin, and L.C. Russell Hsiao, "The Chinese People's Liberation Army Signals Intelligence and Cyber Reconnaissance Infrastructure," Project 2049 Institute, November 11, 2011, http://project2049.net/documents/pla_third_department_sigint_cyber_stokes_lin_hsiao.pdf.

[8] Mark A. Stokes, "China's Nuclear Warhead Storage and Handling System," Project 2049 Institute, March 12, 2010, 3.

Missile Bases

The Second Artillery leadership also oversees an expanding operational and support infrastructure that is distributed among six corps-level "missile bases," which are roughly analogous to Russian rocket armies (see **Figure 1**). The six missile bases integrate the capabilities of launch brigades and support regiments under their purview, while a seventh base manages the centralized system for storage and handling of nuclear warheads (see **Table 1** and **Figure 2**).

In the event of a crisis, one or more missile bases would make up a corps-level Second Artillery component under a JTC, along with selected brigades, support regiments, and staff elements under the Second Artillery's general headquarters. For example, in a notional Taiwan scenario, the CMC could direct the formation of a JTC that would integrate staff elements from the GSD, Nanjing Military Region, PLAN, PLAAF, and Second Artillery.[9]

FIGURE 1   Second Artillery missile bases

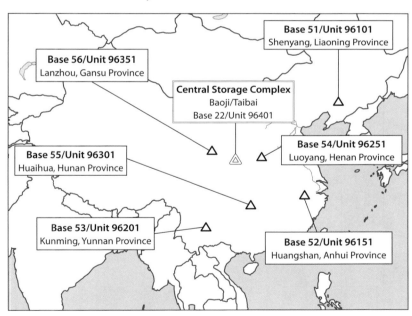

---

[9] For background on wartime command and control (C2), see Dean Cheng, "Zhanyixue and Joint Campaigns," in *China's Revolution in Doctrinal Affairs: Emerging Trends in the Operational Art of the Chinese People's Liberation Army*, ed. James Mulvenon and David M. Finkelstein (Alexandria: CNA Corporation, 2005), 101–15.

TABLE 1 Second Artillery missile bases

	HQ (city)	Units	Deployed (provinces)	Known conventional capabilities	Known nuclear capabilities	Details
Base 51	Shenyang, Liaoning	≥4 brigades	Liaoning Shaanxi Jilin Shandong Shanxi	1 MRBM brigade with possible conventional capabilities	1 ICBM brigade with DF-31 (or DF-31A)	• Oversees first unit equipped with DF-31 variant and final unit equipped with DF-3 liquid-fueled IRBM
Base 52	Huangshan, Anhui	7–9 brigades	Anhui Jiangxi Fujian Zhejiang Guangdong	≥7 brigades, including: • ≥2 DF-21 MRBM/IRBM brigades • ≥2 DF-15/16 brigades • 2 DF-11A brigades • possible integrated missile brigade previously subordinate to Nanjing MR	2 brigades with DF-21	• The largest and most powerful missile corps • Operational planning focus on Taiwan • May include UAV-equipped brigade previously under Nanjing MR
Base 53	Kunming, Yunnan	5 brigades	Yunnan Guizhou Guangxi Guangdong	≥3 brigades, including: • 1 LACM brigade • 1 brigade possibly equipped with DF-21D ASBM • conventional missile brigade previously subordinate to Guangzhou MR	2 IRBM or ICBM brigades, one with a DF-21 variant and the other with either DF-21A or DF-31	• Equipped with the most diverse range of missile systems • Likely oversaw the initial introduction of LACMs and ASBMs • May also support a service-wide training facility near Guiyang • May include UAV-equipped brigade • 1 brigade recently relocated and possibly converted to DF-31 ICBM

Table 1 continued.

Base 54	Luoyang, Henan	3 ICBM brigades	Henan	—	≥1 brigade with silo-based DF-5	• May host DF-31 brigade • Indications of a new test brigade, speculated to be a mobile MIRV ICBM brigade
Base 55	Huaihua, Hunan	2 ICBM brigades and 1 GLCM brigade	Hunan Jiangxi	—	≥1 brigade with DF-5 or DF-5A and 1 brigade probably equipped with DF-31 variant	• In a contingency, the GLCM brigade may be assigned to a JTF Second Artillery component command
Base 56	Lanzhou, Gansu (was Xining, Qinghai, until 2010–11)	3 brigades	Gansu Qinghai Xinjiang	1 brigade with known conventional capabilities	1–2 ICBM brigades with DF-31A and 1 brigade with conventionally capable DF-21C	• May also manage northwest test and training base • Principal operating area for a conventional Indian contingency likely to be near Kurle, Xinjiang
Base 22	Baoji, Shaanxi	—	—	—	—	• Responsible for storage and handling of nuclear weapons

SOURCE: Mark A. Stokes, "The PLA Second Artillery Force Handbook 2012," Project 2049 Institute (unpublished manuscript, 2012).

NOTE: HQ = headquarters. MR = military region. MRBM = medium-range ballistic missile. IRBM = intermediate-range ballistic missile. ASBM = antiship ballistic missile. ICBM = intercontinental ballistic missile. GLCM = ground-launched cruise missile. LACM = land-attack cruise missile.

FIGURE 2   Missile base structure

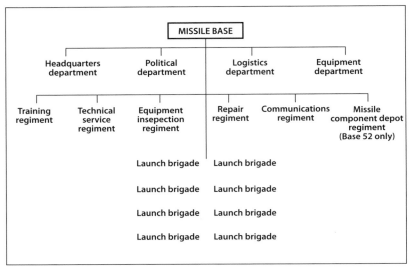

Launch Brigades and Support Regiments

Second Artillery operations are centered on launch brigades. The number of launch brigades, the basic firepower unit of the Second Artillery, has expanded from 15 in 1991 to at least 28 today. A launch brigade consists of 6 subordinate launch battalions of 2 companies each.[10] The number of launchers assigned to each company varies by missile type. Conventional SRBM brigades under the purview of Base 52, the missile base focused on a Taiwan scenario, are assigned 36 transporter-erector-launchers, or 6 launchers per battalion (3 per company). Launch brigades rely on central depots and uninterrupted rail and road services for delivery of missile systems and warheads (see **Figure 3**).

Adopting the Soviet model for missile operations, a technical battalion is responsible to the brigade commander for preparing a missile round for launch, including inspection and testing of components, missile assembly

---

[10] Roughly equal in status to a U.S. Air Force wing, a launch brigade is typically commanded by a senior colonel (roughly equivalent to a U.S. brigadier general). Brigade headquarters are structured along similar lines as the general headquarters and missile bases, with staff functions carried out by a headquarters department, political department, logistics department, and equipment department.

and warhead mating, targeting, and other tasks.[11] Mobile missile brigades oversee a site-management battalion that is responsible for launch positions, storage, and handling facilities. A brigade's technical service battalion provides warning, camouflage, and weather support. Over the last decade, newly formed Second Artillery brigades have formed ECM battalions for self-protection against air attack, which have been noted participating in training during deployments to northwest China.[12] Finally, a launch

FIGURE 3   Missile brigades under Base 52 and Base 53

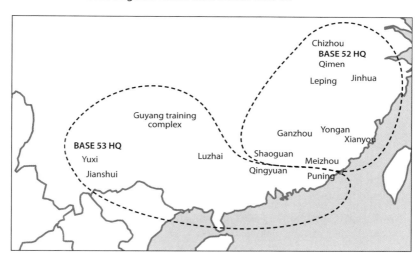

---

[11] B.P. Voronin, and N.A. Stolyarov, "Podgotovka k pusku i pusk raket," *Voyennoye*, 1972, translated by U.S. Foreign Technology Division as "Launch Preparation and Rocket Launching," May 23, 1991, http://www.dtic.mil/dtic/tr/fulltext/u2/a238929.pdf.

[12] For example, media highlighted ECM battalion training in northwest China on October 19, 2010. See Zhang Tiehan, "Di Er Paobing mou lü dianzi duikang fendui fashe yanmu gannao dan" [A Second Artillery Brigade's Electronic Warfare Unit Launches Smoke Interference Shells], *Zhongguo junshi tupian zhongxin*, October 25, 2010, http://tp.chinamil.com.cn/2010-10/25/content_4320362.htm. Confirmed brigades with ECM battalions include the 96164 Unit (820 Brigade in Jinhua), 96215 Unit, and 96363 Unit in Tianshui. See "Longnan: Er Pao Guanbing zai Huangzhu dajian shouge zhangpeng cun" [Longnan: The Second Artillery Corps Establishes Its First Tent Village at Huangzhu], *Jiefangjun bao*, August 23, 2010, http://news.sohu.com/20100823/n274392447.shtml; Zhang Tiehan, Li Junjie, and Yu Wenwu, "Di Er Paobing mou lü kaizhan taolun bianxi jifa guanbing reqing" [A Brigade of the Second Artillery Conducts Discussions and Analysis on Inspiring Soldiers' Enthusiasm], *Jiefangjun bao*, May 19, 2009, http://www.chinamil.com.cn/site1/jbzsc/2009-05/19/content_1768818.htm; and Li Zhiyang, Sun Erpeng, Chen Yang, and Zhang Huabin, "Er Pao mou bu wanshan jili jizhi guahao ganbu guanli" [A Unit of the Second Artillery Improves the Incentive Mechanism to Properly Conduct Cadre Management], *Renmin wang*, October 7, 2008, http://military.people.com.cn/GB/42967/8140815.html.

brigade's communications battalion is the glue that binds together elements within the brigade (see **Figure 4**).[13]

Each missile base also oversees a number of support regiments that are responsible for training, transportation, warhead and missile storage, vehicle repair and maintenance, and communications:

- The base's training regiment is responsible for standardized training of new personnel, coordination of deployment and live-fire exercises, and other training activities.

- A specialized transportation regiment is responsible for delivery of warheads and missiles to a brigade's depot and other technical positions for assembly, mating, and other pre-launch missions. Means of transportation include both rail and vehicular, as well as airlift in cases of extreme emergency. Transportation regiments oversee rail transfer facilities, which appear to be managed by a rail-transport battalion.

- A so-called equipment-inspection regiment is responsible for storage and handling of warhead and missile components and fuel.[14] Battalions under the regiment manage at least three weapon-storage and handling sites, with each having as many as seven subordinate facilities. Missiles appear to be stored and handled separately from warheads. An additional specialized regiment oversees conventional-missile storage and handling.[15]

- A repair and maintenance regiment ensures the readiness of launchers and other support vehicles.

- A communications regiment links base headquarters, support regiments, and launch brigades. In addition to a dedicated Second Artillery fiber-optic network, communications regiments also likely rely on satellite communications, including commercial systems.

---

[13] Leveraging static fiber-optic networks and satellite terminals for brigade liaison with upper echelons, the communications battalion most likely relies on tactical line-of-sight communications for intra-brigade communications. A brigade may have its own fiber-optic network anchoring a brigade to selected pre-survey launch sites and technical positions. However, reliance on wireless line-of-sight communications would indicate that launch battalions operate within a one-hundred kilometer radius of a brigade's command center.

[14] With most nuclear warheads centrally stored in the Taibai mountain area, equipment-inspection regiments possess a minimal number of nuclear warheads at any one time.

[15] See Stokes, "China's Nuclear Warhead Storage."

FIGURE 4 Missile brigade structure

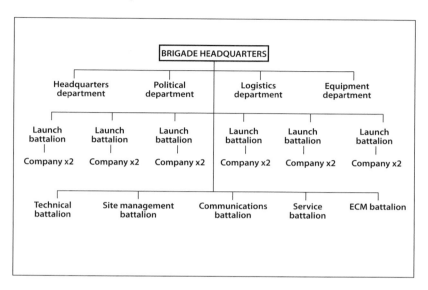

Wartime Command and Control

A future PLA military campaign likely would require a highly centralized strategic and operational C2 system that would be linked tightly with the political leadership. In a crisis situation, the CMC may direct establishment of a JTC that would be would be responsible for operational-level C2.[16] Specifically, the C2 system would include a basic command hub that houses the individual centers for decision-making, firepower, intelligence, information operations, and communications. The system also would include alternative, forward, and rear command centers. The reserve post would assume duties as the primary command post if the latter is neutralized.

Staff from the Second Artillery Headquarters Department and a missile base headquarters may form the basis for the JTC's Second Artillery component. The Second Artillery corps-level command center would have operational authority over a handful of assigned conventional missile brigades. However, due to the unique operational characteristics of the Second Artillery, there could be situations in which the campaign

---

[16] Strike operations would be controlled, directed, and coordinated within the JTC. Subordinate service-level C2 entities would include conventional Second Artillery missile and navy corps-level commands, as well as a range of cells directly supporting the JTC.

command could come under the direct authority of the Second Artillery general headquarters in Beijing.

PLA officers envision the Second Artillery implementing a four-phase operational plan: (1) operational preparations, (2) the campaign-mobility phase, (3) the missile-strike phase, and (4) the enemy-counterattack phase. Limited firepower assets would be used against targets whose destruction or suppression can achieve the greatest effects. Primary targets for the application of firepower include C2 systems and associated communications; strategic infrastructure; the most advanced capabilities of the opponent, including its air-defense system; defense industries; and airbases and ports. From the PLA's perspective, air and conventional theater-missile strikes are the most important means of firepower against deep targets. Second Artillery conventional doctrine emphasizes synchronized, multi-axis strikes as a fundamental principle.

A key requirement for strike operations would be real-time sensor information, especially for persistent surveillance of aircraft carrier battle groups. Targeting cells would need to establish links with central authorities, the JTC, and lateral service commands for real-time feeds from domestic military and civilian satellite imagery and other sensors. Ballistic computer cells would be responsible for computer updates to launchers' and missiles' onboard computer systems. The PLA would also need to plan for possible high-tempo operations, normally involving three echelons—the peacetime garrisons, the operational area's central depot and transfer points, and pre-surveyed launch areas. Most launch preparations for both the missile and warhead are carried out in the central depot, between the garrison and pre-surveyed launch sites.

Second Artillery Operational Training and Professional Education

Second Artillery operational training has been growing in sophistication and focusing on joint operations. In 2009, China's state-run media announced that the Second Artillery and PLAAF had conducted one of the largest joint exercises to date in northwest and northeast China. Deploying from home bases in southeast China, the Second Artillery contingent was the lead service in the exercise and was represented by five thousand soldiers from four SRBM brigades. They were supported by two PLAAF divisions and a radar brigade.[17] However, a preliminary survey indicates that the Second Artillery has yet to exercise a synchronized raid of more than a half-dozen missiles.

---

[17] ECM and intelligence, surveillance, and reconnaissance (ISR) elements from the brigades participated in the exercise as well. "Er Pao yu kongjun shouci jinxing shibing shidan daokong lianhe yanxi" [Second Artillery and Air Force Conduct Joint Live-Fire Exercise for the First Time], Xinhua, July 19, 2009, http://war.news.163.com/09/0719/13/5EJBGC2P00011MTO.html.

The Second Artillery's operational training and professional military education system is gradually expanding. Before assignment to units, education for new officers is carried out at the Second Artillery Engineering College in Xian. This educational facility supplies approximately 88% of all launch-brigade commanders, 75% of the brigade chiefs of staff, and 90% of Engineering Department directors.[18]

The force's principal operational testing and training ground is located in the northwestern provinces of Qinghai and Xinjiang. For live-fire training, selected battalions from each brigade are deployed annually to the test and training base in northwest China, headquartered in the Qinghai city of Delingha. Another training base in northeastern China hosts Second Artillery "blue force" exercises that simulate operations in a realistic threat environment. A third training base with an unknown mission is located near the southwestern city of Guizhou.[19]

Evolving Operational Capabilities

The PLA's growing organizational infrastructure and expanding arsenal of increasingly accurate and lethal ballistic and land-attack cruise missiles serve as the PLA's primary instruments of power projection and strategic attack. The Second Artillery relies on a sophisticated C4ISR (command, control, communications, computers, intelligence, surveillance, and reconnaissance) system, including space-, air-, and surface-based sensors for targeting. But despite fielding increasingly capable long-range precision-strike assets, the Second Artillery's operational system exhibits some vulnerabilities. Targeting is an intelligence problem, and any military organization trying to conduct a complex campaign, regardless of how big, has single points of failure. Second Artillery theater command, control, computer, and communication networks; supporting sensor architecture; and transportation networks are likely to remain vulnerable to interdiction by defending forces.[20]

Acquisition and Technology Policy

The PLA relies on an increasingly efficient and effective system for leveraging military-related technologies that could enable the fielding of

---

[18] "Er Pao daodan lü 88% lüzhang biye yu Di Er Paobing Gongcheng Xueyuan" [Second Artillery Engineering Academy Produces 88% of Brigade Commanders], *Jiefangjun bao*, October 20, 2009, http://info.cndsi.com/html/20091020/74096110715.html.

[19] Mark A. Stokes, "The PLA Second Artillery Force Handbook 2012," Project 2049 Institute (unpublished manuscript, 2012).

[20] See Jan van Tol, Mark Gunzinger, Andrew Krepinevich, and Jim Thomas, "AirSea Battle: A Point-of-Departure Operational Concept," CSBA, 2010, xiii.

new long-range precision-strike capabilities over the next ten to fifteen years. The Second Artillery leadership establishes long-term operational requirements for development and relies on an expansive defense-industrial R&D sector and manufacturing supply chain for its weapons and systems. The Second Artillery Equipment Department works closely with the PLA's General Armaments Department (GAD) to leverage technology development programs at the national level and manage R&D, manufacturing, and follow-on support contracts.

Two large state-owned enterprises—the China Aerospace Science and Industry Corporation (CASIC) and the China Aerospace Science and Technology Corporation (CASC)—design, develop, and manufacture missile systems for the Second Artillery based on general policies established by the GAD.[21] While maintaining a long-term perspective, force planners and the defense industry rely on conservative, incremental upgrades to existing missile variants. China's missile R&D strategy has its roots in a directive issued by Nie Rongzhen in the 1960s. The strategy, "three moves in a chess game," calls for three variants of each missile model to be in the R&D cycle at any one time. Under this concept, the variants should be in three increasingly advanced stages of R&D: (1) preliminary research, (2) model R&D, involving design, development, testing, design reviews, and then the "freezing" or finalization of the design, and (3) low-rate initial production. Preliminary or basic research matures technologies, which in turn reduces research and development time. After the completion of preliminary research, a review process determines if risks have been sufficiently mitigated to move into the next R&D stage.

Upon entering the model R&D phase, the GAD or Second Artillery is assigned a chief designer from the defense industry, a small handful of deputy chief designers, and a program manager. The design team is responsible for the technical aspects of R&D, including coordinating with a vast supply chain. The program manager oversees the budgetary and administrative aspects of R&D, production, and testing. The R&D phase draws to a close once the missile-system design has successfully passed flight testing and is approved by a PLA design-finalization committee. After the design is finalized, the missile enters into low-rate initial production and is assigned to seed units for operational testing and evaluation.[22]

---

[21] Among various sources, see John Wilson Lewis and Hua Di, "China's Ballistic Missile Programs: Technologies, Strategies, and Goals," *International Security* 17, no. 2 (1992): 5–40.

[22] See State Council of the People's Republic of China (PRC), "Wuqi zhuangbei yanzhi shejishi xitong he xingzheng zhihui xitong gongzuo tiaoli" [General Work Regulations on the R&D Designer System and Program Management System for Weapons Development], April 4, 1984, http://www.people. com.cn/item/flfgk/gwyfg/1984/112801198402.html. These regulations are unlikely to have changed.

The Second Artillery command appears to direct the formation of an operational testing and evaluation group, or seed unit, consisting of a select number of field-grade officers. The testing and evaluation group is often collocated with an existing brigade that is equipped with a similar missile variant. To facilitate introduction of the new variant into the inventory, the unit works closely with the R&D design team and manufacturing facilities, develops tactics and maintenance procedures, and certifies simulation systems for training purposes. Once the equipment nears operational capability, the unit may transition to its permanent garrison location and convert to brigade status.[23]

Expanding the Operational Battlespace

Since the deployment of its first ballistic missile in the 1960s, the PLA and China's space and missile industry have steadily taken incremental steps toward greater range, survivability, accuracy, and effectiveness against a broader range of targets. Based on a similarly incremental approach to R&D, production, and operational testing and evaluation, the PLA is gradually extending and diversifying the warfighting capacity of the Second Artillery's ballistic-missile force as a core element of its A2/AD strategy. Space-based, airborne, and ground-based sensors can facilitate C2 and provide crucial strategic intelligence, theater-awareness, targeting, and battle-damage assessment information. Authoritative Chinese writings indicate research into, and development of, increasingly accurate and longer-range conventional strategic-strike systems that could be launched from Chinese territory against land- and sea-based targets throughout the Asia-Pacific region in a crisis situation. The PLA appears to have a long-term, phased approach for development of a conventional global precision-strike capability.

Taiwan and the deployment of SRBMs with a range of six hundred kilometers was the focus of an initial phase. Following the decision in 1988 to deploy ballistic missiles in a conventional role, the initial deployment of conventionally armed theater missiles began with establishment of a seed unit on August 1, 1991. Until 2000, the Second Artillery's conventional missile force was limited to one regiment-sized unit in southeastern China. Today, the SRBM force has grown to at least five SRBM brigades subordinate to the Second Artillery's 52 Base. Brigade garrisons and operating areas, strategically positioned as far north as Zhejiang and as far south as Guangdong, are

---

[23] See "Laizi Er Pao jundaishi de baogao" [Report from the Second Artillery Representative Offices], *Jiefangjun bao*, April 25, 2001, http://health.eastday.com/epublish/gb/paper200/1/class020000007/hwz274633.htm.

designed to fire salvos from multiple axes in order to confuse, saturate, and exhaust missile defenses on Taiwan.[24]

As its SRBM force developed, Second Artillery planners entered a second phase that sought to extend the range of the Second Artillery's missile force and field a rudimentary ability to strike targets on land and moving targets at sea out to 1,500–2,000 km.[25] An extended-range SRBM variant, which appears to be designated as the DF-16, could bridge the range between the SRBMs and the DF-21C medium-range ballistic missile (MRBM) or DF-21D antiship ballistic missile (ASBM). The DF-21C and DF-21D are the centerpieces of the Second Artillery's extended-range conventional strike capability. Launched from positions near permanent garrisons, these systems could be used for conventional strikes against targets throughout Japan, northern India, Southeast Asia, the western Pacific Ocean, and the South China Sea. The terminally guided DF-21C can deliver a 2,000-kilogram warhead to a range of at least 1,750 km with a circular error probability of less than 50 meters. In addition, by the end of 2010, the CASC First Academy had completed conceptual-design flight tests for a two-staged conventional ballistic missile that remained within the atmosphere.[26]

The Second Artillery has at least eight, and possibly as many as ten, brigades equipped with the DF-21 missile system. Conventionally capable DF-21 variants may be replacing at least a portion of the force's DF-21 and extended-range DF-21A inventory. The conventionally capable DF-21C force structure appears similar to that of a SRBM brigade (e.g., six subordinate launch battalions with two companies each). With conventionally capable MRBM brigades equipped with a minimum of twelve launchers, current effectiveness of operations against targets in Japan, India, and elsewhere in the region may be limited. However, China's defense-industrial and operational infrastructure indicates significant room for growth, with capacity for MRBM production having doubled between 2002 and 2006. Existing

---

[24] See Mark A. Stokes and Ian Easton, "Evolving Aerospace Trends in the Asia-Pacific Region: Implications for Stability in the Taiwan Strait and Beyond," Project 2049 Institute, May 27, 2010, http://project2049.net/documents/aerospace_trends_asia_pacific_region_stokes_easton.pdf.

[25] For detailed assessments of China's antiship ballistic-missile program, see Andrew S. Erickson and David D. Yang, "On the Verge of a Game-Changer: A Chinese Antiship Ballistic Missile Could Alter the Rules in the Pacific and Place U.S. Navy Carrier Strike Groups in Jeopardy," U.S. Naval Institute Proceedings 135, no. 5 (2009): 26–32; and Mark A. Stokes, "China's Evolving Conventional Strategic Strike Capability: the Anti-Ship Ballistic Missile Challenge to U.S. Maritime Operations in the Western Pacific and Beyond," Project 2049 Institute, September 14, 2009. Also see Eric Hagt and Matthew Durnin, "China's Antiship Ballistic Missile: Developments and Missing Links," Naval War College Review 62, no. 4 (2009): 87–115.

[26] "Qi Rundong, Zhu Xuejun, Fan Shiwei jiben qingkuang ji jianyao shiji" [Accomplishments and Deeds of Qi Rundong, Zhu Xuejun, and Fan Shiwei], Zhongguo yukang xuehui, September 16, 2010, http://www.csaspace.org.cn/CMS/xhdt/ArticleShow.asp?ArticleID=877.

brigades deployed in southeast China and currently equipped with SRBMs may convert to extended-range MRBMs in the future.

Many of the basic technologies needed for a rudimentary maritime variant—such as the DF-21D—have been in development for more than twenty years. At the core of this capability is an advanced missile-borne sensing and data-processing system supported by strategic cueing from a dual-use maritime-surveillance network. Manufacturing facilities for solid rocket motors associated with an initial ASBM variant appear to have been completed in 2009, with flight testing of a new motor and airframe likely being in the advanced stages. An operational testing and evaluation unit was established as early as 2006 and appears to be based in the Guangdong city of Qingyuan. The ASBM brigade also appears to have conducted one of its first major field exercises at an unspecified joint-training center in early spring 2011.[27]

In addition to MRBMs, the PLA's extended-range conventional strike capability also includes ground- and air-launched LACM systems. Since successful completion of operational testing in October 2003, the PLA's inventory of ground-launched cruise missiles has expanded significantly. LACMs appear to have a relatively high priority due to their ability to penetrate missile defenses and strike selected targets out to a range of at least two thousand kilometers. Around one hundred LACMs enter into the operational inventory each year. Based in south-central and southwest China, two or possibly three Second Artillery ground-launched cruise missile brigades would be able to rapidly forward deploy in a crisis situation.[28]

A third phase may extend these capabilities to a range of three thousand kilometers by the conclusion of the twelfth five-year plan in 2015. Supported by an expanding persistent-surveillance architecture, the goal may be suppression of air operations on Guam, throughout the South China Sea, and in other locations in the region. Systems are under development that may place U.S. military facilities on Guam at risk by the middle of this decade.[29] For example, China's aerospace industry has been analyzing alternatives to extend the range of its ASBMs while maintaining precision.

The options include a more advanced solid motor and a "boost-glide" trajectory that would complicate mid-course missile defenses. Initial

---

[27] See Stokes, "China's Evolving Conventional Strike"; and Mark Stokes, "Expansion of China's Ballistic Missile Infrastructure Opposite Taiwan," Project 2049 Institute, AsiaEye web log, April 18, 2011, http://blog.project2049.net/2011/04/expansion-of-chinas-ballistic-missile.html.

[28] The 2007 Department of Defense report to Congress on PRC military power said that first- and second-generation LACMs should be deployed "in the near future." The 2008 Department of Defense report to Congress noted that 50–250 LACMs and 20–30 launchers were deployed, and the 2009 report assessed that the PLA has 150–350 LACMs and 40–55 launchers in its inventory.

[29] Wayne A. Ulman, "China's Emergent Military Aerospace and Commercial Aviation Capabilities," testimony before the U.S.-China Economic and Security Review Commission, Washington, D.C., May 20, 2010.

aerospace-vehicle R&D is believed to rely on conventional ballistic-missile technology for ascent into a suborbital trajectory in or near space.[30] The missile would then release a post-boost vehicle to glide and maneuver toward the intended target. Chinese engineers appear to be conducting preliminary research into a conceptual design for a suborbital flight vehicle or strike system that adopts a boost-glide trajectory. Instead of flying on a normal ballistic path that takes the missile into space before returning to earth, the boost-glide missile skips in and out of near space, those altitudes between twenty and one hundred kilometers. Aerodynamically configured to glide toward its target, the flight vehicle adopts hybrid characteristics of both ballistic and cruise missiles. In addition to complicating mid-course missile defenses, boost-glide flight vehicles are said to extend the range of existing ballistic missiles. One study, for example, asserts that a basic boost-glide capability would extend the range of a missile by 31.2%.[31] There also are indications that an antiship variant of the DH-10 LACM, with a range of three thousand kilometers, may also be under development.[32]

A subsequent fourth phase may seek to extend China's conventional precision-strike capability to eight thousand kilometers before the end of the thirteenth five-year plan in 2020. Since 2002, CASIC Third Academy designers and engineers have argued their case in prominent, authoritative industry journals that cruise missiles could be adjusted to fulfill the requirements of longer-range precision strikes—at least out to eight thousand kilometers— against a broad range of targets, including ships at sea. Engineers analyzed the relative operational effectiveness of cruise and ballistic missiles, and judged the latter as the preferred option for the strategic counter-carrier program. Designers proposed new propulsion systems, smaller radar cross sections, increased maneuverability, and a suborbital trajectory through near space to ensure the missiles could penetrate maritime defenses.

Analysts may envision a final phase involving a global precision-strike capability by 2025. Authoritative Chinese publications indicate the existence of feasibility and conceptual-design studies of a boost-glide capability with global reach. Such writings suggest that the U.S. Prompt Global Strike program is considered a model, and CASC designers have identified ten critical technologies required for global precision strike. PLA and defense-

---

[30] For an overview of the key players involved in technology policy oversight, see Zhan Shige, Mei Qingguo, Liu Qingquan, and Ji Peiwen, "Linjin kongjian feixingqi de fazhan qushi he zhongda jichu kexue wenti yantaohui zaijing zhaokai" [Conference Opens on Near Space Flight Vehicle Development Trends and Issues in Major Basic Technology Programs], *Qingkuang jiaoliu*, no. 15, May 12, 2006, http://www.nsfc.gov.cn/Portal0/InfoModule_375/1111.htm.

[31] Xu Wei, Sun Pizhong, and Xia Zhixun, "Integration Design and Optimization for Boost Glide Missile," *Journal of Solid Rocket Technology* 31, no. 4 (2008): 319.

[32] See Stokes, "China's Evolving Conventional Strike."

industrial designers, for their part, have assessed the feasibility of global post-boost vehicles and appear confident in their ability to overcome the technical obstacles to fielding such a system. CASC engineers have highlighted ramjet-engine technology as capable of supporting a post-boost vehicle, though they have also cited technical bottlenecks such as heating and the utility of infrared terminal sensors for both land targets and ships at sea. Assuming bottleneck issues can be addressed, CASC designers believe that a global-strike vehicle could enter R&D during the twelfth five-year plan.[33]

Sensor Architecture and Integrated-Strike Operations

The PLA is improving its ability to monitor events in the Asia-Pacific region through an expanded system of space-based remote sensing, communications, and navigation satellites. As its persistent-sensor and C2 architecture increases in sophistication and range, the PLA's ability to hold at risk an expanding number of targets throughout the western Pacific Ocean, the South China Sea, and elsewhere around its periphery is expected to grow. The PLA's ability to conduct strategic and operational strike missions is likely to be restricted by the range of its persistent surveillance.

Since as early as 2004, a guiding PLA objective for developing its armed forces has been "informationization." This principle stresses the centrality of information technology in weapon systems and their application.[34] The PLA still considers itself in the early stages of informationization, with a goal of achieving a fully informationized PLA by 2050.[35] PLA joint-firepower operations theory envisions a seamless connection between the sensors and shooters of the PLAAF, the Second Artillery, and other firepower custodians.

To expand its battlespace awareness, the PLA is investing in at least four capabilities that could enable it to monitor activities in the western Pacific, South China Sea, and Indian Ocean: (1) space-based sensors, (2) near-space flight vehicles, (3) unmanned aerial vehicles (UAV), and 4) land-based over-the-horizon (OTH) radar systems.

Space-based sensors. Space assets enable the monitoring of naval activities in surrounding waters and the tracking of air force deployments into the region. Space-based reconnaissance systems also provide imagery necessary for mission-planning functions, such as navigation and terminal guidance for

[33] See Stokes, "China's Evolving Conventional Strike."

[34] See, for example, Wang Baocun, "Xinxi huoli zhan jiexi" [Information-Firepower Analysis], *Jiefangjun bao*, April 22, 2004, http://news.xinhuanet.com/mil/2004-04/22/content_1434792.htm. Also see "Zhongshi yanjiu xinxi huoli zhan ying cheng duli zuozhan yangshi" [Stress the Study of Information-Firepower Warfare as an Independent Form of Operation], *Jiefangjun bao*, March 4, 2008, http://www.china.com.cn/military/txt/2008-03/04/content_11509946.htm.

[35] "Zhongshi yanjiu xinxi huoli zhan ying cheng duli zuozhan yangshi."

LACMs. Satellites also offer a survivable means of communication that will become particularly important as the PLA operates further from its territory.

The General Staff Department oversees a broad and diffuse sensor infrastructure that could support long-range strike operations. A regional-strike capability would rely on high-resolution images from dual-use synthetic aperture radar (SAR) based in space, as well as electrooptical (EO) and possibly electronic intelligence (ELINT) satellites for surveillance and targeting. China has focused its resources on increasingly capable EO satellites employing digital camera technology, as well as space-based radar for all-weather, 24-hour coverage. These capabilities are being augmented with electronic-reconnaissance satellites able to monitor radar and radio transmissions. China is also deploying a robust weather satellite capability, oceanography satellites, specialized satellites for survey and mapping, and possibly space-based sensors capable of providing early warning of ballistic-missile launches. Based in the northern Beijing suburb of Qinghe, the GSD Space Reconnaissance Bureau appears to be primarily focused on EO and SAR remote-sensing operations.[36]

With the first dedicated military system launched in 2006, SAR satellites are a core component of militarily relevant surveillance architecture supporting OTH targeting of surface assets. To augment its SAR and EO systems, the PLA likely fields a basic electronic-reconnaissance architecture. Chinese military analysts view electronic reconnaissance as necessary to accurately track and target U.S. carrier strike groups in near real-time from lower-earth orbit, which would form part of China's long-range precision-strike capability, including its ASBM system. In a crisis situation, China may have the option of augmenting existing space-based assets with microsatellites launched on solid-fuel vehicles. Existing and future data-relay satellites and other communications systems that do not require line of sight could transmit targeting data to and from the theater and the Second Artillery's operational-level command center.[37]

Near-space sensors. Chinese analysts view the domain between the atmosphere and space—near space—as an emerging area of strategic competition. Near space is defined as the region between 20 and 100 km (65,000 to 328,000 feet) in altitude. Assuming technical challenges can be addressed, near-space flight vehicles may emerge as a dominant platform

---

[36] More specifically, the key organization is the GSD Second Department Technology Bureau, also known as the Beijing Institute of Remote Sensing Information or GSD Space Technology Reconnaissance Bureau. See Mark A. Stokes and Dean Cheng, "China's Evolving Space Capabilities: Implications for U.S. Interests," Project 2049 Institute, report prepared for the U.S.-China Economic and Security Review Commission, April 26, 2012, http://www.uscc.gov/RFP/2012/USCC_China-Space-Program-Report_April-2012.pdf.

[37] See ibid.

for a persistent region-wide surveillance capability during crisis situations, due to their relative cost-effectiveness. The Second Artillery has become increasingly interested in near-space flight vehicles for surveillance, communications relay, electronic warfare, and long-range precision-strike operations. For reconnaissance missions, SAR surveillance and ELINT appear to be priorities.[38]

UAV sensors. The PLA has an ambitious UAV program to support long-range precision-strike operations. UAV programs appear focused on EO, SAR, ELINT, and sensors; electronic warfare; communications relay; and integrated strike and reconnaissance. The GSD and the Second Artillery are among the principal users of the UAV program, with Second Artillery requirements likely to be the most stressful due to range, radar cross-section, and altitude considerations. UAVs would support conventional SRBM and possibly MRBM targeting and battle-damage assessment. UAVs would likely support ASBM operations, with an expected range requirement of at least two thousand kilometers. The Second Artillery's Headquarters Department would likely control UAV operations through a battalion subordinate to the Second Artillery Reconnaissance Group (Unit 96637).

OTH radar systems. In addition to space-based, near-space, and airborne sensors, OTH backscatter radar systems would be a central element of an architecture for air and maritime surveillance with extended range. Skywave OTH radar systems emit a pulse in the lower part of the frequency spectrum, from 3 to 30 megahertz (MHz), with the pulse bouncing off the ionosphere to illuminate a target—either air or surface—from the top down. As a result, detection ranges for wide area surveillance can extend out from one thousand to four thousand kilometers. In addition to resolution issues, Chinese engineers cite challenges stemming from sea clutter that makes it difficult to discriminate between ocean targets. However, engineers are confident in the ability of OTH radar systems to detect aircraft carriers, airborne assets, and other targets operating within range of the radar system. Known as the "skywave brigade," a PLAAF unit mans a watch center south of Xiangyang city in Hubei Province. The brigade also operates transmitter and receiver sites, as well as ionosphere-measuring stations along China's southeast coast.[39]

---

[38] See Stokes, "China's Evolving Conventional Strike."

[39] "The PLA Air Force Over the Horizon Radar Brigade," Taiwan Link web log, December 24, 2009, http://thetaiwanlink.blogspot.com/2009/12/pla-air-force-over-horizon-radar.html.

Global and Regional Implications

The Second Artillery has emerged as a cornerstone of Chinese warfighting capabilities. It is central to the PLA's emerging capacity to not only complicate U.S. power projection and freedom of operations in the Asia-Pacific region but also challenge regional powers' attempts to deny the PLA air superiority and command of the seas. The PRC's ability to conduct a regional aerospace campaign complicates its territorial disputes with states around its periphery. As China's military strength increases relative to that of its neighbors, the PRC could feasibly become more assertive in its claims. Along this trajectory, miscalculations, accidents, disputes over sovereignty, or other unforeseen events have the potential to escalate into armed conflict between the PRC and its neighbors.

Taiwan

The Republic of China (ROC) remains a principal driver for conventional-force modernization of the Second Artillery Corps. The CCP is diversifying its military options and enhancing its ability to use coercive force against Taiwan's political leadership in an increasingly cost-effective manner. The PLA also seeks to deny or complicate the ability or willingness of the United States to intervene in response to China's use of force. Should a decision be made to use military force, the PLA most likely would seek to compel a political concession swiftly with minimal effort.[40] A broad range of options for military coercion may be available to CCP leaders as they calibrate the use of force to manipulate the cost-benefit calculus of an opposing political and military leadership.

While the PLA likely seeks an ability to do so, annihilation involving the physical occupation of Taiwan is the least likely course of action. When viewed from a coercive context, Beijing is at war with Taiwan every day. The PLA's use of force spans along a continuum from deterrence warfare, perhaps best demonstrated by Beijing's deployment of five Second Artillery SRBM brigades opposite Taiwan, all the way to annihilation. PRC decision-makers are most likely to resort to coercive uses of force, short of a full-scale invasion, in order to achieve limited political objectives. However, a minimal-warning invasion is the most stressful and dangerous for PLA planners and defenders alike.

---

[40] Among various sources, see Chung Chien, "High-Tech War Preparation of the PLA: Taking Taiwan without Bloodshed," *Taiwan Defense Affairs* 1, no. 1 (2000): 141–62. The guiding principle is contained in the eight character slogan of "victory with the first fight, rapid war and rapid resolution" (*chuzhan juesheng, suzhan sujue*).

In a scenario involving a PLA amphibious invasion and physical occupation of Taiwan, air dominance is a necessary precondition. It is envisioned that large-scale SRBM salvos will be carried out against ground-based air defenses, airbases, and other critical military infrastructure, and followed up by conventional PLAAF strikes to ensure air defenses remain suppressed. The Second Artillery's ability to suppress ground-based air defenses and damage runways would give the PLAAF the necessary advantage to attain air superiority over the Taiwan Strait. If successfully able to operate in the skies over Taiwan with impunity, PLAAF interdiction missions could effectively support an amphibious invasion.[41]

In the Taiwan Strait, political considerations trump simple military solutions. Weapon systems and capabilities transcend the pure military realm and are fielded not only for their operational value but also to achieve political outcomes. Second Artillery SRBM brigades have significant military value, but their primary utility lies in their political and psychological effects. In a similar vein, the political value of PAC-3 (Patriot Advanced Capability-3) missile systems, F-16s, and Hsiungfeng 2E (HF-2E) LACMs is equally as important as their military utility to Taiwan. A reduced U.S. political and military commitment could create opportunities and incentives for Beijing's political and military leadership to assume greater risk in cross-strait relations, including resorting to force to resolve political differences.

Taiwan has long maintained an ability to carry out deep-strike missions in order to interdict military targets in southeast China. To counter PRC coercion, Taiwan stresses maintenance of military strength, the ability to survive a first-strike attack, and the ability to carry out a second-strike retaliation. For example, media reports alleged that Taiwan's leadership communicated to U.S. interlocutors its intent to strike a range of PRC airbases, missile bases, radar installations, and supply depots with indigenous fighters and tactical missiles during the March 1996 crisis. As British air strategist Vice Marshal Tony Mason explained in January 2001:

> Any attack from the mainland, regardless of its timescale, would depend upon tight coordination to achieve its political objectives. Consequently, any delay, disruption or dislocation inflicted by even small-scale ROCAF [ROC Air Force] attacks could have a disproportionate strategic and ultimately political impact.

Among the most significant aspects of missile-force suppression and other defenses include a newly deployed force of HF-2E LACMs, conventional air force assets, missile defenses, and other capabilities for the suppression of enemy air defenses. In 2005, media reports alleged that at least 24 launchers

---

[41] David A. Shlapak et al., *A Question of Balance: Political Context and Military Aspects of the China-Taiwan Dispute* (Arlington: RAND Corporation, 2009), 42.

had been manufactured, along with an unknown number of missiles that could cover over twenty targets in southeast China.[42] More recently, media reports have highlighted further testing of HF-2E cruise missiles in 2010, with plans to produce at least 80 of the missiles with a range of more than five hundred kilometers by the end of the year.[43]

The ROCAF has been evaluating how to best maximize its ability to sustain flight operations after initial strikes. Central to its strategy are early warning systems, ground-based integrated air and missile defenses to thin out incoming missile raids, two hardened shelters on the east coast of the island, rapid runway-repair capabilities, and swift clearing of unexploded ordnance. Underground aircraft-storage facilities adjacent to Hualien Airbase and near Taidong are able to house more than half of the ROCAF's total fleet. These two bases were designed to preserve the combat strength of the air force in the event of a first strike by the enemy.[44] While the facilities are formidable, Second Artillery LACMs could attempt to target vulnerabilities around the periphery of the bunkers. In order to open windows to generate sorties, the ROCAF and Taiwan's R&D community have been evaluating options and investing in rapid runway-repair and unexploded ordnance equipment. Taiwan is also investing in early warning and terminal missile defenses in order to undercut the coercive utility of Second Artillery theater missiles.

Japan

Unlike Taiwan, Japan's security concerns are primarily directed at North Korea. The chances for armed conflict between the PRC and Japan are slim, despite historical animosity and budding nationalist sentiments. However, unresolved territorial disputes and a more assertive China could lead to a crisis in the future. Competing territorial claims to the Senkaku/Diaoyu Islands could lead to a confrontation. In this unlikely yet possible scenario, the PLA could attempt to establish local air superiority over the contested area. This could be extended to include control of the skies in the southern part of

---

[42] See "Taiwan to Deploy LACM," *Taiwan Defense Review*, September 6, 2005; and Mark A. Stokes, "The Chinese Joint Aerospace Campaign: Strategy, Doctrine, and Force Modernization," in Mulvenon and Finkelstein, *China's Revolution in Doctrinal Affairs*, 291–302.

[43] "Chuan Taiwan jiang shi she Xiong-2E xunhang daodan, ke gongji dalu" [Taiwan to Produce Hsiungfeng-2E Cruise Missiles That Can Hit Mainland China], *Huanqiu wang*, March 25, 2010, http://mil.huanqiu.com/Taiwan/2010-03/755709.html.

[44] See Wendell Minnick, "Taiwan's Hidden Base Will Safeguard Aircraft," *Defense News*, May 3, 2010, http://minnickarticles.blogspot.com/2010/05/taiwans-hidden-base-will-safeguard.html; Lin, "Balance in the Taiwan Strait," 579; and Brian Hsu, "Chen Visits Mountain Air Force Base," *Taipei Times*, December 15, 2000.

Japan.[45] However, air dominance over the whole of Japan appears unlikely to succeed due to the large number of airfields throughout the Japanese islands.

Nevertheless, the PLA's ambitious force modernization could pose challenges for the Japan Self-Defense Forces (JSDF) in the years ahead. Given advancements in ballistic- and cruise-missile technology; electronic, cyber, and anti-satellite capabilities; C4ISR developments; and conventional air-modernization programs, trends suggest PLA capabilities relative to the JSDF could enable the PLA to attain local air superiority over competing territorial claims at the outset of any future conflict. Much depends on the resilience of Japan's regional air- and missile-defense commands. Like Taiwan, Japan's challenges may include inadequate hardening at key airbases and C2 facilities, shortcomings in cruise-missile defense, and uncertainties surrounding procurement of a suitable next-generation fighter.[46]

As time goes on, should the U.S.-Japan alliance prove incapable of deterring PLA military action over a territorial dispute, an inability to defend against conventional MRBMs and ground-launched cruise missiles could prompt future political leadership in Tokyo to rethink the self-imposed restrictions on the development of long-range precision-strike systems. Past media reporting indicates Tokyo has at least considered the procurement of strike systems such as Tomahawks.[47]

South China Sea

The Second Artillery's role in a future conflict with Southeast Asian neighbors over territorial claims or freedom of navigation in the South China Sea likely would be limited. Outdated air-defense systems in Southeast Asia likely would encourage JTC and Second Artillery commanders to hold limited missile rounds in reserve and leverage a steadily modernizing PLAAF to assume primary precision-strike responsibility. In the event of U.S. intervention, the Second Artillery might consider employing limited ASBM assets against U.S. naval combatants conducting escort missions or freedom-of-navigation missions, or perhaps even against ships within a carrier battle group. A ballistic-missile strike against a U.S. naval asset in a limited South China Sea scenario, with a multitude of political off-ramps, could be viewed

---

[45] Shlapak et al., *A Question of Balance*, 42. At least 100 airfields in Japan may be capable of handling fighter operations, although the military only operates 32. In a detailed analysis by RAND, runways shorter than nine thousand feet would require a single ballistic missile to temporarily halt flight operations, and only two missiles would be needed for runways longer than nine thousand feet.

[46] Russell Hsiao, "China's Fifth Generation Fighters and the Changing Strategic Balance," Jamestown Foundation, China Brief, November 19, 2009, http://www.jamestown.org/single/?no_cache=1&tx_ttnews%5Btt_news%5D=35745.

[47] Nao Shimoyachi, "Japan Mulled Buying Cruise Missiles for Pre-Emptive Self-Defense: Ishiba," *Japan Times*, January 25, 2005, http://www.japantimes.co.jp/text/nn20050125f2.html.

as highly escalatory. Such strikes could result in a joint campaign firepower suppression against the JTC, Second Artillery component command, and ASBM brigade infrastructure by the U.S. Navy and Air Force.

India

The Second Artillery's conventional MRBM brigades likely would play a prominent role in a territorial dispute with India over two areas of land in eastern and northern India—Aksai Chin, which is currently administered by the PRC as part of Xinjiang Province, and Arunachal Pradesh, which is currently administered by India. While the competing claims are unlikely to erupt in conflict, it is worth noting that China and India did go to war over these territories in 1962, and that the experience has severely conditioned Indian threat perceptions of China. For all of the PRC's attempts to resolve border disputes with its neighbors, the one with India is still outstanding.

Similar to the Taiwan and Japan scenarios, brigades equipped with systems of conventionally capable theater missiles could strike a limited number of strategic- and operational-level targets, such as national or theater command centers, critical nodes in theater air-defense systems, and key airfields. Assuming a sufficient number of missiles, the Second Artillery could enable conventional air operations to be conducted at less risk. In response, India is enhancing its aerospace power with a significant investment into modernizing its air force, theater missiles, and missile defense.[48]

Conclusion

The gradual expansion of the Second Artillery's lethal range is altering the regional strategic landscape. Due to their speed, precision, and difficulties in fielding viable defenses, the force's missile systems—if extended in range and deployed in sufficient numbers—have the potential to provide the PLA with a decisive military edge in the event of a conflict over territorial or sovereignty claims. Largely driven by a Taiwan scenario, China's capacity to conduct a successful aerospace campaign to swiftly gain a decisive air advantage may surpass defenses that its neighbors—including Taiwan, Japan, perhaps India, and even U.S. forces operating in the western Pacific—are able to field. The Second Artillery long-range precision-strike capability is contributing to a growing imbalance in the regional security situation. An

---

[48] For an excellent overview of China-India military dynamics, see Srikanth Kondapalli, "The Chinese Military Eyes South Asia," in *Shaping China's Security Environment: The Role of the People's Liberation Army*, ed. Andrew Scobell and Larry M. Wortzel (Carlisle: U.S. Army War College, 2006), 197–282, http://www.strategicstudiesinstitute.army.mil/pdffiles/PUB709.pdf.

evolving sensor network supports missile operations, cueing strike assets and offering situation awareness around China's periphery. The PLA has made significant progress in the air defenses needed to protect Second Artillery strike assets from interdiction on the ground. Resilient C2, effective computer-network operations, and extensive use of underground facilities also reduce vulnerabilities.

There are indications that the PRC's defense industry is looking beyond the successful fielding of a regional-strike capability. With advanced missile-borne sensing and data processing, based only on rough initial strategic cueing from a dual-use maritime surveillance network, the initial deployment of ASBMs gives the PLA a precision-strike capability against U.S. and allied ships, including aircraft carriers, at ranges between 1,500 and 2,000 km. A follow-on ASBM and its land-attack variants are likely to extend the Second Artillery's operational range out to 3,000 km, as the corps fields more sophisticated boost-glide trajectory and missile-defense countermeasures. Subsequent technological advances could extend a conventional precision-strike capability out to 8,000 km. Perhaps mirroring similar U.S. programs, technical writings indicate the desire for a global conventional precision-strike capability over the long term. A successful effort could present additional challenges, however, given that it may allow the PLA to reach targets deep inside an enemy's territory without relying on forward bases.

The Second Artillery is expanding its infrastructure and developing an increasingly complex operational system that could give the PLA a decisive edge in securing control over the skies around its periphery should territorial disputes erupt into conflict. The ability to dominate the airspace over a given geographic domain has the potential to create instability should political disagreements flare up. The more confident that a regime is of military success, the greater the chance that force could be assertively applied in pursuit of political demands. Balance and stability require that no one single power be assured of air superiority. A strategic shift in regional aerospace balance may also increasingly unravel the fabric of U.S. alliances and prompt allies and friends to consider weapons of mass destruction as a means of security.[49]

U.S. missile defenses are likely unable to counter more sophisticated and larger Chinese ballistic-missile raids.[50] As a result, the United States and its allies and partners in the Asia-Pacific region need to rely on hardening and counterstrikes for defense.

---

[49] For perspectives on the implications of China's rising power, see Paul Giarra and Michael Green, "Asia's Military Balance at a Tipping Point," *Wall Street Journal Asia*, July 17, 2009; and Shlapak et al., *A Question of Balance*.

[50] Department of Defense, "Ballistic Missile Defense Review Report," February 2010, http://www.defense.gov/bmdr/docs/BMDR%20as%20of%2026JAN10%200630_for%20web.pdf.

Over the next five to ten years, follow-on missile variants flying at a boost-glide trajectory, the incorporation of maneuvering post-boost vehicles, and multiple independently targeted warheads would likely stress the ability of U.S. midcourse missile-defense interceptors. Forced to operate out of range of PLA ballistic missiles, the effectiveness of carrier-based assets, such as the F/A-18E/F strike fighter, would be even more limited than they already are.

Barring quick-reaction counterstrikes and deployment of effective defenses, U.S. aircraft carriers and other ships operating within two thousand kilometers of brigade operating areas could be vulnerable to ASBM strikes. As time goes on, the United States may need to re-examine priorities and rely more on smaller ships, a greater number of affordable submarines able to operate in littoral areas, unmanned air platforms for long-range combat, and the hardening of U.S. military bases and facilities throughout the region, including Kadena Air Base on Okinawa and the facilities in Guam and Hawaii. The principal means of defending against PLA long-range precision strike is interdiction of the JTC and Second Artillery infrastructure. Degradation of the GSD sensor network that supports missile operations becomes critical. While destruction of satellites in orbit risks escalation, communication links between ground stations and satellites can be jammed and ground control sites neutralized. Airfields supporting UAV operations might also be targeted.

With concerns mounting over the anti-access challenge to bases in the western Pacific and area-denial capabilities that could restrict U.S. naval operations, pressure to reduce the U.S. footprint in Japan and elsewhere could intensify. Noting the emergence of an arms race, Robert Kaplan foresees a shift in U.S. basing—moving away from allied territories to Guam and the South Pacific Islands—and a greater U.S. naval presence in the Indian Ocean.[51] Reliance on ballistic missiles and extended-range LACMs also incentivizes other militaries to develop similar capabilities. The PLA's expansion of its aerospace capabilities is at least partially driving a modest shift in U.S. regional defense policies.[52]

Addressing these challenges requires maintaining or developing the means to undercut the political and military utility of the PLA's theater

---

[51] See, for example, Krepinevich, "Why AirSea Battle?"; and Robert D. Kaplan, "The Geography of Chinese Power: How Far Can Beijing Reach on Land and at Sea?" *Foreign Affairs*, May/June 2010. Anti-access strategies aim to prevent U.S. forces from operating from fixed land bases in a theater of operations. Area-denial operations aim to prevent the freedom of action of maritime forces operating in the theater.

[52] Erickson and Yang, "Verge of a Game-Changer"; Paul S. Giarra, "A Chinese Anti-Ship Ballistic Missile: Implications for the USN," testimony before the U.S.-China Economic and Security Commission, Washington, D.C., June 11, 2009, http://www.uscc.gov/hearings/2009hearings/written_testimonies/09_06_11_wrts/09_06_11_giarra_statement.pdf; Krepinevich, "Why AirSea Battle?"; and Roger Cliff et al., *Entering the Dragon's Lair: Chinese Anti-Access Strategies and Their Implications for the United States* (Arlington: RAND Corporation, 2007), http://www.rand.org/pubs/monographs/2007/RAND_MG524.pdf.

missile–centric strategy and striving for a balance that could deter the CCP from resorting to force or other means of coercion. Counterstrikes launched from Taiwan, Guam, or the continental United States against critical nodes in the PLA's JTC and the Second Artillery's operational system could halt a campaign and restore a safe environment for operations in the western Pacific.

To counter the PLA's growing capacity to carry out an extended-range aerospace campaign, the goals of air-sea battle and the new joint operational access concept could include investing in the ability to withstand initial strikes and limit damage to U.S. allies, ad hoc coalition partners, and bases of all defending parties. A defender requires the means to strike any target within the battlespace from which the Second Artillery's offensive operations are being launched. If the infrastructure of a JTC or Second Artillery component command can be mapped out in detail, vulnerabilities or single points of failure will become apparent. Targeting is an intelligence problem, and any military organization trying to conduct a complex campaign, regardless of how big, has single points of failure. Operations would seek to neutralize the PLA's C2 networks, suppress the PLA's theater-sensor architecture and theater-strike systems, and sustain initiative in the air, on and under the sea, in space, and within the cyber domain.[53] Forward, land-based regional-strike vehicles and prompt global-strike systems launched from U.S. bases in Japan or Guam may augment the deep-interdiction capabilities of allies and friends.[54]

Large, sustained, and synchronized missile salvos are complex operations to coordinate. Preliminary research indicates that the Second Artillery has not exercised a synchronized launch of more than a half dozen missiles at one time. Regardless of the numbers of missile rounds, single points of failure in the Second Artillery's operational system exist. The JTC and the Second Artillery's component, launch-brigade, and battalion-command centers and key communications nodes may be considered operational centers of gravity and thus priority targets. Skip-echelon C2—command arrangements that allow a commander two levels above a launch unit—complicates operations, and the isolation of individual launch-unit commanders and political commissars reduces their capacity for coordinated raids. Base- and brigade-level missile depots would be situated in underground facilities and would thus be difficult targets. However, striking unhardened infrastructure critical for depot operations could have systemic effects on missile-launch preparations. Neutralizing nodes in the regional rail and road networks used by transportation regiments could have a serious impact on the effectiveness of

---

[53] See Jan van Tol et al., "AirSea Battle: A Point-of-Departure Operational Concept," CSBA, May 18, 2010, xiii, http://www.csbaonline.org/wp-content/uploads/2010/05/2010.05.18-AirSea-Battle.pdf.

[54] For an excellent overview, see Bruce M. Sugden, "Speed Kills: Analyzing the Deployment of Conventional Ballistic Missiles," *International Security* 34, no. 1 (2009): 113–46.

the Second Artillery. Special operations forces could play a role in campaigns to suppress enemy air defenses and ballistic missiles.

A concerted campaign to suppress the Second Artillery offensive operations would first require access to or over a brigade's area of operations. The PLAAF's defenses are the front line of Second Artillery force protection. A regional defender's campaign to suppress air defenses would likely target the PLAAF air corps, radar brigades, C2 systems for air-defense missile brigades, and subordinate assets standing between U.S. or other defenders' forces and critical nodes in the Second Artillery's operational system.

Addressing challenges posed by the Second Artillery and its efforts to suppress air defenses requires not only greater collaboration within the U.S. defense establishment but also effective leveraging of the talents of allies and ad hoc coalition partners in the region. The United States has reportedly begun examining how to diversify defense relations with traditional allies in the region, such as Japan, South Korea, and Australia. Yet little consideration appears to have been given to the significant role that Taiwan could play in an evolving U.S. defense strategy, including the joint operational access and air-sea battle concepts. Because Taiwan's democratic system of government—an alternative to mainland China's authoritarian model—presents an existential challenge to the CCP, the PLA continues to rely on military coercion to compel concessions on sovereignty. Beijing's large infrastructure of SRBMs opposite Taiwan fosters mistrust and discourages meaningful political dialogue that could lead toward a resolution of differences in a manner acceptable to people on Taiwan and the international community.

Taiwan is the only security partner in the region that is willing and able to develop the kind of force needed for networked, integrated deep-interdiction operations in an A2/AD environment. As the defender, Taiwan has the moral high ground and enjoys an asymmetrical advantage in the political stakes involved (e.g., survival of a free and open society under an independent, sovereign political system). Taiwan's knowledge of single points of failure in JTC operational air and missile systems could someday save the lives of young U.S. Air Force and Navy pilots. Taiwan's capacity to interdict single points of failure in the Second Artillery and the broader PLA A2/AD system could relieve the United States of part of its heavy operational burden and reduce risks of escalation.

U.S. policymakers and defense planners may consider an alignment of political interests with those on Taiwan calling for a drawdown of missile forces opposite Taiwan as a precondition for political talks. The political and military value of a drawdown by the Second Artillery depends on what exactly would be withdrawn, how, and where these units are withdrawn to. The gradual deployment of five SRBM brigades (and a sixth in 2010) opposite

Taiwan over the last fifteen to twenty years is what has changed the military equation. These missile brigades have given the PLA a relative advantage. Removal of the five or six brigades under Base 52, along with closure of missile depots, would return the dynamic balance of power to pre-1991 levels. MRBM and LACM brigades farther away from Taiwan under Base 53 or Base 55 have many fewer (and much more expensive) missiles in their inventory, and they have a mission that involves not just Taiwan but also India and Southeast Asia.

A brigade could conduct a cross-regional operation and return to operational areas opposite Taiwan. But if a brigade's logistics infrastructure is moved back with the missiles, then redeploying back to areas opposite Taiwan opens up logistical vulnerabilities that could be exploited. If the PLA were to agree to shut down or re-subordinate several brigades organized under Base 52 and renounce the use of force, then that would be a truly substantive demonstration of peaceful intent.

The PLA's growing capacity to exercise its aerospace power around its periphery provides an incentive for neighbors to shore up defenses and develop similar strike capabilities. The most effective and efficient means of defending against theater missiles is neutralizing the missile infrastructure on the ground. The PLA's expanding aerospace capabilities are influencing the development of similar capabilities in other defense establishments, including the United States. In the absence of a common set of norms governing the horizontal and vertical proliferation of ballistic and ground-launched cruise missiles, countries throughout the region are by necessity increasing investment into long-range precision-strike systems in order to maintain a conventional deterrent and ensure effective defense should deterrence fail.

Alternative approaches could seek to moderate the Second Artillery's force posture and address underlying security dilemmas through cooperative threat-reduction programs. A conventional global-strike capability risks escalation, since an adversary may misinterpret the launch of missiles with conventional warheads and conclude that the missiles carry nuclear weapons.

The demonstrated coercive value of the world's largest and most sophisticated arsenal of medium- and intermediate-range ballistic missiles creates a demand for similar capabilities around the world. The Second Artillery's successes in fielding advanced long-range precision-strike systems dilutes international efforts to stem proliferation of the means of delivery for weapons of mass destruction. This may encourage other countries to follow suit, especially as China's global leadership and standing increase.

Ballistic and ground-launched cruise missiles have long been of sufficient concern to warrant international agreements to limit their horizontal and vertical proliferation. The Missile Technology Control Regime and Hague

Code of Conduct against Ballistic Missile Proliferation both intend to stem the proliferation of unmanned delivery systems capable of delivering WMDs.

China's missile-centric strategy also could undermine one of the most successful and enduring arms control agreements to date—the Intermediate Nuclear Forces (INF) Treaty. The 1987 INF Treaty led to the elimination of U.S. and former Soviet land-based ballistic and cruise missiles with ranges between 500 and 5,500 km. In 2007, senior Russian officials announced a possible withdrawal from the INF Treaty unless it was implemented on a global basis. Opinion leaders in Moscow cited particular concern over the expansion of neighboring theater-missile forces. Defense against land-based theater missiles requires a combination of infrastructure hardening, early warning, and missile-defense interceptors, as well as interdiction operations against missile forces on the ground. As time goes on, neighbors around China's periphery may feel compelled to field similar capabilities in order to address the growth in Chinese long-range precision-strike assets.

EXECUTIVE SUMMARY

This chapter examines the implications of China's advances in space, cyber, and electronic warfare technologies.

MAIN ARGUMENT:
China's rapid progress in space, cyber, and electronic warfare technologies holds important implications for Asian security. Chinese military observers and scholars argue that in order to guarantee victory in a modern war, the People's Liberation Army (PLA) must first achieve superiority in the information domain, preferably by striking first. The PLA thus intends for its space, cyber, and electronic warfare operations both to gain an asymmetric advantage over the U.S. military and to fulfill its mandate under the "new historic missions" rubric in order to protect China's interests in space and the electromagnetic sphere.

POLICY IMPLICATIONS:
- Advances in these technologies will improve China's capabilities to protect its national interests and to project power, not just in Asia but also globally.

- Chinese emphasis on information warfare strikes at the heart of a U.S. military whose superiority is based in large part on networked forces. China's progress in these areas raises the possibility that U.S. military forces could be delayed or disrupted while the PLA achieves rapid information dominance over a smaller, less advanced military.

- PLA analysts' tendency to accentuate the positive offensive outcomes of information warfare while ignoring its limitations and unintended consequences may lead Chinese leaders to use the full spectrum of space, cyber, and electronic warfare capabilities.

Controlling the Information Domain: Space, Cyber, and Electronic Warfare

Kevin Pollpeter

Since the late 1990s, China's military has been rapidly modernizing its forces. The increasing role of information in warfare has focused the attention of the People's Liberation Army (PLA) on using information and denying its use to enemies. In particular, the role of space-based assets, the ubiquity of electronic systems, and their linkage to computers and computer networks to create systems and "systems of systems" have led to the identification of space operations, electronic warfare, and computer network operations as playing critical roles in information warfare. Chinese advances in these technologies reflect a military that is less focused on conducting a traditional "people's war" campaign and more focused on using networked information systems to locate, track, and target an enemy while at the same time striking at enemy information systems to deny that enemy these same capabilities.

This chapter discusses Chinese advances in space, cyber, and electronic warfare technologies. It argues that the PLA views space, cyberspace, and the electromagnetic spectrum as distinct domains that must be seized and defended, and is thus developing technologies and strategies to achieve information superiority. In each technology area China has made significant progress, and in at least two areas—space and cyberspace—the PLA has reached advanced technology levels. The chapter also finds that Chinese strategists advocate using these technologies in decisive first strikes in order to seize the

Kevin Pollpeter is Deputy Director for the East Asia Program at Defense Group Inc. He can be reached at <kevin.pollpeter@defensegp.com>.

The author would like to thank Anton Wishik for his research assistance.

initiative early in a conflict. For less advanced militaries, China's advances in information warfare portend a PLA that is able to achieve rapid information dominance by using precision strikes against an enemy's command, control, communications, computers, intelligence, surveillance, and reconnaissance (C4ISR) capabilities. For the most advanced militaries, China's improvements in information warfare pose an anti-access/area-denial (A2/AD) threat. Specifically, China could target critical systems to overcome U.S. defenses, disrupt offensive operations, and delay the entry of U.S. forces. Continued austerity measures in the United States will only exacerbate this threat.

This chapter first discusses Chinese writings on information warfare and the PLA's "new historic missions" to gain an understanding of China's information warfare strategy and its place within PLA operational planning. The chapter then discusses the PLA's advancements in space, cyber, and electronic warfare technologies, as well as its strategies for their employment. This analysis is followed by a discussion of the likely consequences of such progress for potential contingencies in the western Pacific. Finally, the chapter offers conclusions on the overarching implications of the PLA's advances in information warfare, based on the likelihood of the use of force by China and its consequences for the U.S. military and China's neighbors.

Information Warfare

The PLA's belief that space, cyber, and electronic warfare technologies do not just enable operations but are also separate domains that must be seized and denied to an adversary is rooted in the military's view of modern warfare. The PLA has nearly shed its doctrine of people's war and now focuses on fighting and winning "local wars under informationized conditions." According to this concept, information operations are the most important operational method of modern wars. Chinese writings regard information collection, processing, and transmission, as well as the denial of those capabilities to an adversary, as vital to the successful prosecution of a modern high-tech war and the precondition for achieving supremacy in the air, at sea, and on the ground.[1]

The PLA bases its emphasis on the role of information in warfare on the performance of the U.S. military in multiple wars since the early 1990s. Conflicts in Iraq, Afghanistan, and Yugoslavia demonstrated the utility of networked forces using advanced information technology. Over the past twenty years, the U.S. military has become increasingly adept at the collection,

---

[1] Peng Guangqian and Yao Youzhi, *Zhanluexue* [The Science of Strategy] (Beijing: Military Science Press, 2001), 358.

transmittal, processing, fusion, and dissemination of information. It has been able to use this advantage to improve battlefield situational awareness to achieve rapid dominance over its opponents, which resulted in quick resolutions of the initial, more conventional stages of these conflicts.[2]

The performance of the U.S. military has also influenced the PLA to focus on ways that it can defeat a powerfully armed opponent equipped with advanced weapon systems. As such, PLA doctrine no longer focuses on annihilating an enemy's forces. Instead, attacks focus on an adversary's "center of gravity." Under this type of strategy, the PLA would not try to conduct a wholesale destruction of enemy forces but would determine a target or set of targets so critical that its destruction would gravely affect the adversary's operations.[3]

Chinese military writings often refer to C4ISR systems as the main target of modern military operations. Although the PLA views the reliance of the U.S. military on information and information systems as a great source of strength, it also regards this reliance as a potential Achilles' heel that, if properly struck, can slow down or even paralyze the U.S. military. By striking enemy information systems, the PLA can take out the "eyes, ears, brain, and nervous system" of weapon systems, thereby causing paralysis and achieving a Chinese victory with lower costs and in a shorter amount of time.[4]

The PLA, however, need not achieve absolute superiority over an entire campaign and instead may try to create windows of opportunity where it can achieve superiority for periods long enough to successfully strike key targets, paralyze the enemy, and potentially cause unacceptable casualties.[5] Central to this strategy is conducting offensive operations at the beginning of a campaign in order to seize the initiative. The focus on seizing the initiative has led to an emphasis in Chinese writings on the concept of "gaining mastery by striking first," including preemption and surprise attacks.[6]

Indeed, whereas China's overall military strategy is active defense, its information warfare strategy is active offense. This strategy is based on the

---

[2] See, for example, Chang Xianqi, *Junshi hangtianxue* [Military Astronautics] (Beijing: National Defense Industry Press, 2002), 257–58; Cai Fengzhen and Tian Anping, *Kongtian yitihua zuozhanxue* [Integrated Air and Space Operations Studies] (Beijing: People's Liberation Army Press, 2006), 59; Cai Fengzhen and Tian Anping, *Kongtian zhanchang yu Zhongguo kongjun* [The Air-Space Battlefield and China's Air Force] (Beijing: People's Liberation Army Press, 2004), 19, 22; and Wang Wenrong, ed., *Zhongguo jundui di san ci xiandaihua lungang* [On the Third Modernization of the PLA] (Beijing: People's Liberation Army Press, 2005), 45.

[3] He Diqing, *Zhanyixue jiaocheng* [A Course on the Science of Campaigns] (Beijing: Military Science Press, 2001), 244.

[4] Zhang Yuliang, ed., *Zhanyixue* [Campaign Studies] (Beijing: National Defense University Press, 2006), 157.

[5] Wang Mingliang, "Xinxihua zhanzheng tezheng jianxi" [An Analysis of the Features of Information Warfare], *Zhongguo junshi kexue* [China Military Science] 1 (2005): 25, 26.

[6] Wang Houqing and Zhang Xingye, eds., *Zhanyixue* [Science of Campaigns] (Beijing: National Defense University Press, 2000), 108–10.

assertion that unlike traditional defensive operations, which can reduce an enemy's combat power, defensive information operations merely fend off attacks without weakening an opponent.[7] As a result, Chinese military doctrine calls for an aggressive assault against an adversary's C4ISR systems from the outset of hostilities.

The establishment of outer space and the electromagnetic sphere as domains in which China has interests that must be defended was codified under the rubric of the new historic missions. These missions were introduced by President Hu Jintao in 2004 and subsequently ratified by the Communist Party in 2007. They outline four broad areas of responsibilities for the PLA and implicitly require the PLA to develop the technologies and doctrine to carry out these missions:

- *Guarantee Chinese Communist Party rule.* The PLA is to remain the ultimate backer of the Communist Party.

- *Safeguard the strategic opportunity for national development.* The PLA is to serve as a powerful defensive force that can deter aggression against China and protect its national sovereignty and territorial integrity so that China may develop economically.

- *Safeguard national interests.* The PLA must defend China's interests, not only within its land borders, territorial waters, and territorial airspace but also in distant waters, outer space, and the electromagnetic sphere.

- *Play an important role in world peace.* China must maintain a defensive military strategy and participate in UN peacekeeping missions and international cooperation on counterterrorism.[8]

The new historic missions reflect the leadership's intent for the PLA to be able to address China's 21st-century security challenges. Most notably, this new doctrine also charges the PLA with protecting not only China's interests within its land borders and territorial airspace and waters, but also China's interests in distant waters, outer space, and the electromagnetic sphere. This new mandate implicitly directs the PLA to develop technologies to carry out these missions.[9]

The new historic missions are not mere pabulum. Since 2004, China's military has expanded operations and improved technology in areas that are

---

[7] Zhang, *Zhanyixue*, 159.

[8] "Lun xinshiji xinjieduan wojun de lishi shiming—xiezai *Jiefangjun Bao* chuan chuangkan 50 zhounian zhiji" [On Our Military's Historic Missions in the New Century, New Stage—Written on the 50th Anniversary of the Founding of the Liberation Army Daily], *Jiefangjun Bao* [PLA Daily], January 9, 2006.

[9] "Lun xinshiji xinjieduan wojun de lishi shiming."

directly relevant. In 2008, the Chinese navy began counterpiracy operations in the Gulf of Aden, and China is the UN Security Council's largest contributor of forces to peacekeeping missions. China's technological advancements have also been impressive—it conducted anti-satellite (ASAT) tests in 2007 and a missile-defense test in 2010 and began sea trials for its first aircraft carrier in 2011. Consequently, the identification of outer space and the electromagnetic sphere as domains of Chinese interest requires the PLA to develop technologies and operational concepts concerning space, computer network attacks, and electronic warfare. The following sections will discuss China's efforts to fulfill its new mission responsibilities in these three technological areas.

Space Technologies

According to the U.S. Defense Intelligence Agency (DIA), "China's space program, including ostensibly civil projects, supports China's growing ability to deny or degrade the space assets of potential adversaries and enhances China's conventional military capabilities."[10] A nearly universal theme in Chinese writings on space is that "whoever controls space will control the Earth."[11] According to Chinese observers, space will become the dominant battlefield of future wars given its ability to provide critical C4ISR capabilities. Chinese authors point to the use of space by the U.S. military for communications, intelligence collection, navigation and positioning, and meteorology and conclude that space assets have facilitated much of the success of recent U.S. operations.[12] As a result, space takes on a strategic nature, in which China must develop the capabilities to exploit space for its economic and military value as well as to both defend its systems from threats and deny an adversary's use of space.[13]

Space-based C4ISR

A robust, space-based C4ISR system is often described as a critical component of a future networked PLA. The necessity to develop space-based

[10] Ronald L. Burgess, Jr., "Annual Threat Assessment," statement before the Senate Armed Services Committee, Washington, D.C., February 16, 2012, 19, http://www.dia.mil/public-affairs/testimonies/2012-02-16.html.

[11] See, for example, Chang, *Junshi hangtianxue*, 146.

[12] Ibid., 257–58; and Chi Yajun and Xiao Yunhua, *Xinxihua zhanzheng yu xinxi zuozhan lilun qingyao* [The Fundamentals of Informationized Warfare and Information Operations Theory] (Beijing: Military Science Press, 2006), 38–39.

[13] Pan Youmu, "Zhaoyan kongtian yitihua tansuo guojia kongtian anquanzhanlue" [Exploring National Air and Space Security Strategies in View of Air and Space Integration], *Zhongguo junshi kexue* [China Military Science] 9, no. 2 (2006): 65.

C4ISR systems appears to derive largely from the requirement to develop power-projection and precision-strike capabilities. The development of long-range cruise missiles and antiship ballistic missiles for attacks over the horizon requires the ability to locate, track, and target enemy ships hundreds of kilometers away from China's shores, as well as the ability to coordinate these operations with units from multiple services. Such missile development also requires the long-range C4ISR capabilities that space best provides. Additionally, space-based assets can offer targeting and battle-damage assessment information that could help deny adversaries the use of airbases, ports, and other facilities.[14]

Chinese analysts assess that the employment of space-based C4ISR capabilities requires the PLA to develop capabilities to attack space systems. China must be able to both protect its systems from attack and deny the use of space to an adversary. Based on the assessment that the use of space systems facilitated the success of U.S. military operations, Chinese analysts surmise that the loss of critical sensor and communications capabilities could imperil the U.S. military's ability to achieve victory or to achieve victory with minimal casualties.[15]

Chinese scholars discuss a range of attacks against enemy space targets, including both "soft kill" and "hard kill" attacks. Soft-kill measures, such as jamming or temporarily blinding satellite sensors, are preferred over hard-kill measures because they do not produce debris and because their effects can be temporary and less observable than other types of strikes. Soft-kill methods can also be used against third-party satellites to avoid permanent disabling or destruction. Hard-kill measures, such as kinetic-kill vehicles, are not to be completely dispensed with, however. Instead, hard kills can complement soft kills when soft kills are ineffective or unsuitable for the mission.[16]

China's intent to carry out force-enhancement and counter-space operations is seen in the rapid development of its space program since 2000, with the most visible activity being its human spaceflight program. From the testing of its first space capsule in 1999, China graduated to manned

---

[14] See, for example, Pan Changpeng, Gu Wenjin, and Chen Jie, "Junshi weixing dui fanchuan daodan gongfang zuozhan de zhiyuan nengli fenxi" [Analysis of the Capabilities of Military Satellite Support of Antiship Missiles in Offensive and Defensive Operations], *Feihang daodan* [Winged Missile Journal], May 2006: 12; and Chen Xuan and Wang Jiasheng, "Meiguo tianji xinxi xitong fazhan yu weilai wangluo zhongxin zhan" [Development of Space-Based Information Systems in the U.S. and Network-centric Warfare in the Future], *Hangtian dianzi duikang* [Aerospace Electronic Warfare] 6 (2007): 20.

[15] See, for example, Zhao Shuang, Zhang Shexin, Fang Youpei, and Wang Liping, "Research on the Status and Development of the U.S. and Russia's Space Target Surveillance," *Hangtian dianzi duikang* [Aerospace Electronic Warfare] 1 (2008): 27.

[16] Chang, *Junshi hangtianxue*, 258, 273–74, 295–96; and Cai and Tian, *Kongtian zhanchang yu Zhongguo kongjun*, 28.

spaceflight in 2003 and in 2012 docked a manned Shenzhou space capsule with the Tiangong-1 space station. Although the United States has abandoned military human spaceflight, Chinese writers describe manned platforms as more responsive than unmanned platforms and able to employ a variety of weapons.[17] One author even writes that manned platforms "are not only the best space weapon for attacking satellites in low earth orbit, synchronous orbit, and high orbit, they are also the best method for conducting near attack operations."[18]

China has also made remarkable progress in space-based remote-sensing capabilities and plans to establish a "high-resolution Earth observation system" capable of stable all-weather, 24-hour, multispectral, and various-resolution observation.[19] Since 1999, China has launched 31 remote-sensing satellites and now has several series of them. Its Ziyuan satellites, the latest of which is the Ziyuan-3, are each equipped with three high-resolution panchromatic cameras and an infrared multispectral scanner with spectral resolutions ranging from 2.1 to 6.0 meters and a ground swath resolution ranging from 51.0 to 52.3 kilometers, depending on the sensor used.[20]

China has also launched three new types of remote-sensing satellites since 2000: the Yaogan, Huanjing, and Haiyang series (see **Table 1**). The most numerous of these satellites are those in the Yaogan series, with China having launched seventeen Yaogan satellites since 2006. Although this series is the least understood, it is widely believed that Yaogan satellites are a mixture of optical imagery, synthetic aperture radar (SAR), and electronic intelligence satellites. If true, the use of optical imagery and SAR satellites gives the Chinese military the capability to take images during both day and night and in cloud cover. Moreover, the resolution of these satellites' sensors is much improved over that of previous Chinese satellites and is reported to be 1.0 meter for optical imagery and 1.5 meters for SAR imagery.[21] In March 2010, China launched three Yaogan satellites. The satellites formed a constellation similar to that of the U.S. Navy's Naval Ocean Surveillance System (NOSS), which performs electronic intelligence missions to locate and track ships.

---

[17] Li Yiyong, Li Zhi, and Shen Huairong, "Linjin kongjian feixingqi fazhan yu yingyong fenxi" [Analysis on Development and Application of Near Space Vehicle], *Zhuangbei zhihui jishu xueyuan xuebao* [Journal of the Academy of Equipment Command and Technology] 19, no. 2 (2008): 64; and Chang, *Junshi hangtianxue*, 118–19.

[18] Li Guangchang, Cheng Jian, and Zheng Lianqing, *Kongtian yiti Xinxi zuozhan* [Integrated Aerospace Information Operations] (Beijing: Military Science Press, 2004), 218.

[19] China Information Office of the State Council, "China's Space Activities in 2011," December 29, 2011.

[20] Rui C. Barbosa, "China Opens 2012 with ZiYuan-3 Launch via Long March 4B," NasaSpaceFlight. com, January 8, 2012, http://www.nasaspaceflight.com/2012/01/china-opens-2012-ziyuan-3-launch-long-march-4b.

[21] "Yaogan," SinoDefence.com, http://www.sinodefence.com/satellites/yaogan6.asp; and "Yaogan," SinoDefence.com, http://www.sinodefence.com/satellites/yaogan5.asp.

TABLE 1   Selected Chinese satellites

Satellite	Type	Capabilities
Yaogan-1, 3, 6, and 10	Synthetic aperture radar (SAR)	1.5-meter resolution
Yaogan-2, 4, 5, 7, 8, 9a, 9b, 9c, 11, 12, 13, 14, and 15	Electrooptical	1-meter resolution
Huanjing	Electrooptical	30-meter resolution
Haiyang	Ocean monitoring	Ocean color scanners and electrooptical
Tianlian	Data relay	Ka- and S-band communications
Beidou	Navigation	10-meter accuracy
Chinasat-20A	Communication	Secure voice and data communications
Chinasat-1A	Communication	Ku- and Ka-band transponders

SOURCE: Sinodefence.com.

China's remote-sensing satellite series also includes the Huanjing ("environment") satellites, which China has launched two of since 2008. These satellites carry electrooptical imagery sensors with resolution of 30 meters and two infrared sensors with imagery resolution of 100 meters and 150 meters, respectively.[22] In addition, China has launched two Haiyang ("ocean") satellites. These satellites are equipped with scanners and electrooptical imagery sensors to conduct environmental monitoring of the ocean, such as chlorophyll concentration, surface temperature, suspended silt charge, soluble organic matter, and pollution. China is planning eight satellites in the Huanjing program that are capable of visible, infrared, multispectral, and SAR imaging.[23]

Linking these satellites together are two data-relay satellites called Tianlian ("sky link"). Due to their higher orbit, these satellites can facilitate communication both between satellites and between satellites and ground stations. Without them, China's remote-sensing satellites would have to fly within the line of sight of a ground-receiving station to send their images to Earth. With these satellites, China can now cover 85% of the globe, greatly

[22] "Huanjing Series (China), Spacecraft - Earth Observation," Janes.com, http://articles.janes.com/articles/Janes-Space-Systems-and-Industry/Huanjing-series-China.html.

[23] Office of the U.S. Secretary of Defense, *Annual Report to Congress: Military and Security Developments Involving the People's Republic of China* (2011), 35.

increasing the timeliness of its space-based intelligence, surveillance, and reconnaissance (ISR) data.

China has also launched two satellite navigation and positioning constellations since 2000. The first constellation, Beidou-1, was established in 2007 and consisted of three satellites that covered a large portion of China and Asia. This constellation utilized a radio determination satellite service (RDSS) that depended on a satellite–ground station linkage for positioning and provided accuracies of up to twenty meters. In 2011, China established a second satellite navigation and positioning constellation, Beidou-2 (also known as Compass), which operates according to the same principles as the United States' global positioning system (GPS). This 9-satellite system provides coverage for China and most of Asia but will eventually expand to a 35-satellite constellation to provide global coverage. The accuracy of Beidou-2 is 10 meters, much less than the 3.0–7.8 meter accuracy of GPS.

Counter-space Technologies

China is assessed to have a broad-based development program for counter-space technology that consists of jammers, direct-ascent ASAT weapons, and directed-energy weapons.[24] In 2007, the PLA destroyed an aging weather satellite with a direct-ascent kinetic-kill vehicle, and in 2010 demonstrated a de facto ASAT capability when it successfully intercepted a ballistic missile in mid-course using a ground-based missile.

China has also acquired or developed electronic warfare systems to jam common satellite communication and GPS signals and is developing lasers and high-powered microwave and particle beam weapons. China could also detonate a nuclear weapon in space to destroy satellites through both the blast and the electromagnetic pulse generated by the explosion. The use of a nuclear weapon in space, however, would also affect China's satellites, as well as those of third parties.[25]

The dual-use nature of space technology means that many of the technologies and techniques used in China's ostensibly civilian or non-offensive programs can be used in a counter-space role. For example, the development of a telemetry, tracking, and control (TT&C) system to support China's human spaceflight and lunar exploration programs enables China to better monitor the satellites of potential adversaries. The TT&C system could also provide the ability to use co-orbital satellites in order to crash into an adversary's satellite or move in orbit close enough to attack a satellite

---

[24] Office of the U.S. Secretary of Defense, *Annual Report to Congress: Military and Security Developments Involving the People's Republic of China* (2012), 9.

[25] Office of the U.S. Secretary of Defense, *Annual Report to Congress* (2011), 37.

with weapons. Unlike the weapons discussed above that only enable China to attack satellites in low earth orbit, co-orbital satellites would provide the capability to attack targets in medium or high earth orbit, such as GPS and communication satellites.

China's human spaceflight program has practical applications for intercepting spacecraft. The successful docking of a Shenzhou space capsule with the Tiangong space station provides China with a nascent counter-space capability. In addition, in conjunction with the Shenzhou-7 mission, China released a small companion satellite, the BX-1, from the space capsule, which orbited around Shenzhou-7 and captured imagery of it. The BX-1 also came within 25 kilometers of the International Space Station, demonstrating a potential ability for China to inspect and attack an adversary's satellite, even though the BX-1 was in a different orbit and had no ability to intersect the station.

Cyberwarfare

Cyberwarfare has emerged as the most pernicious threat from China. In recent years, Chinese cyberwarfare units and civilian hackers have most likely conducted widespread and effective espionage against targets around the world. The extent and effectiveness of these attacks accentuates the priority that China places on cyberattacks and the potential for their use during wartime. Specifically, cyberwarfare provides China with three capabilities. First, it allows China to identify vulnerabilities in targeted computer networks that can be exploited to exfiltrate data. Second, cyber operations can target logistical, communication, and commercial networks to constrain an adversary's actions or slow its response time. Finally, cyber operations "can serve as a force multiplier when coupled with kinetic attacks during times of crisis or conflict."[26]

Chinese writers refer to cyberwarfare as network warfare: "opposing sides fighting for network superiority by crippling or destroying the information and effectiveness of the enemy's computer network system while also protecting one's own network systems in order to safely conduct information war operations."[27] The interest in network attack is based on its assessment that computer networks are the "brains" and "nerve centers" of military information systems, and thus strikes on an enemy's core information systems can greatly reduce its command and control capabilities and even

---

[26] Office of the U.S. Secretary of Defense, *Annual Report to Congress* (2011), 4–5.

[27] Xu Xiaoyan, ed., *Xinxi zuozhanxue* [The Science of Information Operations] (Beijing: People's Liberation Army Press, 2002), 158.

cause paralysis. Based on this assessment, units would be unable to function cohesively with the loss of computer capabilities, even if personnel and equipment remain unharmed.[28]

Network warfare holds many advantages over more traditional types of warfare. First, network warfare is low cost, especially in relation to the weapon systems that it counters.[29] Second, network warfare can achieve rapid effects: for example, malware can be inserted into a computer network in a matter of seconds or minutes and can rapidly spread. Third, network warfare is covert. Computer attacks may go undetected for some time, and even if an adversary has security software, it is only effective against known malware. Computer attacks are also conducted more easily than other types of warfare and at almost any location. Finally, Chinese analysts describe network warfare as possessing a large destructive capability.[30] In fact, some Chinese observers equate the destructive power of cyberattacks with that of a nuclear attack. For example, two prominent authors predict that computer attacks will become so destructive that they will become the main form of warfare and may even develop into a deterrent capability similar to nuclear weapons.[31]

Indeed, military networks are not the only targets for network attacks. Chinese analysts have also identified civilian networks, including communication, financial, and transportation centers, as potential targets. According to one analyst, attacking a combination of military and civilian networks can "directly affect an enemy's strategic policy decisions and overall strategic situation, [and] completely weaken and paralyze the enemy's political, military, economic, and cultural war potential."[32]

One of the most important uses of network operations is to gather intelligence, an activity known as "computer reconnaissance."[33] According to Chinese analysts, the main peacetime mission of cyber forces is to collect and analyze the computer networks of potential adversaries in order to identify vulnerabilities, critical equipment, and their dispositions.[34] Computer reconnaissance is important to the PLA because the military assesses that it will likely face a superior opponent capable of defeating the PLA if it is

---

[28] Xu, *Xinxi zuozhanxue*, 161, 167.

[29] Ibid., 157–58.

[30] Guo Shengwei, *Xinxihua zhanzheng yu wangdian budui* [Informationized War and Network Electronic Units] (Beijing: National Defense University Press, 2008), 257–59, 364.

[31] Dai Qingmin, *Wangdian yitizhan yinlun* [An Introduction to the Theory of Integrated Network Electronic Warfare] (Beijing: People's Liberation Army Press, 2002), 32; and Xu, *Xinxi zuozhan xue*, 166–67.

[32] Dai, *Wangdian yitizhan yinlun,* 7.

[33] Ibid., 33.

[34] Guo, *Xinxihua zhanzheng yu wangdian budui*, 218.

allowed to fully prepare. Under this scenario, the PLA must act decisively at the outset of a conflict. Computer reconnaissance facilitates early actions by providing vital information on the disposition of enemy forces and identifying weaknesses in the adversary's computer networks that could be exploited during conflict.[35]

Chinese analysts also discuss hacking and using malware against an adversary, including the use of logic bombs, back doors, and Trojan horse and other computer viruses.[36] Malware can be installed on a computer system through a variety of means. These include directly hacking into a computer system, using honeypots and spear phishing (email impersonation).[37] Chinese analysts also discuss inserting incorrect information into enemy information systems to deceive the enemy.[38]

Chinese writers suggest strikes at the strategic, operational, and tactical levels, including attacks against space systems,[39] airborne early warning-and-control (AEW&C) aircraft, command and control centers, important radar sites and wireless computer networks, air-defense networks, and antiship missile systems.[40] Chinese analysts point to the success of alleged cyberattacks to prove their value. For example, Chinese authors state that before the outbreak of the 1991 Gulf War, the United States put viruses into the air defense–system computer systems that Iraq had purchased, which, in conjunction with electronic warfare attacks, resulted in "weapons and equipment almost completely losing their operational capabilities."[41] Chinese analysts also assert that Serbian cyber forces inserted malware into the flight control systems of the USS *Nimitz*, which shut down flight operations for more than three hours, and they point to the distributed denial-of-service (DDoS) attacks that shut down the White House website.[42]

Chinese Computer Network Operations

China's cyber activities have grown both in sophistication and in number since 2001. According to the DIA, "the pace of foreign economic collection and industrial espionage activities conducted by foreign intelligence services, corporations, and private individuals against major U.S. corporations and

---

[35] Dai, *Wangdian yitizhan yinlun*, 115, 33.

[36] Guo, *Xinxihua zhanzheng yu wangdian budui*, 255.

[37] Ibid., 312.

[38] Dai, *Wangdian yitizhan yinlun*, 197.

[39] Guo, *Xinxihua zhanzheng yu wangdian budui*, 255.

[40] Dai, *Wangdian yitizhan yinlun*, 191, 203.

[41] Ibid., 7.

[42] Ibid., 26.

government agencies is accelerating. China is likely using its computer network exploitation capability to support intelligence collection against the United States."[43]

One of the earliest examples of Chinese hacking is the 2001 U.S.-China hacker war. In 2001, the hacker group Honker Union of China declared a week-long cyberwar against the United States to protest the collision of a Chinese fighter plane with a U.S. reconnaissance aircraft that resulted in the death of the Chinese pilot. Most of the group's attacks defaced websites.[44] At this time, the U.S. Department of Defense assessed that China had "the capability to penetrate poorly protected U.S. computer systems and potentially could use computer network attack to attack specific U.S. civilian and military infrastructures," and that Chinese cyber activity would likely "occur during periods of tension or crises. Chinese hacking activities likely would involve extensive web page defacements with themes sympathetic to China."[45]

Chinese cyber capabilities improved in the following years. In 2007, the U.S. Defense Department reported that the PLA established network attack units to attack enemy computer systems and networks and has increased the role of computer network operations in its exercises. In a 2005 exercise the PLA began to incorporate offensive operations into its exercises using computer network attack as first strikes against enemy networks.[46] Around this time, U.S. government offices began to report more sophisticated cyber intrusions. In 2008, Congressman Frank Wolf revealed that in 2006 Chinese hackers infiltrated four of his office computers containing information on Chinese political dissidents, as well as other computers in the House of Representatives.[47] Also in 2006, the U.S. Department of Commerce revealed that the computer network of its Bureau of Industry and Security, which manages U.S. technology exports, had been compromised. Though no official determination of the origin of the attack was made public, widespread speculation focused on China.[48]

Chinese computer espionage has only increased since these activities. According to the U.S. Office of the National Counterintelligence Executive, "U.S. corporations and cyber security specialists also have reported an

---

[43] Burgess, "Annual Threat Assessment," 26.

[44] Rose Tang, "China-U.S. Cyber War Escalates," CNN.com, May 1, 2001; and Craig S. Smith, "May 6–12; The First World Hacker War," *New York Times*, May 13, 2001.

[45] Office of the U.S. Secretary of Defense, *Annual Report on the Military Power of the People's Republic of China* (2002), 31–32.

[46] Office of the U.S. Secretary of Defense, *Annual Report on the Military Power of the People's Republic of China*, (2007), 22.

[47] Thomas Claburn, "U.S. Rep. Wolf Says Chinese Hackers Targeted Him for Criticizing China," *Information Week*, June 12, 2008.

[48] John Leyden, "Chinese Crackers Attack US.gov," *Register*, October 9, 2006.

onslaught of computer network intrusions originating from Internet Protocol (IP) addresses in China."[49] In February 2011, computer security company McAfee attributed an intrusion that it called "Night Dragon" to China. Beginning in 2009, employees of global oil, energy, and petrochemical companies were subjected to spear-phishing emails that resulted in the theft of proprietary information on the financing of oil- and gas-field bids and operations.[50] McAfee described these attacks as "not very sophisticated" yet well coordinated, targeted, and "very successful."[51]

China apparently conducted a more complex cyberattack, named "GhostNet" by the risk consultancy SecDev Group, against hundreds of political, economic, and media targets around the world, including diplomats, military attachés, private assistants, secretaries to prime ministers, and journalists.[52] According to a SecDev Group investigation conducted between June 2008 and March 2009, "close to 30 percent of the infected computers can be considered high-value," including those in foreign ministries, the Asian Development Bank, the ASEAN Secretariat, and NATO headquarters.[53]

GhostNet is described as a "covert, difficult-to-detect and elaborate cyber-espionage system capable of taking full control of affected systems."[54] The attack was conducted using spear-phishing techniques in which emails designed to appear from trusted sources were used to entice victims into downloading malware. Once a computer was compromised, the malware not only spread to other infected computers through additional fraudulent emails but also allowed the perpetrators to take "full control of infected computers, including searching and downloading specific files, and covertly operating attached devices, including microphones and web cameras."[55]

A third set of intrusions linked to China were conducted against the company RSA in March 2011.[56] RSA manufactures two-factor authentication devices that are widely used by U.S. government agencies, contractors, and banks to secure remote access to sensitive networks. The attacks, described

---

[49] Office of the U.S. National Counterintelligence Executive, "Foreign Spies Stealing U.S. Economic Secrets in Cyberspace: Report to Congress on Foreign Economic Collection and Industrial Espionage, 2009–2011," October 2011, 5.

[50] Ibid.

[51] Brian Prince, "McAfee: Night Dragon Cyber-Attack Unsophisticated but Effective," eWeek.com, February 10, 2011, http://www.eweek.com/c/a/Security/McAfee-Night-Dragon-Cyber-Attack-Unsophisticated-But-Effective-303870/.

[52] "Tracking GhostNet: Investigating a Cyber Espionage Network," Information Warfare Monitor, March 29, 2009, 47.

[53] Ibid., 5.

[54] Ibid., 6.

[55] Ibid., 6–7.

[56] Elinor Mills, "China Linked to New Breaches Tied to RSA," CNET, June 6, 2011.

by RSA as "extremely sophisticated," first involved intrusions into RSA networks that resulted in the compromise of information concerning the company's SecurID two-factor authentication products.[57] The perpetrators of the attack then used phishing emails to trick employees of firms using RSA's technologies into downloading malware in order to gain access to their login information. Following RSA's announcement, U.S. defense contractors Lockheed Martin, L-3 Communications, and Northrop Grumman reported intrusions that stemmed from the breach of RSA's systems.[58]

Chinese cyberattacks have been growing in number and sophistication over the past ten years. The high-profile attacks summarized here reflect that these attacks focus on exploiting human fallibilities to gain entry into a computer system rather than brute-force hacking. Such attacks reveal both a knowledge of the vulnerabilities of operating systems and a sophisticated understanding of their human targets and social engineering. While these attacks have mainly involved the theft of information and have not been conducted to sabotage the activities of the U.S. government, military, utilities, or industry, they do have many commonalities with such attacks. As the U.S. Defense Department concludes, "the accesses and skills required for these intrusions are similar to those necessary to conduct computer network attacks."[59]

Electronic Warfare

Electronic warfare, also called electronic countermeasures, consists of operations conducted to weaken and destroy electronic equipment and systems and to protect one's own electronic equipment and systems and their normal operation.[60]

In Chinese scholarship, one source refers to electronic warfare as the core of information operations due to the expansion of the use of microelectronics, communications, computer, and multimedia technologies.[61] Indeed, electronic

---

[57] Art Coviello, "Open Letter to Customers," RSA website, http://www.rsa.com/node.aspx?id=3872.

[58] Elinor Mills, "Report: Data Stolen in RSA Breach Used to Target Defense Contractor," CNET, June 1, 2011.

[59] Office of the U.S. Secretary of Defense, *Annual Report to Congress* (2011), 5.

[60] Academy of Military Sciences, Operational Theory and Regulations Research Department, and the Informationized Operational Theory Laboratory, *Xinxihua zuozhan lilun xuexi zhinan— Xinxihua zhuozhan 400 ti* [Informationized Operations Theory Study Guide—400 Questions on Informationized Operations] (Beijing: Military Science Press, 2005), 93–94.

[61] Chi and Xiao, *Xinxihua zhanzheng yu xinxi zuozhan*, 164.

warfare is considered to be a precursor to any military operation and critical for achieving electromagnetic superiority in the air and space domains.[62]

This assessment is partially based on U.S. military operations during the 1991 Gulf War, in which coalition forces conducted kinetic and non-kinetic strikes against Iraqi command and control sites that "effectively eliminated the command system of the Iraqi military."[63] According to Chinese sources, coalition forces used a large number of ELINT (electronic intelligence) capabilities against Iraq to collect intelligence. When operations began, coalition forces integrated jamming and kinetic strikes to conduct attacks against key command, control, communications, and intelligence (C3I) systems.[64]

The goal of electronic warfare is to achieve electromagnetic superiority, which is defined as achieving control over the electromagnetic spectrum during a certain time and at a certain location. This allows the attacker to achieve freedom of action in the electromagnetic spectrum while depriving an adversary of such freedom.[65] According to the U.S. military, "the PLA is believed to be able to conduct both defensive and offensive EW [electronic warfare] operations. Basic objectives of an electronic attack campaign are to conceal PLA operational preparations, weaken enemy air defense early warning, and paralyze or disrupt enemy integrated air defense systems."[66] According to Chinese sources, electronic warfare comprises electronic strikes, reconnaissance, and defense.

Electronic strikes refer to the use of jamming and kinetic attacks to weaken and destroy an adversary's electronic systems and requirements.[67] The main activities of jamming are to suppress enemy air-defense systems through the use of high-powered, ground-based stations and chaff by airplanes, jamming radar sites and GPS, and by conducting electronic deception.[68] Kinetic strikes, on the other hand, include the use of anti-radiation missiles such as the AGM-88 high-speed anti-radiation missile (HARM) and anti-

---

[62] Yuan Wenxuan, *Lianhe zhanyi xinxi zuozhan jiaocheng* [A Course on Joint Campaign Information Operations] (Beijing: National Defense University Press, 2009), 321–22.

[63] Xu, *Xinxi zuozhanxue*, 153–54.

[64] Chi and Xiao, *Xinxihua zhanzheng yu xinxi zuozhan*, 366–69.

[65] Academy of Military Sciences, *Xinxihua zuozhan lilun xuexi zhinan*, 280.

[66] Office of the U.S. Secretary Of Defense, *Annual Report on the Military Power of the People's Republic of China*, (2004).

[67] Academy of Military Sciences, *Xinxihua zuozhan lilun xuexi zhinan*, 95; and Air Force Officer Handbook Committee, *Zhongguo renmin jiefangjun kongjun junguan shouce* [China PLA Air Force Officer Handbook] (Beijing: Blue Sky Press, 2006), 352.

[68] Yuan, *Lianhe zhanyi xinxi zuozhan jiaocheng*, 179–80.

radiation unmanned aerial vehicles (UAV). HARM missiles in particular are described as important weapons for the PLA.[69]

Chinese writings discuss targets for electronic warfare strikes in different types of operations. For example, during air operations, the PLA would conduct attacks against communication nodes, radars, command centers, and air-defense weapon-control systems.[70] In supporting conventional missile attack operations, electronic warfare forces would conduct jamming and anti-radiation strikes against the enemy's early warning systems and missile-defense weapon-control systems. In establishing sea control, the PLA would use electronic warfare aircraft, ground-based high-power jamming systems, and ship-based electronic warfare forces against enemy ships and airborne and sea-based anti-missile systems.[71] In counter-space operations, electronic warfare forces would attack space-based systems of reconnaissance and intelligence, positioning and navigation, and communication.[72]

Electronic reconnaissance refers to collecting and analyzing the enemy's electromagnetic radiation signals. The mission of such reconnaissance is to discover enemy wireless communications, radar, guidance remote control, and telemetry; ascertain and analyze the nature and threat characteristics of electronic targets; determine the effectiveness of electronic strikes; and provide intelligence for electronic defense and offense.[73] Electronic defense refers to preventing one's own electromagnetic signals from discovery, identification, and suppression by an enemy and to maintaining the normal operation of electronic systems and equipment.

Electronic Warfare Technologies

China has a number of electronic warfare technologies and platforms (see **Table 2**). These include the Gaoxin series of aircraft based on the Y-8 transport platform, anti-radiation missiles, electronic countermeasures pods carried under the wings of aircraft, and electronic warfare technologies that are organic to aircraft and ships. Research programs for electronic warfare reportedly receive high-level visibility and support from senior leaders in the Communist Party,[74] and they have made steady progress since 2000. At that time, the PLA's electronic warfare systems derived mostly

---

[69] Yuan, *Lianhe zhanyi xinxi zuozhan jiaocheng*, 287.

[70] Ibid., 299, 315.

[71] Ibid., 299.

[72] Ibid., 321–22.

[73] Academy of Military Sciences, *Xinxihua zuozhan lilun xuexi zhinan*, 94–95.

[74] Office of the U.S. Secretary Of Defense, *Annual Report on the Military Power of the People's Republic of China*, 2004.

TABLE 2   PLA electronic warfare platforms and systems

Platform/system	Type	Specifications
Gaoxin-1	Aircraft	Electronic intelligence
Gaoxin-2	Aircraft	Signals intelligence
Gaoxin-4	Aircraft	Electronic warfare or signals intelligence
Gaoxin-7	Aircraft	Electronic warfare
BM/KJ 8602	Airborne	Radar-warning receiver designed for tactical and other combat aircraft
BM/KJ 8608	Airborne	Electronic intelligence
BM/KG 8601/8605/8606	Airborne	Radar jammers for fixed-wing aircraft
BM/KG300G	Airborne	Radar-warning receiver for fixed-wing aircraft
KZ800	Airborne	Electronic intelligence suite for use on medium- and large-sized aircraft
JN1102	UAV-based	Communications jamming
DZ9001	Vehicle-based	Electronic intelligence
JN1105A	Vehicle-based	Communications jamming
JN1601	Vehicle-based	Communications jamming
DZ9002	Fixed or mobile	Electronic intelligence
DZ9300	Man portable	Electronic intelligence
FT-2000	Missile	Anti-radiation

SOURCE: IHS Jane's Defence and Security Intelligence & Analysis database.

from a combination of technologies from the 1950s to 1980s. In 2004, the U.S. Defense Department assessed that while Chinese electronic warfare systems had made marked improvements, they were still "simple by modern standards."[75] By 2006, however, the Defense Department assessed that China's investments in advanced electronic warfare programs had given the PLA Air Force "technological parity with or superiority over most potential adversaries."[76] By 2012, the PLA appeared to have designed specific electronic

---

[75] Office of the U.S. Secretary of Defense, *Annual Report on the Military Power of the People's Republic of China*, (2004).

[76] Office of the U.S. Secretary of Defense, *Annual Report: The Military Power of the People's Republic of China* (2009), viii.

warfare platforms to target all of the U.S. military's high-value assets.[77] For example, according to Chinese defense industry representatives, the KG300G J-band electronic warfare jammer pod "can overcome the frequency-hopping capability of the newest-generation active electronic scanning array (AESA) radars, such as the F-22A's Northrop Grumman AN/APG-77." The KG300G is also described as having digital radio frequency memory (DRFM) capabilities, an advanced radar-jamming technology.[78]

Integrated Electronic Warfare and Cyberwarfare Operations

The PLA's focus on electronic warfare and cyberwarfare has led some PLA analysts to conclude that electronic warfare and cyber operations should be merged into one organic whole. The combining of these two types of warfare was first introduced under the rubric of "integrated network electronic warfare" (INEW) and has since been reformulated under different names by other military analysts. INEW and its subsequent reformulations propose using "electronic warfare, computer network operations, and kinetic strikes to disrupt battlefield information systems that support an adversary's warfighting and power projection capabilities."[79] The original impetus for INEW was the realization that by acting as individual services with separated units for electronic warfare and network warfare, the PLA could not defeat an enemy as powerful as the United States. Only by acting in a joint manner could the PLA hope to have success against the U.S. military.[80]

Writings on integrated network warfare and electronic warfare emphasize a combined approach to defeating an adversary's network-centric forces. In doing so, they emphasize offensive action, especially first strike. While Chinese writings on integrated electronic warfare and network warfare operations were originally conceived as a solution to the problem of how best to organize the PLA's inferior electronic warfare and cyber forces, technological advancements since 1999 have shown that Chinese writers were prescient in their concept, even if they were unaware of the coming technological changes. One prominent example of the melding of electronic warfare and cyber capabilities was supposedly demonstrated in the Israeli bombing of the Syrian nuclear facility in 2007, in which non-stealthy F-15 and F-16 aircraft reportedly slipped into Syrian airspace undetected. Instead

---

[77] David Fulghum and Bill Sweetman, "Cyberthreats, Shortfalls Threaten USAF Plans," *Aviation Week*, March 8, 2012.

[78] Reuben F. Johnson, "Further Details Emerge for the BM/KJ 8602 Radar Warning Receiver," *International Defence Review*, January 1, 2008.

[79] Office of the U.S. Secretary of Defense, *Annual Report to Congress* (2011), 25.

[80] Dai, *Wangdian yitizhan yinlun*, 116.

of jamming Syrian air defenses, which would have revealed the attack, the Israelis apparently used an airborne network-attack system that allowed them to gain access to Syrian radar systems using malicious algorithms inserted through the system's radar antennas. This access allowed the Israelis to either spoof the radars with false signals or take control of the systems.[81] The United States and other countries are developing these technologies to such an extent that an electronic attack cannot be separated from a cyberattack.[82]

Chinese analysts have realized the potential of such attack methods. According to one article, as weapon systems become more network-based, offensive information-warfare measures such as those reportedly employed by the Israeli Air Force will become more effective.[83] Another article goes even further, stating that such cyber weapons have overturned the traditional theory of air strike and air defense, as well as the traditional method of electronic countering, and thus constitute a grave challenge to the air-defense system's operation and training. The article also states that such technologies provide a "new inspiration" to the PLA, and by having the capability to invade "the enemy's tactical internet, interrupting its operations command process and damaging its command and control network," the PLA "can achieve effects that cannot be achieved through conventional electronic warfare."[84]

Implications

The next section will assess China's space, cyber, and electronic warfare capabilities in relation to the types of missions that the PLA may be called on to conduct in the future. The implications will depend on the PLA's mission as well as the adversary's technological level, ability to operate in these domains, and societal connectedness. For example, PLA modernization in space, cyber, and electronic warfare will complicate many aspects of U.S. military operations. These same capabilities, however, will be less consequential for Somali pirates because their operations do not depend on or derive significant advantages from high-tech operations.

---

[81] David A. Fulghum, "Why Syria's Air Defenses Failed to Detect Israelis," Ares web blog, *Aviation Week*, October 3, 2007.

[82] Fulghum and Sweetman, "Cyberthreats, Shortfalls Threaten USAF Plans"; and David A. Fulghum, "China, U.S. Chase Air-to-Air Cyberweapon," *Aviation Week*, March 9, 2012.

[83] Xu Kang, Hu Defeng, and Gu Jingmin, "Dianzi xianfeng—meijun 'shute' gongji xitong [The Electronic Warfare Vanguard: The U.S. "Suter" Attack System], *Guofang* [National Defense] 8 (2010): 78.

[84] Lu Xiangyang, Chai Qi, and Zhou Yongsheng, "Guanyu weilai dianzi duikang zhisheng zhidao de jidian sikao" [Several Thoughts on the Way of Achieving Victory in Electronic Warfare in the Future], *Guofang keji* [National Defense Science and Technology] 5 (2011): 75.

Space

China's burgeoning space program has two military missions. The first is force enhancement to support combat operations and improve the effectiveness of military forces. The force-enhancement mission for space includes the following: ISR; integrated tactical warning and attack assessment; command, control, and communications; navigation and positioning; and environmental monitoring. The second component is counter-space missions to protect PLA forces while denying space capabilities to the adversary.

Force enhancement. The PLA is planning to integrate space into warfighting through the development of space-based C4ISR systems. Chinese writings on the use of space for force-enhancement missions reflect the country's need for long-range precision strikes, usually against U.S. forces. China's space-based C4ISR and navigation capabilities can be used against any opponent, however, with the current focus of the PLA being on developing capabilities to support regional efforts. Space-based capabilities will become more important due to China's lack of airborne ISR assets, especially to cover the long distances to targets in the western Pacific and South China Sea. With its current constellation of ISR satellites, China is able to image a target near Taiwan 35 times per day.[85] The PLA can use this constellation to identify land-based and sea-based targets across Asia. With space-based ISR, PLA aviation and missile forces could adjust fire, restrike targets, or verify that a target was destroyed, greatly enhancing the effectiveness of the kinetic portion of an operation. The PLA could also identify new targets and, depending on the speed and efficiency of its targeting process, attack them in almost real time.

China can also use its space-based ISR capabilities in a maritime role against surface ships. The PLA would most likely use this capability in conjunction with over-the-horizon radar and airborne and naval ISR for more precise targeting. Most threatening is the combination of these systems with the antiship ballistic missile (ASBM) DF-21D, which has a range of 1,500 kilometers. With adequate ISR support, the DF-21D would allow China to engage surface ships while keeping its own navy out of range of the adversary's surface ships. These attacks could also force the U.S. Navy to operate well beyond the optimal limits of its carrier-based aircraft, shortening the amount of time that these aircraft could stay on station.

China's improving satellite navigation and positioning system will also give its military increased capabilities. While the Beidou system only provides ten-meter accuracy, it does provide the PLA with autonomy that

---

[85] Eric Hagt and Matthew Durnin, "Space, China's Tactical Frontier," *Journal of Strategic Studies* 34, no. 5 (2011): 741.

it could not obtain from using a foreign satellite-navigation system. Such autonomy would immunize China from U.S. efforts to reduce the accuracy of GPS signals and would allow the PLA to jam GPS signals while continuing to use its own Beidou system.

Counter-space. China's counter-space capabilities are more limited in usage than its force-enhancement capabilities, mainly owing to the limited number of potential adversaries who have space programs. The U.S. military is the obvious priority. U.S. reliance on space suggests that the destruction or debilitation of some portion of the U.S. military's space capability could achieve catastrophic effects, including the loss of a significant portion of its communications and ISR capabilities.

The 2011 U.S. National Security Space Strategy states that space is "vital to U.S. national security" because it enables a country "to understand emerging threats, project power globally, conduct operations, support diplomatic efforts, and enable global economic viability." The loss of critical sensor and communications capabilities could imperil the military's ability to operate effectively in the western Pacific or, at the very least, to win victories with minimal casualties. China's ASAT capabilities, such as directed-energy and kinetic-kill vehicles, threaten satellites in low earth orbit, such as ISR satellites. The development of co-orbital satellites, on the other hand, would provide China the means of attacking satellites in medium and high earth orbits, such as GPS and communication satellites.

Other countries, however, are not as dependent on space. While many rely on commercial communication and remote-sensing satellites and GPS, no nation's military is as dependent on space as the U.S. military is, and no nation would suffer as significantly as the United States from the loss of space capability. Taiwan, for example, has just one remote-sensing satellite. Japan, the most technologically advanced country in Asia, has no Earth remote-sensing satellites and no communication satellites. India has the largest Asian space program with ten communication satellites and eleven remote-sensing satellites.

Cyberwarfare

China's cyberwarfare capabilities also appear to be quite advanced. Though it is impossible to fully evaluate Chinese cyber capabilities with open sources, the success of multiple, sophisticated Chinese cyberattacks against government, military, and civilian information systems indicates advanced levels of sophistication. This should not be surprising. Developing malware to go after specific vulnerabilities is neither as technologically demanding nor as resource-intensive as developing traditional weapon systems.

Chinese cyberattacks to date have aimed at intelligence collection. The emphasis on intelligence gathering suggests that Chinese-origin computer network operations serve several purposes. The first is to gather intellectual property from foreign companies. China's defense industry, in order to jump-start its own development programs, has in some cases relied heavily on the acquisition of foreign technology, both legal and illegal. These acquisitions have enabled Chinese engineers to make gains more quickly than if they had relied on their own efforts. A second purpose of these attacks is to prepare the battlefield. Information collected from the theft of defense-related programs can allow the Chinese military to develop counterdefenses to foreign weapon systems.

During a conflict, China could conduct more destructive cyberattacks. The large numbers of patriotic Chinese hackers could be encouraged, implicitly or explicitly, by the government to conduct attacks, as they were in the 2001 U.S.-China hacker war. In this context, the case of Russian cyberattacks against Georgia and Estonia may serve as a useful benchmark to assess the impact of such offensives. While the Russian attacks against each country were similar, the target countries were not. Georgia, a relatively undeveloped country with low rates of Internet usage, had just 7 Internet users per 100 people and thus was less vulnerable to cyberattacks. Estonia, on the other hand, as one of the world's most connected countries with 57 Internet users per 100 people, was much more vulnerable to the Russian cyberattacks.[86] During the 2008 conflict between Russia and Georgia, Georgian Internet infrastructure was attacked repeatedly by large numbers of patriotic Russian hackers. These attacks resulted in the defacement of the websites of the president, the National Bank of the Republic of Georgia, and the Ministry of Foreign Affairs.[87] Denial of service (DoS) and DDoS attacks were conducted against a wide variety of targets, including government, news and media websites, and a bank.[88] Like the Georgian attacks, Russian attacks against Estonia in 2007 were DDoS attacks against a broad set of targets, including the "Estonian presidency and its parliament, almost all of the country's government ministries, political parties, three of the country's six big news organizations, two of the biggest banks, and firms specializing in communications."[89]

---

[86] Eneken Tikk et al., "Cyber Attacks against Georgia: Legal Lessons Identified," Cooperative Cyber Defence Centre of Excellence, November 2008, 5.

[87] Ibid., 7.

[88] Ibid., 8.

[89] Ian Traynor, "Russia Accused of Unleashing Cyberwar to Disable Estonia," *Guardian*, May 16, 2007.

Despite the unprecedented scale of these offensives, it is unclear how much serious damage occurred. Chinese attacks against a country's media and commercial operations, while aggravating, may not seriously disrupt its ability to conduct military operations or demoralize its populace. The ability of Georgia and Estonia to release information over the Internet was affected, but print, television, and radio media was unaffected in both countries. Banking was affected but not debilitated. In Georgia, electronic banking services shut down for ten days,[90] and in Estonia, the attacks prevented credit card and ATM transactions for several days, shut down a number of governmental and commercial websites, and reportedly cost at least one bank $1 million.[91] The attacks, however, neither brought the countries to their knees nor caused any permanent damage.

A more serious type of cyberattack involves the disruption of military operations. In this case, Chinese cyber-intelligence operations conducted in peacetime could identify network vulnerabilities that could be exploited during wartime. These involve the slowing or disabling of websites or the insertion of false information, a practice known as spoofing. These types of attacks could disrupt operations by degrading email or Internet access and could force units to become more paper-based or use alternative forms of communication. As with the attacks on Estonia and Georgia, however, these attacks need not be completely disabling. An example of one such attack occurred against the U.S. Department of Commerce, which debilitated the organization's computer networks. Yet the attack only slowed operations and did not fully paralyze the office.[92]

Spoofing, on the other hand, could result in false or altered troop deployments or logistics orders. Such attacks are more insidious and could be more debilitating than disabling military websites because the victim may not realize that it has been attacked or what information has been altered. Such attacks could also slow the deployment of forces and interfere with the adequate resupply of forces.

The most serious type of cyberattack, called a supervisory control and data acquisition (SCADA) attack, can be directed against industrial processes and infrastructure, such as power plants and water utilities. The use of the Stuxnet worm against Iranian nuclear facilities was the first confirmed use of this type of attack. Unlike other cyberattacks, the development of a Stuxnet-like worm is only possible through the dedicated efforts of a small number of very capable

---

[90] Tikk et al., "Cyber Attacks against Georgia," 16.

[91] Stephen Herzog, "Revisiting the Estonian Cyberattacks: Digital Threats and Multinational Responses," *Journal of Strategic Security* 4, no. 2 (2011): 51–52.

[92] Lisa Rein, "For Agency, A Loss of Technology Has Had Down- and Upsides," *Washington Post*, April 9, 2012.

cyber specialists. According to one expert, there might be as few as ten world-class cyber specialists capable of developing Stuxnet.[93] The sophistication of Chinese cyberattacks and the possession of the Stuxnet malware suggest that Chinese cyberwarfare entities could devise a similar weapon.

Chinese writings on the use of cyberattacks against civilian transportation, government utilities, and financial centers raise the specter of attacks against these targets. Possession of the Stuxnet worm could enable the PLA to reengineer the malware or gain valuable information from its design. The widespread manufacture of industrial control technologies and electronic subcomponents in China would facilitate such attacks by allowing the implantation of malware into components at the time of manufacturing.

Considering Chinese peacetime efforts at cyberwarfare, it is highly likely that China will conduct some type of cyberattack against an adversary during a conflict. The effects of these attacks would be dependent upon the level of connectivity of the adversary and its ability to defend against such attacks. More advanced societies, such as Japan or Taiwan, may be more susceptible to attacks while less developed countries like Vietnam will be less susceptible. Although some of these attacks may only result in inconveniences rather than serious disabilities, the effect of many low-level attacks could demonstrate China's resolve and reinforce the cost of the conflict to an adversary's public. Effective SCADA attacks, by contrast, could cause serious disruption to a country's military operations and society and would likely raise the costs of a conflict significantly.

Electronic Warfare

Chinese advances in electronic warfare are more difficult to assess from open sources, but what is available suggests increasing sophistication. Kinetic and non-kinetic electronic warfare attacks are especially important in air and naval warfare. Debilitating enemy air-defense radar at the outset of an operation prepares the way for main-force air and missile units to conduct kinetic attacks. The combination of cyberattack methods with electronic warfare represents a new threat that will be a major part of any operation involving an advanced military power. The ability to insert malicious algorithms into any antenna to affect the operation of a system means that electronic warfare must now be fully integrated with cyber operations and that systems not protected against such attacks will be vulnerable.

---

[93] Peter Apps and William Maclean, "Militaries Scramble For New Cyber-Skills," Reuters, February 15, 2012.

Such attacks become more serious considering the reported vulnerabilities of active electronically scanned array (AESA) radar. This type of radar, present on many U.S. aircraft as well as on Japan's F-2 fighter, is capable of observing the battlefield with high-resolution, wide-angle surveillance, but in doing so also looks for unknown signals, which provides an easy pathway for the insertion of malware. Further, more advanced aircraft are more susceptible to cyberattack. According to the U.S. Air Force's chief scientist, "90 percent of the F-35's, 70 percent of the F-22's, 60 percent of the B-2's, and 20 percent of the F-15's functionalities are cyber-based."[94] According to press reports, such vulnerabilities could greatly complicate U.S. Air Force operations and would most likely be an even greater threat to less capable militaries.

Deterrence

While China's development of space, cyber, and electronic warfare capabilities have a definite warfighting purpose, these capabilities are also designed to preserve China's freedom of action, not only in their respective domains but in a larger military and geopolitical context, by increasing the costs of war to a potential adversary to such an extent that it is not in the adversary's interest to engage in armed conflict.[95] According to China's 2008 defense white paper, PLA strategy stresses "deterring crises and wars." Chinese researchers often refer to Sun Tzu's precept that "to subdue the enemy without fighting is the acme of skill," and conclude that deterrence fits strongly with Chinese military strategy.[96] In fact, one book suggests that deterrence is an inherently Chinese concept due to the self-perceived national predilection to avoid war at all costs. According to this source, "the difference between Western and Chinese military strategists is that Chinese strategists advocate being cautious in war....This represents to the greatest extent possible adopting non-war measures to reduce the scale of the war and to achieve political goals."[97]

Chinese writers define deterrence as "countries or national groups displaying the will to use armed force or the will to prepare to use armed force to compel the other side not to rashly conduct hostile activities or conduct

---

[94] David A. Fulghum, "Cyberwar Strategy," *Aviation Week*, April 9, 2012, 51.

[95] Elements of this section are taken from Kevin Pollpeter, "PLA Space Doctrine," in *Chinese Aerospace Power: Evolving Maritime Roles*, ed. Andrew S. Erickson and Lyle J. Goldstein (Annapolis: Naval Institute Press, 2011), 61.

[96] See, for example, Cai and Tian, *Kongtian zhanchang yu Zhongguo kongjun*, 146.

[97] Zhao Xijun, ed., *Daodan weishe zonghengtan* [A Comprehensive Review of Missile Deterrence] (Beijing: National Defense University Press, 2003), 2.

escalatory activities."[98] The goal is to force the opponent to do a cost-benefit analysis of entering into armed conflict with China by demonstrating that China can inflict unacceptable losses on the opponent. Chinese military writers are unanimous in their judgment that for deterrence to be effective, China must not only possess real military capability but also display the will to use it. Indeed, they deem real power as indispensable to deterrence and that having a credible deterrent force with an "empty fortress" will be difficult.[99] Moreover, such capabilities must be made known. In this respect, China's ASAT tests and cyber operations have an inherent deterrent aspect by demonstrating the country's capabilities publicly.

China has also designed its deterrence measures to protect it from coercion by other powers. For example, Beijing points to numerous U.S. actions that it interprets as having both an extant counter-space capability and a doctrine for use. These include the 1985 ASAT kinetic-kill test, the 1997 mid-infrared advanced chemical laser (MIRACL) test, various Schriever war games, and Operation Burnt Frost in 2008 to shoot down an errant U.S. satellite. Similar attitudes are prevalent within China's cyber community. According to one author, "the network deterrence of hegemonic countries must be countered and any one sovereign country must develop its own network strike capabilities."[100]

Conclusion

China's advances in space, electronic warfare, and cyber capabilities represent a determined effort on the part of the PLA to "fight and win local wars under informationized conditions." China has made significant progress in all three areas since 2000. Chinese writings on space, cyber, and electronic warfare also indicate that the PLA will attempt to seize control of these domains and that achieving such control is essential to achieving victory. Indeed, in future conflicts, opponents can expect China to mount a full-scale information-warfare campaign at the outset of an operation, perhaps even before its opponent is prepared to engage in conflict. The PLA does not need to conduct a war of annihilation. Chinese military writings assess that the PLA only needs to strike targets that can debilitate a military long enough to accomplish its goal. These targets, identified as "centers of gravity," can differ according to the opponent.

---

[98] Zhao, *Daodan weishe zonghengtan*, 1–2. See also Sun Haiyang and Chang Jin'an, "Junshi weishe de xinxingshi—taikong weishe" [A New Type of Military Deterrence—Space Deterrence], *Junshi xueshu* [Military Art Journal] 10 (2003): 32.

[99] Zhao, *Daodan weishe zonghengtan*, 6.

[100] Dai, *Wangdian yitizhan yinlun*, 32.

A troubling aspect of China's military writings on information warfare is a lack of thorough analysis on its use and consequences. Chinese writings assume that because these weapons exist, they can be used just like any other weapon. For example, the belief that "space is the ultimate high ground" ignores the primacy of offense in space, the increasingly congested nature of low earth orbit, and the difficulty of rapidly replacing satellites. There are over 1,100 active systems in orbit, and, as the 2007 Chinese ASAT test reinforced, the destruction of satellites can create large fields of debris. An attack of sufficient quantity between two warring parties could render the environment in low earth orbit dangerous for all satellites, including those belonging to countries not involved in the conflict. Moreover, no country keeps a stockpile of satellites in reserve, and a degraded fleet would take years to be replenished.

Chinese operational research on cyberwarfare has also not reached a sufficient level of sophistication. As with space warfare, there is no discussion of collateral damage or unintended consequences. For example, the U.S. military and intelligence agencies considered conducting cyberattacks against Iraq's financial system before invading the country in 2003 but refrained from doing so because they could not guarantee that their effects would be limited to Iraq.[101] No such discussions have been found in Chinese writings. In addition, Chinese scholarship tends to exaggerate the effectiveness of cyber weapons. The assessment that cyberwarfare can be as destructive as nuclear warfare ignores the real destructive power of nuclear weapons and their ability to lay waste to civilization. The apocryphal story of the shutdown of flight operations on the USS *Nimitz* also exaggerates cyberwarfare's effectiveness.

In each case, Chinese military analysts overemphasize the positive offensive benefits of information warfare while downplaying its limitations. This selective analysis can adulterate the decision-making process and may make top civilian and military leaders more willing to approve the use of such techniques. Moreover, because of the belief that the United States already has the capabilities described in this chapter and has used or is preparing to use them, dissuading or deterring China from developing and using these weapons may be difficult.

China's increasing military capabilities have most often been analyzed in the context of their ability to thwart U.S. military intervention, most often in the case of a conflict over Taiwan. Indeed, the impetus behind much of China's military modernization is to defeat the U.S. military in that conflict. China's development of information-warfare technologies has concentrated on exploiting the asymmetries between the two militaries. As a technologically inferior power, China can place little confidence in defeating

---

[101] John Markoff and Thom Shanker, "U.S. Weighs Risks of Civilian Harm in Cyberwarfare," *New York Times*, August 2, 2009.

the United States in a direct conflict. By following an asymmetric approach, however, the PLA can strike at perceived vulnerabilities to achieve maximum affect. Chinese military planners may opt to attack a few critical assets that open a window of opportunity to conduct follow-on strikes against targets whose debilitation or destruction could nullify the United States' overall military superiority. These advancements demonstrate the stated intent of PLA doctrine to target an opponent's C4ISR systems. Such advancements thus strike at the heart of the U.S. military, whose superiority relies in large part on networked information systems.

China's military modernization can no longer be viewed strictly through the lens of asymmetric warfare, however. The new historic missions doctrine is clear in charging the PLA with defending China's expanding national interests, including its interests in outer space and the electromagnetic sphere. Beijing's investment in space, cyber, and electronic warfare capabilities reflects this ambition. Defending China's expanding interests could motivate the PLA to become expeditionary, which would require it to support units far from home that can respond to various contingencies, ranging from disaster relief and noncombatant evacuation to armed conflict. In this regard, advances in space and cyber capabilities increase China's power-projection capabilities. Unlike the United States, which can rely on long-range bombers and aircraft carriers to wield power, China's conventional forces lack a global strike capability. C4ISR and navigation capabilities in outer space would enable the PLA to operate farther from China's shores—in the waters to the east of Taiwan, the South China Sea, and beyond. Cyber capabilities likewise allow China to strike targets anywhere on the globe, including in the United States.

Although the PLA is not expected to be able to conduct large-scale operations far from its coast prior to 2020,[102] its rapidly improving capabilities may at some time enable it to conduct a robust information-warfare campaign against less-capable adversaries. If China's current trajectory of military modernization continues, by 2025 the PLA can be expected to field a force capable of carrying out much more advanced information operations than at present. By that time, China will most likely have a robust, space-based C4ISR network made up of imagery satellites with resolutions well below one meter, electronic intelligence satellites, and a global satellite-navigation system linked together by data-relay satellites. At this point, China could likely possess a number of advanced counter-space capabilities, including even more capable kinetic-kill, directed-energy, and co-orbital ASAT capabilities.

In the cyber realm, the acquisition and reverse-engineering of the Stuxnet and Flame malware could enable Chinese hackers to develop even more

---

[102] Office of the U.S. Secretary of Defense, *Annual Report to Congress* (2010), 27.

sophisticated malware to identify weaknesses in computer networks, exfiltrate information, and thereby debilitate government and military computer systems and civilian infrastructure. Assisted by such cyber espionage, the PLA could also continue to develop effective counters to U.S. electronic systems. In particular, Chinese efforts to defeat AESA radar technologies through DRFM or the insertion of malware into aircraft antennas could seriously undermine opposing efforts to maintain control of the electromagnetic sphere.

With such improvements, China's neighbors who do not have the resources to match the PLA in either size or sophistication would be at a distinct disadvantage. PLA analysts write about conducting "information blockades" against opponents, which they refer to as "comprehensive countermeasures to block the enemy collection and exchange of information."[103] Such actions could enable PLA aviation and naval forces to act with relative impunity, much as the U.S. Air Force and Navy have done since the early 1990s. Such a possibility could draw China's neighbors closer to the United States as nations attempt to balance the growing power of China, since no single nation may be able to successfully face the PLA alone.

Ironically, as the PLA becomes more capable in these areas, it may motivate other militaries to develop asymmetric means to defeat it, especially as it becomes more reliant on networked information systems. Attempts to challenge China in space or in the electromagnetic domain may be difficult, however. Developing space and counter-space technologies is beyond the expertise of most Asian countries, and purchasing such technologies may be politically unpalatable for other space powers due to the sensitivity of space weapons. It is more likely that countries would develop their own cyber forces due to the fewer resources required; however, the ability to make a counterforce that could be effective against a Chinese strike may be problematic. Cyberattacks to date have only caused minor damage, and the development of a Stuxnet-like capability requires highly skilled programmers, a resource that nearly all countries lack, rather than a large number of patriotic hackers.

The PLA's rate of technological advancement, if sustained, also holds important implications for the U.S. military. China's advances in information warfare pose an A2/AD threat in which China can target certain critical systems to overcome U.S. defenses, disrupt U.S. offensive operations, and delay the entry of U.S. forces into a conflict. This strategy gains more salience when pitted against the U.S. concept of air-sea battle (ASB), which emphasizes

---

[103] Air Force Informationization Working Office, Air Force Specialized Informationization Experts Consulting Committee, *Kongjun xinxihua zhishi: gainianbian* [Air Force Informationization Knowledge: Concepts Volume] (Beijing: Military Science Press, 2009), 71.

stealth, electronic warfare and cyberwarfare, ISR, and standoff weaponry to penetrate and defeat A2/AD systems.[104]

Chinese efforts to develop A2/AD capabilities and the U.S. effort to counter them through ASB thus present a dynamic in which both sides are developing advanced C4ISR technologies to enable long-range precision strikes while at the same time developing the means to deny these capabilities to their adversary. In effect, in their pursuit of offensive capabilities designed to suppress each other's information systems, both sides must also increase their reliance on them. As a result, while China is now pursuing an asymmetrical advantage over the United States, in the long-term view both sides are actually responding symmetrically to the threat posed by the other to prepare for a potential conflict in which national will, technology, training, and the ability to withstand attrition will decide the outcome of a conflict rather than fundamental differences in their approaches to war.

The U.S. military may face difficult challenges under this scenario. China, with its claims to Taiwan and portions of the South China Sea, would characterize any conflict over these areas as a struggle of national sovereignty and would most likely be able to generate a higher level of sustained national will than the United States could, given that the United States has no territorial claims in these areas. In addition, an emphasis on the competing claims of technological advantage and a high attrition rate would also appear to disfavor the United States, which must ship forces across the Pacific. The PLA's emphasis on striking first in the information domain would also mean that the U.S. military might have to weather a robust first strike against its C4ISR systems. Given its increasing reliance on a relatively small number of highly capable platforms, the United States would thus be at a disadvantage if it sustained heavy losses, especially at the beginning of the conflict.

The authors of ASB acknowledge that significant attrition could occur to U.S. forces, and they make numerous suggestions for ameliorating U.S. losses in a potential conflict with China. These include both the hardening of U.S. bases and developing the following capabilities:

- more capable ballistic-missile defense systems
- long-range strike capabilities and a persistent strike platform
- short-range ballistic-missile capabilities
- manned and unmanned low-observable platforms
- stealthy land-attack cruise missiles
- long-range antiship missiles

---

[104]David Fulghum, "Navy Aviation in the Crosshairs," *Aviation Week*, April 9, 2012, 49.

- improved mine-laying capabilities and smart mobile mines
- counter-space capabilities
- low-observable, long-range penetrating, and stand-off electronic attack capabilities
- wide-area airborne networks
- complementary or backup systems to GPS
- long-range UAVs
- a new class of nuclear cruise-missile submarines
- sufficient numbers of munitions, aerial-refueling aircraft, maritime-patrol aircraft, lower-end warships, and obscurants and decoys[105]

The austerity measures that the United States will likely need to make in the coming decades, however, suggest that the military will only be able to afford a small percentage of these capabilities. China, on the other hand, if it maintains sufficient economic growth, could sustain adequate numbers of platforms needed to frustrate U.S. operations. Even if these platforms were not as advanced as U.S. weapons, they could be effective enough to damage U.S. forces to a level that greatly complicates the U.S. military's ability to achieve its goals.

Consequently, China's advances in information warfare portend a conflict that will be unlike any other in its emphasis on the control of information and its extension into space, cyberspace, and the electromagnetic spectrum. If the trends described in this chapter continue, China will be able to pose a serious threat to the U.S. military's expeditionary nature, where the melding of space, cyber, and electronic warfare with ISR is critical to operating in an A2/AD environment. China's advances could also enable the PLA to achieve rapid information dominance over smaller, less advanced militaries. China's ability to keep the U.S. military at bay while defeating a lesser opponent would pose challenges to U.S. influence in Asia, as countries decide whether to balance or bandwagon. Such a scenario suggests that the United States must bolster relationships with its Asian partners to foster a more collective response to Chinese military modernization, while at the same time finding a way to match military requirements with fiscal austerity.

---

[105] Jan van Tol with Mark Gunziger, Andrew Krepinevich, and Jim Thomas, "AirSea Battle: A Point of Departure Operational Concept," Center for Strategic and Budgetary Assessments, 2010, 81–94.

STRATEGIC ASIA 2012–13

REGIONAL IMPACT
AND RESPONSES

EXECUTIVE SUMMARY

This chapter examines the impact of China's military modernization on the strategic and defense postures of Japan, South Korea, and Taiwan—the principal U.S. security partners in Northeast Asia.

MAIN ARGUMENT:
China's military modernization and probing behavior pose serious challenges for the territorial and maritime interests of Japan, South Korea, and Taiwan. Their particular concerns revolve around symmetric threats from China's buildup of its air defense and blue water naval power and asymmetric threats stemming from its A2/AD strategy. These countries seek engagement with China but are increasingly hedging militarily. In terms of internal balancing, they are augmenting their own air defense and naval power to counter China symmetrically, but also looking to respond to asymmetric threats. Japan is pursuing a new dynamic defense force doctrine, South Korea is adopting a more comprehensive defense policy that looks beyond immediate security issues on the Korean Peninsula, and Taiwan is moving toward a posture reliant on asymmetric capabilities. At the same time, enabled by reduced fears of abandonment and entrapment, all three countries have swung back firmly into the U.S. security fold to redouble external balancing against China.

POLICY IMPLICATIONS:
- Greater friction between U.S. partners and China heightens the risk that the U.S. will become entrapped in potential conflicts. The fact that Japan, South Korea, and Taiwan are now aligned in seeking U.S. security engagement enhances Washington's options to shape the regional environment.

- In order to inject substance into its rebalancing toward the Asia-Pacific, the U.S. needs to (1) reassure these countries of its future forward-deployed presence, (2) maintain sufficient supplementary and unique military capabilities in the region, and (3) increase the political credibility of its security guarantees.

China's Military Modernization: U.S. Allies and Partners in Northeast Asia

Christopher W. Hughes

Japan, the Republic of Korea (ROK), and the Republic of China (ROC) all harbor significant national security concerns vis-à-vis China's rise and its military modernization. For Taiwan, the People's Republic of China (PRC) is the prime security concern. For Japan, China likewise increasingly looms as the greatest medium- to long-term threat to national security. Although South Korea is immediately preoccupied with North Korea, China represents a threat standing behind Pyongyang on the Korean Peninsula, and in its own right the PRC constitutes a longer-term threat to the ROK's wider security interests. Japan, South Korea, and Taiwan's individual diplomatic and military responses, along with the subsequent Chinese counter-reactions, will strongly test China's grand strategy and deployment of military capabilities in the Asia-Pacific region. Moreover, given the combination of the relative size of the military forces of Japan, South Korea, and Taiwan and the core national security issues involved on all sides, the fundamental mismanagement of bilateral relations with China contains real potential for interstate conflict and the destabilization of the entire region.

Due to Japan's, South Korea's, and Taiwan's status as a U.S. ally or partner, respectively, their responses to the modernization of the People's Liberation Army (PLA) carry implications not just for their own national security and China's stance in the region, but also for the United States and the overall regional security order. In responding to challenges from China, these allies and partners will inevitably look to the United States for diplomatic and

Christopher W. Hughes is Head of the Department of Politics and International Studies (PAIS) at the University of Warwick and Professor of International Politics and Japanese Studies in PAIS. He can be reached at <c.w.hughes@warwick.ac.uk>.

military cooperation. Washington thus is confronted with its own set of tests regarding its future strategic intent and maintenance of capabilities in the region. The United States' capacity to support these particular allies and partners in responding to China's rising power may speak volumes about the credibility of its continued military commitment to the region and the likely sustainability of the entire U.S.-led infrastructure of security in the Asia-Pacific.

This chapter will address the following interconnected policy issues. First, it will analyze the impact of China's military modernization on Japan's, South Korea's, and Taiwan's military capabilities; on each country's strategic relations with China; and more widely on regional stability. Second, the chapter will examine the impact of trends in Japanese, South Korean, and Taiwanese military modernization on the United States' maintenance both of its own military capabilities and of its alliances and partnerships in the region, and consequently the continuation of its role as the principal guarantor of regional security in Northeast Asia.

In examining these issues, this chapter makes four major arguments about Japan's, South Korea's, and Taiwan's common challenges and responses, and consequently about the United States' efforts to manage its military ties with regional allies and partners. The first is that these three countries often share concerns about the development of specific Chinese military capabilities. These concerns then serve as common drivers for these states' own military modernization programs.

The second argument is that all three countries are simultaneously seeking engagement with China to dampen security dilemmas and hedging against its rise through varying degrees of internal military balancing. Yet just as they share common modernization ambitions, Japan, South Korea, and Taiwan also confront common domestic obstacles, such as political and budgetary constraints, that limit their capacity for internal balancing against China.

The third argument is that Japan, South Korea, and Taiwan display convergent trends in external balancing efforts and in rethinking their individual military ties with the United States. All three have oscillated in their degree of attachment to the United States, influenced both by concerns over maintaining engagement and growing economic interdependence with China and by fears of abandonment and entrapment stemming from the United States' reformulation of its regional and global military postures. More recently, however, these fears have diminished. Consequently Japan, South Korea, and Taiwan have moved more firmly back into the U.S. security fold.

The fourth major argument, which follows from the third, is that despite the recent discussion of the United States having "lost Asia" in the face of a rising China, the key U.S. allies and partners in Northeast Asia are now moving away from China on security issues. Japan, South Korea, and Taiwan are increasingly hedging hard internally, as well as seeking renewed security assistance from the United States externally.[1] In this situation, rising military competition between China and U.S. allies and partners in Northeast Asia presents the United States with regional security challenges, but also with fresh opportunities to shape the regional security outlook through maintaining its role as the chief security guarantor.

The first section of this chapter concentrates on Japan, arguably the most important U.S. ally in Northeast Asia, if not the entire Asia-Pacific region. It investigates Japan's overall grand strategy toward China in terms of long-term and more recent patterns of engagement, rising security tensions, and hedging through the U.S.-Japan alliance. This is followed by a discussion of Japanese concerns regarding China's development of specific military capabilities. Japan's internal balancing response is then examined, as well as its external balancing, including recent attempts to strengthen the U.S.-Japan alliance and relations with other U.S. partners. The second and third sections follow this pattern by examining South Korea's and Taiwan's grand strategies, specific concerns over Chinese capabilities, and internal and external balancing efforts. The conclusion considers in more depth the implications of these trends for U.S. strategy and military deployments in the Asia-Pacific region.

Japan: A Fundamental Military Transformation?

Japan's Grand Strategy and China

Japanese grand strategy for most of the postwar period has included a strong commitment toward the engagement of China. Japan's policymakers, even in the midst of the Cold War, were relatively sanguine about the threat from Chinese Communism and more concerned about the risks that internal Chinese political unrest and disintegration posed for regional stability. In the post–Cold War period, Japan has attempted to accelerate engagement of China by assisting with internal economic reform, political stabilization, and integration into the regional political economy partly in order to moderate China's external behavior.[2] The two countries' economic interdependence has continued to deepen as well. Thus, even in the face of concerns about

---

[1] T.J. Pempel, "How Bush Bungled Asia: How Militarism, Economic Indifference, and Unilateralism Have Weakened the U.S. across Asia," *Pacific Review* 21, no. 5 (2008): 547–81; and Victor Cha, "Winning Asia: Washington's Untold Success Story," *Foreign Affairs* 86, no. 6 (2007): 98–113.

[2] For a full evaluation of the development of Japan's China strategy in the postwar period, see Mike M. Mochizuki, "Japan's Shifting China Strategy toward the Rise of China," *Journal of Strategic Studies* 30, no. 4/5 (2007): 739–76.

rising Chinese economic and military power, Japan has looked to maintain its default position of engagement. This strategy is reflected in Tokyo's attempts since 2006 to inject substance into a "strategic and mutually beneficial partnership" with China, involving cooperation on a range of economic and political issues. Indeed, Japan's economic gravitation toward China—which surpassed the United States as Japan's largest trade partner in 2006—has been seen at times as a step toward potential bandwagoning with a potential Sino-centric regional order.

The Democratic Party of Japan's (DPJ) displacement of the Liberal Democratic Party (LDP) from power in 2009 initially seemed to augur this type of shift. Japan's new top leaders courted and were courted by their Chinese counterparts. The DPJ also seemed to distance itself from the U.S.-Japan alliance over issues such as the relocation of the U.S. Marine Corps' (USMC) Futenma Air Station in Okinawa Prefecture and the withdrawal of the Japan Self-Defense Forces (JSDF) in 2010 from Indian Ocean refueling missions designed to support the U.S.-led coalition in Afghanistan.

Yet such interpretations of DPJ intentions appear to have been mistaken. DPJ policymakers never entertained any real interest in bandwagoning with China or undermining the U.S.-Japan alliance. The new administration redoubled engagement with China—in part by demonstrating a more autonomous stance vis-à-vis the United States—in order to assume greater responsibility for Japan's own foreign and security relations in East Asia. The government thereby hoped to induce greater Chinese cooperation in projected regional formats such as an East Asian community (EAC), which could help collectively shape and constrain China's rising power. Regarding the Futenma Air Station, the DPJ has been looking to shift the alliance onto a stronger and more sustainable track by resolving the issue in a way that does not consolidate the USMC presence and prolong the disproportionate burden on Okinawa Prefecture. Instead, the DPJ has focused on tightening alliance cooperation closer to Japan itself and the surrounding region.[3]

Moreover, Japan's heightened engagement of China has always been tempered by a corresponding strengthening of hedging activities through the U.S.-Japan alliance. Japan, even as it pursued engagement with China in the 1990s, took steps under LDP governments—through the so-called reconfirmation or redefinition of the alliance and the accompanying process of revising the U.S.-Japan Defense Guidelines in 1997—to hedge against China's rising power by clarifying the interoperability of the alliance and its ability to respond to regional contingencies, including a Taiwan Strait crisis. Similarly, the DPJ, even during the supposed heyday of its bandwagoning

---

[3] Christopher W. Hughes, "The Democratic Party of Japan's New (but Failing) Grand Strategy: From Reluctant Realism to Resentful Realism?" *Journal of Japanese Studies* 38, no. 1 (2012): 109–140.

with China in 2009, maintained support for U.S. bases and force realignments on the Japanese mainland, endorsed a revised U.S. nuclear strategy, and continued bilateral cooperation on ballistic missile defense (BMD). Since 2010, the DPJ has arguably cooperated with the United States and hedged against China's rising military power with an even harder edge than previous LDP administrations through cooperation with the United States. Given increasing pressure from perceived Chinese provocations, the DPJ, despite its initial intentions to maintain engagement, may actually be obliged to consider an overall tilt toward a containment-style strategy.

Japanese concerns under LDP governments, and now under the DPJ, relate to China's apparent ambitions to project military power outside its immediate territory. These ambitions include not only the protection of core Chinese interests in the Taiwan Strait but now increasingly the assertion of territorial and resource interests in the East China Sea, South China Sea, and the sea lines of communication (SLOC) in the Asia-Pacific region and beyond to the Persian Gulf. The frequent dispatch of "research ships" and PLA Navy (PLAN) vessels into Japan's exclusive economic zone (EEZ) around the disputed Senkaku Islands has served to reinforce Japan's concerns about China's expanding area of maritime operations. Likewise, tensions further north in the East China Sea have been intensified by overlapping EEZs and territorial claims to energy resources. Despite the two countries reaching an agreement in principle in 2008 for joint development of gas fields, Japan has been frustrated by China's apparent reluctance to proceed with bilateral development plans and remains suspicious that China is already moving to exploit the fields unilaterally. In addition, Japanese policymakers see China's refusal to recognize the territory of Okinotorishima as an islet—thereby negating Japan's claims to the surrounding EEZ in the Philippine Sea—as another challenge to the territorial status quo.

Finally, the confrontation between a Japan Coast Guard (JCG) vessel and a Chinese fishing trawler in late 2010 forced Japanese policymakers to recognize China's intentions on territorial issues. The DPJ administration's decision to not only detain but then indict the captain of the Chinese trawler for attempting to ram the JCG vessel sparked a major diplomatic row. China was especially offended by Japan appealing to the United States for security guarantees under the assumption that the Senkaku Islands were covered by the bilateral U.S.-Japan security treaty. Beijing reacted by exerting intense diplomatic and economic pressure on Japan. It suspended all high-level contacts and working-level talks, including negotiations on the gas fields in the East China Sea, and halted exports of vital rare earth minerals. The latter move was viewed in Japan as a form of economic warfare. In the end, the DPJ government partly buckled under Chinese pressure, releasing the trawler captain without charges and eventually restoring barely cordial ties with China by early 2012.

Japan's defense planners have viewed China's recent maritime activities as shadowboxing for potentially aggressive future territorial designs. In November 2004, the Japan Maritime Self-Defense Force (MSDF) tracked a PLAN Han-class nuclear-powered attack submarine (SSN) navigating in Japanese territorial waters. In September 2005, five PLAN ships, including a Sovremenny-class guided-missile destroyer (DDG), traveled in the vicinity of the disputed gas fields in the East China Sea; and in October 2008 another Sovremenny-class DDG and four other warships made the first passage by PLAN vessels through the Tsugaru Strait and then circled the rest of the Japanese archipelago. In November 2008, a PLAN flotilla including destroyers passed between the main island of Okinawa and Miyako Island, on course toward the Pacific Ocean; and in March 2010 a group of six PLAN warships, including a Luzhou-class DDG repeated this passage. Japan looked on askance as the PLAN dispatched ten warships on the same route in April 2009, including two destroyers, one of which was Sovremenny-class; three frigates; three support vessels; and two Kilo-class attack submarines (SSK). Japanese policymakers took particular note of the size and composition of this PLAN squadron, described in some media sources in rather hyperbolic terms as an "armada."[4] The squadron not only was the largest to date, but the variety of vessels it included, replete with air-defense destroyers, pointed to the type of force necessary to support a future aircraft-carrier battle group. Moreover, PLAN bravado was evident in two incidents of the squadron's helicopters buzzing MSDF vessels that were shadowing the destroyers and also in the fact that the Kilo-class SSKs were willing to surface. In July 2010, another PLAN flotilla of one Luzhou-class DDG and a frigate again passed through the Okinawa and Miyako Island route; and in June 2011 the PLAN sent a still larger squadron of eleven warships, including a Sovremenny-class DDG, through the same route.[5]

Meanwhile, China's maritime activities vis-à-vis other powers in the region have been taken by Japan as evidence of potentially aggressive intent. Japanese defense analysts have noted Chinese actions—such as the surfacing of a PLAN Song-class SSK near the USS *Kitty Hawk* close to Okinawa in October 2006, and the "harassing" of the U.S. naval surveillance vessel the USNS *Impeccable* operating within China's EEZ, 75 miles south of Hainan in the South China Sea—as challenges to the U.S. presence in the region and

---

[4] "MSDF Tracks China Armada Off Okinawa," *Japan Times*, April 14, 2010, http://www.japantimes.co.jp/text/nn20100414a2.html.

[5] Boeishohen [Ministry of Defence], *Boei hakusho 2011* [Defense White Paper 2011] (Tokyo, Zaimusho Insatsukyoku, 2011), 85–88.

more widely the principle of the freedom of navigation.[6] The intensification of PLAN activities in the South China Sea in recent years has compounded Japanese views of China's willingness to use intimidation in pursuit of territorial claims. The National Institute for Defense Studies (NIDS), which is under the Japan Ministry of Defense (JMOD), stated in 2011 that it "can be inferred that the reason why the PLAN is focusing on the South China Sea is that it is aiming to resolve territorial issues in its own favor regarding the Spratly Islands…based on the flaunting of overwhelming military power."[7] In turn, Japan's policymakers have watched with great interest China's expansion of naval activity outside the Asia-Pacific and noted the country's enhanced capabilities to project sustained naval power across SLOCs. For example, the PLAN has dispatched ships to engage in antipiracy escort and naval diplomatic activities in the Gulf of Aden and off the coast of Somalia, thereby advancing key interests in the Middle East and Africa.

Japanese analysts acknowledge that China's expanded military ambitions may be driven by an understandable concern for the protection of SLOCs and the country's now global economic interests and that in many cases even potentially provocative behavior, such as sending squadrons close to Japanese territory, has to be tolerated under international conventions. Nevertheless, Japan entertains deep anxieties that China's rising military power is no longer focused simply on "access denial" and preventing Taiwan independence but is now looking to assert the longer-term aim of "area control" over the "first island chain" of the East and South China seas. Japan worries that China will pursue this goal by transgressing established international norms relating to freedom of navigation and EEZs, and thereby gradually neutralize the Japanese and U.S. naval presence in the region. Japanese analysts are fond of reporting that China is engaged in tactics of media, legal, and psychological warfare designed to cow the surrounding powers into submission, and they see this strategy as increasingly backed by the acquisition of asymmetric and symmetric capabilities.[8]

Japan's Concerns over China's Military Modernization

Japanese perceptions of Chinese military modernization coincide closely with those of other states in the region. Japan sees the PLA as set on procuring capabilities that will serve the immediate asymmetric warfare ends of anti-access/area-denial (A2/AD) in the sea and air space surrounding China, as

---

[6] Boeisho Boeikenkyushohen [National Institute for Defense Studies], *Chugoku anzen hosho repoto* [China Security Report] (Tokyo, Boeikenkyujo, 2011), 17.

[7] Boeisho Boeikenkyushohen, *Chugoku anzen hosho repoto*, 15.

[8] Boeishohen, *Boei hakusho 2011*, 76.

well as the longer-term symmetric warfare ends of penetrating neighboring air, sea, and land defenses and projecting power equal to other great powers in the Asia-Pacific and beyond.

The Japan Air Self-Defense Force (ASDF) has long been accustomed to maintaining qualitative superiority among the region's powers, but the PLA Air Force (PLAAF) has begun for the first time to pose air-defense challenges for Japan. The PLAAF's introduction of fourth-generation fighters since the late 1990s—including the J-10, J11-B, Su-27, Su-30MKK, and Su-30MK2, which together constituted around one-third of China's fleet in 2010—has now raised concerns that the ASDF's aging fleet of F4-Js and F-15Js may be rapidly losing its edge in air superiority.[9] Indications since 2009 that the PLAAF will introduce a fifth-generation J-20 "stealth" fighter, along with its current deployment of KJ-2000 early warning and control aircraft and H-6U and Il-78 in-flight refueling aircraft, have only exacerbated ASDF fears. Official statistics show that the ASDF scrambled its fighters 83 times by mid-2011 to intercept Chinese aircraft, which is three times as often as it did over the same period in 2010 and on pace to far exceed the total intercepts for that entire year.[10]

The ballistic-missile forces of the PLA's Second Artillery Corps, although clearly directed primarily at Taiwan rather than Japan, nevertheless raise concerns in that they are capable of striking JSDF and U.S. forces stationed in Japan. Specifically, Japanese policymakers might envision a Taiwan contingency in which DF-15/CSS-6 short-range ballistic missiles (SRBM) are used to target U.S. Air Force (USAF) units at Kadena in Okinawa—or DF-3/CSS-2 intermediate-range ballistic missiles (IRBM) are used to attack U.S. military assets at Iwakuni, Misawa, and Yokota in Honshu—in order to deter the United States and Japan from intervention.[11] Similarly, PLAAF DH-10 or CJ-10 cruise missiles are seen as posing problems for Japan's defense of key military infrastructure. Perhaps even more worrying for Japan in the long-term is China's development of antiship ballistic missiles (ASBM) capable of striking U.S. aircraft carriers operating out of Japan and in the Asia-Pacific,

---

[9] U.S.-China Economic and Security Review Commission, *2010 Report to Congress of the U.S.-China Economic and Security Review Commission*, 111th Congress, 2nd session (Washington, D.C., 2010), 76, http://www.uscc.gov/annual_report/2010/annual_report_full_10.pdf.

[10] "Kuji no kinkyu hasshi, tai-Chugokuki ga 3baizo, konnendo hanki" [ASDF Scrambles in First Half of Year Triple against Chinese Aircraft], *Asahi Shimbun*, October 13, 2011, http://www.asahi.com/politics/update/1013/TKY201110130527.html.

[11] David A. Shlapak, "The Red Rockets' Glare: Implications of Improvements in PRC Air and Missile Strike Capabilities," in *New Opportunities and Challenges for Taiwan's Security*, ed. Roger Cliff, Philip Saunders, and Scott Harold (Santa Monica: RAND, 2011), 75; and U.S.-China Economic and Security Review Commission, *2010 Report to Congress*, 90.

which might severely undermine the U.S. force projection and deterrence posture in the region.[12]

MSDF concerns about China revolve around its modernization of a range of anti-access and blue water maritime capabilities. The PLAN has introduced Kilo-, Yuan-, and Song-class diesel-powered and Shang-class nuclear-powered submarines with quieting technologies. These developments may complicate the MSDF's traditional defensive role in keeping the seas around Japan free from enemy submarines in order to enable the U.S. Seventh Fleet to concentrate on the effective projection of offensive power. The PLAN has also introduced Luyang-class and Luzhou-class DDGs with a fleet air-defense role, combined with Sovremenny-class DDGs capable of targeting U.S. aircraft carriers, as well as Jiangkai-class guided-missile frigates (FFG) with stealth characteristics. These developments demonstrate China's potential ability to deploy modern fleet formations and thereby complicate Japanese and U.S. naval dominance in the region. China's pursuit of aircraft carriers through the refit of the ex-Soviet carrier *Varyag* has likewise generated intense interest in Japan. While Chinese carriers lag far behind those of the United States in capability, they are nevertheless taken as yet another sign of China's determination to pursue offensive power projection and challenge the United States' effective monopoly in this area. An additional concern for Japanese planners is China's upgrading of its amphibious warfare capabilities with the addition of Yuzhao-class landing ships, which might help China seize Japanese far-flung islands in a contingency.

Beyond these air and maritime capabilities, the other principal sources of concern for Japan's military planners are China's space and cyberspace capabilities. China's successful anti-satellite (ASAT) weapon test in January 2007 poses obvious future problems for both the United States' and Japan's space-based military information-gathering and early warning systems. Japan has already felt the possible impact of China's emerging cyberspace capabilities. Frequent attacks originating from China have been made on the JMOD and civilian ministries' infrastructure, and attempts were also made in September 2011 to hack into the systems of Mitsubishi Heavy Industries, Japan's largest defense contractor.

Japan's Internal Balancing in Response to China

Japan's long-term reform of its national military capabilities under successive National Defense Program Guidelines (NDPG) has been driven by the two principal concerns of North Korea and China. North Korea's nuclear- and ballistic-missile programs have served as the most immediate

---

[12] Boeishohen, *Boei hakusho 2011*, 81.

driver for major changes in Japan's military posture. The range of security problems that these programs present should not be underestimated, not least in how Pyongyang's provocations have at times threatened to drive a wedge between the United States and Japan over differing immediate attachments to the nuclear and missile threats. North Korea's missile programs have thus tested the alliance's political solidarity more than its military strength.[13] However, North Korea has arguably functioned more as a secondary driver, and indeed at times a convenient legitimizing pretext, for an agenda of change in a Japanese defense policy driven more fundamentally by the rise of China and the associated looming military challenges. The latter are of a far greater magnitude than those of North Korea. Hence, even though the North Korean and Chinese threats have worked in combination over the past two decades to exert pressure on Japan to revise its defense policies, as well as introduce more mobile and technologically advanced JSDF capabilities, it is actually China that demonstrates the greatest propensity to deliver radical change in Japan's military posture over the longer term.

The function of China as the underlying primary driver for Japan's defense modernization is demonstrated in the JMOD's past NDPGs and most strikingly in the latest revised NDPG of 2010. The 1996 National Defense Program Outline (NDPO) omitted any direct reference to China, but the revised 2004 NDPG noted China's modernization of its nuclear- and ballistic-missile forces and increasing ambitions for out-of-area operations, and recommended that Japan "remain attentive to its [China's] future actions."[14] The NDPG then stated that the JSDF would increasingly reorient its capabilities to respond to scenarios such as ballistic-missile attacks, invasion of Japan's offshore islands, and violations of Japanese sea and air space—all indirect references to China's military activities. The 2010 NDPG went much further, emphasizing China's rapid military modernization and development of power projection and the accompanying lack of transparency in defense spending and procurement. The 2010 guidelines stressed that all of this was a "concern for the regional and global community," which is oblique Japanese language for China's growth as a

[13] Christopher W. Hughes, "Supersizing the DPRK Threat: Japan's Evolving Military Posture and North Korea," *Asian Survey* 49, no. 2 (2009): 291–311.

[14] Boeishohen, "Heisei 8 nendo iko ni kakawaru Boei Keikaku no Taiko" [NDPO for 1996 Onward] (Tokyo, November 28, 1995), http://www.mod.go.jp/j/approach/agenda/guideline/1996_taikou/dp96j.html; and Boeishohen, "Heisei 17 Nendo iko ni kakawaru Boei Keikaku no Taiko ni tsuite" [NDPG for 2005 Onward] (Tokyo, December 10, 2004), http://www.mod.go.jp/j/approach/agenda/guideline/2005/taikou.html.

significant threat.[15] The 2012 NDPG added responses to cyberwarfare to its list of anxieties clearly related to China's capabilities.

Most importantly, though, the 2010 NDPG initiated a potential step-change in Japanese defense doctrine—apparently derived principally from concerns over Chinese activities and capabilities—in that it moved to abandon the concept of the basic defense force (BDF) in favor of a new dynamic defense force (DDF). The BDF was essentially a Cold War construct first established in the 1976 NDPO, which was the forerunner of the NDPG, and used to justify the development and maintenance of the minimum JSDF capabilities sufficient to deter Soviet aggression, while still allowing for the possibility of ramping up the size of forces if Japan were threatened with large-scale aggression.[16] Hence, the BDF made for a JSDF posture limited to a static defense of Japanese territory and characterized by the buildup of heavy land forces concentrated in northern Japan, especially in Hokkaido, to prevent Soviet incursions. The JSDF did depart somewhat from the BDF in the late 1980s with a significant expansion of air interceptor and destroyer capabilities. This shift enabled the JSDF to fulfill a greater defensive role around the Japanese archipelago and SLOCs and helped free up U.S. forces for greater power projection against the rising Soviet threat. Nevertheless, the BDF remained intact through the remainder of the Cold War and in the 1996 NDPG. It was not until the 2004 NDPG that Japan edged away from the concept by arguing for the adoption of more mobile, flexible, and multifunctional forces capable of responding to various contingencies regionally and out of area.

The 2010 NDPG's formal abandonment of the BDF and adoption of the DDF continues the trend of attempting to extricate Japan's military from the legacy posture of the Cold War by emphasizing a shift toward lighter and more technologically advanced forces with power-projection capabilities. The DDF even more crucially emphasizes that the JSDF should not only enhance the quality of its capabilities but now look to utilize these more actively than in the past. In other words, the JSDF should move from just building the force by adding equipment to actually operating it effectively for national defense.[17]

---

[15] Boeishohen, "Heisei 23 Nendo iko ni kakawaru Boei Keikaku no Taiko ni tsuite" [NDPG for 2011 Onward] (Tokyo, December 17, 2011), http://www.mod.go.jp/j/approach/agenda/guideline/2011/taikou.html. Japan's Ministry of Foreign Affairs echoes this line in its Diplomatic Bluebook for 2012, which stresses the lack of transparency in China's military buildup and increasing maritime activities around Japan, and the consequent concerns for regional and international security. See Gaimusho [Ministry of Foreign Affairs], *Gaiko Seisho Yoshi 2012* [Diplomatic Bluebook 2012], April 2012, http://www.mofa.go.jp/mofaj/gaiko/bluebook/index.html, 22.

[16] "Showa 52 nendo iko ni kakawaru Boei Keikaku no Taiko" [NDPO for 1977 Onward], October 29, 1976, http://www.ioc.u-tokyo.ac.jp/~worldjpn/documents/texts/docs/19761029.O1J.html.

[17] Boeisho Kenkyushohen, *Higashi Ajia senryaku gaiyo* [East Asian Strategic Review] (Tokyo: Boei Kenkyusho, 2011), 230–33.

The NDPG charges the JSDF with the responsibility to raise and sustain the tempo of operations; increase patrolling and intelligence, surveillance, and reconnaissance (ISR) activities; deal swiftly with probing or *fait accompli* occupation activities in Japan's air and sea space; and strengthen general preparedness for regional and global contingencies. In short, Japan seeks to devise a defense posture that is dynamic and capable of responding rapidly and flexibly to diverse threats—no longer just to Japan itself, but in the Asia-Pacific region and beyond.

Japan's decision to attempt a radical transformation of its defense doctrine through finally adopting the DDF concept is a deep reflection, if not indeed a direct product, of the influence of China's recent military modernization and the security concerns it has created over territory and SLOCs. Although Japan's policymakers, anxious about counter-reactions from their counterparts, refrain from explicitly identifying China as a threat and the prime motivation for revisions to defense policy, the DDF is clearly designed primarily to meet the mounting military challenges from China. In turn, Japan's defense planners have followed through with this transformation of military doctrine by instituting corresponding changes to JSDF deployments and capabilities.

In recent years, Japanese policymakers have progressively shifted the weight of key JSDF capabilities away from the outmoded Cold War emphasis on northern Japan and instead turned southward in order to meet the emerging challenges from China. Since 2009, the ASDF has begun to deploy its most capable fighter, the F-15J, in Okinawa Prefecture; announced that it would redeploy two fighter squadrons to Okinawa; improved the operation of E-2C aircraft from Okinawa; deployed mobile radar equipment closer to Taiwan—on Miyako, Yonaguni, Ishigaki, and Iriomote-jima, the four southernmost Japanese islands; and upgraded three ground-based radar sites on Miyako and Okinoerabu islands, located just north of Okinawa. The ASDF is further looking to improve its airlift capability to support the deployment of Ground Self-Defense Force (GSDF) defensive reinforcements to the southern islands and the stationing of ballistic missile defense PAC-3 batteries in Okinawa. In December 2011 the GSDF, ASDF, and MSDF conducted joint exercises in Honshu, supported by the United States, based on the scenario of needing to retake one of the southern islands. These involved deploying ASDF F-2s and MSDF P-3Cs to remove enemy warships from surrounding waters and deplete enemy air defenses, and then using ASDF F-15Js to provide air cover for ASDF C-130s to drop GSDF parachute forces.[18]

---

[18] "Jieitai ga rito dakkan kuren, Nansei Shoto sotei shi 12 gatsu" [JSDF Drills for Retaking Distant Islands in December, Envisaging the Southern Islands among Others], *Yomiuri Shimbun*, August 19, 2010, http://www.yomiuri.co.jp/politics/news/20100819-OYT1T00023.htm.

The GSDF has now been charged with strengthening the defenses of Miyako, Yonaguni, Ishigaki, and Iriomote-jima through deploying a new coastal surveillance unit, as well as forming a first-response unit to gather information and defend the islands. In addition, the GSDF is forming a new anti-aircraft artillery group for rapid air-transport deployment to the southern islands. The GSDF and ASDF were subsequently able to rehearse these operations in the run-up to North Korea's test missile launch in April 2012. The Japanese government, fearful of debris from the missile falling on Okinawa, inserted PAC-3 units into Miyako and Ishigaki and five hundred GSDF personnel into Miyako, Ishigaki, and Yonaguni.[19] Meanwhile, even further afield, the continued deployment of MSDF destroyers and P-3Cs in antipiracy operations in the Gulf of Aden—including the construction of the JSDF's first postwar overseas military base in Djibouti in mid-2011—has enabled Japan to monitor China's maritime activities in this region.[20]

In terms of the development of specific military capabilities, Japan has largely sought to counter China's modernization with a symmetrical buildup of JSDF assets. The 2010 NDPG and accompanying Mid-Term Defense Program (MTDP) emphasize focusing on the characteristics of readiness, mobility, flexibility, sustainability, versatility, and jointness. In practice, this policy has meant the continuing reduction of main battle tanks and artillery originally procured to deter the Soviet Union and a switch to investments in lighter, more mobile, and technologically advanced forces capable of responding to regional contingencies (see **Tables 1**, **2**, and **3**).

The ASDF has first sought to slow any movement in the balance of air-defense power in China's favor by investing in recent upgrades to the radar and AAM-5 air-to-air missiles of its F-15Js, especially to improve aerial dog-fighting and anti–cruise missile capabilities. However, the ASDF has also looked to push the air-defense balance firmly back into its own favor in the medium to long term by acquiring a new F-X fighter.

The ASDF's avowed aim has been to acquire an air superiority interceptor to replace its obsolete F-4Js. It first sought to procure the F-22A as a means to trump China's current fourth-generation inventory and any fifth-generation future ambitions in air power. Japan was eventually denied the F-22A because the U.S. Congress refused to lift its blanket ban on the export of the aircraft for fear of the loss of sensitive technology. The Bush and Obama administrations were also concerned that this aircraft would too decisively shift the air power

---

[19] "PAC-3 haibi de ondosa: Nansai Shoto no boeiryoku kyoka" [Differences in Enthusiasm for PAC-3 Deployments: Strengthening the Defensive Power of the Southern Islands], *Asahi Shimbun*, April 1, 2012, 4.

[20] "Jieitai hajimete no "kaigai kichi" kaizoku taisaku de Jibuchi ni" [The JSDF's First Overseas Base in Djibouti for Anti-Piracy], *Yomiuri Shimbun*, May 28, 2011, http://www.yomiuri.co.jp/politics/news/20110528-OYT1T00450.htm.

TABLE 1 Ground Self-Defense Force (GSDF) organization and primary equipment

		1976 NDPO	1996 NDPO	2004 NDPG	2010 NDPG
Personnel	Total GSDF personnel	180,000	160,000	155,000	154,000
	Regular personnel	–	*145,000*	*148,000*	*147,000*
	Ready reserve personnel	–	*15,000*	*7,000*	*7,000*
Major units	Regionally deployed units	12 divisions	8 divisions	8 divisions	8 divisions
	Mobile operation units	2 combined brigades	6 brigades	6 brigades	6 brigades
		1 armored division	1 armored division	1 armored division	1 armored division
		1 airborne brigade	1 airborne brigade	Central Readiness Group	Central Readiness Group
		1 helicopter brigade	1 helicopter brigade	–	–
	Ground-to-air missile units	8 anti-aircraft artillery groups	8 anti-aircraft artillery groups	8 anti-aircraft artillery groups	7 anti-aircraft artillery groups
Main equipment	Battle tanks	~1,200	~900	~600	~400
	Artillery	~1,000	~900	~600	~400

SOURCE: Japan Defense Agency, *Nihon no boei 1995: Boei hakusho* [Defense of Japan 1995: Defense White Paper] (Tokyo: Okurasho insatsukyoku, 1995), 312, 321; and Japan Ministry of Defense, *Nihon no boei 2011: Boei hakusho* [Defense of Japan 2011: Defense White Paper] (Tokyo: Zaimusho insatsukyoku, 2011), 175.

TABLE 2 Maritime Self-Defense Force (MSDF) organization and primary equipment

		1976 NDPO	1996 NDPO	2004 NDPG	2010 NDPG
Major units	Destroyer units (for mobile operations)	4 flotillas	4 flotillas	4 flotillas	4 flotillas
	Destoyer units (regional district units)	10 divisions	7 divisions	5 divisions	6 brigades
	Submarine units	6 divisions	6 divisions	4 divisions	6 submarine units
	Minesweeping units	2 flotillas	1 flotilla	1 flotilla	1 flotilla
	Land-based patrol aircraft units	16 squadrons	13 squadrons	9 squadrons	9 squadrons
Main equipment	Destroyers	~60	~50	47	48
	Submarines	16	16	16	22
	Combat aircraft	~220	~170	~150	~150

SOURCE: Japan Defense Agency, *Nihon no boei 1995*, 312, 321; and Japan Ministry of Defense, *Nihon no boei 2011*, 175.

TABLE 3   Air Self-Defense Force (ASDF) organization and primary equipment

		1976 NDPO	1996 NDPO	2004 NDPG	2010 NDPG
Major units	Aircraft control and warning units	28 groups	8 groups	8 groups	4 warning groups
		1 squadron	20 squadrons	20 squadrons	28 squadrons
		–	1 airborne early warning squadron	1 airborne early warning squadron	1 airborne early warning squadron
	Interceptor units	10 squadrons	9 squadrons	12 squadrons	12 squadrons
	Support fighter units	3 squadrons	3 squadrons	–	–
	Air reconnaissance units	1 squadron	1 squadron	1 squadron	1 squadron
	Air transport units	3 squadrons	3 squadrons	3 squadrons	3 squadrons
	Ground-to-air missile units	6 groups	6 groups	6 groups	6 groups
Main equipment	Combat aircraft	~400	~400	~350	~340
	Fighters	~350	~300	~260	~260

SOURCE: Japan Defense Agency, *Nihon no boei 1995*, 312, 321; and Japan Ministry of Defense, *Nihon no boei 2011*, 175.

balance toward Japan vis-à-vis China and trigger a destabilizing regional arms race.[21] Japan then launched an F-X competition, finally selecting in December 2011 the Lockheed-Martin F-35A over the BAE Systems Eurofighter Typhoon and Boeing F/A-18. Japan's choice of the F-35A was controversial because it is not strictly an air superiority fighter, unlike the Eurofighter; is not yet operationally capable or combat-tested; will likely not be delivered until the end of the decade; and is expensive at an estimated 10–20 billion yen per aircraft. The Japanese defense industry will also receive minimal or possibly zero opportunities to maintain its competency in fighter production by purchasing an essentially off-the-shelf import.[22]

Nevertheless, Japan's procurement of a fleet of 42 F-35As will eventually provide the ASDF with a formidable fifth-generation multirole aircraft. The F-35A features stealth characteristics and should match up well with, if perhaps not totally supersede, future Chinese capabilities. Just as interestingly, Japan's attachment of importance to the stealth capabilities of the F-35A, along with its greater associated strengths as an air defense–penetration fighter rather than an air superiority fighter, suggests a future ASDF interest in developing an offensive counter-air doctrine. This type of Japanese capability might be used to strike against North Korean missile bases and even the Chinese mainland in a contingency and would mark a radical departure from Japan's defense-oriented posture. Meanwhile, the other key air power development, partially in response to China's military modernization, has been the ASDF's procurement of the indigenously produced C-2 transport. This aircraft will provide the necessary airlift around the Japanese archipelago to respond to possible invasions of offshore islands.

Japan's reaction to China's missile forces has again been largely symmetric in attempting to neutralize these capabilities through the deployment of BMD. The 2010 NDPG mandates the ASDF to maintain six anti-aircraft groups equipped with PAC-3 batteries, and the MSDF to maintain six Aegis DDGs equipped with BMD SM-3 interceptors. The JSDF now deploys, after the United States, the most sophisticated BMD capabilities in the Asia-Pacific, and thus pursues deterrence by denial of China's ballistic-missile threat. However, Japan still might entertain the prospect of edging toward a form of "deterrence by punishment" if it were to deploy the F-35A for strikes on missile launchers, armed with the joint direct attack munitions (JDAM) introduced by the ASDF in 2009. Although cruise missiles are usually discussed as a means of striking

---

[21] Christopher Bolkcom and Emma Chanlett-Avery, "Potential F-22 *Raptor* Export to Japan," Congressional Research Service, CRS Report for Congress, RS22684, March 11, 2009.

[22] "F35 sentoki: kakaku kosho ni seifu kuryo nesage kosho muzukashiku" [F-35 Fighter: Government Suffering at the High Cost, Difficulty of Negotiations for Lowering Price], *Mainichi Shimbun*, May 9, 2012, http://mainichi.jp/select/news/20120510k0000m010107000c.html.

at North Korean missile launch pads and are not yet openly contemplated as an option for responding to China's missiles, the MSDF might value a cruise-missile capability as another form of deterrence by punishment.

Given that Japan's primary concerns over China relate to maritime security, the MSDF has embarked on the most significant buildup of capabilities under recent NDPGs, many of which are designed to negate both the PLAN's access-denial and blue water naval strategies. Under the 2010 NDPG and MTDP, the MSDF is set to increase the SSK fleet by more than one-third, from 15 to 22 boats. The destroyer force is maintained at 48 in number, and Japan as part of this buildup continues to introduce helicopter-carrying destroyers (DDH). The MSDF has taken delivery of two 7,000-ton Hyuga-class 16DDHs, with a regular complement of four helicopters but capable of carrying up to eleven. It is then set to procure two additional 19,000-ton 22DDHs, capable of carrying up to fourteen helicopters. MSDF DDHs are the largest vessels built for service in the postwar period and are light helicopter carriers in all but name. The prime function of these assets is to provide a very powerful antisubmarine warfare (ASW) capability, clearly aimed against China's access-denial strategy. But Japan's venturing back into carrier technology presages a possible Sino-Japanese carrier arms race, and analysts suspect that the MSDF might eventually attempt to operate fixed-wing aircraft from the 22DDHs, such as the maritime variant of the F-35. Japan's maritime air and ASW capability will be further strengthened through the procurement of a replacement for its P-3Cs: the indigenously developed P-1 patrol surveillance aircraft. The P-1 will be able to sweep over a range of eight thousand kilometers.

Japan is also beginning to try to match China in other potential combat spheres. The Cabinet Secretariat's 2009 Basic Plan for Space Policy contains highly ambitious goals for the development of early warning satellites to assist the BMD program; and the JMOD's Committee on the Promotion of Space Development and Use established basic guidelines in the same year that argue for taking measures to protect satellites against attack and improve C4ISR (command, control, communications, computers, intelligence, surveillance, and reconnaissance). The Information Security Policy Council and JMOD are jointly looking to counter Chinese asymmetric warfare through devising measures to defend information networks against cyberattack.[23]

Consequently, Japan's internal balancing efforts vis-à-vis China have markedly strengthened in recent years. These internal military efforts are, however, predictably accompanied by concomitant domestic constraints. Japanese policymakers still hold out hope that diplomacy and engagement

---

[23] Boeishohen, *Boei hakusho 2011*, 208, 210.

will curb China's future military ambitions, and the continuing strength of anti-militaristic sentiment among Japan's citizenry means that the Japanese state remains reluctant to openly resort to military deterrence. Yet a bipartisan consensus is emerging between the DPJ and LDP, reflected in the defense measures outlined above, that Japan must face up to and hedge harder against the impending threats from China's military modernization. Prior to losing power to the DPJ, the LDP sought to characterize the DPJ as a party soft on defense issues. However, the DPJ has actually followed very closely and then superseded the LDP in terms of reinforcing Japan's national defense capabilities, with the result that the two parties' defense policies appear indistinguishable in relation to China. This process of convergence was only accelerated by the Sino-Japanese spat over the Senkaku Islands in 2010. Moreover, public opinion may also be converging with the views of policy elites. According to a Cabinet Office survey following the 2010 Senkaku Islands incident, 78% of the public feels no affinity with China, the highest percentage since the conclusion of the Sino-Japanese Treaty of Peace and Friendship in 1980.[24]

The principal domestic constraint on Japan's ability to hedge hard against the potential threat from China is not denial of the risk involved but the limited availability of resources to address competing priorities. Japan's struggling economy and the growing demands for welfare expenditure— compounded by the need for reconstruction funds following the March 2011 earthquake and tsunami and the ensuing crisis at the Fukushima Daiichi nuclear power plant—have meant that the defense budget continues to be squeezed. Japan's persistence in limiting defense expenditure to 1% of GNP in an era of declining GNP inevitably constrains the budget. Since the mid-1990s, defense spending has remained limited to around 6% of total government expenditures and a de facto ceiling of 5 trillion yen (see **Figure 1**). An even greater constraint on Japan's military modernization is that the proportion of the defense budget available for procuring new equipment has now shrunk to 17% (see **Figure 2**), further reducing the volume of new platforms produced (see **Figure 3**).[25] These constraints make it all the more important for Japan to leverage internal balancing efforts in conjunction with external balancing against China through the U.S.-Japan alliance.

---

[24] "Gaiko ni kansuru Yoron Chosa" [Public Opinion Poll on Diplomacy], Naikakufu Daijin Kanbo Seifu Kohoshitsu, January 30, 2012, http://www8.cao.go.jp/survey/h23/h23-gaiko/zh/z10.html.

[25] For a full analysis of Japan's defense budget and the impact on the Japan Self Defense Forces' ability to procure new equipment and national strategic autonomy, see Christopher W. Hughes, "The Slow Death of Japanese Techno-Nationalism? Emerging Comparative Lessons for China's Defense Production," *Journal of Strategic Studies* 34, no. 3 (2011): 451–79.

FIGURE 1   Japanese defense expenditure, 1985–2011 (millions of yen)

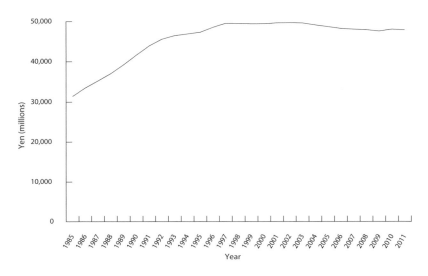

SOURCE: Japan Defense Agency and Japan Ministry of Defense, *Nihon no boei: Boei hakusho* [Defense of Japan: Defense White Paper], various years.

FIGURE 2   Percentage of the Japanese defense budget spent on equipment procurement, 1988–2011

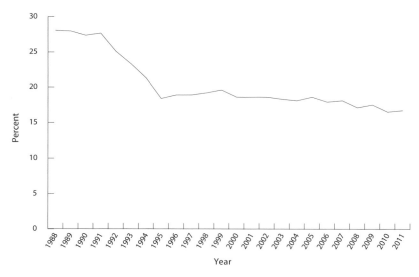

SOURCE: Japan Defense Agency and Japan Ministry of Defense, *Nihon no boei*, various years.

FIGURE 3   Japanese procurement of weapon platforms, 1990–2010

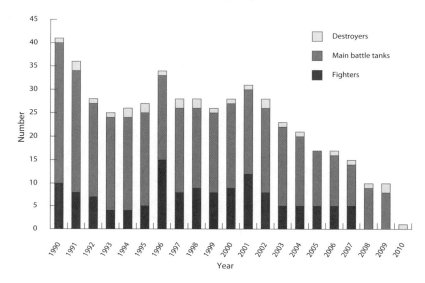

SOURCE: Japan Defense Agency and Japan Ministry of Defense, *Nihon no boei*, various years.

Japan's External Balancing through the U.S.-Japan Alliance

Japanese policymakers, as noted above, have consistently utilized the U.S.-Japan alliance as an indispensable, if not indeed their principal, hedge against China's military rise. This dependency, as the junior partner in the bilateral framework, on the United States, and Japan's consequent possibility of finding itself confronting not just its own bilateral strategic pressures from China but also being caught between the interactions of its U.S. ally and China, has always carried the alliance-dilemma risks of abandonment and entrapment. Japanese foreign and defense policy planners have feared U.S. abandonment in the event of strategic accommodation between the United States and China, especially if Japan's security interests are not deemed by the United States to converge with its own core interests and warrant the mobilization of U.S. forces in defense of Japan. Some Japanese analysts suspect that the defense of the Senkaku Islands, even though it is included under the scope of Article 5 of the bilateral security treaty, could be just such an issue where the United States would be reluctant to intervene on Japan's behalf for fear of putting the entire Sino-U.S. relationship at risk. In particular, they worry that if China were to seize the islands first, the United States would be reluctant to help Japan recover the territories through a full-scale conflict, even if it is willing to assist in deterring such aggression.[26] Indeed, this lack of faith in U.S. security guarantees has apparently spurred Tokyo governor Shintaro Ishihara's provocative move, publicly announced in April 2012, for his municipal government to attempt to purchase the Senkaku Islands from their private owners. Ishihara hopes to cajole the central Japanese government into possibly taking its own actions to procure the islands in order to bolster national territorial claims and defenses.[27]

Japanese abandonment concerns are exacerbated by the fact that the United States might lack not only the commitment to intervene in these types of regional conflicts but also the necessary military power to counter China's probing and access-denial strategy. The consequence is that Japanese defense planners and analysts have increasingly focused on assessing the degree of implementation of the United States' air-sea battle (ASB) concept as a means to judge the surety of U.S. capabilities to face off against China. Additionally, they have stressed the need for Japan's own military strategy and capability to complement ASB planning.[28]

Conversely, Japan must consider the possibility of not only confronting bilateral strategic pressure from China but also being caught in the strategic interactions between China and the United States. Entrapment concerns have historically revolved around the possibility of Japan becoming embroiled in a Sino-U.S. conflict, such as in the Taiwan Strait, that does not fully converge with its own core interests.

As a result of these fears of abandonment and entrapment, all Japanese administrations have attempted to obviate these types of dilemmas through a mixture of engagement with China to dampen conflict and elaborate hedging games within and outside the U.S.-Japan alliance to preserve limits

---

[26] Magosaki Ukeru, "Nichibei Domei o zettai shisubekarazu: Beigun ga Nihon o mamoru to kagiranai Riyu," in *Nihon no Ronten 2012* [Japan's Debating Points in 2012], ed. Bungei Shunjuhen (Tokyo: Bungei Shunju, 2012), 120–23; and Magosaki Ukeru, *Fuyukai no genjitsu: Chugoku no taikokuka, Beikoku no senryaku Tenkan* [Unpleasant Realities: China's Rise to Great Power, America's Change of Strategy] (Tokyo: Kodansha Gendai Shinsho, 2012), 130–34.

[27] Ishihara Shintaro, *Shin Darukuron: Gayoku to Tenbatsu* [New Depravity Theory: Egoism and Heaven's Judgment] (Tokyo: Shincho Shinsho, 2011), 78–81.

[28] Yoichi Kato, "Japan's Response to New U.S. Defense Strategy: 'Welcome but…,'" Center for Strategic and International Studies (CSIS), PacNet, no. 17, March 15, 2012, http://csis.org/files/publication/Pac1217.pdf; and Michael McDevitt, "The Evolving Maritime Security Environment in East Asia: Implications for the U.S.-Japan Alliance," CSIS, PacNet, no. 33, March 31, 2012, http://csis.org/publication/pacnet-33-evolving-maritime-security-environment-east-asia-implications-us-japan-alliance.

on Japanese military commitments to the United States.[29] As noted earlier, the DPJ initially pursued this type of strategy. The party worked to redouble engagement with China and strengthen U.S.-Japan alliance ties in certain areas, while at the same time attempting to back away from the LDP's previous military commitments to broader U.S. military campaigns and strategy, which it saw as increasing the risk of entrapment in various security scenarios.

Nevertheless, as argued above, the DPJ is now swinging back firmly, and perhaps more firmly than the LDP ever did, toward recentralizing the United States within Japan's grand strategy in order to cope with China's rise. This prioritization of the U.S.-Japan alliance has clearly been catalyzed by the DPJ's failure to gain traction in moderating China's assertiveness over territorial issues in the East China Sea and the general trajectory of its military buildup. Thus, Japan has currently demoted its concerns about entrapment and seeks above all to prevent military abandonment by the United States at this crucial juncture in Sino-Japanese relations.

Japan's recentering of the United States in its grand strategy toward the Asia-Pacific region and vis-à-vis China is demonstrated politically by the DPJ's move away from active support for an EAC as its preferred future mechanism for macro-regional cooperation and toward a new emphasis on the East Asian Summit (EAS). The United States was not envisaged as a member of the former, whereas it has been a full participant in the latter since 2011. Thus, Japan can bring the United States' presence to bear in checking Chinese influence in designing regional frameworks and pushing alternatives such as the ASEAN +3. Economically, the DPJ has indicated since November 2010 that it intends to participate in the Trans-Pacific Partnership (TPP) in order to facilitate the larger, long-term goal of creating a free trade area for the Asia-Pacific. The United States has emerged as the de facto leader of efforts to negotiate the TPP, while China is unlikely to become a participant. Japan has not abandoned participation in other emerging frameworks for economic cooperation that are also viewed as building momentum for a free trade area encompassing the entire region, such as an East Asian free trade area, the Comprehensive Economic Partnership for East Asia, and a Northeast Asia trilateral free trade agreement, which all include China as a member. Nevertheless, the fact that Japan is now attempting to prioritize the TPP in the face of stiff domestic opposition signifies that it intends to push a U.S.-led and Asia-Pacific–dominant standard for regional cooperation. Japan hopes

---

[29] Eric Heginbotham and Richard J. Samuels, "Japan's Dual Hedge," *Foreign Affairs* 81, no. 5 (2003): 110–23.

that China will ultimately have to subscribe to this standard and accept limits on its ability to lead a counter-region centered on East Asia.[30]

In security terms, the DPJ has clearly accelerated moves to strengthen the alliance following the 2010 incident over the Senkaku Islands. The 2010 NDPG was devised with close linkages to the United States' own 2010 Quadrennial Defense Review (QDR), and Japan's reorientation toward the United States has coincided in general with Washington's own rebalancing toward the Asia-Pacific, announced in January 2012.[31] Japan's confidence in U.S. security guarantees received a boost in September 2010 following the Senkaku Islands incident, when Secretary of State Hillary Clinton and then secretary of defense Robert Gates offered swift assurances that Article 5 of the security treaty encompassed the islands. The U.S.-Japan alliance was further strengthened in the wake of the March 11 disasters. The United States launched Operation Tomodachi (literally "Operation Friend"), which utilized the full panoply of U.S. military assets in Japan and the Pacific, including 20 U.S. Navy (USN) vessels, 140 aircraft, and 20,000 USMC personnel, to support the JSDF's mobilization of 100,000 troops for disaster relief.

The DPJ's early attempts to revisit plans under the 2006 Defense Policy Review Initiative (DPRI) for the relocation of the Futenma Air Station inside Okinawa Prefecture were a political and diplomatic debacle. Since mid-2010, the party has advocated reverting to the original bilateral agreements, despite continued local opposition to the implementation of this policy. The DPJ has been assisted in these plans by Washington's easing of immediate pressure for the relocation of Futenma. In February 2012 the United States agreed to relocate 4,700 USMC personnel, rather than the full 8,000 originally requested, from Okinawa to Guam without predicating these moves on a resolution of the Futenma issue. Japan's cooperation with the United States on base realignments under the DPRI has continued with support for the relocation of the USS George Washington's carrier wing to Iwakuni on Honshu. More generally, the DPJ's support for the U.S. military presence in Japan was demonstrated by its agreement in 2010 to maintain host-nation support at the same levels for 2011–15 in spite of budgetary pressures. Moreover, in regard to BMD—perhaps the most important long-term driver of U.S.-Japan military integration—cooperation under the DPJ has rolled forward. Japan and the United States have continued to jointly develop the SM-3 Block IIA interceptor missile, and the U.S.-Japan Security Consultative Committee

---

[30] Takashi Terada, "Trade Winds: Big Power Politics and Asia-Pacific Economic Integration," *Global Asia* 7, no. 1 (2012): 90–95.

[31] Boeisho Kenkyushohen, *Higashi Ajia senryaku gaiyo 2012*, 224–25; Hillary Clinton, "America's Pacific Century," *Foreign Policy*, November 2011, 56–63; and U.S. Department of Defense, "Sustaining U.S. Global Leadership: Priorities for 21st Century Defense," January 2012, 2, http://www.defense.gov/news/Defense_Strategic_Guidance.pdf.

(SCC) agreed in June 2011 that Japan would make an exemption to its arms export ban in order to permit the export of the missile to other countries.[32] Furthermore, in April 2012, Japan and the United States completed DPRI plans for collocation of the ASDF Air Defense Command with that of the USAF at Yokota Air Base near Tokyo. The move is intended to improve information-sharing in response to missile attacks.[33]

Japan under the DPJ has also picked up the pace of cooperation by updating the 2005 and 2007 "common strategic objectives" of the bilateral alliance during the 2011 SCC process. Japan and the United States pledged to continue to press China on its military transparency; noted the complementarities of Japan's DDF concept in the NDPG and the U.S. commitment in the QDR to meeting the regional challenges posed by China's ballistic-missile program and A2/AD strategy, as well as to ensuring cyber and maritime security; and agreed that both sides would enhance cooperation in responding to regional contingencies through measures such as strengthened joint ISR.[34]

The SCC's update of the common strategic objectives also strongly endorsed Japan's support for the U.S. presence in the region through the building of security links with a range of other U.S. partners. Japan and Australia's security ties have advanced relatively steadily since the "Joint Declaration on Security" in 2003, and the DPJ administration concluded an acquisition and cross-servicing agreement (ACSA) with Australia in 2010 for the sharing of military logistical support in peacetime and UN operations. Modeled on Japan's ACSA with the United States signed in 1996 and revised in 1999, the agreement clearly provides a template compatible for possible trilateral logistical cooperation among Japan, the United States, and Australia in the future.

In contrast, Japanese security ties with India have proceeded more slowly since their initial Joint Declaration on Security and Cooperation in 2008. But the DPJ administration appears willing to step up cooperation with this emerging U.S. partner. Japan conducted the foreign ministry's first-ever trilateral security talks at the director level with the United States and India in December 2011 and reached an agreement with India to hold joint naval maritime security exercises in 2012.

---

[32] Hillary Clinton et al., "Toward a Deeper and Broader Alliance: Building on 50 Years of Partnership," Joint Statement of the Security Consultative Committee, June 21, 2011, 9, http://www.mofa.go.jp/region/n-america/us/security/pdfs/joint1106_01.pdf. The SCC comprises the two countries' defense and foreign ministers and is the principal coordinating mechanism for the alliance.

[33] "ASDF Command Now at Yokota Base," *Japan Times*, March 27, 2012, http://www.japantimes.co.jp/text/nn20120327a2.html.

[34] Clinton, "Toward a Deeper and Broader Alliance," 4, 7–8.

Similarly, Japan and the DPJ government have been more willing to explore meaningful ties with South Korea, another important U.S. partner. MSDF officers for the first time observed U.S.-ROK military exercises in July 2010 as a demonstration of trilateral unity in the wake of the *Cheonan* incident. South Korean naval officers then participated as observers for the first time in large-scale U.S.-Japan military exercises in December 2010, this time following North Korea's bombardment of Yeonpyeong Island. Since early 2011, Japan and South Korea have been considering, and in April 2012 were reportedly close to signing, an ACSA and general security of military information agreement for the exchange of BMD early warning intelligence, although in May 2012 the South Korean government shied away from finally concluding the agreements due to domestic political sensitivities over military cooperation with Japan. Japan and South Korea attempted to sign the agreements again in June, only for the South to again pull out twenty minutes before the ceremony, precipitating the resignation of President Lee Myung-bak's advisers in the face of domestic criticism of the secretive nature by which the agreements had been negotiated.[35]

In addition, Japan has followed the U.S. agenda in supporting the ASEAN states against pressure from China in the South China Sea. The JCG continues to demonstrate Japanese maritime presence in the region through cooperation on antipiracy. Japan and Indonesia also held their own strategic dialogue on maritime issues in February 2011, and Japan concluded a joint statement on enhancing its strategic partnership with ASEAN in November 2011, which pledged to promote cooperation on maritime security in the region.[36]

Japan's support for the U.S. agenda has thus moved the United States squarely back into the center of Japan's strategic calculations for responding to the rise of China. Nevertheless, Japan's external balancing with the United States is still likely to encounter obstacles. Both countries must contend with immediate problems in their joint management of the alliance that could undermine its stability. Operation Tomodachi undoubtedly improved the alliance's political confidence, but contrary to some predictions has not created sufficient momentum to help achieve a decisive breakthrough on the Okinawa issue. The United States' decoupling of Futenma from the rest of the DPRI is helpful in the short term but has created other concerns for Japan. Specifically, it may reduce the incentives for both sides to resolve the issue in the longer term, leading to the USMC facility remaining in its

---

[35] "Nikkan Boei 2 kyoryoku, sakiokuri: Kankokunai de shinchoron" [Postponing Two Japan–South Korea Defense Cooperation Agreements: Caution Due to Domestic Politics], *Yomiuri Shimbun*, May 19, 2012.

[36] Japan Ministry of Foreign Affairs, "Joint Statement for Enhancing Japan-ASEAN Strategic Partnership for Prospering Together (Bali Declaration)," November 18, 2011, 3, http://www.mofa.go.jp/region/asia-paci/asean/conference/pdfs/bali_declaration_en_1111.pdf.

current location and engendering further local opposition to U.S. bases in Okinawa. Recent U.S. requests for Japan to fund the repair of the Futenma runway in the absence of any immediate prospect for relocation only compound fears of the issue remaining unresolved. Moreover, the United States' failed requests for Japan to increase funding for USMC realignment to Guam, despite the fact that with the decoupling of Futenma the scale of the reduction of burden on Okinawa would have actually decreased, could have generated bilateral frictions.[37]

But even more important for the success of Japan's external balancing efforts will be a shared sense of the credibility of U.S. security guarantees. From the Japanese perspective, China's maritime activity in the East China Sea poses an increasingly important test of the threshold necessary for the United States to support Japan's territorial integrity and broader security. Japan's new DDF doctrine may to some extent deter Chinese activity and thus help avert any probing of this threshold. However, Japanese anxieties over the United States' willingness to intervene in these types of scenarios may ultimately expose weaknesses in the alliance that need to be addressed.

Hence, Tokyo continues to harbor doubts about Washington's budgetary ability to back up its commitments and strategies with the deployment of hard military capabilities. These doubts will persist even if Japanese policymakers look to support ASB through the DDF and encourage the United States' shift of naval and air assets to the Asia-Pacific—having drawn reassurance from Secretary of Defense Leon Panetta's indication in June 2012 that the United States will deploy 60% of its naval assets to the region.[38] Similarly, although North Korea remains a second-order security issue for Japan compared with China, any sign of failure of U.S. implacability to contain North Korea in response to missile and nuclear tests will be taken as a wider indication of the lack of U.S. commitment to support Japan against China.

---

[37] "Futenma koteika no kennen: hoshuhi yokyu" [Concerns at the Immovability of Futenma: Requests for Additional Funding], *Asahi Shimbun*, April 5, 2012, 3.

[38] Leon Panetta, "The U.S. Rebalance Towards the Asia-Pacific" (remarks at the Shangri-La Dialogue of the 11th IISS Asia Security Summit, Singapore, June 2, 2012), http://www.iiss.org/conferences/the-shangri-la-dialogue/shangri-la-dialogue-2012/speeches/first-plenary-session/leon-panetta/; and "Ajia Taiheiyo no Beikaigun kyoka, kinketsu tsuzuki jitsugen futomei" [The Strengthening of the U.S. Navy in the Asia-Pacific, A Lack of Clarity in Implementation as a Lack of Funds Continues], *Yomiuri Shimbun*, June 6, 2012, http://www.yomiuri.co.jp/world/news/20120602-OYT1T00833.htm.

South Korea: The Korean Peninsula and Post-Reunification Concerns toward China

South Korea's Grand Strategy and China

Among the three powers analyzed in this chapter, South Korea is the one that has been forced to react the least and most indirectly to China's military modernization. The ROK's most immediate security concern remains North Korea. Nonetheless, South Korean policymakers increasingly recognize the need for a grand strategy to contend with China's rise and the associated military challenges both from growing Chinese influence over North Korea and directly from Chinese military modernization. Likewise, they now recognize the importance of pursuing hedging strategies through internal balancing and also external balancing via the U.S.-ROK alliance.

Since the normalization of ROK-China relations in 1992, South Korea has emerged as a highly committed engager of China. Efforts at engagement have been spectacularly successful economically, with China surpassing the United States to become South Korea's largest trading partner in 2004 and the number-one destination for South Korean FDI in 2000 (including a near 300% increase between 2003 and 2004).[39] In turn, South Korea's growing interdependence with China, especially economically, has begun to generate questions about South Korean grand strategy, as recent presidential administrations have wrestled with the implications of China's rise.

The administration of President Roh Moo-hyun (2003–8), in line with booming Sino–South Korean economic interdependence and China's growing influence over North Korea, appeared to pursue a pronounced "tilt" toward China in its grand strategy. The flip side of this growing strategic convergence with China was a degree of diplomatic distancing from the United States. Roh attempted to establish more equidistance between the two great powers through elaborating the concept of the South as a regional balancer in Northeast Asia.[40] In terms of defense policy, the Roh administration's call for a "cooperative self-reliant" military posture indicated its intention to shift away from exclusive strategic reliance on the United States. More generally, Roh seemed to contribute to a mood in wider South Korean society of disaffection

---

[39] David Kang, "South Korea's Embrace of Interdependence in Pursuit of Security," in *Strategic Asia 2006–07: Trade, Interdependence, and Security*, ed. Ashley J. Tellis and Michael Wills (Seattle: National Bureau of Asian Research, 2006), 146–47; Samuel S. Kim, *The Two Koreas and the Great Powers* (Cambridge: Cambridge University Press, 2006), 75–80; and Jonathan D. Pollack, "The Korean Peninsula in U.S. Strategy: Policy Choices for the Next President," in *Strategic Asia 2008–09: Challenges and Choices*, ed. Ashley J. Tellis, Mercy Kuo, and Andrew Marble (Seattle: National Bureau of Asian Research, 2008), 140–41.

[40] Sukhee Han, "From Engagement to Hedging: South Korea's New China Policy," *Korean Journal of Defense Analysis* 20, no. 4 (2008): 336.

with the U.S.-ROK alliance, even to the point of anti-Americanism.[41] The Roh administration's policies have even been construed as the beginnings of South Korea as a small power being drawn into China's strategic orbit and thus bandwagoning with an emerging Sino-centric regional order.

In fact, a more straightforward interpretation is that South Korea was initiating strategic hedging behavior, confronted for the first time by the dilemma of navigating strategic relations with two major partners. Even though the Roh administration oversaw the significant strengthening of the U.S.-ROK alliance, this process was perceived to contain significant alliance dilemmas of abandonment and entrapment vis-à-vis the United States and concomitantly security dilemmas vis-à-vis China. Navigating these risks necessitated strategic hedging by South Korea.

If the Roh administration tilted South Korea toward China for reasons of economic interdependence and strategic hedging, then this logic has dictated that, under the successor administration of President Lee Myung-bak, the South has swung back toward the U.S. strategic fold as more negative views of China's rise have taken hold. In the earlier stages of the Roh administration, China's rise was viewed as predominantly benign in nature, but by the administration's later stages Sino–South Korean relations began to deteriorate over a range of issues, reflecting fears of increasing Chinese dominance. These issues included China's assertions over the historical origins of the Goguryeo Kingdom in the northern part of the Korean Peninsula, creating suspicions that Beijing might entertain territorial claims; disregard for human rights in returning escapees back to North Korea; apparent lack of will in cooperating with the South and the international community to halt the North's nuclear program; and growing economic dominance over the South in trade relations.[42] The result is that, according to a 2011 poll, China was seen by 63% of Koreans as the greatest threat to Korea post-unification, whereas only 21% and 12% of respondents, respectively, perceived Japan and the United States as threats.[43]

This changing perception of China's rise, interlinked with dissatisfaction toward the Roh administration's North Korea policy, has forced a general recalibration of North Korea strategy, U.S.-ROK alliance ties, and Sino–South Korean relations under the Lee administration. As will be explained below,

---

[41] Gi-Wook Shin, *One Alliance, Two Lenses: U.S.–South Korea Relations in a New Era* (Stanford: Stanford University Press), 2010, 197–200; and National Institute for Defense Studies, *East Asian Strategic Review* (Tokyo: Japan Times, 2006), 91.

[42] Jae Ho Chung, "China's 'Soft' Clash with South Korea: The History War and Beyond," *Asian Survey* 49, no. 3 (2009): 468–74; and Scott Snyder, *China's Rise and the Two Koreas: Politics, Economics, Security* (Boulder: Lynne Rienner, 2009), 94–104.

[43] Karl Friedhoff, "South Korea 2011: The Asan Institute's Annual Survey," Asan Institute for Policy Studies, 2012, 16, http://asaninst.org/eng/01_research/public_list.php.

this strategic agenda involves arresting South Korea's move away from the United States and instituting a new harder hedge against China's military modernization through internal and external balancing.

South Korean Concerns over China's Doctrines and Capabilities

Defense Reform 2020, which was released by the Korean Ministry of National Defense (MND) in 2006 as the principal document for initiating new military planning for the ROK armed forces, provides a sense of the types of concerns that China's military modernization has engendered in South Korea. In some ways the product of the Roh administration's heavy engagement with North Korea and China, Defense Reform 2020 estimated that the possibility of full-scale war on the Korean Peninsula was declining. The plan was reluctant, though, to designate alternative sources of threat due to apparent fears of creating new regional antagonisms. Moreover, the Korean MND shortly thereafter was obliged to revise its estimates of Korean Peninsula security in reaction to North Korea's renewed threat posture, especially in terms of the North's asymmetric capabilities to penetrate South Korea's defenses, as seen in the *Cheonan* sinking and Yeonpyeong bombardment incidents of 2010. The result is Defense Reform 307, which was adopted in 2011 and modifies Defense Form 2020 in order to bolster South Korea's ability to respond to North Korean asymmetric threats, specifically through enhanced early warning and command and control.

Even though North Korea has returned to the forefront of the Korean MND's immediate security concerns, Defense Reform 2020 and its longer-term plans to institute new structures and capabilities for the ROK military—beyond those necessary to respond to North Korean threats—hint at China as a future priority for national defense efforts. South Korean defense planners appear to envisage a number of scenarios for national security arising from China's military modernization.

The ROK military still must plan for a full-scale conflict on the Korean Peninsula, which might trigger Chinese military intervention. But more specifically, in a conflict short of all-out war, many analysts believe that China might choose to intervene primarily through maritime access-denial activities aimed at complicating U.S. naval deployments and South Korean SLOCs in the Yellow Sea.[44] China's strong objections to exercises between the USN and ROK Navy (ROKN) in the Yellow Sea in November 2010, following the Yeonpyeong incident, may reflect its concern with any resistance to future

---

[44] Bruce W. Bennett, *A Brief Analysis of the Republic of Korea's Defense Reform Plan* (Santa Monica: RAND, 2006), 18.

Chinese dominance in this area.[45] Similarly, scenarios of North Korean collapse, whether occurring peacefully or otherwise, raise clear concerns for Korean MND planners with regard to Chinese military power. The ROK military needs sufficient capabilities to move north in order to meet a PLA southward intervention to secure North Korea's nuclear weapons; to conduct stability operations in the North during a possible PLA occupation of other parts of the country; and, eventually, to maintain border security with China in a reunited Korea.[46]

Even more interestingly, South Korea now appears to be preparing for an entirely new set of threats from China not entirely related to the Korean Peninsula and primarily derived from China's maritime modernization. These threats include increasing pressure from China over maritime disputes in the Yellow Sea, such as the dispute over the sovereignty of Socotra Rock (also known as Ieodo or Suyan) in 2006, violent clashes between trawlers over fishing grounds in 2010 and 2011, and tensions over SLOCs, as both countries compete for stable energy supplies. In addition, South Korea is planning for the possibility that it may become caught, in classic middle-power style, in a Sino-Japanese maritime arms race, necessitating a more robust ROKN presence to fend off these two larger powers.[47]

South Korea's Internal Balancing in Response to China

Defense Reform 2020 and subsequent revisions of this plan in the Lee administration's defense master plan of 2009 have initiated a significant strengthening of the ROK military. The plans again largely address North Korea's growing asymmetric threat but at the same time add capabilities to ensure against threats outside the immediate Korean Peninsula, including China's rise.

The defense master plan emphasizes an overall modernization of South Korea's defense posture: a reduction of the total number of personnel from 655,000 in 2009 to 517,000 by 2020 (originally planned for 500,000 under

---

[45] Chung Min Lee, "Coping with Giants: South Korea's Response to India's and China's Rise," in *Strategic Asia 2011–12: Asia Responds to Its Rising Powers—China and India*, ed. Ashley J. Tellis, Travis Tanner, and Jessica Keough (Seattle: National Bureau of Asian Research, 2011), 180.

[46] Chung Min Lee, "Reassessing the ROK-U.S. Alliance: Transformation Challenges and the Consequences of South Korea's Choices," *Australian Journal of International Affairs* 57, no. 5 (2003): 297–98; and Bruce W. Bennett and Jennifer Lind, "North Korean Collapse: Military Missions and Requirements," *International Security* 36, no. 2 (2011): 84–119.

[47] Jae Ho Chung, "China's Place in South Korea's Security Matrix," in *Beyond North Korea: Future Challenges to South Korea's Security*, ed. Byung Kwan Kim, Gi-Wook Shin, and David Straub (Stanford: Shorenstein Asia-Pacific Research Center, 2011), 143–44; National Institute for Defense Studies, *East Asian Strategic Review 2007* (Tokyo: Japan Times, 2007), 87; and Tae-Hyo Kim, "Korea's Strategic Thoughts toward Japan: Searching for a Democratic Future in the Past-Driven Present," *Korean Journal of Defense Analysis* 20, no. 2 (2008): 147.

Defense Reform 2020), the greater professionalization of the military by increasing the proportion of volunteers, and a general rebalancing of the military away from the ROK Army (ROKA), which currently accounts for around 80% of personnel, toward the ROK Air Force (ROKAF) and the ROKN. The MND's objective is furthermore to create a more technologically advanced military, one that is capable of network-centric warfare and joint operations, by replacing up to half of its total weaponry with new systems.[48]

The ROKA is to be strengthened through the introduction of a multiple-launch rocket system, the upgraded K1A1 and new K2 main battle tanks, the K-21 infantry fighting vehicle, and unmanned aerial vehicles (UAV). The ROKAF is investing in 60 F-15K fighters and the Boeing 737 AEW&C, and has plans to acquire a fifth-generation KF-X fighter. However, it is the ROKN that has undergone the most striking developments. The Korean navy has procured Aegis air-defense systems in the new KDX-3 (Sejong-class) DDG; the multipurpose KDX-2 (Chungmugong Yi Sun-shin–class) DDH; the 14,000-ton Dokdo (LPH-6111), which offers improved amphibious capability and is in essence a light helicopter carrier; and Type 214 (Son Won-il–class) SSKs.[49] These new technologies have converted South Korea into a serious blue water naval power in Northeast Asia and provide the capability to meet China's expanding maritime activities symmetrically.

Despite South Korea's ambitious plans to acquire a more flexible military with enhanced power-projection capabilities, there remain considerable domestic constraints on internal balancing. Domestic politics and the differences in policies toward North Korea between the Roh and Lee administrations obviously play a role in influencing security strategy. That said, there is actually significant agreement between Defense Reform 2020 and the defense master plan in terms of projecting a stronger military posture beyond the Korean Peninsula itself. Instead, the principal domestic constraint is the inability of governments to prevent the politicization of defense expenditure. Defense Reform 2020 set the goal of annual 10% increases in defense expenditure from 2006 to 2010, followed by 9% annual increases until 2015 and then 1% increases until 2020. But the 10% goal was lowered to 7% in 2006 and then revised to 7.6% in the defense master plan

---

[48] Bennett, *A Brief Analysis of the Republic of Korea's Defense Reform Plan*, 87; and Michael Raska, "RMA Diffusion Paths and Patterns in South Korea's Military Modernization," *Korean Journal of Defense Analysis* 23, no. 3 (2011): 378–80.

[49] Yoji Koda, "The Emerging Republic of Korea Navy," *Naval War College Review* 63, no. 2 (2010): 23–26.

of 2009, though in fact there was only a 3.6% increase in 2010.[50] Hence, in spite of the impressive increase of government resources for defense (see **Figure 4**), it appears that the Korean MND is falling short of the pace and level necessary to fund all of its defense programs.

FIGURE 4   South Korean defense budget, 1998–2010 (trillions of won)

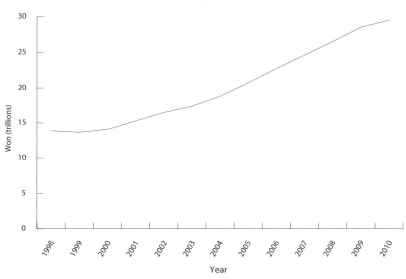

SOURCE: International Institute for Strategic Studies, *The Military Balance* (London: Routledge, various years).

South Korea's External Balancing through the U.S.-ROK Alliance

The U.S.-ROK alliance is certainly crucial for South Korea's current deterrence of North Korea and for future deterrence of a rising China. As noted earlier, however, the alliance has been strained in recent years, precipitating more pronounced South Korean strategic hedging. Thus, future external balancing of China through the bilateral alliance is unlikely to proceed in a smooth, linear fashion.

---

[50] Bennett, *A Brief Analysis of the Republic of Korea's Defense Reform Plan*, 21–22; National Institute for Defense Studies, *East Asian Strategic Review 2010* (Tokyo: Japan Times, 2010), 96–97; and ROK Ministry of National Defense, *2010 Defense White Paper* (Seoul, 2010), 407, http://www.mnd.go.kr/cms_file/info/mndpaper/2010/2010WhitePaperAll_eng.pdf.

In many ways these pressures are actually the product of substantial bilateral achievements in recent years that boosted the military strength of the alliance, even under the supposedly anti-alliance Roh administration. The U.S. Global Posture Review (GPR) and the 2003 Future of the U.S.-ROK Alliance Policy Initiative succeeded in the realignment objectives of consolidating the U.S. Army and USAF military presence in South Korea south of the Demilitarized Zone (DMZ) around Osan and Pyeongtaek (in contrast to the still partially gridlocked process of realignment in Japan). The solidity of the alliance was further demonstrated by the dispatch of ROKA medical personnel and engineers to Iraq between 2003 and 2008, in the face of considerable domestic opposition. The Korean contingent in Iraq had a regular complement of six hundred personnel but at one point reached more than three thousand.

Nevertheless, these moves to strengthen the bilateral alliance have simultaneously enhanced the risks of abandonment and entrapment for South Korea. The U.S. realignment of forces south of the DMZ signaled for some South Korean policymakers that this crucial "tripwire" presence had been removed. They worried that the North might be emboldened to attack but that the United States would no longer be obligated to intervene. Moreover, the U.S. determination under the GPR to free up forces to respond to other regional and global contingencies raised questions about the denuding of the U.S. security presence in South Korea. Conversely, Korean policymakers were afraid that the withdrawal of U.S. forces to south of the DMZ might enable Washington to launch preemptive attacks on the North. Furthermore, they grew concerned that the United States might seek to use its new hubs at Osan and Pyeongtaek to support intervention in a Taiwan Strait crisis, thus drawing South Korea into an undesirable war with China.[51]

The Lee administration, though, has largely succeeded in overriding South Korean fears of entrapment. Instead, it has emphasized the need to avoid abandonment in the face of North Korean provocations and respond to new concerns about the rise of Chinese military power. Consequently, the Lee administration has swung firmly back into the U.S. security fold with the announcement of the Joint Vision for the Alliance of the ROK and the United States in 2009 and has pledged to reinforce military cooperation as well as for the United States to maintain extended nuclear deterrence over South Korea.[52] Moreover, as noted previously, South Korea has appeared more willing than

<hr>

[51] Chang-hee Nam, "Relocating the U.S. Forces in South Korea: Strained Alliance, Emerging Partnership in the Changing Defense Posture," *Asian Survey* 46, no. 4 (2006): 626; and Jonathan D. Pollack, "The Strategic Future and Military Capabilities of the Two Koreas," in *Strategic Asia 2005–06: Military Modernization in an Era of Uncertainty*, ed. Ashley J. Tellis and Michael Wills (Seattle: National Bureau of Asian Research, 2005), 153.

[52] Republic of Korea Ministry of National Defense, *2010 Defense White Paper*, 78–79.

before to pursue trilateral security cooperation with the United States and Japan. A public opinion poll in 2011 even indicated that 54% of South Koreans were in favor of an ROK-Japan alliance to fend off China in the event of Korean reunification.[53] However, historical animosities regarding the colonial past and the territorial dispute over the Dokdo/Takeshima Islands, as well as possible perceptions of a remilitarized Japan as a threat to national security, continue to hamper fuller South Korean participation in trilateral security.[54]

Taiwan: Asymmetric Balancing of China's Asymmetric Capabilities

Taiwan's Strategy and Views of China's Military Modernization

Taiwan's grand strategy and defense policy are driven overwhelmingly by the condition of relations with China and assessments of its military modernization. Nevertheless, even within these relatively tightly defined strategic parameters, transitions in domestic politics have meant that different Taiwanese administrations have in varying degrees both engaged with China and concomitantly resorted to hedging by means of strengthening national military power or attempts to reinforce quasi-alliance ties with the United States. Chen Shui-bian's Democratic Progressive Party (DPP) administration (2000–2008) managed not only to alienate China through intimating moves toward *de jure* independence but also to gradually disaffect U.S. Democratic and then Republican administrations, which similarly disapproved of the potential destabilization of the political status quo across the Taiwan Strait. In contrast, Ma Ying-jeou's Kuomintang (KMT) administration has shown a willingness for closer engagement of China and preservation of the status quo, while more skillfully maneuvering to improve U.S.-Taiwan relations.

As will be detailed later, even though the DPP and KMT may diverge in their assessments of the optimal means to respond to China's rise, both parties at least share an understanding of the scale of the mounting challenges posed by Chinese military modernization. Recent analysis of the balance of power in the Taiwan Strait argues that China has gained ascendancy in a number of crucial capabilities.[55] China's deployment of up to one thousand DF-11 and DF-15 SRBMs along the coasts of its southeastern provinces poses a massive

---

[53] Friedhoff, "The Asan Institute's Annual Survey."

[54] Note that Dokdo is the class name of the ROKN's largest amphibious ship, while the Sejong-class DDG is named after a monarch who defeated Japan in the fifteenth century. Donald Keyser, "Regional and Global Challenges to South Korea's Security," in Kim, Shin, and Straub, *Beyond North Korea*, 56–57.

[55] U.S. Office of the Secretary of Defense, *Military Developments Involving the People's Republic of China* (Washington, D.C., 2011), 47, http://www.defense.gov/pubs/pdfs/2011_cmpr_final.pdf.

asymmetric threat to Taiwan's military defense infrastructure.[56] The PLAAF also now appears to be gaining mastery in air defense over the Taiwan Strait with its deployment of fourth-generation fighters.[57] In addition, the verdict seems to be that the PLAN is acquiring both a quantitative and qualitative advantage in destroyers and submarines, which could provide it with the capacity to launch amphibious assaults, blockade Taiwan, and impose access-denial vis-à-vis U.S. attempts at intervention in the Taiwan Strait.

Taiwan's Internal Balancing in Response to China

In the face of this new reality, Taiwan's military strategy has abandoned previous pretensions of maintaining sufficient offensive power to impose its political objectives on the mainland (including the historical goal, however outlandish, of overthrowing the Communist Party) and prevail decisively in any conflict situation. Instead, Taiwan's strategy has shifted to a predominantly defense-oriented stance that is focused on achieving the more straightforward goal of national survival. This strategy aims to maintain adequate deterrent capabilities and to exact high enough costs on the PLA to prevent China from imposing its reunification objectives on Taipei.[58]

Defense planners in Taiwan continue to have hopes for a symmetrical response to China's military buildup. In part, this includes developing capabilities for air-to-air, naval-to-naval, and ground-to-ground defensive interdiction, as well as acquiring counter-force and counter-value offensive weaponry.[59] In the dimension of air defense, the ROC Air Force is attempting to match up to China's ballistic missiles and advanced fighters by procuring from the United States the PAC-3 system and requesting F-16C/Ds. Similarly, the ROC Navy has procured P-3Cs and Kidd-class DDGs, as well as requesting from the United States the Aegis system and diesel submarines, in order to meet the PLAN's enhanced submarine and destroyer capabilities.

However, the growing recognition by Taiwanese policymakers that they simply cannot succeed in a symmetric arms competition with China has encouraged recent consideration of the need to switch to a more asymmetric defense posture.[60] The Ma administration has encouraged this trend,

---

[56] Shlapak, "The Red Rockets' Glare," 74–75.

[57] U.S.-China Economic and Security Review Commission, *2010 Report to Congress*, 150–52.

[58] Michael D. Swaine and Roy D. Kamphausen, "Military Modernization in Taiwan," in Tellis and Wills, *Strategic Asia 2005–06*, 393; and Robert S. Ross, "Explaining Taiwan's Revisionist Diplomacy," *Journal of Contemporary China* 15, no. 48 (2006): 446–47.

[59] Swain and Kamphausen, "Military Modernization in Taiwan," 394, 400.

[60] Alexander Chieh-cheng Huang, "A Midterm Assessment of Taiwan's First Quadrennial Defense Review," Brookings Institution, February 3, 2012, 4, http://www.brookings.edu/papers/2011/02_taiwan_huang.aspx.

apparently influenced by U.S. assessments advocating that Taiwan adopt a defense-oriented "porcupine" strategy.[61] Increasingly, Taiwanese defense planners are emphasizing the need for the hardening of critical infrastructure, such as airfields and ports, to survive PLA missile bombardments, as well as for investment in hardware such as mines, fast missile boats, attack helicopters, and special forces. This strategy is designed to raise the costs for China of an assault on Taiwan and to buy time for a hoped-for U.S. intervention.

The first QDR of 2009 by Taiwan's Ministry of National Defense and subsequent national defense reports (NDR) significantly rethink defense policy and attempt to meet China's asymmetric threats with Taiwan's own asymmetric capabilities.[62] These reports argue for a significant transformation of Taiwan's defense posture by promoting an all-volunteer military; streamlined forces, with a reduction in total personnel from 275,000 to 215,000; and an increased capacity for joint operations between the three services. The QDR and NDR talk of "a rock-solid and impregnable defensive force that, by implication, could not be dislodged, shattered, or breached by a numerically superior enemy force during an attempt to attack or invade ROC territory."[63]

The modernization of Taiwan's defense policy in reaction to China's modernization, however, is likely to be shaped and impeded by continuing domestic contentions. Taiwan's MND is not likely to shift entirely to an asymmetric response but rather will continue to require the replacement and updating of aging equipment. For example, Taiwan continues to ask the United States for F-16C/Ds, the provision for which is seen as a key means to test the seriousness of commitments under the Taiwan Relations Act.[64] Even more importantly, just as in Japan and South Korea, the trajectory of military modernization will be dictated by the availability of national budgetary resources. Defense procurements have been regularly subject to budget disputes between the DPP and KMT in the Legislative Yuan. The two parties have disagreed over whether plans to procure equipment from the United States fit Taiwan's defense profile, represent value for money, and are overly

---

[61] Baohui Zhang, "Taiwan's New Grand Strategy," *Journal of Contemporary China* 20, no. 69 (2011): 278–80; and William S. Murray, "Revisiting Taiwan's Defense Strategy," *Naval War College Review* 61, no. 3 (2008): 13–37.

[62] Julia M. Famularo, *The Taiwan Quadrennial Defense Review: Implications for U.S.-Taiwan Relations*, Project 2049 Institute, June 22, 2009, 3, http://project2049.net/documents/the_taiwan_quadrennial_defense_review_implications_for_US_taiwan_relations.pdf.

[63] Republic of China (ROC) Ministry of National Defense, *Quadrennial Defense Review 2009*, 10; and ROC Ministry of National Defense, *National Defense Report 2011*, http://2011mndreport.mnd.gov.tw/en/info07html.

[64] Famularo, *The Taiwan Quadrennial Defense Review*, 9; and U.S.-China Economic and Security Review Commission, *2010 Report to Congress*, 151–52.

provocative toward China.[65] Moreover, despite the fact that Taiwan is pitted against rising Chinese military expenditure, the defense budget continues to fall with the deterioration of the national economy in the midst of the global financial crisis (see **Figure 5**). This trend suggests a lack of serious prioritization of the military.[66]

FIGURE 5   Taiwan defense budget, 1998–2011 (billions of Taiwan dollars)

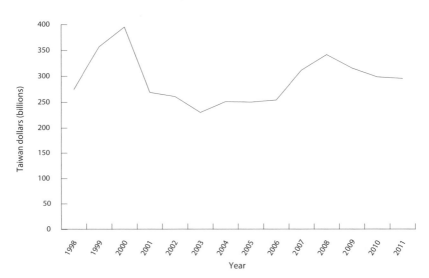

SOURCE: International Institute for Strategic Studies, *The Military Balance*, various years.

Taiwan's External Balancing through U.S.-Taiwan Relations

Taiwan's internal balancing efforts vis-à-vis China are clearly highly dependent also on external balancing with the United States, either through the continued supply of advanced military weaponry or the possible eventuality of U.S. intervention in a Taiwan Strait conflict. As seen with other

---

[65] Shirley A. Kan, "Taiwan: Major U.S. Arms Sales since 1990," Congressional Research Service, CRS Report for Congress, RL30957, September 15, 2011, 33–43; and Swain and Kamphausen, "Military Modernization in Taiwan," 398.

[66] Huang, "A Midterm Assessment of Taiwan's First Quadrennial Defense Review," 3.

U.S. partners in Northeast Asia, however, Taiwan's dependency on the United States raises concerns of abandonment (though not entrapment, given that Taiwanese policymakers would dearly like to be more closely integrated with U.S. security strategy). These abandonment anxieties spring partially from the fact that the United States maintains no formal alliance or security guarantee with Taiwan. Further, the U.S. approach toward Taiwan is more influenced by the condition of Sino-U.S. relations than are U.S. policies toward Japan and South Korea. Strategic accommodation between the United States and China thus always carries the risk for Taiwan of abandonment by the United States—a risk that was underscored by U.S. reluctance under the George W. Bush administration to supply Taiwan with certain types of weaponry.[67] Moreover, the DPP administration's inability to secure funding for arms procurement only compounded the problem of weakening ties between Taipei and Washington.

Nonetheless, the KMT administration has now, in a fashion similar to other U.S. partners, returned to the U.S. strategic fold. President Ma's re-engagement with China, emphasis on maintaining the cross-strait status quo, and follow-through on arms procurement packages reassured the Bush and now the Obama administrations that Taiwan is a reliable partner.[68] The Obama administration's release in 2011 of a $6.4 billion arms package to Taiwan—including Black Hawk UH-60s, PAC-3s, Harpoon antiship cruise missiles, Osprey-class mine-hunting ships, and multifunctional information distribution systems for C4ISR—is a manifestation of the United States' renewed commitment to Taiwan's defense. The improved U.S.-Taiwan relationship should thus provide the Ma administration with more flexibility to hedge against China's rise through external balancing.

Moreover, the Ma administration appears to be reconsidering its strategic relations with Japan, after initially neglecting ties, and has called for a special partnership to recognize implicit, mutually shared security concerns. Nonetheless, security ties will continue to be constrained by both sides' concerns over Chinese reactions, Japanese anxieties over entrapment in a Taiwan Strait contingency, and an apparent lack of KMT affinity with Japan over issues of territorial sovereignty and the colonial past.[69]

---

[67] Zhang, "Taiwan's New Grand Strategy," 280–81.

[68] Shirley A. Kan and Wayne M. Morrison, "U.S.-Taiwan Relationship: Overview of Policy Issues," Congressional Research Service, CRS Report for Congress, R41952, August 4, 2011.

[69] Thomas S. Wilkins, "Taiwan-Japan Relations in an Era of Uncertainty," *Asia Policy*, no. 13 (2012): 113–32.

Conclusions and Implications for U.S. Policy

China's military modernization has precipitated common challenges and responses for the United States' key allies and partners in Northeast Asia. The first conclusion is that China's strategic and military rise is increasingly impinging on the security of Japan, South Korea, and Taiwan in terms of their territorial integrity and access to SLOCs. This trend is especially manifested in the PLAN's recently expanded maritime activities and probing behavior toward these countries' respective national defenses. In turn, defense planners in Japan, South Korea, and Taiwan maintain similar concerns over China's development of specific military capabilities. All three countries view the PLA's expansion of its air defense and maritime power-projection capabilities as posing a symmetric threat through its fourth-generation fighters, advanced destroyers, and aircraft carriers, as well as an asymmetric threat through its ballistic-missile forces and submarines that can be deployed for access-denial.

The second conclusion is that Japan, South Korea, and Taiwan seek to continue to engage China in order to minimize growing security dilemmas, but at the same time are utilizing hedging options through internal military balancing. All three countries are pursuing similar military modernization in terms of building symmetric air-defense and maritime capabilities. Japan and South Korea, in particular, are looking to procure fifth-generation fighters and continue to augment their powerful blue water navies by equipping them with air-defense destroyers, helicopter carriers, and ASW capabilities. Japan and Taiwan are seeking to counter Chinese asymmetric capabilities in areas such as Aegis and PAC-3 missile defense. Japan, South Korea, and Taiwan further share an approach to military modernization characterized by an emphasis on joint operations, mobile forces, professionalization of the military, and technological advancement. Meanwhile, the current and future challenges posed by China have been sufficient to initiate a fundamental change in military doctrines. Japan has moved toward a more active response to China's probing behavior through the DDF concept, while Taiwan appears to be contemplating a radical shift toward a defense posture that counters China's asymmetric capabilities through a far deeper asymmetric posture of its own. But despite these common impulses for internal balancing and military modernization, Japan, South Korea, and Taiwan are also encountering common domestic impediments for their defense efforts. Domestic political divisions over the extent of the threat posed by China and competing priorities for state finances have limited the ability to fully fund modernization plans: in Japan the defense budget remains stagnant; in South Korea it continues to rise, though not fast enough to keep pace with modernization efforts; and in Taiwan military expenditure is now falling significantly.

The third conclusion is that Japan, South Korea, and Taiwan all demonstrate a marked degree of convergence in their external balancing and re-adhesion to military ties with the United States. These three allies and partners have wavered in recent times in their degree of attachment to political and security relations with the United States. They have been anxious to maintain engagement with China and also concerned about abandonment and entrapment in U.S. military strategy. Entrapment and alliance dilemmas were especially prevalent during the George H.W. Bush administration but have increasingly abated during the George W. Bush administration and the Obama administration. The United States' disengagement from its riskier military expeditions in the Middle East, the continuing rise of China, and domestic political leadership changes in Japan, South Korea, and Taiwan have helped reduce fears of entrapment and abandonment, with the result that these three allies and partners have swung firmly back into the U.S. security fold. The United States thus remains indispensable to their attempts to deal with China's rise.

The final set of conclusions concerns the implications of both China's military modernization and the reactions of allies and partners for the United States' strategic position in Northeast Asia and security in the wider Asia-Pacific region. China's rise presents the United States with both challenges and opportunities. On the one hand, Washington must recognize the risks associated with the growing suspicions of its allies and partners toward China's rise. A quiet arms race is developing in Northeast Asia that could incite highly destabilizing interstate conflicts that jeopardize U.S. interests. In particular, the possibility exists for tensions to rapidly escalate over issues of territorial sovereignty, such as the Senkaku Islands. Although in relative terms, such issues are not very strategically important to the United States, they are politically vital to its allies and partners and could entrap the United States in regional conflicts. On the other hand, the fact that these allies and partners are increasingly aligned in emphasizing the crucial role of the United States in their external balancing against China's rise enhances Washington's strategic leverage in Northeast Asia.

The United States is thus presented with opportunities to not just maintain but also further augment its security relations with Japan, South Korea, and Taiwan, while actively shaping the region's security structures in readiness for the developing challenges from China. The Obama administration's "rebalancing" of U.S. strategic priorities toward East Asia is already helping advance this security agenda. Japan, South Korea, and Taiwan have all proved receptive to the United States' renewed emphasis on East Asia, as seen by their return to the U.S. strategic fold, whether through demonstrating flexibility on base realignments, extended nuclear deterrence, or arms sales packages.

However, the analysis presented above indicates that the United States cannot take for granted this renewed influence over allies and partners in Northeast Asia. In the first place, these countries' economic interdependence with China—mirroring the United States' own interdependence—constrains their freedom of strategic action for open balancing and even hedging. Moreover, despite the United States' continued efforts, corralling its Northeast Asian partners into cooperating more closely with each other is proving to be slow work, given residual Japan–South Korea suspicions and apparent Japan-Taiwan disaffection. Consequently, in order to amplify its influence, the United States will need to carefully calibrate its military capabilities and management of individual alliances to allow it to maintain its indispensability for Japan, South Korea, and Taiwan. At the same time, the United States must be careful to avoid exacerbating its own security tensions with China, as well as tensions between Beijing and its partners and allies. In particular, Washington needs to bolster its rebalancing strategy through demonstrating to allies and partners how the United States will maintain its role as a regional guarantor of security, given cuts to the U.S. defense budget and the quantitative drawdown of force deployments.

The first step in reassuring allies and partners about U.S. rebalancing is to maintain a robust forward-deployed military presence in Northeast Asia. The Bush administration's emphasis on strategic flexibility and realignments in the GPR was the principal driver of abandonment and entrapment dilemmas for Japan and South Korea, which damaged their alliances with the United States. Similarly, relations with Taiwan proved hard to improve given the fears of abandonment generated by Sino-U.S. strategic accommodation. The 2010 QDR's stress on forward-deployments should help reassure allies and partners about the strength of the U.S. presence in the region and reduce anxiety about abandonment and entrapment scenarios. Nevertheless, U.S. policymakers are still tasked with explaining in exact terms how rotation and dispersal to sites such as Guam will prevent a reduction in the long-term U.S. military presence.

The next crucial step in reassuring Japan, South Korea, and Taiwan will be for the United States to maintain not just a presence per se but also the actual disposition of capabilities in the region. Washington may seek to nudge its allies and partners to maintain or boost their own defense budgets. However, given the constraints on local efforts to pursue internal balancing of China, the United States will need to continue to provide supplementary and unique capabilities for the implementation of the ASB concept, for instance. The United States can reinforce symmetric air-defense and maritime responses to Chinese military modernization through the deployment of its most powerful inventory of F-22s, air-defense destroyers, and attack submarines and the continued forward-basing of aircraft carriers. In terms of asymmetric threats and responses, U.S. ballistic-missile defenses and cybersecurity capabilities are areas for continued cooperation with Northeast Asian allies and partners. Moreover, even though the United States has removed tactical nuclear weapons from East Asia, it will also be crucial that Japan, South Korea, and Taiwan feel that the United States can provide nuclear deterrence from a distance.

The final priority for U.S. security planners is to look beyond the presence and disposition of capabilities in Northeast Asia and concentrate on the political credibility of the U.S. commitment to regional security. For example, recent Chinese probing behavior in the East China Sea, especially the 2010 Senkaku Islands incident, constitutes a test not just for Japan's material defenses but also for the political and psychological solidity of the U.S.-Japan alliance. Japan is attempting through the DDF concept to take more responsibility for defense against such provocations in order to avoid needing to test the U.S.-Japanese alliance. However, this stance is a means to stave off a still genuine fear that the United States may not come to Japan's assistance in the East China Sea. Meanwhile, confidence in the alliance was further undermined by North Korea's missile test in April 2012. The launch generated calls from Japan for stern action against the North but drew a milder response from the United States, which is still more concerned about the North's nuclear proliferation. The incident thus opened up divisions between the two allies. In these areas the United States will need to convince its allies and partners in the region that their interests coincide with U.S. interests and that the threshold for U.S. support is not so high as to leave the potential for abandonment in the face of Chinese provocations.

Concomitantly, U.S. policymakers would also do well to avoid attempting to impose U.S. interests on allies with the assumption that they are automatically shared. The Bush administration's focus on the Middle East made the United States appear as a distracted superpower to allies unconvinced of the war-on-terrorism agenda. To the extent that the Bush administration did pay attention to the Asia-Pacific, it gave the appearance of prioritizing U.S. interests over those of allies and partners, as seen with the perceived strategic accommodation of China or the lack of implacability in maintaining its own red lines for North Korea's missile and nuclear programs. Hence, if the Obama administration's strategic rebalancing toward the Asia-Pacific is to succeed, the United States will need to work with allies and partners to forge joint security agendas.

EXECUTIVE SUMMARY

This chapter examines how Australia and several key countries in Southeast Asia are responding to Chinese military modernization.

MAIN ARGUMENT:
The dominant response of Australia, Vietnam, Indonesia, and many other regional countries to Chinese military modernization is balancing. This approach, however, takes different forms depending on the country and its circumstances. Extensive soft balancing, including efforts to build stronger regional security institutions, is increasingly combined with a trend across the region toward harder forms of balancing. This combined approach of soft and hard balancing is driven largely by China's growing military capabilities and assertiveness, particularly in the maritime domain.

POLICY IMPLICATIONS:
- Concerns in Southeast Asia and Australia about China's military capabilities and future intentions mean that countries are likely to continue strengthening security ties with the U.S. as a hedge, although each relationship faces its own inherent constraints.

- Preparedness to continue developing closer defense links with the U.S. will depend on internal dynamics in each country; China's future diplomatic and military behavior, particularly in the South China Sea; and Washington's ability to persuade the region that its rebalancing strategy is a long-term commitment matched by resources.

- Reductions in U.S. military power in the region following further cuts to its defense budget or a slackening of U.S. diplomatic engagement would erode, and in time potentially reverse, the trend toward strengthening security relationships.

- Security relationships might also erode if Washington appears to back away from strong positions on freedom of navigation.

Southeast Asia and Australia: Case Studies in Responding to China's Military Power

Andrew Shearer

Southeast Asia is growing in geopolitical importance and has come to play a vital role in the global economy by virtue of straddling maritime chokepoints between the western Pacific and the Indian Ocean. Australia is one step removed from the direct consequences of China's military modernization compared with maritime Southeast Asia, and two steps removed compared with mainland Southeast Asia. Yet the increasing prominence of the Indian Ocean, the intensifying great-power competition in Asia as a result of the rise of China and India, and the growing range of Chinese weapons together are rendering Australia a more central player in the region. This chapter notes the integrative effects of intraregional economic ties and institution-building efforts but also highlights the diversity of Southeast Asia, the growing role of outside powers (especially China but also India), and the relative weakness of regional security structures.

Although there continues to be an important continental dimension to security dynamics in and around Southeast Asia, China's emergence (or re-emergence) as a major seagoing power is the trend with the most profound implications for the structure of security interactions in Southeast Asia and beyond. The contemporary Asia-Pacific security agenda is thus largely (although not exclusively) set by maritime developments. Chinese naval modernization is a particular focus for Vietnam, Indonesia, and Australia. This chapter examines how Australia and several key Southeast Asian countries are interpreting the military modernization of the People's

Andrew Shearer is a Deputy Secretary in the Victorian Department of Premier and Cabinet in Australia. He can be reached at <ajshearer66@gmail.com>.

The views expressed in this chapter are the author's own and not those of the Victorian Government.

Liberation Army (PLA) and assesses their strategic responses. Rather than attempting to provide an exhaustive survey of Southeast Asian security perceptions and policies or a review of current tensions in the South China Sea, it considers several case studies—with a particular emphasis on Vietnam, Indonesia, and Australia.

Based on this analysis, the chapter argues that claims of a Southeast Asian arms race are overblown and that China is not the only driver of regional defense policies: enduring intraregional differences, internal security challenges, economic growth, and transnational challenges remain strong influences. Beijing's development of maritime power-projection capabilities, however, is starting to generate force-structure responses in Southeast Asia and further afield in Australia (as well as reactions from extraregional powers), thereby influencing regional security dynamics more broadly. This is a significant departure because traditionally China has exercised influence in Southeast Asia as a land power rather than as a seagoing one.[1] These changing dynamics can be seen in the South China Sea, where they intersect with growing competition for energy among Asia's great powers. Specifically, China's growing military presence and increasing assertiveness since mid-2010 have caused Southeast Asian claimant nations and other regional countries to question Beijing's long-term strategic intentions as new capabilities come online. Tensions between China and the Philippines over Scarborough Shoal are only the latest manifestation of a pattern that goes back to the 1970s and 1980s but has recently taken on a sharper edge because of Beijing's increased clout and confidence, the increasing capabilities of the PLA Navy (PLAN), and greater prospects for the United States and its allies to be drawn into a conflict.

The first section of this chapter outlines the growing strategic importance of Southeast Asia and Australia. The next section addresses how the security perceptions of key regional countries themselves are changing and examines the different factors that are shaping these countries' responses to China. Following that discussion is a treatment of the strategies adopted by Australia and key countries in Southeast Asia in response to the shifting security environment, with a particular focus on the maritime security domain. This section highlights common elements across strategies, dealing in turn with internal balancing, or measures a country takes to strengthen its own capabilities; external balancing through formal treaty relationships; and softer forms of balancing (e.g., through thickening security ties with other regional countries or through institution-building). The section attempts to explain how regional states weight these elements differently in their own specific

---

[1] See Robert S. Ross, "China's Naval Nationalism: Sources, Prospects, and the U.S. Response," *International Security* 34, no. 2 (2009): 46–81.

strategic mix. Following President Barack Obama's late 2011 regional tour promoting the U.S. rebalancing strategy toward Asia, the final section of the chapter analyzes responses in Australia and Southeast Asia to this policy. The chapter then concludes by discussing implications for future policy.

The Strategic Importance of Southeast Asia and Australia

U.S. military planners have long understood Southeast Asia's vital importance. Given the region's location at the strategic intersection of the Pacific and Indian oceans, control of the region's vital maritime chokepoints is indispensable to any major power looking to maintain secure sea lines of communication (SLOC). This recognition dates back to the United States' colonialist past and is reflected in its mindset today as a Pacific power. The region's importance was reinforced by Japan's attempt to dominate the western Pacific and Indian Ocean during World War II and the Soviet navy's 1970s foray into the Indian Ocean. Organizationally, it is reflected in the fact that the U.S. Pacific Command's area of operations stretches west to include India.

Nonetheless, for most of the Cold War—with the obvious exception of the conflict in Vietnam—Northeast Asia loomed much larger in U.S. strategy than Southeast Asia. Japan's proximity to the Soviet Union, the unresolved conflict on the Korean Peninsula, and the U.S. commitment to Taiwan combined to ensure that Washington's focus remained largely on the northern reaches of the western Pacific. After the U.S. withdrawal from Vietnam, the main risks of war in Asia involving the United States remained in Northeast Asia, particularly on the Korean Peninsula and across the Taiwan Strait. The continuing presence of large U.S. military forces in Japan and South Korea after U.S. bases in the Philippines closed in the early 1990s helped cement this preoccupation.

Now, however, this focus is starting to shift, and Southeast Asia is taking a more central place both in U.S. strategy and in the calculations of other major powers, including China and India. Likewise, Australia's location makes access to facilities there increasingly attractive to U.S. military planners.

China's military modernization, although an important factor, is not the only reason for this shift. Terrorism and other transnational threats, disaster-relief operations, and requests by regional governments for opportunities to train with U.S. forces create bona fide reasons for a more "distributed" U.S. military presence in Asia. The role of a number of Southeast Asian countries, such as Thailand, in production networks has heightened their importance to the world economy, as have these countries' resource endowments. Many of the burgeoning economic links between the major economies of East Asia and the countries of South Asia and the Middle East run through Southeast Asia—either over land (via a growing network of pipelines, roads, and railways) or by sea through the Malacca Strait and the South China Sea. There is also an ideational component, with China looking to dilute or neutralize traditional patterns of alignment with the United States through diplomatic suasion and coercion, economic inducements, and aid. These broad trends are reinforced by a renewed focus among strategists and commentators, such as Robert Kaplan, on the importance of the Indian Ocean, including its Southeast Asian littoral.[2] For all these reasons, since the end of the Cold War the United States has been moving to strengthen its diplomatic, military, and economic engagement with Southeast Asia and Australia.

Nonetheless, responding to China's developing military capabilities is a big factor in Washington's renewed focus on the region, particularly in more recent changes to U.S. force posture. Growing Chinese anti-access and area-denial (A2/AD) capabilities are making U.S. forward-deployed forces in Northeast Asia more vulnerable and therefore militate in favor of dispersal of U.S. forces and access to facilities farther south—out of the range of many of China's missiles. Moreover, China is highly dependent on SLOCs across the Indian Ocean and running through Southeast Asian chokepoints. Chinese and American strategists alike recognize that U.S. military forces with ready access to the Indian Ocean and proximity to the Southeast Asian straits can exploit that vulnerability and thereby possibly influence China's behavior. China's recent assertive behavior in the South China Sea has only given greater impetus to these efforts and is making many potential U.S. partners more receptive to the United States than they may otherwise have been. This is not necessarily the way many commentators expected events to play out.

Shifting Regional Security Perceptions

For much of the decade leading up to 2010—the period of Beijing's so-called smile diplomacy—the dominant narrative regarding China's interaction with Southeast Asia was one of ever-closer economic integration and steadily warming political ties. As China emerged at the center of a growing regional manufacturing web, Beijing pursued adroit trade diplomacy and began to abandon its traditional suspicion of multilateral forums. Economic integration is accelerating further following the 2010

---

[2] Robert D. Kaplan, *Monsoon: The Indian Ocean and the Future of American Power* (New York: Random House, 2011).

ASEAN-China free trade agreement (FTA), with two-way trade growing by 24% in 2011. China is already the leading trading partner for many countries in Southeast Asia, as well as for Australia, and ASEAN is forecast to become China's largest trading partner by 2015. As a result, some observers have reached exaggerated estimates of Chinese "soft power" and speculated that countries traditionally aligned with the United States may drift increasingly into Beijing's orbit—or "bandwagon" with China, in international relations parlance.[3] These concerns were shared in some Washington policy circles.

Markets and Maritime Muscle-Flexing

Economic power clearly brings with it a degree of influence, and a number of countries in the region have made concessions to Beijing out of concern for offending China. Indeed, as China's confidence and assertiveness grow, Southeast Asian countries find themselves facing tough decisions. There has been anxiety in the Philippines, for example, that the government's stand over Scarborough Shoal is jeopardizing profitable banana exports to China and much-needed Chinese tourist visits, both of which have been frozen, according to media reports.[4] Manila has sought to de-escalate the dispute, replacing the naval ship it had sent to the area with a civilian vessel and handing over detained Chinese fishermen and their catch. Other regional governments—particularly those with overlapping claims in the South China Sea—have been watching developments closely.

Although some analysts argue that Beijing's ability to convert raw economic power into strategic leverage has been exaggerated,[5] China's attempts to wield the country's lucrative domestic market as a diplomatic weapon are likely to strengthen regional concerns about the PLA's continuing modernization and its preparedness to use its growing naval capabilities assertively in the western Pacific, particularly in the South China Sea. Together these developments are altering Southeast Asian threat perceptions and the regional security outlook. China's maritime buildup is clearly aimed at developing the capacity to deny other powers access to the waters of the "first island chain," in the first instance around Taiwan.[6] The construction of Yulin Naval Base, a large facility on Hainan Island for

---

[3] See, for example, Joshua Kurlantzick, *Charm Offensive: How China's Soft Power Is Transforming the World* (New Haven: Yale University Press, 2007); and Kishore Mahbubani, "Smart Power, Chinese Style," *American Interest*, March/April 2008.

[4] "The China-Philippines Banana War," *Asia Sentinel*, June 6, 2012.

[5] John Lee, "Lonely Power, Staying Power: The Rise of China and the Resilience of U.S. Pre-eminence," Lowy Institute for International Policy, Strategic Snapshot, no. 10, September 2011, 3.

[6] See Toshi Yoshihara and James R. Holmes, *Red Star over the Pacific: China's Rise and the Challenge to U.S. Maritime Strategy* (Annapolis: Naval Institute Press, 2010).

submarines and surface vessels—together with the upgrading of the PLAN's South China Sea Fleet[7]—has highlighted the strategic priority Beijing places on the South China Sea. The sea is important to Beijing both as a lifeline for critical oil shipments from the Middle East and as a potential source of undersea resources.[8] Now China is developing the capacity to send forces further south and to sustain them for longer periods.[9]

The transformation of the PLAN is changing the strategic context of the South China Sea dispute.[10] The deployment of new Chinese capabilities has coincided with a pattern of more assertive behavior by Chinese naval and paramilitary forces in the South China Sea, resulting in a spate of incidents over the past few years. The mid-2012 stand-off over Scarborough Shoal is only the most recent installment. In 2009, Chinese vessels harassed the USNS *Impeccable* in the South China Sea west of the Paracels, and a PLAN submarine collided with the USS *John S. McCain*'s towed array sonar off the Philippines. In 2010, the PLAN conducted a major maritime exercise in the South China Sea. At the ASEAN Regional Forum (ARF) meeting in July of that year, Secretary of State Hillary Clinton, supported by most regional governments, reaffirmed the United States' national interest in freedom of navigation through the South China Sea. The ensuing angry outburst by Chinese foreign minister Yang Jiechi and his abrupt putdown of "small countries" caused disquiet in Southeast Asian capitals.[11] Tensions reignited between China and the Philippines in April 2012, when a Philippine naval vessel confronted Chinese fishing boats near Scarborough Shoal and Beijing pushed back hard. The July 2012 grounding of a Chinese frigate near Half Moon Shoal, in waters claimed by the Philippines, and Beijing's move the same month to establish a municipal government for its Sansha outpost in the Paracels (following a PLA announcement that it would establish a military garrison there) have further upped the stakes.[12]

---

[7] Improvements include the addition of large amphibious vessels and Jin-class nuclear submarines.

[8] See "Behind Recent Gunboat Diplomacy in the South China Sea," International Institute for Strategic Studies, Strategic Comments, no. 28, August 2011; and Patrick M. Cronin and Robert D. Kaplan, "Cooperation from Strength: U.S. Strategy and the South China Sea," in *Cooperation from Strength: The United States, China and the South China Sea*, ed. Patrick M. Cronin (Washington, D.C.: Center for a New American Security, 2012), 7.

[9] Carlyle A. Thayer, *Southeast Asia: Patterns of Security Cooperation* (Canberra: Australian Strategic Policy Institute, 2010), 36.

[10] Ian Storey, "Asia's Changing Balance of Military Power: Implications for the South China Sea Dispute," in "Maritime Resources in Asia: Energy and Geopolitics," National Bureau of Asian Research (NBR), NBR Special Report, December 2011.

[11] Donald K. Emmerson, "China's 'Frown Diplomacy' in Southeast Asia," Center for Strategic and International Studies (CSIS), PacNet, no. 45, October 6, 2010.

[12] Jane Perlez, "China Asserts Sea Claim with Politics and Ships," *New York Times*, August 13, 2012.

China's maritime and diplomatic posturing since 2009 has undone many of the gains of a decade of patient smile diplomacy, pushing Southeast Asian governments closer to the United States.[13]

Factors Influencing Regional Security Perceptions

Perceptions in Southeast Asia and Australia of China's military buildup vary, underlining the region's diversity and the analytic and policy pitfalls associated with viewing it as a monolith. The way countries interpret China's military modernization, actions, and intentions is shaped by a range of factors.

Geopolitics. Proximity to China is an important factor in the way different Southeast Asian countries view the threat represented by China's military buildup. Burma, Laos, and Vietnam, for example, all share a land border with China. Burma is particularly important because it offers overland access from China to the Indian Ocean. Each country deals with its proximity differently, however. Vietnam is the only one of China's neighbors to have repeatedly and recently fought wars with China, clashing at sea over the Paracel Islands in the 1970s and the Spratly Islands in the 1980s. The two sides also fought a brief conflict on land in 1979, in which Vietnam inflicted significant damage on invading Chinese forces. By contrast Laos, despite strong links with Vietnam, has largely accommodated China, and until recently Burma seemed to have done the same. The countries of maritime Southeast Asia, separated from China by sea, have somewhat more latitude, although China's growing maritime capabilities are eroding this advantage. Australia is one step further removed China, lying beyond the range of many of its ballistic missiles.

History. China's links with Southeast Asia date back centuries and are based on long-standing trade contacts and a very substantial and established regional Chinese diaspora. By contrast, substantial contact with Australia is more recent, dating back to the 1850s. Thailand and Vietnam have long and deeply complicated historical relationships with China involving elements of civilizational pride, independence, and tension but also of cultural and economic affinity and integration. On the other hand, suspicion of China's motives and ambivalence about the Chinese diaspora have been engrained in Indonesia, particularly since the 1950s.

Competing territorial claims. Vietnam, the Philippines, Malaysia, and Brunei have overlapping territorial claims with China (and Taiwan) in the South China Sea, and China's "nine-dotted line" claim incorporates waters

---

[13] Ian Storey, "China's Missteps in Southeast Asia: Less Charm, More Offensive," *China Brief,* December 17, 2010, 7.

within the exclusive economic zone (EEZ) around Indonesia's Natuna Islands. But the most acute tensions have involved Vietnam and more recently the Philippines. Conflict over the Spratly and Paracel island chains goes back to the 1970s, and South China Sea tensions have flared up again during the last few years: Chinese maritime patrol vessels tangled with Vietnamese survey ships inside Vietnam's EEZ during 2011 and Chinese authorities engaged in an angry stand-off with a Philippine naval vessel at Scarborough Shoal in April 2012. Competition to control important fishing grounds contributed to earlier tensions, but more recently the suspected presence of undersea gas deposits has raised the stakes, particularly given China's burgeoning demand for energy.[14]

Economics. Almost all Southeast Asian countries are increasingly economically dependent on China. This dependence is largely the result of the dispersal of manufacturing production chains among lower-cost economies but also reflects China's insatiable demand for commodities. China has made extensive economic inroads in Burma, Cambodia, Laos, and Thailand, although Beijing's leverage in Burma may be weakening as a result of recent developments. China likewise recently overtook Japan to become Australia's largest trading partner. Cambodia's economic dependence on China is widely cited as a major factor in its refusal as chair during the July 2012 ASEAN foreign ministers' meeting to issue a final communiqué referring explicitly to Scarborough Shoal. Yet Beijing's efforts to leverage these burgeoning economic ties into political and strategic influence have in other instances met with less success. Growing Chinese commerce with Australia, the Philippines, Vietnam, and other regional countries has not dissuaded them from pursuing security choices at odds with Beijing's preferences, including closer defense ties with Washington. Indeed, there is growing evidence that economic dependence often tends to reinforce rather than alleviate concerns about China's military modernization and the country's influence more broadly.

Strength or weakness. Power matters, and power relativities affect threat perceptions. Smaller, more vulnerable Southeast Asian countries may feel more threatened by China's growing military power than larger, more resilient nations. Moreover, power is shifting within Southeast Asia. Indonesia, for example, could—based on present projections—emerge as a major regional power in its own right some time after 2035, but only if it consolidates its democratic transition and maintains pro-growth

---

[14] According to Chinese studies cited in 2008 by the U.S. Energy Information Administration, the unproven oil reserves believed to lie under the South China Sea may be almost as large as Saudi Arabia's proven reserves. See "Oil Fuels South China Sea Disputes," *Australian Financial Review*, August 14, 2012.

economic policies. The country's long-term prospects risk being damaged by an upsurge in economic populism and a failure to come to terms with corruption and cronyism. Vietnam is also a large, resilient country, albeit one facing its own challenges to political and economic reform. Although it held its own against the PLA in the 1979 war, today the best Vietnam could hope for is to make any incident or series of incidents at sea sufficiently messy to damage China's image (which itself may have a restraining effect on Beijing). Cambodia and Laos, by contrast, lack such clout and have demonstrated less readiness to stand up to Beijing, despite their close links to Vietnam. Both countries will also find it hard to resist being drawn further into China's sway as a result of proximity and economic dependence.

Competing threats. China's military modernization is not the only potential security threat faced by Southeast Asian countries. The Philippines and Indonesia continue to face internal challenges from extremists and separatist movements. The region has enjoyed several decades of peace, during which ASEAN has played a useful role in fostering cooperation and tamping down traditional rivalries. Nonetheless, long-standing tensions between states remain and sometimes rise above the surface: Malaysia and Singapore are wary of each other, and both are suspicious of Indonesia; Thai and Cambodian forces recently exchanged fire over an unresolved border dispute. Such conflicts could displace attention from China's military modernization.

Alignment. Given the reality of Sino-U.S. strategic competition in the western Pacific, the way regional states perceive China's military modernization will be influenced by the extent of their strategic alignment with the United States—whether as formal treaty allies (Australia, the Philippines, and Thailand), as non-treaty "strategic partners" (Singapore), as states that deliberately eschew alignment (Indonesia, traditionally), and as states that lean more obviously toward China (Burma, at least until recently when its government terminated the huge Chinese-backed Myitsone dam project, and Cambodia). Yet there is not always a clear correlation between a country's formal alignment with the United States and its threat perception of China. For example, at different times Thailand and the Philippines have each demonstrated reluctance to support U.S. policy positions out of concern about Beijing's reaction.

Domestic politics. The factors discussed above tend to be long-term, structural influences on Southeast Asian threat perceptions, but domestic political developments can also have an effect. The 2010 elections in the Philippines, for example, ushered in a government that has expressed more reservations about China's military capabilities and intentions than its predecessor and has been more prepared to stand up to Chinese pressure (or arguably on occasion to provoke Beijing). In addition, political reforms in Burma opened the way to the possible normalization of relations with the United States. In Australia, the Rudd government's first major defense policy statement included noticeably sharper language on China.[15]

The factors outlined very briefly above interact to shape Australia's and Southeast Asian countries' perceptions of China's military modernization. They are also important drivers of the decisions regional states make about defense policy, military strategy, and diplomacy.

Responding to Chinese Military Modernization: Regional Defense and Security Choices

For countries bordering China and for the other nations of mainland Southeast Asia, the strategic challenge today is still recognizably the one they have dealt with for centuries: how to coexist with a major continental power. Yet China's post–Cold War turn to the sea and growing military capabilities pose a very different challenge, particularly for the countries of maritime Southeast Asia but also for Australia and other regional powers. The overlay of Sino-U.S. strategic competition is another complicating factor. China's growing missile capabilities profoundly affect the contours of the security landscape in the western Pacific, while its rapidly developing space, cyber, and electronic warfare systems also pose increasing challenges for U.S. and allied forces. Yet PLA naval and air capabilities and actions are the dominant drivers to date of regional security responses to China's rise and are foremost in the minds of Southeast Asian and Australian defense planners.

Responses to the challenges posed by China can take a number of forms: internal balancing, or building up national defense capabilities; external balancing, or building up formal defensive alliances; and soft balancing through the use of tacit, informal, and institution-based offsetting approaches.[16] One of the characteristics of soft balancing is that informal security arrangements and cooperative exercises can readily be upgraded "to open, hard-balancing strategies if and when security competition becomes intense and the powerful state becomes threatening."[17]

---

[15] Department of Defence of the Australian Government, *Defending Australia in the Asia Pacific Century: Force 2030* (Canberra, 2009).

[16] See, for example, Robert A. Pape, "Soft Balancing: How States Pursue Security in a Unipolar World" (paper presented at the annual meeting of the American Political Science Association, Chicago, September 2–5, 2004).

[17] T.V. Paul, "The Enduring Axioms of Balance of Power Theory and Their Contemporary Relevance," in *Balance of Power Revisited: Theory and Practice in the 21st Century*, ed. T.V. Paul, James J. Wirtz, and Michel Fortmann (Stanford: Stanford University Press, 2004), 3.

"Bandwagoning"—when weaker states join forces with a stronger power because the cost of balancing outweighs the benefits—is also an option for responding to China's growing military power.[18] As noted above, Cambodia and other mainland Southeast Asian countries have shown clear signs of this behavior. This phenomenon would be more likely to spread should the ideational and balancing reasons for alignment with the United States weaken significantly or were excessive U.S. defense cuts to undermine regional confidence in the United States' commitment to Asia. Even if regional countries do not bandwagon with China, its growing influence may over time sway them sufficiently to prevent their bandwagoning with the United States, which would seriously complicate the U.S. position in Asia.

Elements of each strategy feature in the responses of Southeast Asian countries to China's military—and in particular naval—modernization. The remainder of this chapter examines the mix of strategies adopted by key regional states, particularly Vietnam, Indonesia, and Australia, and argues that the dominant approach is soft balancing (albeit one that is moving toward harder forms of balancing), accompanied by hedging through acquisitions of sophisticated naval and air capabilities (see **Table 1** in the next section for a summary of the balancing strategies employed by countries in the region). The final section addresses attitudes in key Southeast Asian countries and Australia toward the possibility of U.S. strategic retrenchment.

Beefing Up: Internal Balancing in Southeast Asia and Australia

According to the Stockholm International Peace Research Institute (SIPRI), in 2010 the rate of growth of military expenditure in Asia slowed, and Southeast Asian military expenditure grew at less than half the rate for East Asia as a whole.[19] Nonetheless, Southeast Asian defense spending was still 60% higher in 2010 than in 2001—confirming that Southeast Asia has not been a bystander in what the International Institute for Strategic Studies (IISS) calls the "increasing militarization" of Asia.[20] A number of Southeast Asian countries, as well as Australia, have been growing their

---

[18] See Kenneth Waltz, *Theory of International Politics* (Boston: McGraw-Hill, 1979).

[19] Stockholm International Peace Research Institute (SIPRI), *SIPRI Yearbook 2011: Armaments, Disarmament and International Security* (Oxford: Oxford University Press, 2011), 185.

[20] Ibid.; and International Institute for Strategic Studies (IISS), *The Military Balance 2012* (London: Routledge, 2012), 204.

TABLE 1 Southeast Asian and Australian regional strategies

Country	South China Sea claimant	Mix of strategies
Australia	No	• External balancing (strengthening U.S. alliance, including through marine and aircraft rotations) • Internal balancing (boosting maritime capabilities) • Soft balancing (strengthening bilateral security links with regional countries and institutional balancing, including through the EAS)
Brunei	Yes	• Maintaining a low profile in South China Sea disputes • Institutional balancing (through ASEAN) • Limited military capabilities
Burma/ Myanmar	No	• Previously bandwagoning with China • Now signs of soft balancing (e.g., repositioning toward the U.S.)
Cambodia	No	• Bandwagoning with China (e.g., in chairing of July 2012 ASEAN meetings)
Indonesia	No	• Soft balancing (traditionally nonaligned, but strengthening security ties with the U.S., India, and other regional powers; institutional balancing, including through ASEAN and the EAS) • Limited internal balancing (e.g., acquiring submarines)
Laos	No	• Bandwagoning with China
Malaysia	Yes	• Soft balancing (strengthening security ties with the U.S.) • Internal balancing (boosting maritime and air capabilities)
Philippines	Yes	• External balancing (considering enhanced U.S. military presence) • Internal balancing (boosting maritime capabilities, albeit from a low base) • Soft balancing (through regional institutions and strengthening security ties with regional powers, such as Australia)
Singapore	No	• Internal balancing (maintenance of Southeast Asia's most sophisticated military forces) • Soft balancing (strong security links with the U.S., including hosting U.S. Navy littoral combat ships, and with other regional powers, including India and Australia; institutional balancing, including through ASEAN and the EAS)
Thailand	No	• Elements of both bandwagoning with China and balancing (e.g., allowing U.S. military access under the alliance)
Vietnam	Yes	• Internal balancing (boosting maritime capabilities) • Soft balancing (strengthening security links with the U.S. and regional powers, including India; institutional balancing, including through ASEAN and the EAS)

NOTE: Although Indonesia is not a South China Sea claimant, China's "nine-dotted line" claim overlaps with Indonesia's exclusive economic zone.

defense budgets and building up their naval, air, and missile capabilities, in particular.[21]

Defense procurement decisions in Southeast Asia tend to reflect a complex and diffuse set of calculations, including long-standing intraregional rivalries and competition over borders, resources, and history; traditional patterns of alignment and nonalignment; economic growth and measures to develop greater resources and defense industrial capacity; and a growing awareness of regional strategic uncertainty, especially about U.S. staying power in Asia. The increasing presence in Southeast Asia of percieved outside powers in addition to China may also be a factor.[22]

Southeast Asian countries are loath to criticize China openly. Understandable caution about alienating a rising power is no doubt a major factor, and in some cases there may be an element of ingrained deference from countries habituated to tributary relationships with China during its previous period as a great power. Some regional states may also be hedging against the possibility of U.S. retrenchment. Economics play a major part, however: the incorporation of Southeast Asian economies into regional production chains means they are increasingly dependent on China for their current and future prosperity and are therefore unlikely to be too strident in expressing concern about Beijing's military capabilities and intentions (even if, as noted above, their security actions do not always please Beijing). The declaratory policies of Southeast Asian countries generally avoid giving unnecessary offense to China.[23] Nevertheless, it has become increasingly clear—particularly since tensions in the South China Sea started to escalate in mid-2010—that China's ambitious program of military modernization and increasingly assertive military, paramilitary, and diplomatic behavior have taken greater prominence in the defense plans of Southeast Asian countries and Australia and are influencing force-structure decisions.

A range of Southeast Asian countries are increasing their defense spending in order to acquire capabilities that can be used offensively—or even preemptively—against enemy maritime forces and surface vessels in particular.[24] These include modern submarines, combat aircraft, and antiship

---

[21] IISS, *The Military Balance 2012*, 206.

[22] W. Lawrence S. Prabhakar, "The Regional Dimension of Territorial and Maritime Disputes in Southeast Asia: Actors, Disagreements and Dynamics," in *Maritime Security in Southeast Asia*, ed. Kwa Chong Guan and John K. Skogan (London: Routledge, 2007), 39–40.

[23] Vietnam's 2009 defense white paper is a case in point. It notes in general terms rising regional territorial tensions and military capabilities, without singling out China, and emphasizes the gradual modernization of Vietnam's military for purely defensive purposes. See Vietnam Ministry of National Defence, *Vietnam National Defence* (Hanoi, December 2009), 13–30.

[24] IISS, *The Military Balance 2012*, 206–7; and "Military Spending in South-East Asia: Shopping Spree," *Economist*, March 24, 2012.

missiles. The weight of scholarly opinion is that this competition does not amount to a classic arms race—at least not yet.[25] Nonetheless, China's military modernization is undoubtedly causing a ripple effect in Southeast Asia; as IISS points out, in some cases these acquisitions have the unstated purpose of deterring adventurism by China as well as by other neighboring states.[26] Regional governments took the view that China's four high-profile naval exercises in 2010, intended to reinforce its diplomatic claims in the South China Sea, amounted to "a demonstration that China was rapidly developing the capacity to sustain larger naval deployments deep into the South China Sea."[27] The following discussion considers this situation more closely through an examination of recent defense decisions by Vietnam, Indonesia, and Australia.

Vietnam

Vietnam has had a complicated relationship with China for centuries, marked by both interdependence and sharp rivalry. The two clashed over the Paracel Islands in 1974, with China gaining possession. They subsequently fought a brief but bloody land war in 1979 and clashed periodically over their respective claims in the South China Sea during the 1980s and early 1990s. Vietnam (along with the Philippines) has been a target of China's increasing assertiveness over the last several years. During the first half of 2011, a Chinese vessel reportedly severed a Vietnamese oil-exploration survey cable inside Vietnam's EEZ off the country's south central coast, and in return the Vietnamese navy is believed to have chased away Chinese civilian vessels.[28] Vietnam and China both later conducted live-fire exercises in nearby waters. These tensions abated somewhat during the second half of 2011, when both sides reached an agreement on basic principles and established a crisis hotline.[29] Nonetheless, rising concern in Hanoi about China's intentions in

---

[25] Christian LaMiere, "Waves of Concern—Southeast Asian States Plan Naval Defences," *Jane's Intelligence Review*, April 14, 2011.

[26] Prabhakar, "Regional Dimension of Territorial and Maritime Disputes," 39–40; IISS, *The Military Balance 2012*, 208; and Richard Bitzinger, "Military Modernization in the Asia-Pacific: Assessing New Capabilities," in *Strategic Asia 2010–11: Asia's Rising Power and America's Continued Purpose*, ed. Ashley J. Tellis, Andrew Marble, and Travis Tanner (Seattle: National Bureau of Asian Research, 2011), 78–111.

[27] Carlyle A. Thayer, "The United States, China and Southeast Asia," in *Southeast Asian Affairs 2011*, ed. Daljit Singh (Singapore: Institute of Southeast Asia Studies, 2011), 21.

[28] Rory Medcalf, Raoul Heinrichs, and Justin Jones, *Crisis and Confidence: Major Powers and Maritime Security in Indo-Pacific Asia*, Lowy Institute for International Policy, Report, June 2011, 9; and IISS, *The Military Balance 2012*, 207.

[29] "China, Vietnam Ink Agreement, Set Up Hotline on Disputed Seas," Press Trust of India, October 12, 2011, http://news.in.msn.com/international/article.aspx?cp-documentid=5507853.

the South China Sea has been a clear driver of Vietnam's efforts to boost naval and air capabilities.[30]

Vietnam's decision to acquire six Kilo-class conventional submarines created headlines around Asia. No doubt this was the intention: the announcement was made at the regional Shangri-La Dialogue in June 2011, immediately after the incident noted above in which a Vietnamese survey cable was reportedly severed.[31] The Kilo-class is among the world's quietest and most capable conventional submarines, and the acquisition thus represents a significant capability improvement.[32] Scheduled for delivery between 2014 and 2017,[33] the six submarines are clearly a direct response to the perceived military threat from China—in particular, from the Chinese submarine buildup on Hainan. They will be augmented by approximately half a dozen new surface combatants over the next decade and will help Vietnam implement an anti-access strategy off its southeast coast and in the Spratlys.[34]

Vietnam is also upgrading its air-combat capability. A 2009–10 order for 20 additional Su-30MK aircraft will expand the country's existing fleet of Su-27 and Su-30 aircraft to around 60.[35] These aircraft, however, will not redress the existing significant air-combat imbalance favoring China, and Vietnamese defense planners can be under no illusions about the future prospect of a PLA Air Force capable of conducting strategic strike missions at extended ranges—perhaps as far as three thousand kilometers by 2030.[36] In addition to submarine and aircraft purchases, Vietnam is also reportedly stepping up technical collaboration with Russia to develop unmanned aerial vehicles and antiship missiles.[37] Like the Kilo-submarine purchase, increased Vietnamese air-combat capabilities can contribute to a sea-denial strategy, helping reinforce Vietnam's territorial claims, complicate Beijing's strategic calculations, and reduce the potency of a strategy designed perhaps as much to coerce neighbors as to defeat them.

---

[30] IISS, *The Military Balance 2012*, 207.

[31] Wendell Minnick, "Vietnam Confirms Kilo Sub Buy at Shangri-La," *DefenseNews*, June 5, 2011, http://www.defensenews.com/article/20110605/DEFSECT03/106050301/Vietnam-Confirms-Kilo-Sub-Buy-Shangri-La.

[32] LaMiere, "Waves of Concern."

[33] IISS, *The Military Balance 2012*, 207.

[34] "Military Spending in South-East Asia."

[35] LaMiere, "Waves of Concern."

[36] Mark A. Stokes and Ian Easton, "Evolving Aerospace Trends in the Asia-Pacific Region: Implications for Stability in the Taiwan Strait and Beyond," Project 2049 Institute, May 27, 2010, 18.

[37] John Grevatt, "Russia, Vietnam Step up Technical Collaboration in UAVs and Anti-ship Missiles," *Jane's Defence Weekly*, March 16, 2012.

Australia

Australia is the other country in the region that is most obviously augmenting its maritime force. This development was announced, with considerable fanfare, in the former Rudd government's 2009 defense white paper. The *Force 2030* white paper outlined Australia's intention to focus on enhancing its maritime capabilities and develop by the mid-2030s "a more potent and heavier maritime force" built around an expanded fleet of twelve submarines, cruise missiles, and more capable surface combatants optimized for antisubmarine warfare.[38] For the first time in a public, official document, the Australian government expressed concern about China's military modernization, which was one factor in the downturn in Sino-Australian relations during 2009–10. The white paper noted that "pronounced military modernization in the Asia-Pacific region is having significant implications for our strategic outlook" and made explicit that the government saw the *Force 2030* plan as a "'strategic hedge' against future uncertainty."[39]

Until recently, Australia's defense budget has been growing at 3% annually in real terms since the former Howard government began rebuilding the Australian Defence Force in 2000. Over several decades, maintaining a capability edge in the region has been a keystone of Australian defense policy, but this is becoming much more costly and difficult. The proliferation in the region of precision-guided munitions and electronic warfare systems in particular is providing an acute challenge for Australian defense planners. In 2011 Australia spent almost as much on defense ($27.7 billion) as all of Southeast Asia ($32.9 billion).[40] The new maritime capabilities outlined in Australia's 2009 white paper would augment other weapons systems already on order, including three air-warfare destroyers (equipped with the Aegis air-combat system and therefore interoperable with U.S. and potentially Japanese and South Korean missile-defense forces); two large amphibious ships, each capable of carrying more than one thousand troops, one hundred armored vehicles, and twelve helicopters; manned and unmanned long-range surveillance aircraft; upgraded frigates; and other naval weapon and communications systems.[41] Australia has also indicated its intention to purchase up to one hundred F-35 air-combat aircraft.

[38] Department of Defence of the Australian Government, *Force 2030*, 13.

[39] Ibid., 16, 28.

[40] IISS, *The Military Balance 2012*, 209.

[41] Stephen Smith (presentation at the Royal Australian Navy Sea Power Conference, January 31, 2012).

On the face of it, the *Force 2030* plan would amount to a significant buildup of Australian capabilities in response to a regional defense environment made more challenging by the introduction of sophisticated new capabilities by neighboring Southeast Asian countries, whether in response to China or to each other's acquisitions. However, the initial skepticism of some Australian commentators (including this author) about the white paper's commitments has been borne out.[42] Rudd was widely regarded as the main driver of *Force 2030*, and in the first budget following his departure, the successor Gillard government in May 2011 cut A\$4.3 billion from the defense budget to 2019 and deferred A\$2.4 billion of investment until after 2014.[43] The May 2012 budget cut an additional A\$5.5 billion over four years, while redirecting A\$2.9 billion, mostly from investment in new equipment, to meet other pressures within the defense budget. As a result, Australia's 2013 defense budget will fall by 10.5%. Defense spending as a share of GDP will fall to 1.56%, its lowest level since 1938.[44]

With the air-warfare destroyer and F-35 projects already running behind schedule and over budget, *Force 2030* is under growing pressure and will be reviewed in a white paper previously scheduled for 2014 but now hastily moved up to 2013. This pressure applies in particular to the proposed force's centerpiece: the ambitious program to replace the existing Collins-class fleet of six submarines with twelve boats of greater range, longer endurance on patrol, and expanded capabilities. The existing submarine fleet is afflicted with serious capability, reliability, and maintenance problems. According to a recent report by the Australian Strategic Policy Institute (ASPI), it will not be possible to develop a submarine force of the specified size and capability even by the mid-2030s. Therefore, absent drastic remedial action, Australia faces an inevitable submarine capability gap into the late 2020s, and even the possibility of a period with no submarines.[45] Options canvassed by ASPI include extending the life of the existing Collins-class fleet, buying or building a smaller and less capable off-the-shelf submarine, and acquiring a nuclear attack submarine. Each alternative presents military, political, or financial risks.

---

[42] Andrew Shearer, "Australia Bulks Up," *Wall Street Journal Asia*, May 6, 2009, 15.

[43] See "The Cost of Defence: ASPI Defence Budget Brief 2011–2012," Australian Strategic Policy Institute (ASPI), May 2011.

[44] See "The Cost of Defense: ASPI Defence Budget Brief 2012–2013," ASPI, May 2012.

[45] Andrew Davies and Mark Thomson, "Mind the Gap: Getting Serious about Submarines," APSI, Strategic Insights, no. 57, April 2012.

Indonesia

Indonesia's military retains its traditional internal security focus and remains relatively poorly funded, accounting for only 16% of Southeast Asian defense expenditure despite the country's vast territory and large population.[46] However, uncertainty about the Asia-Pacific security outlook and Jakarta's renewed regional leadership ambitions are driving increased defense spending, which has been further facilitated by healthy economic growth. Indonesian military expenditure has risen from just $2.6 billion in 2006 to $8 billion in 2012.[47] There are also signs that Indonesian concerns about interference by outside powers and rivalries with neighbors have motivated a more outward-looking military posture aimed at sea-denial. For example, Jakarta ordered three new conventional submarines from South Korea in January 2012, has tested Russian-built SS-N-26 antiship missiles, and is also working with Chinese companies to develop antiship missiles.[48]

Other Regional Countries

Vietnam, Australia, and Indonesia are not the only regional countries engaged in significant internal balancing. Singapore, for example, spends more on defense than any Southeast Asian country (accounting for roughly 30% of the region's military expenditure) and maintains the most sophisticated and capable forces in Southeast Asia.[49] It is introducing F-15SG fighter aircraft and took delivery of the first of two modern submarines in August 2011. China's South China Sea claims and military modernization have been a driver of Malaysia's defense program since the late 1980s.[50] Malaysia's two modern Scorpene-class submarines are moving toward operational status and will deploy from Sabah, and Malaysia is better placed than other Southeast Asian parties to defend its claims in the South China Sea.[51] Domestic political pressures have, however, curbed Malaysia's planned increases in defense spending, delaying the MiG-29 fighter aircraft replacement project.[52] Thailand, too—although preoccupied for several years by border clashes with neighboring Cambodia—is introducing Grippen multirole combat aircraft and is interested in acquiring up to

---

[46] IISS, *The Military Balance 2012*, 211.

[47] "Military Spending in South-East Asia."

[48] IISS, *The Military Balance 2012*, 206.

[49] Ibid.

[50] Storey, "Asia's Changing Balance of Military Power."

[51] Ibid.

[52] IISS, *The Military Balance 2012*, 206.

six submarines.[53] The Philippine government almost doubled its defense budget last year to nearly $2.5 billion.[54] The United States has agreed to transfer two former coast guard vessels to the Philippine Navy and is reportedly contemplating providing F-16 fighters and coastal radar. Manila is also reportedly looking to acquire military equipment from U.S. allies, including patrol boats from Japan.[55] Nonetheless, the Philippines' capacity to uphold its claims in the South China Sea is likely to remain weak.[56]

Doubling Up and Reaching Out: Hard and Soft Balancing Strategies

The collapse of the Soviet Union and the end of the Cold War were widely expected to undermine the rationale for the U.S. alliance system in Asia. On the face of it, the eviction of U.S. forces from the Philippines and a gradual tilt toward Beijing in Thailand and other mainland Southeast Asian countries such as Cambodia seemed to bear this out, particularly during the period of China's smile diplomacy in the late 1990s and early 2000s (although Singapore remained quietly in the U.S. security camp). More recently, the growing reliance of the Australian economy on China as a market for minerals and energy—accentuated since the global financial crisis—has triggered a lively public debate among Australia's academic, business, and political elites about the sustainability of a close alliance with the United States. Both major political parties remain committed to a strong U.S. alliance, and mainstream public opinion is also supportive.[57] But a succession of scholars, business leaders, political figures on both sides, and retired military commanders have warned that closer defense ties with the United States could jeopardize relations with China and hence Australia's future prosperity.[58]

---

[53] IISS, *The Military Balance 2012*, 207.

[54] "Military Spending in South-East Asia."

[55] "U.S. Adds Firepower to Philippine Defence," *Guardian*, August 6, 2012.

[56] Storey, "Asia's Changing Balance of Military Power."

[57] Andrew Shearer, "Uncharted Waters: The U.S. Alliance and Australia's New Era of Strategic Uncertainty," Lowy Institute for International Policy, Lowy Institute Perspectives, August 2011.

[58] See Hugh White, "Power Shift: Australia's Future between Washington and Beijing," *Quarterly Essay*, no. 39 (September 2010); Peter Ker, "Palmer Blasts Obama's Marines Plan for NT," *Brisbane Times*, November 22, 2011, http://www.brisbanetimes.com.au/business/palmer-blasts-obamas-marines-plan-for-nt-20111122-1ns63.html; Andrew Bolt, "Keating: Gillard Let Herself Be Verballed by Obama," *Herald Sun*, Andrew Bolt web log, November 24, 2011, http://blogs.news.com.au/heraldsun/andrewbolt/index.php/heraldsun/comments/keating_gillard_let_herself_be_verballed_by_obama; and Mark Dodd and Matthew Franklin, "General Peter Leahy Warns of U.S.-China Collision," *Australian*, April 12, 2012, http://www.theaustralian.com.au/national-affairs/defence/general-peter-leahy-warns-of-us-china-collision/story-e6frg8yo-1226324341958.

China's military modernization has not yet generated classic hard-balancing behavior in Southeast Asia. That is, new formal, treaty-based defensive alliances have not come into being as a result of threat perceptions about China's rise. Nor do new formal security alliances with the United States seem likely in the foreseeable future (despite occasional hyperbole to the contrary).[59] The only formal U.S. treaty partners in the region remain Australia, the Philippines, and Thailand—alliances that have their roots in the Cold War and even earlier. (Singapore, the United States' strongest Southeast Asian defense partner, is not a treaty ally.) Yet predictions of the demise of traditional U.S. alliances in Asia seem to have been premature. Australia, the Philippines, and Thailand have each sought to reinvigorate their respective alliances with the United States; for example, all three sent military forces to Iraq. Although these efforts have not been expressly in reaction to China's growing military capabilities, uncertainty caused by the disruptive effects of China's rise and growing misgivings about its longer-term strategic intentions have been a common element.

Balancing at the Harder End? Australia Welcomes Back the Marines

In Australia's case the commitment to revitalizing the alliance dates back to the advent of the conservative Howard government in 1996 and has been sustained by subsequent Labor governments under Rudd and Gillard. During this period, the Australia-U.S. alliance—already close—has deepened and broadened appreciably.[60] Australia committed military forces to U.S.-led coalition operations in Afghanistan and Iraq. In most of the major defense acquisition decisions outlined above, Canberra placed a deliberate premium on the ability of the Australian Defence Force to operate effectively with the U.S. military. The two countries expanded their long-standing intelligence links and signed a defense trade cooperation treaty to streamline collaboration between their defense industries. More recently, they have extended traditional defense cooperation into the critical new realms of space and cyberspace.[61]

Significantly, during President Obama's tour of Asia in late 2011, he and Prime Minister Gillard announced that U.S. forces would enjoy expanded

---

[59] See, for example, Robert Kaplan's speech to the Carnegie Council on November 30, 2010, in which he forecast that Vietnam would become a U.S. ally, available at YouTube, http://www.youtube.com/watch?v=eAd7B-S3tvo.

[60] For a detailed treatment, see Greg Sheridan, *The Partnership: The Inside Story of the U.S.-Australian Alliance under Howard and Bush* (Sydney: University of New South Wales Press, 2006).

[61] "Australia–United States Ministerial Consultations (AUSMIN) 2011 Joint Communiqué," Australian Minister for Foreign Affairs, Media Release, September 15, 2011, http://foreignminister.gov.au/releases/2011/kr_mr_110916b.html.

access to defense bases and training ranges in Australia's north. A U.S. marine air-ground task force, building over time to 2,500 personnel with supporting ships and aircraft, will spend six months each year in the Northern Territory training with Australian forces. In addition, the use of airbases across Australia's north by the U.S. military will increase significantly.[62] The announcement drew frosty responses in Beijing and, initially, Jakarta. The initial two hundred marines arrived in Darwin in April 2012 and the number will continue to build over the next five years. Australia's defense minister announced in August 2012 that Australia, Indonesia, and the United States were planning to hold a trilateral disaster-relief exercise in 2013 under the auspices of the East Asia Summit (EAS).

Softly, Softly: Balancing in Southeast Asia

While President Obama was in Australia in November 2011 to commemorate the 60th anniversary of the Australia-U.S. alliance, Secretary of State Clinton was in the Philippines to mark the same milestone in the U.S.-Philippines Mutual Defense Treaty. Like a number of other ASEAN countries, the Philippines has sought since the end of the Cold War to balance its alliance with the United States with its burgeoning economic relationship with China. Yet after a period in which the Philippines seemed to drift closer to Beijing, China's increasing maritime assertiveness has seen Manila seek to strengthen defense ties with the United States.[63] During Secretary Clinton's visit, the two countries reaffirmed their alliance in the Manila Declaration, which expressed their shared interest in maintaining freedom of navigation and cooperating on maritime security.[64] The two militaries conduct frequent combined exercises, and the Philippines is a major recipient of funding from the U.S. International Military and Education Training (IMET) program.[65] Discussions are underway between Washington and Manila regarding enhanced U.S. military access to Philippine facilities, including the former U.S. naval base at Subic Bay, but these talks are less advanced than parallel negotiations with Australia and Singapore. Manila's balancing efforts appear to have gained new urgency since tensions ignited over Scarborough Shoal:

---

[62] "Australia–United States Force Posture Initiatives," Prime Minister of Australia, Media Release, November 16, 2011, http://www.pm.gov.au/press-office/australia-united-states-force-posture-initiatives.

[63] See Renato Cruz de Castro, "Between the Clawing Eagle and Ascendant Dragon: The Demise of the Philippines' Policy of Hedging," Lowy Institute for International Policy, Strategic Snapshot, no. 7, January 2011.

[64] "Manila Declaration on U.S.-Philippine Alliance," U.S. Department of State, November 16, 2011, http://translations.state.gov/st/english/texttrans/2011/11/20111116141458su0.2878338.html #axzz1t0AG9ZlN.

[65] Thayer, *Patterns of Security Cooperation*, 16.

in August 2012 the Philippines Senate ratified an agreement allowing Australian soldiers to train with the Philippines military in-country, after a four-year delay.[66]

Thai military cooperation with the United States has declined since the Cold War, and Bangkok has moved diplomatically closer to Beijing.[67] Moreover, Thailand remains a weakened reed owing to unresolved domestic political divisions. Yet Thailand is watchful of China's rise and has also chosen to maintain its alliance with the United States despite—or perhaps more correctly, as a hedge against—its proximity to and economic integration with China. It provides access and support to the U.S. military and hosts the annual Cobra Gold exercise led by U.S. Pacific Command, which has been expanding and is now the largest multinational exercise conducted in the Asia-Pacific region.[68]

However, the most prevalent response in Southeast Asia to China's military modernization and rising regional uncertainty takes the form of soft balancing—an inherently more ambiguous form of strategic behavior involving tacit balancing of a potentially threatening state or rising power, short of formal alliances. In addition to limited arms buildup, typical manifestations of soft balancing include the development of security understandings, *ad hoc* exercises, and collaboration in regional or international institutions.[69] Soft-balancing behavior in the region has intensified markedly in the last few years in direct response to concerns about China's rapidly growing military capabilities and unclear strategic intentions. This web of new, informal security linkages takes three main forms:

- strategic partnerships between the United States and nontraditional allies

- strategic partnerships with other major powers outside the immediate region—in some cases U.S. allies such as Japan, but also with India, for example

- strategic partnerships among Southeast Asian nations

---

[66] Luke Hunt, "Philippines Sign-off on Australian Troops," *Diplomat*, ASEAN Beat web log, July 26, 2012.

[67] Catharin E. Dalpino, "An Old Alliance for the New Century: Reinvigorating the U.S.-Thailand Alliance," NBR, NBR Special Report, no. 40, June 2012.

[68] Thayer, *Patterns of Security Cooperation*, 17.

[69] Paul, "Axioms of Balance of Power Theory," 3. See also Robert A. Pape, "Soft Balancing: How States Pursue Security in a Multipolar World" (paper presented at the Annual Meeting of the American Political Science Association, Chicago, September 2–5, 2004).

Despite speculation about U.S. decline and widespread predictions that Southeast Asian countries would bandwagon with China—particularly in the wake of the global financial crisis—almost all the countries in the region have moved to strengthen their security ties with the United States. The nascent Burma-U.S. rapprochement could prove the most recent example of this wider trend. China's development of advanced military capabilities, the escalation of tensions in the South China Sea since 2009, and the Obama administration's rebalancing toward Asia are factors in the acceleration of this trend.[70] However, the strengthening of ties between the United States and Southeast Asia goes back significantly further, to the period of uncertainty in the 1990s following the collapse of the Soviet Union and the first flutterings of concern in Asia about the risk of U.S. retrenchment and possible Chinese dominance.

Singapore and Malaysia, in different ways, both follow this pattern. Singapore—while pursuing a policy of "complex interdependence" with China—signed a strategic framework for defense cooperation with the United States in 2005 and has emerged as the United States' closest security partner in Southeast Asia, hosting visits by U.S. warships (including aircraft carriers) and aircraft. As part of the current round of changes to U.S. force posture in Asia, Singapore will host the deployment of up to four littoral combat ships.[71] Similarly, Malaysia, despite the anti-Western rhetoric of former prime minister Mahathir Mohamad, has for more than two decades been quietly building a defense relationship with the United States that one analyst calls "one of the region's best-kept 'secrets.'"[72] Malaysian and U.S. forces work together in around fifteen bilateral and multilateral exercises, including the major Cobra Gold and Rim of the Pacific (RIMPAC) series; Malaysia dispatched a medical team to Afghanistan; almost one hundred Malaysian military personnel train annually in the United States; Malaysia operates F/A-18 aircraft and is considering further acquisitions of U.S. defense equipment; and the number of annual U.S. Navy ship visits has risen from around 10 to over 30 in the past decade. Significant as these growing partnerships are, however, the emerging Vietnamese and Indonesian defense and security relationships with the United States are potentially of greater long-term importance to the region because of both countries' strategic weight.

---

[70] For a discussion of U.S. strategic rebalancing, see Michael Green and Dan Twining, "Dizzy Yet? The Pros and Cons of the Asia 'Pivot,'" *Foreign Policy,* Shadow Government web log, November 21, 2011, http://shadow.foreignpolicy.com/posts/2011/11/21/dizzy_yet_the_pros_and_cons_of_the_asia_pivot.

[71] See Jessica Brown, "Southeast Asia's American Embrace," Centre for Independent Studies, Foreign Policy Analysis, no. 7, March 29, 2011, 6; and John T. Bennett, "Singapore Willing to Host More U.S. Warships," *U.S. News,* DOTMIL web log, April 6, 2012, http://www.usnews.com/news/blogs/dotmil/2012/04/06/singapore-willing-to-host-more-us-warships.

[72] Thayer, *Patterns of Security Cooperation,* 44.

Despite the legacy of the Vietnam War, Washington and Hanoi took the first tentative steps toward normalizing relations in 1991 and achieved normalization in 1995. Since 2000, shared concern over China's growing strength has been a key driver of closer defense relations between the former adversaries, with Vietnamese officials looking to encourage a greater U.S. presence in Southeast Asia in order to counter China's ambitions.[73] The George W. Bush administration initiated annual bilateral summits and held four from 2005 to 2008. Washington successfully advocated unconditional normal trade relations status for Vietnam and WTO membership in 2007, and concluded a landmark bilateral trade agreement with Hanoi, which was ratified by Congress in 2011. As a result of these efforts, bilateral trade has burgeoned. The Obama administration has continued this high-level diplomatic momentum, with Secretary Clinton visiting Vietnam twice during 2010 and former secretary of defense Robert Gates once.[74]

Unsurprisingly, defense ties have developed more slowly than economic relations. U.S. policymakers have been keen to expand security and military cooperation with Vietnam since the early 2000s, whereas Hanoi has been more cautious.[75] Hanoi fears inconstancy in U.S. policy—not least because it knows Vietnam matters less to the United States than China does—and is resigned to having to limit its defense and other ties with the United States out of deference to China. Economic leverage is part of this equation, with Sino-Vietnamese trade growing fast and Vietnam partly dependent on China for electricity. Human rights concerns, on the other hand, remain the major constraint on the U.S. side, particularly in Congress.

Spurred by Vietnamese concern about China, however, early trust-building steps have led in recent years to a dramatic deepening in military-to-military relations. Nearly twenty U.S. naval vessels visited Vietnam between late 2003 and late 2010, including a highly symbolic visit by the USS *John S. McCain* to Da Nang Harbor in August 2010.[76] In addition, the two countries reached an IMET agreement in 2005, allowing Vietnamese officers to visit the United States for English-language training. Washington also began supporting Vietnam through the Foreign Military Financing program in 2009. In August 2010 the United States and Vietnam held an inaugural high-level dialogue on defense policy, and Vietnamese shipyards repaired two ships for the U.S. Military Sealift Command.[77] At the second

---

[73] Mark E. Manyin, "U.S.-Vietnam Relations in 2011: Current Issues and Implications for U.S. Policy," Congressional Research Service, CRS Report for Congress, R40208, July 26, 2011, 3–4.

[74] Ibid., 7.

[75] Ibid., 19–21.

[76] Thayer, *Patterns of Security Cooperation*, 44.

[77] Manyin, "U.S.-Vietnam Relations in 2011," 19–20.

dialogue in 2011, the two countries signed an agreement on military medical collaboration, which was their first formal military cooperation since normalization. Perhaps most significantly, in 2010 the United States and Vietnam worked closely in regional forums to mobilize a multilateral response to China's assertiveness in the South China Sea. The following year they conducted a combined naval exercise off the coast of Vietnam. Secretary of Defense Leon Panetta visited Hanoi in June 2012 to discuss possible military cooperation, and in August 2012 the United States began the first clean-up of the toxic chemical Agent Orange near Da Nang Airbase.

Predictably, China has not welcomed the warming of U.S.-Vietnam security relations. U.S. ship visits to Vietnam during 2010 and the transit through Vietnam's EEZ of the aircraft carrier USS *George Washington* drew warnings to Hanoi in China's state-controlled media not to become a "strategic pawn" of the United States.[78] Walking the delicate diplomatic tightrope between siding with the United States and appeasing China, Vietnam has taken steps since June 2011 to defuse tensions with Beijing. Recent actions include sending a special envoy to agree to a joint statement on peaceful resolution of the two countries' disputes at sea, breaking up domestic protests against China's actions in the South China Sea, and agreeing with its fellow ASEAN members and China to a July 2011 set of confidence-building guidelines.[79]

As a maritime Southeast Asian nation, Indonesia enjoys more strategic depth than Vietnam vis-à-vis China and faces very different defense challenges. Nonetheless, Jakarta has its own complicated history with China and must perform a difficult balancing act as it seeks to strengthen strategic links with Washington without alienating Beijing. Indonesia's decision to break with decades of nonalignment and sign a (subsequently lapsed) security agreement with Australia in 1995 was largely driven by long-term anxiety about China.[80] Although the country's forthcoming presidential election is a cause of some uncertainty, the long-term trend is a gradual movement away from nonalignment, at least in what Jakarta does, if not always in what it says.

After the fall of pro-Western strongman president Suharto in 1998, Indonesia grappled with a series of demanding internal challenges, including democratic transition and political decentralization, economic reform, the separation of East Timor, and a range of domestic security problems. Under the leadership of President Susilo Bambang Yudhoyono, however, the

---

[78] Storey, "China's Missteps in Southeast Asia," 6.

[79] Manyin, "U.S.-Vietnam Relations in 2011," 1–2.

[80] Ralf Emmers, "The Influence of the Balance of Power Factor within the ASEAN Regional Forum," *Contemporary Southeast Asia* 23, no. 2 (2001): 275–90, 282.

country has begun to re-emerge as the natural leader of Southeast Asia as well as a major power in its own right, with a seat in the group of twenty (G-20) and a respected voice on global issues. Over the same period, Indonesia has become more confident in its diplomatic dealings with China.[81] Yet, paradoxically, this new confidence has coincided with the emergence of China's rise as Indonesia's overriding security concern. Indonesian defense planners worry about China's growing power-projection capabilities and what they portend for the growing PLA presence in the Malacca Strait, the South China Sea, and the Indian Ocean—all critical strategic areas for Jakarta.[82] As noted above, China claims waters overlapping with Indonesia's EEZ around the Natuna Islands.

Nonetheless, Indonesian policymakers are divided in their attitudes toward Washington and have been cautious in re-embracing the United States as a security partner. Indonesian policy is shaped by a variety of factors, including domestic politics and the nation's traditional stance of nonalignment; the experience of sudden U.S. policy shifts, such as Congress's decision to sever defense ties in 2000 over human rights concerns; and a desire to avoid needlessly offending China. This ambivalence has hitherto been reinforced by the assessment that China does not yet have the military capabilities to pose a direct threat to Southeast Asia.[83] Indonesia is also wary of being dragged into a U.S.-led effort to "contain" China. Potential candidates to replace Yudhoyono as president are likely to be less overtly pro-American, at best. A Prabowo Subianto presidency, for example, could be problematic for U.S.-Indonesia relations—and in particular for defense cooperation—given Subianto's unsavory human rights record as a special forces officer.

Yet, notwithstanding these nuances and limitations, Indonesia-U.S. security ties have quietly but steadily intensified, particularly since the Bush administration moved to restore formal security ties in 2005 and resumed defense sales, military training, and bilateral exercises. Since then, the United States has helped provide Indonesia with maritime surveillance radar systems covering archipelagic waters, including the Malacca and Makassar straits. Washington has also provided funding to improve Indonesian capabilities to address smuggling, piracy, and trafficking. Furthermore, in 2009 the two countries hosted Garuda Shield, a major multilateral peacekeeping

---

[81] Rizal Sukma, "Indonesia's Response to the Rise of China: Growing Comfort amid Uncertainties," in *The Rise of China: Responses from Southeast Asia and Japan*, ed. Jun Tsunekawa (Tokyo: National Institute for Defense Studies, 2009), 139–55.

[82] Jessica Brown, "Jakarta's Juggling Act: Balancing China and America in the Asia-Pacific," Centre for Independent Studies, Foreign Policy Analysis, no. 5, February 3, 2011, 1, 3.

[83] Amitav Acharya, "Seeking Security in the Dragon's Shadow: China and Southeast Asia in the Emerging Asian Order," Institute of Defence and Strategic Studies, Working Paper, no. 44, March 2003.

exercise.[84] That same year, Secretary Clinton included Indonesia on her first official trip to Asia, and in June 2010 Presidents Obama and Yudhoyono signed a comprehensive partnership agreement.[85] The two governments also signed a defense framework agreement to boost security cooperation. On a visit to Jakarta the following month, then secretary of defense Robert Gates announced that military cooperation would gradually resume with the controversial Indonesian special forces unit Kopassus. Although the initial impetus for restoring defense relations may have come from a shared interest in prosecuting the war on terrorism, there is little doubt that uncertainty generated by China's military modernization is a factor sustaining Indonesia-U.S. defense cooperation in 2012. Indonesia remains "uncertain and anxious" about China's long-term role and intentions, both in economic and military terms.[86]

Southeast Asian countries may be drawing closer to the United States, but Indonesia is not the only one retaining its postcolonial antipathy to dependence. Regional states partly keep their strengthening defense ties with the United States low-key to avoid giving China overt cause for offense. Yet their colonial legacy is also a factor. Singapore, Vietnam, and Indonesia are all looking to diversify their partnerships with capable, strategically weighty powers other than the United States. India, for example, has a prominent place in the strategic calculations of all three.

Singapore, in particular, is a master at this aspect of soft balancing. The country not only has cultivated both a strong strategic relationship with the United States and comprehensive economic ties with China, but also has developed offsetting partnerships with the wider region's major maritime democracies—India, Japan, Australia, and South Korea. For instance, Singapore has been a strong supporter of New Delhi's "look east" policy since its inception at the end of the Cold War. Since 1993, the two nations have also conducted annual combined naval exercises known as SIMBEX (Singapore India Maritime Bilateral Exercise). SIMBEX has evolved from straightforward antisubmarine warfare training to advanced naval warfare exercises with air, surface, and subsurface dimensions. The most recent exercise was held in April 2012 in the Andaman Sea and Bay of Bengal.[87] Additionally, the two countries signed a defense cooperation agreement in 2003 and a bilateral agreement in 2007 to further facilitate combined

---

[84] Thayer, *Patterns of Security Cooperation*, 44.

[85] "The U.S.-Indonesia Comprehensive Partnership," White House, Press Release, June 27, 2010, http://www.whitehouse.gov/the-press-office/us-indonesia-comprehensive-partnership.

[86] Sukma, "Indonesia's Response to the Rise of China," 140, 153.

[87] "Singapore, Indian Navies Conduct Bilateral Maritime Exercise," *Channel News Asia*, April 1, 2012, http://www.channelnewsasia.com/stories/singaporelocalnews/view/1192489/1/.html.

training and exercises in India. Both militaries dispatched maritime forces as part of the core group that responded to the 2004 Boxing Day tsunami. As a result of these developments, as well as burgeoning economic links, Singapore has become India's most important political partner in Southeast Asia.[88]

Singapore likewise enjoys a close security relationship with Australia, which includes shared participation in the Five Power Defence Arrangements (along with Malaysia, New Zealand, and the United Kingdom) and extensive use of Australian training facilities by Singapore military aircraft and ground forces. Singapore and Japan also recently established a bilateral maritime security dialogue, which will add to existing security cooperation in areas such as counterterrorism.

Vietnam is implementing its own soft-balancing strategy in which, as noted above, India has an important place. Cultural and economic ties between the two countries go back centuries. They forged a close strategic relationship during the Cold War, when both countries looked to Moscow for military equipment and economic support. In addition, India was one of a few non-Communist countries to support Vietnam during its war with Cambodia in the late 1970s. Since 2000, Indian and Vietnamese naval forces have conducted combined naval exercises, and in June 2010 Hanoi and New Delhi agreed to increase the frequency of Indian ship visits to Vietnam. Later that year, Prime Minister Nguyen Tan Dung announced that Vietnam would open the former U.S. naval base at Cam Ranh Bay to foreign navies— including submarines and aircraft carriers—for repair and re-provisioning.[89] This move apparently tested Beijing's patience: in September 2011, Chinese naval vessels harassed an Indian warship off the coast of Vietnam, according to media reports.[90]

Indonesia is also developing closer security ties with India, with the two sides having conducted joint maritime patrols of the Malacca Strait since 2002. Similarly, Australia signed a formal security framework agreement with Indonesia (2006) and security declarations with Japan (2007), South Korea (2009), and India (2009).

---

[88] David Brewster, "India's Security Partnership with Singapore," *Pacific Review* 22, no. 5 (2009): 597.

[89] Storey, "China's Missteps in Southeast Asia," 7.

[90] "South China Spree: Beijing Has Much to Gain by Observing International Rules," *Financial Times*, September 2, 2011. In June 2012, PLAN vessels reportedly insisted on "escorting" a flotilla of four Indian naval vessels through international waters in the South China Sea en route to a port call in Shanghai. See Ananth Krishnan, "In South China Sea, a Surprise China Escort for Indian Ships," *Hindu*, June 14, 2012, http://www.thehindu.com/news/national/article3524965.ece.

Institutional Balancing: Multilateral Security Diplomacy in the Asia-Pacific

Finally, Southeast Asian nations are adept at institutional forms of soft balancing and have continued to demonstrate this in their responses to China's military modernization and behavior in the South China Sea. There are important intraregional reasons for the establishment of ASEAN and the subsequent development of other regional institutions based on and around it.[91] A desire to overcome long-standing enmities and allow very different political and economic systems to coexist, the need to develop common solutions to shared transnational problems and to present a more united front to outside powers, and the imperatives of economic integration during the era of globalization have all been drivers of Southeast Asian regionalism.

However, there has also been a strong external impetus. Soon after the collapse of the Soviet Union, Southeast Asian governments turned their minds to the possibility of destabilizing U.S. retrenchment. The U.S. withdrawal from the Philippines in 1992 heightened concerns about China's growing influence, and by 1993 China's rising power had become regional countries' main source of concern.[92] They recognized the importance of the U.S. alliance system in Asia but saw the building of regional multilateral security institutions—with ASEAN at their core—as a means of balancing China by locking in U.S. strategic engagement in a post-Soviet world and binding China into peaceful norms of behavior before it became too powerful to influence. Hence, when the ASEAN Regional Forum was established in 1994, a key purpose was "to engage the United States, Japan and the PRC in a structure of multilateral dialogue in order to promote a stable distribution of power in the Asia-Pacific."[93] Multilateral institutions offer the additional advantage to Southeast Asian countries of "safety in numbers": Beijing strongly prefers a bilateral approach to contending claims in the South China Sea, but Southeast Asian countries have astutely sought to use regional bodies to avoid being singled out by China and to instead play it against the United States.

Despite the ARF's modest track record (which certainly has fallen conspicuously short of the forum's foundational aim of moderating China's

---

[91] These include the ASEAN Regional Forum (formed in 1994 as a forum for discussion of regional security issues and to foster security cooperation), ASEAN +3 cooperation (established in 1997 between ASEAN and China, Japan, and South Korea to focus on a range of economic and transnational issues), and the East Asia Summit (an annual regional summit first held in 2005 and expanded in 2010 to include the United States and Russia).

[92] Emmers, "Influence of the Balance of Power Factor," 281.

[93] Ibid., 280.

behavior) and the relative weakness of multilateral security institutions in Asia, this logic has continued to underpin Southeast Asian attitudes toward regional architecture. The ASEAN countries do not trust China sufficiently to embrace Beijing's "ASEAN +3" institutional model as a construct for maintaining regional security. Hence, they see the security focus of the newer East Asia Summit as a hedge against Chinese assertiveness.[94] Singapore campaigned actively, with support from Indonesia and Japan, to persuade Australia and India—and later, the United States—to join the EAS in order to counterbalance China. Vietnam has successfully exploited the EAS, as well as the relatively new ASEAN Defence Ministers' Meeting-Plus (ADMM-Plus), as a forum to internationalize the South China Sea issue.

Notwithstanding ASEAN's industrious institution-building, the two most significant developments in terms of regional architecture have been China's embrace of regional multilateralism—and particularly the exclusive ASEAN +3 model—in the latter half of the 1990s as a means of countering U.S. influence in Asia, and the Obama administration's shift from ambivalence to active participation in regional institutions, particularly the EAS. Regarding the EAS, President Obama called for the dialogue to be broadened to include traditional strategic challenges, including maritime security.[95] As a result of these dynamics, the chief importance of the EAS and other key regional organizations may be that they are increasingly becoming another diplomatic front where Sino-U.S. strategic competition plays out.

Southeast Asian countries are using these groups as part of their strategy to ensure that the United States stays closely engaged—particularly when things heat up in the South China Sea, as they did in April 2012 between China and the Philippines—and to keep other major external powers in the equation for balance. Regional states become equally concerned, however, if tensions between Beijing and Washington rise too much. After Secretary Clinton's remarks (made largely in response to regional concern) grabbed world headlines at the ARF in July 2010, Southeast Asian governments looked to turn down the temperature, reportedly softening language in the communiqué of the second U.S.-ASEAN summit held in New York the following September (subsequent statements, including at the 2010 EAS, were stronger).[96] Whether the EAS develops into a substantial mechanism remains to be seen, however, particularly as the next three EAS chairs are Cambodia, Brunei, and Burma. In the words of one Southeast Asia expert,

---

[94] Donald K. Emmerson, "U.S., China Role Play for ASEAN," *Asia Times Online*, November 19, 2011.

[95] Ralph A. Cossa and Brad Glosserman, "Regional Overview: A Pivotal Moment for U.S. Foreign Policy?" Pacific Forum CSIS, Comparative Connections 13, no. 3, January 2012.

[96] Storey, "China's Missteps in Southeast Asia."

"the EAS to date is little more than an annual conversation."[97] The jury is similarly out on the ADMM-Plus: it meets only once every three years, and the first meeting in October 2010 produced modest results, although five working groups have been established to develop practical regional cooperation on humanitarian assistance and disaster relief, maritime security, military medicine, counterterrorism, and peacekeeping.[98]

The limitations of institutional balancing as a strategy were sharply exposed by the acrimonious breakdown of July 2012 ASEAN foreign ministers' talks in Phnom Penh. As noted above, the meeting failed to issue a communiqué after the host Cambodian government, at China's behest, rejected a push led by the Philippines and Vietnam to include a reference to current tensions over Scarborough Shoal. This outcome highlighted deep divisions within ASEAN over China's rise, the hardening of positions on the South China Sea, and the rising risk of miscalculation. It will also likely reinforce the efforts of Southeast Asian countries will to hedge by strengthening their own defense capabilities as well as bilateral links with the United States and other regional partners.

Positioning for the Pivot: Regional Reactions to U.S. Rebalancing

An increased U.S. emphasis on Southeast Asia has been an explicit element of the U.S. "pivot," or rebalancing, to Asia. Whereas the Obama administration can point to a number of concrete achievements in the region, the George W. Bush administration is often criticized for giving insufficient attention to Southeast Asia or alternatively for seeing the region exclusively through the lens of the global war on terrorism and ignoring individual countries' priorities and interests.[99] This impression was not helped by the Bush administration's occasional failure to attend regional meetings, which, however insubstantial in content, are symbolically important to Southeast Asian countries as a sign of continuing U.S. interest and engagement.

The reality is more complex, however. Many Southeast Asian countries, including Singapore, Indonesia, Malaysia, and the Philippines, shared Washington's concern about terrorism, and there is likewise evidence that the Bush administration recognized the wider strategic importance of Southeast Asia. For example, it took steps to strengthen bilateral security and broader links with the Philippines, Thailand, Singapore, Indonesia, and

---

[97] Emmerson, "U.S., China Role Play for ASEAN."

[98] David Capie and Brendan Taylor, "Two Cheers for ADMM+," CSIS, PacNet, no. 51, October 20, 2010.

[99] See, for example, Thayer, *Patterns of Security Cooperation,* 9, 54.

Vietnam. There is no doubt that terrorism was a major driver of much of this cooperation, which included counterterrorism and capacity-building operations by U.S. forces in the southern Philippines. The United States granted the Philippines and Thailand "major non-NATO ally" status in 2003, and the following year concluded a bilateral FTA with Singapore—the United States' first with an East Asian country. In 2005, Washington signed a strategic framework agreement with Singapore and began the process of normalizing military ties with Indonesia. The inaugural U.S.-Vietnam strategic dialogue was held in October 2008, while signing the ASEAN Treaty of Amity and Cooperation (TAC)—a precondition for U.S. participation in the EAS—was also debated under Bush.[100] Ultimately, however, the latter part of Bush's second term saw the growing threat posed by North Korea's nuclear program become the main U.S. preoccupation in the region, and the United States' broader Asia policy suffered as a result.

Nonetheless, the preceding discussion highlights the underlying continuities in U.S. policy toward Southeast Asia. The Obama administration took office determined to place more emphasis on the region, and there is no doubt it has succeeded in broadening the narrative and, to some extent, the substance of U.S. engagement. This was a deliberate shift that has been helped by the passage of time since September 11 and progress in the war on terrorism. The Obama administration has also abandoned the United States' traditional ambivalence about Asian multilateral security institutions—as symbolized by the decision to sign the TAC, President Obama's attendance at the 2011 EAS in Indonesia, the push to put traditional security issues on the agenda for the EAS, and Washington's support for the ADMM-Plus. Additionally, the administration has deftly encouraged tentative political reforms in Burma by softening its policies and looking to re-engage, albeit cautiously. Secretary of State Clinton even paid a historic visit to the country late in 2011. The State Department has signaled it "gets" Southeast Asia by appointing a resident ambassador to ASEAN, dispatching senior officials (led by the energetic assistant secretary of state for East Asian and Pacific affairs, Kurt Campbell) to the region, and attending major regional meetings. Finally, Obama's advocacy of the Trans-Pacific Partnership (TPP) has helped deal the United States back into the Asian trade policy game, while also underlining that the administration's Southeast Asia policy is broadly based rather than driven only by defense or diplomatic considerations.

Stepped-up U.S. engagement with Southeast Asia has included intensified bilateral and multilateral diplomacy, a series of discrete but coordinated changes to U.S. military posture in the region, a re-energized

---

[100] Prashanth Parameswaran, "U.S.-ASEAN Relations in America's 'Pacific Century,'" Fletcher Forum of World Affairs web log, March 9, 2012, http://www.fletcherforum.org/2012/03/09/parameswaran.

exercise program with allies and partners, and a renewed interest in trade liberalization under the TPP rubric. Washington's firm support for freedom of navigation in the South China Sea—including in regional meetings at which China is present, such as the July 2012 ARF—has also helped reassure increasingly nervous Southeast Asian governments.[101] To date these moves have been widely welcomed in the region, although for reasons discussed above some governments are cautious about expressing that support too openly.

As previously noted, Australia and Singapore have come forward to offer enhanced access to U.S. military forces, and discussions are also underway between the United States and the Philippines. In Australia's case, the talks leading to Obama's announcement were initiated by Canberra and began as early as 2007.[102] Singapore has been more circumspect about publicizing the deployment of littoral combat ships but nonetheless has reportedly offered to double the number of the U.S. naval vessels stationed in the country.[103] In October 2011, Philippine and U.S. forces held a ten-day amphibious landing exercise involving more than two thousand American personnel.[104] Jakarta initially grumbled about the Australian announcement but seems mollified by suggestions that the U.S. marines operating out of Darwin would be available to conduct disaster-relief operations with Indonesian and other regional militaries. President Obama's announcement in November 2011 that the United States would transfer 24 excess F-16 fighter aircraft to Indonesia may also have helped.[105] There are constraints on both sides of the U.S.-Vietnam security relationship, but the steady increase in military-to-military links is likely to continue, albeit from a low base. The United States, Australia, and a number of the Southeast Asian countries discussed in this chapter will likely look for new opportunities to conduct "minilateral" defense and security exercises, particularly in the maritime domain.

---

[101] In August 2012 Washington and Beijing traded angry statements over the Sansha announcement mentioned above. See Geoff Dyer, "Clinton Warns Beijing on Sea Dispute," *Financial Times*, July 12, 2012.

[102] The author was a senior Australian foreign policy adviser at the time.

[103] Bennett, "Singapore Willing to Host."

[104] Cossa and Glosserman, "Regional Overview."

[105] Ibid.

Conclusion

It follows from the analysis in this chapter that the reactions of Australia and countries in Southeast Asia to U.S. rebalancing efforts will vary, as will the strategies these countries adopt to respond to China's ongoing military modernization program. This is just one more manifestation of the diversity and complexity of this increasingly important region. It is possible, however, to draw several overarching policy implications.

The first is that the responses to China's military modernization by Australia and a number of strategically important countries in Southeast Asia are shifting up the spectrum from soft toward harder forms of balancing. This trend is clearly of some concern to Beijing, which responds with bluster, often involving maritime harassment, claims of containment, and efforts to intimidate. Yet, significantly, there is little evidence that China's actions are influencing regional countries' strategic choices in the desired direction. Indeed, they seem to be counterproductive: the first marines have arrived in Australia, Singapore is proceeding with the deployment of littoral combat ships, the Philippines is considering reopening Subic Bay to U.S. vessels, and Vietnam continues to host visits to Cam Ranh Bay by U.S., Indian, and other navies.

Indeed, the second, and related, conclusion is that this situation is in large part China's doing. As one analyst put it, "Chinese muscle-flexing in [2010] did as much for the U.S. position in Asia as a half century of American diplomacy."[106] The receptiveness of governments to U.S. proposals for closer political, military, and economic engagement varies across the region for the reasons outlined in the chapter. Admittedly, moves to strengthen security cooperation in many cases predate China's recent assertiveness: this is certainly the case with U.S.-Australian cooperation and also is true of warming ties with Vietnam and Indonesia, as well as with Singapore and Malaysia. But there is little doubt that China's behavior has accelerated this trend and, at least in the cases of the Philippines and Burma, probably helped trigger a change in direction. It follows that the tempo of strengthening U.S. defense ties with the region will be influenced at least in part by China's future conduct.

The final conclusion—and perhaps the most important one—is that the United States' commitment to Southeast Asia is on trial. Most countries in the region fear U.S. strategic retrenchment, not least because of concern about growing Chinese military capabilities and uncertainty about Beijing's intentions. They have thus welcomed the Obama administration's declared

---

[106] Brad Glosserman, "Caging the Dragon? Asian Regional Integration and the United States," Sigur Center for Asian Studies, Policy Commentary, May 2011.

rebalancing toward Asia and its focus on Southeast Asia in particular. However, regional states still must be convinced that the commitment will be sustained, not just over the next few years but for several decades. In part this is a question of resources: the jury remains out as to whether Obama's pivot will prove sustainable in an era of enforced U.S. austerity. Even more, however, the issue is one of staying power—whether declaratory policy will be matched with the necessary will and persistence to counter determined Chinese efforts to offset key areas of U.S. military advantage and to shape the choices of regional countries. In this sense, current events in the South China Sea are part of a wider series that cumulatively sets precedents and patterns of behavior for how China uses its growing power and how regional countries—and the United States—respond. This means that China's military modernization is not just a problem for the future; that future is being made now, in the waters lapping Scarborough Shoal.

EXECUTIVE SUMMARY

This chapter examines the impact of Chinese military modernization on India's military and strategic posture and outlines the country's response to this growing security concern.

MAIN ARGUMENT:
China's military modernization, capacity-building, infrastructure development in Tibet, and moves into the Indian Ocean pose serious challenges to India's security. China's growing footprint in South Asia and attempts to bring peripheral states into its circle of influence only add to these concerns. There is a duality in approaches to dealing with these challenges: while broader political discourse underscores cooperation and downplays competition, there is nonetheless a growing realization that India needs to develop credible hard power as a dissuasive strategy against China. India's strategic dilemma thus lies in shaping its political response to external balancing. Although there is the understanding of a strategic convergence between India and the U.S., there is little consensus on how to shape this relationship to further India's strategic interests. New Delhi continues to face a policy dilemma about whether to be a regional balancer, a swing state, or a strategic hedge.

POLICY IMPLICATIONS:
- The period between now and 2025 is one of strategic vulnerability for India. India needs to fast-track its plans for military modernization and its procedures for procurement.

- India needs to develop a strong bilateral relationship with the U.S., based on a congruence of strategic interests, as a hedge against China.

- To build its indigenous defense capability and industrial base, India needs to seriously examine the U.S. offer of defense cooperation, particularly in critical areas such as C4ISR, space, IT, and cyberspace.

- India needs to initiate a discussion on fostering maritime cooperation among the Asian littorals in order to establish "rimland security."

China's Military Modernization: Responses from India

Arun Sahgal

India's strategic concerns regarding China arise from the latter's emergence as the most influential actor in Asia—one with the ability to shape the future balance of power. What is even more worrisome to India is growing Chinese influence in South Asia and the extended Indian Ocean region (IOR), where New Delhi believes Beijing is severely depreciating its area of influence. Furthermore, China is backing its aggressive assertions with a steady buildup of comprehensive national power and regional military capability. Its military budget has grown annually by double-digit figures for over two decades, with the current 2012–13 fiscal year (FY) outlay crossing $100 billion. This trend continues to fuel apprehension and concern that China will play an increasingly assertive role in Asia and beyond.

There is a general understanding in India that the main focus of China's military modernization and grand strategy is geopolitical competition with the United States, particularly in light of Washington's recently announced "rebalancing strategy" for the Asia-Pacific. Indian concerns about the modernization of the People's Liberation Army (PLA), however, arise primarily from what Robert Kaplan calls the "collapse of distance brought about by advances in military technology," allowing countries to encroach on each other's sphere of influence.[1] Although China tends to underplay the threat from India, both in terms of India's military modernization and

Arun Sahgal is Joint Director of Net Assessment, Technology, and Simulation at the Institute of National Security Studies in New Delhi and Founding Director of the Indian Net Assessment Directorate. He can be reached at <brigarun.sahgal@gmail.com>.

[1] Robert D. Kaplan, "The India-China Rivalry," Stratfor, Global Intelligence, April 25, 2012.

existing capabilities, Beijing has recently exhibited a tendency to look at these capabilities from the larger perspective of strategic collusion between India and the United States.[2] This tendency reflects a mindset that increasingly perceives India as a "near peer competitor"—one acting in concert with the United States—that could in the long run challenge China's regional and global aspirations for preeminence. This is despite repeated assertions by the Indian leadership that India does not have major security issues with China other than the boundary dispute.[3]

India and China went to war over their 5,045-kilometer (km) undemarcated border in 1962. Today, New Delhi claims China illegally occupies 38,000 square km of its territory, while Beijing periodically asserts ownership over a 90,000-square-km area encompassing the northeastern province of Arunachal Pradesh. Although there has been an upswing in diplomatic, political, economic, and even military ties over the past decade—intensifying from 2004 onward—no resolution to the frontier dispute seems imminent. China's continuing military modernization and incremental upgrading of its military posture in Tibet to enable rapid force deployment, backed by logistics capability and communications infrastructure, are worrisome to India. So are repeated incursions by the PLA across the Line of Actual Control (LAC), including into settled or undisputed areas like Sikkim in northeastern India. India looks upon these actions as coercive tactics to keep tensions alive and New Delhi on the defensive.

Another source of tension is Kashmir, which is divided between India and Pakistan—a close Chinese military and nuclear ally. A large tract of Kashmiri territory was ceded by Pakistan to China in 1963, the future of which is to be decided upon final settlement of the Kashmir issue between India and Pakistan. China has built a military highway in this territory and is unlikely to vacate the region. In recent years, Beijing has subtly joined the Kashmir dispute, weighing in on Pakistan's side and causing New Delhi much discomfort.

Thus, the bilateral relationship is largely dictated by each country's understanding of the other's strategic vision, capabilities, and areas of influence. Any miscalculation of the other side's military capability or core interests could degrade ties and lead ultimately to possible conflict. Given this trouble-ridden backdrop, this chapter aims to address two significant and interconnected policy issues: (1) the impact of China's military modernization on India's security, and (2) how India is responding to these

---

[2] The details of Chinese thinking are outlined in He Zude and Fang Wei, "India's Increasing Troop May Go Nowhere," *People's Daily Online*, November 15, 2011.

[3] "No Issues with China Except Boundary Dispute: SM Krishna," *Jagran Post*, June 6, 2012, http://post.jagran.com/No-issue-with-China-other-than-boundary-dispute-SM-Krishna-1338962561.

proliferating security concerns through diplomacy or foreign policy and military modernization, including the development of capabilities in both the continental and maritime domains. In examining the broader Indian response to China's military modernization, this chapter addresses four topics.

First, it examines the overall nature of India's modernization efforts, with particular reference to capacity-building, including the development of infrastructure in response to Chinese forays into Tibet and the IOR. In the context of this discussion, the chapter considers how China is leveraging economic and military relationships with India's neighbors to establish a containment policy toward India.

Second, the chapter examines the perceptions of India's political elite toward China. Some leaders believe that the burgeoning power differential between the two countries must be addressed through a policy aimed at reducing strategic risks via engagement and economic cooperation. They are thus focused on soft rather than hard power and pursue a middle path of engaging China on a broad spectrum of issues without compromising on India's core security concerns. Other political elites, however, want New Delhi to develop adequate military response capabilities at both the strategic and tactical levels to dissuade or deter China from adventurism.

Third, the chapter discusses the steps India is taking to enhance its overall military capability, even as it seeks a cooperative and balanced relationship of mutual advantage with China. New Delhi aims to manage military asymmetry with China through a strategy of credible dissuasive deterrence. The efficacy of this strategy and the time frame for building new capacities are also examined.

The fourth and final issue examined is whether India's concept of strategic autonomy will be sufficient to face the emerging challenges from China. The chapter argues that in dealing with an assertive China, India will be forced into upgrading its conventional and strategic military posture as well as into seeking adequate external balancing. If India's economy begins to flag, however, the challenge from China will be formidable. The chapter analyzes New Delhi's options in such a scenario, including further accommodation of China and external balancing through a cooperative strategic framework led by the United States.

Indian Concerns about Chinese Military Modernization

Developments in Tibet

There is growing concern over the massive Chinese infrastructure buildup in the Tibet Autonomous Region (TAR). The Indian defense minister, A.K. Antony, recently informed the Indian Parliament about rapid developments being undertaken by China in terms of rail, road, airfield, and telecommunications infrastructure.[4] Indian security and military officials are increasingly concerned about these developments, which they view as largely India-centric. This includes capacity augmentation of the Golmud-Lhasa rail line that according to estimates will enable China to mobilize as many as twelve PLA divisions over a four-week period. Similarly, rail links from Lanzhou to Kashi and onto Lhasa facilitate easy switching of reserves and logistics resources between the Chengdu and Lanzhou military regions bordering India.[5] Additionally, Antony also acknowledged that China has developed a 58,000-km road network and constructed five operational airfields at Gongar, Pangta, Linchi, Hoping, and Gar Gunsa.[6] China's massive program to upgrade its airfields, including the development of advance landing grounds, greatly enhances the Chinese air force's overall offensive potential in Tibet and provides substantial strategic airlift capability, allowing for a rapid buildup of forces and shortening the warning period for India.

According to Monika Chansoria at the Centre for Land Warfare Studies in New Delhi, which is sponsored by the Indian Army, China is upgrading its net-centric warfare capability in the TAR. To support its command and control structures, China has installed 58 very small aperture terminal satellite stations and has rapidly spread its fiber-optic communications network. It is also reported to have laid a fiber-optic network in all 55 counties of the TAR, including remote border areas such as Ali and Chamdo.[7] Secure communications and broadband connectivity allow the fielding of battlefield command systems, which further tilts the cyberwarfare balance in the PLA's favor.

Vagaries of nature and the complexities of high-altitude terrain essentially preclude the rapid and massed application of forces. This to an extent calls into question the PLA's ability to rapidly deploy regular and special forces in a preemptive offensive in the TAR. To address the issue of rapid, contingency-based force application at high altitudes, the PLA is reportedly constructing hyperbaric chambers to facilitate rapid acclimatization of troops inducted from lower regions. It is also building the first batch of oxygen-enriched

---

[4] For more details see, Gurmeet Kanwal and Monika Chansoria, "China Preparing Tibet as Future War Zone," *Deccan Herald*, June 3, 2011.

[5] Kanwal and Chansoria, "China Preparing Tibet."

[6] "China Has Five Airfields in Tibet, Antony Tells House," *Tribune News Service*, March 7, 2011, http://www.tribuneindia.com/2011/20110308/nation.htm#2; and "No Issues with China Except Boundary Dispute." For more details, see Monika Chansoria, "China's Infrastructure Developments in Tibet: Evaluating Trendlines," Centre for Land Warfare Studies, Manekshaw Paper, no. 32, 2011, 14.

[7] Chansoria, "China's Infrastructure Developments in Tibet," 17.

troop barracks at the TAR's Nagchu Military Sub-Command at a height of 4,500 meters.[8]

To fine-tune its force application models, the PLA has increased both the level and the frequency of exercises in Tibet. The scope of these exercises is becoming increasingly sophisticated and showcases Chinese capacities not only in net-centric warfare but in fielding integrated command platforms and providing real-time information and battlefield assessments. For example, in November 2011 the PLA for the first time rehearsed capture of mountain passes in Tibet at heights over five thousand meters with the help of armored vehicles and airborne troops in a live military exercise.[9] The exercise also involved massed rocket and artillery fire that showcased a vertically launched joint-attack rocket and missile system for precision attacks equipped with terminal guidance sensors. In live firing drills, the PLA Air Force (PLAAF) has been employing multirole, air superiority J-10 fighters in a ground-attack configuration using conventional and laser-guided bombs. These exercises are a critical pointer to the PLA's heightened preparedness along the Indian border, especially as it seeks to prepare for joint and integrated operations incorporating air power and upgraded ground and air-defense forces.

In addition, China is building conventional and strategic missile capabilities in Tibet, basing them on the region's growing infrastructure. According to defense analyst Vijai K. Nair, China has been upgrading its nuclear and ballistic missiles to target India. Not only has the number of CSS-2 missiles with a 3,100-km strike range employed by the 53rd Army at Jianshui remained unchanged, but the reported deployment of Dong Feng-21 (CSS-5) medium-range ballistic missiles (MRBM) along India's border further underscores the reality of the Chinese threat.

The proximity of the heavily populated provinces of Uttar Pradesh and Bihar, as well as other eastern states, is a major strategic vulnerability for India. This equation is set to change, however, with India's successful testing of 3,500-km-range Agni 4 and 5,500-km-range Agni 5 MRBMs, bringing the entire coast of China within range. Yet the strategic power differential between India and China will remain until such time as these and other missile variants, including submarine-launched intermediate-range ballistic missiles (IRBM), are produced in adequate numbers.

---

[8] "China Builds Oxygen-Rich Barracks for Soldiers in Tibet," *Tibet News Digest*, June 27, 2010, http://www.tibetinfonet.net/content/news/11303.

[9] Pranab Dhal Samanta, "China Now Rehearses Capture of Tibet Passes," *Indian Express*, November 20, 2011, http://www.indianexpress.com/news/china-now-rehearses-capture-of-tibet-passes/878174/0.

Chinese Forays into the Indian Ocean Region

The Indian Ocean is emerging as the greatest security challenge for China and an arena where its strategic interests clash with those of India, the United States, and Japan. To deal with this strategic vulnerability, China has introduced the concept of "far sea defense" as the driver for developing its long-range naval capabilities. The PLA Navy (PLAN) defines the "far seas" as stretching from the northwest Pacific Ocean to the eastern Indian Ocean and, more recently, the east coast of Africa.[10]

The rapidity with which the PLAN is moving toward securing this goal demonstrates its political intent and focus on capability and technology development, including absorption. In a recent in-house simulation exercise on Chinese naval power based on the PLAN's likely production capacities, it was surmised that by 2025 China will be in a position to deploy at least one carrier battle group in the IOR. This group would be backed by one or two surface action groups and supported by two or three nuclear-powered attack submarines (SSN) and shore-based medium-range missiles, including antiship ballistic missiles covering large swathes of the Bay of Bengal and the Arabian Sea.[11] To support these deployments, China is readying "lily pads" in the Indian Ocean to facilitate the stationing and berthing of vessels by providing technical support, maintenance, refueling, and associated materiel supplies. These pads will spread from the South China Sea to the East African coastline.

Chinese Strategy in South Asia

China is following a three-track balance-of-power strategy in Asia. First, the country is attempting to maximize the power gap between itself and its strong Asian neighbors through focused military modernization and simultaneously leverage its economic and political clout. Second, China is using states such as Iran, Pakistan, the Central Asian republics, and Myanmar, and to a lesser extent Sri Lanka, Bangladesh, and the Maldives, as proxies to gain access to critical oil and gas resources and the Indian Ocean. Last, Beijing is using soft power through multilateral economic and political engagement to enhance its strategic influence across Asia.

---

[10] See Phillip C. Saunders, Christopher D. Yung, Michael Swaine, and Andrew Nien-Dzu Yang, eds., *The Chinese Navy: Expanding Capabilities, Evolving Roles* (Washington, D.C.: National Defense University Press, 2011), 129; and Joseph Y. Lin, "China Focuses on 'Far Sea Defence,'" *Asia Times Online*, July 9, 2010.

[11] This exercise was carried out by Institute of National Security Studies as part of a project on non-contact war and anti-access strategy to evaluate Chinese options in the Indian Ocean region.

The central objective of this multipronged policy is to ensure a peaceful and stable periphery through economic engagement and infrastructure development. Rail and pipeline links from Myanmar to Yunnan Province and various corridors connecting southern and southwestern China with South and Southeast Asia, including railway lines, are all part of this vast and fast-expanding network. Another level of this multilayered strategy is the resolution of boundary disputes: China has resolved most of its land and maritime boundary disputes in South Asia except those with India and Bhutan. Recently, it amicably demarcated its frontier dispute with Tajikistan, forsaking its territorial claims for bilateral benefit.[12] China has lately made similar overtures to Bhutan, seeking to resolve their long-standing boundary dispute in return for permission to open a consular office in Thimphu, much to the chagrin of India.[13]

China's attempts at strategic balancing in South Asia by forging military and economic ties with all of India's neighbors, some of whom have fractious ties with New Delhi, and by expanding its naval power in the IOR have further exacerbated bilateral tensions. Beijing's deft moves are aimed at effectively isolating India and further narrowing New Delhi's traditional strategic space. In the case of Pakistan, China is actively engaged in infrastructure development in western Baluchistan Province, Gilgit-Baltistan, and other parts of Pakistan-occupied Kashmir. Major investments are also afoot to develop strategic land bridges connecting the subcontinent to the Chinese mainland through dedicated pipeline and transport corridors to the Indian Ocean.

Further vitiating the atmosphere is the growing anti-India stridency in Beijing, backed by China's influential media, microblogs, and think tanks. A recent *Global Times* editorial following the successful test flight of India's Agni V IRBM warned India not to be "arrogant" considering that China's nuclear power remained much stronger. The article cautioned New Delhi that it stood "no chance" in an arms race with China[14] and portrayed India as a belligerent nation eager to flaunt its missile capabilities. Similar views are expressed with regard to India's oil-exploration ventures in the South China Sea off the Vietnamese coast.[15] Such provocations only serve to further exacerbate tensions between the two sides.

---

[12] "Tajikistan Ratifies Demarcation Agreement with China in Settlement of Long-Running Dispute," Boundary News, International Boundaries Research Unit, Durham University, January 13, 2011, http://www.dur.ac.uk/ibru/news/boundary_news/?itemno=11360&rehref=%2Fibru%2Fnews%2F &resubj=Boundary+news%20Headlines.

[13] Anuradha Sharma and Vishal Arora, "India Keeps Close Eye on China's Courtship of Bhutan," *World Political Review*, June 2012, 23–29.

[14] "India Being Swept Up by Missile Delusion," *Global Times*, April 19, 2012.

[15] "India's Sea Oil Push Politically Motivated," *Global Times*, July 31, 2012, http://www.globaltimes.cn/content/724439.shtml.

India's China Policy

India's Strategic Focus on China

There is a growing perception within India's strategic community and policy establishment that New Delhi should not underestimate China's determination to assert its territorial sovereignty.[16] The defense minister's 2010 operational directive, which is reviewed every five years and lays down operational priorities for all three services, highlights the growing threat from China in a two-front war scenario that also involves China's close ally Pakistan. The directive asks the Indian military to prepare for a full-spectrum war that could include WMDs.[17] The recently published foreign and security policy document "Nonalignment 2.0," authored by leading Indian diplomats, security experts, and military leaders, asserts that Chinese power is impinging directly on India's geopolitical space. The report acknowledges the widening economic and military power differential and underscores the need to maintain the status quo along the LAC in the north while enlarging and building on India's current edge in the maritime south.[18] Similar sentiments of India being prepared to deal with an assertive China have been expressed by the Naresh Chandra Task Force set up to review national security architecture.[19]

Indian policymakers are thus adopting a view that China is insensitive to Indian security concerns. Consequently, there is a growing understanding within India's national security establishment, particularly among the military services, that Indian strategic and military capacity-building must shift incrementally from a Pakistan-centric approach to focus more directly on China.

Until the end of the twentieth century—i.e., over 50 years after independence—India's doctrinal thinking and military acquisitions had steadfastly maintained a focus on meeting the threat from Pakistan. Since 1947, Pakistan has been to war with India three times (1947, 1965, and 1971) in addition to fighting an eleven-week border skirmish in Kashmir's mountainous Kargil region in 1999, in which some 1,200 soldiers died.

---

[16] B. Raman, "My Thoughts on China," South Asia Analysis Group, Paper 4965, March 16, 2012, http://southasiaanalysis.org/papers50/paper4965.html.

[17] R.S. Chauhan, "Defence Ministry Warns House Panel of 'Asymmetric Threats,'" Rediff, May 2, 2012, http://www.rediff.com/news/report/defence-ministry-warns-house-panel-of-asymmetric-threats/20120502.htm.

[18] Sunil Khilnani et al., "Nonalignment 2.0: A Foreign and Strategic Policy for India in the Twenty First Century," Centre for Policy Research, Working Paper, 13.

[19] Josy Joseph, "Naresh Chandra Panel Recommends Military Preparedness to Deal with Assertive China", Tamil News Network (TNN), July 25, 2012, http://articles.timesofindia.indiatimes.com/2012-07-25/india/32847240_1_india-and-afghanistan-sino-indian-chief-of-defence-staff.

During this extended period, and despite the devastating psychological and physical impact of the Indo-China War of 1962, China did not loom large on India's strategic radar. The Indian military essentially focused on maintaining peace and tranquility along the unresolved LAC in Ladakh and Arunachal Pradesh. Through the 1970s and 1980s, the LAC remained largely free of any major incidents, even though relations between the neighbors were frosty for most of this period.

The China threat surfaced briefly in the early 1980s following the PLA incursion into Sumdorong Chu Valley in Arunachal Pradesh,[20] up to seven kilometers into Indian territory. This action resulted in both sides mobilizing but fortunately did not erupt into conflict. Nevertheless, then prime minister Indira Gandhi ordered a serious review of India's overall defensive posture with regard to China so as to prevent future PLA intrusions. Road communications infrastructure along the LAC was purposely kept in an underdeveloped state as part of a "scorched earth" policy to prevent the rapid intrusion of the PLA into the plains of Assam in the northeast, much like in 1962. This policy forced India to fortify its strong military presence right up to the LAC because the terrain, weather, and infrastructure prevented any large-scale Indian buildup during the warning periods.

At the same time, in the Operation Chequerboard exercise, then army chief General K. Sundarji ordered the mobilization of nearly ten mountain divisions along with the Indian Air Force. Three of the divisions were deployed in Arunachal Pradesh's crucial Wangdung area close to the border in order to test India's defensive posture against a Chinese ingression.[21] Soon after these maneuvers, a conscious decision was made to adopt what is now called the forward posture, which entails moving forward and occupying positions on the LAC to prepare for any surprise Chinese attack. This policy led to new defense works being undertaken, in addition to the redeployment of combat support elements and activation of several abandoned forward advanced landing grounds. While all these developments did for a short time induce tension between New Delhi and Beijing, they were soon overshadowed by other events on both sides of the border, including Operation Brass Tacks during November 1986–March 1987 (a major India-Pakistan military stand-off), Rajiv Gandhi's visit to China in December 1988 (the first by an Indian prime minister in 34 years), and the Tiananmen Square incident in 1989.

These developments collectively had two important consequences. First, the boundary issue once again gained salience, resulting in the establishment of a joint working group in 1989 to delineate the LAC. Following Prime

---

[20] M.L. Sali, *India-China Border Dispute: A Case Study of the Eastern Sector* (New Delhi: A.P.H. Publishing Corporation, 1998), 110.

[21] Ibid., 110.

Minister A.B. Vajpayee's visit to China in June 2003, this working group was upgraded to the level of special representatives at India's suggestion in order to provide a political mechanism for resolving the vexing boundary dispute. Second, the above developments once again focused India's attention on how neglected its northern and eastern regions were in terms of operational preparedness and infrastructure to support military deployment.

India's May 1998 nuclear tests were conducted in response to the existential threat posed by China's atomic arsenal.[22] The tests soured bilateral relations between New Delhi and Beijing, which deteriorated even further after then Indian defense minister George Fernandes called China potentially "India's number one enemy."[23]

Despite this free fall in Sino-Indian relations, the operational focus once again swung back to Pakistan after the 1999 Kargil border skirmish. This was followed by a ten-month mobilization against Pakistan beginning in December 2001 after a terrorist strike on the Indian Parliament and Pakistan's unabated proxy war in Jammu and Kashmir (J&K). These developments forced Indian security planners to review their options for responding to Pakistan and all but relegated the China threat to the back burner.

India's Dual Approach to China

Despite the looming Chinese threat, there is no consensus within India's policy discourse on how to meet it. There is, however, a growing realization that given the prevailing power differential it is imperative to engage China, lower tensions, and build a win-win transactional relationship that underscores cooperation and downplays competition. A senior Indian policymaker put it succinctly when he declared the following:

> India is absolutely committed to a pragmatic approach in dealing with sensitive bilateral issues. India does not want any fights with China. We want to develop a relationship further and faster, but we want to assure that our pride is not hurt in the process because China has risen and India is, still, rising.[24]

The unequal pace of development should not cast a shadow on the spirit of mutual equality and respect. Instead, the senior government official argues

---

[22] For the text of Prime Minister Vajpayee's letter to President Clinton explaining the rationale for the tests, see "Nuclear Anxiety; Indian's Letter to Clinton On the Nuclear Testing," *New York Times*, May 13, 1998.

[23] Praveen Swami, "A Hawkish Line on China," *Frontline*, May 23–June 5, 1998; and Alka Acharya, "Sino-Indian Relations since Pokhran II," *Economic and Political Weekly*, June 5 1999, 1397–1400.

[24] "'Handle China Like a Test Match, Not a Ranji Match,'" Interview with Sheela Bhatt, Rediff, December 14, 2011, http://www.rediff.com/news/slide-show/slide-show-1-handle-china-like-a-test-match-not-a-ranji-match/20111214.htm.

that both India and China will need to find ways to preserve mutual pride while moving ahead with development and growth.[25]

India, therefore, wants to ensure that there is less stress or conflict with China, despite also wanting to display publicly that it can stand up for its convictions regardless of the grossly unequal economic trajectory. This policy approach strives to achieve the right balance of pragmatism and nationalism in pushing Sino-Indian relations forward.[26] A similar sentiment has been expressed by Prime Minister Manmohan Singh, who recently told the Lok Sabha (the Indian parliament's lower house) that, despite prevailing problems with China, there is peace along the border. He also categorically rejected the view that Beijing is preparing to attack India. India and China, Singh said, share "very sensitive relations."[27]

There is also a perception among the optimistic lobby, though one that is not openly articulated, that India needs to hedge its bets against China through strategic partnerships with the United States and other major actors in Asia, notably Japan, South Korea, and important Association of Southeast Asian Nations (ASEAN) members, such as Vietnam and Indonesia.[28] This rationale helped convince the Congress Party–led United Progressive Alliance (UPA) to jettison the Communist parties and sign both the Indo-U.S. nuclear deal and Indo-U.S. defense framework agreement. These actions sent a message to Beijing regarding India's strategic options and leverage, highlighting that while India will continue to strive for a mutually equitable partnership with China, it will not accept Chinese coercion or attempts to shape regional discourse at India's expense.[29]

There is also an articulate "pragmatist" lobby in India's establishment, largely comprising the military and a handful of personnel within the national security establishment and intelligence services. This group argues that China is consciously aiming to alter South Asia's strategic environment in its favor through military activism in Tibet and across India's neighborhood and by overt strengthening of Pakistan's military and nuclear capabilities. In their perception, China wants to deal only with tributaries and not with peers.

What has alarmed India's Ministry of Defence and military is that even after years of tortuous boundary negotiations nothing tangible has been

---

[25] "'Handle China Like a Test Match.'"

[26] Ibid.

[27] "China Won't Attack India: PM," Zee News, December 14, 2011, http://zeenews.india.com/news/nation/china-won-t-attack-india-pm_746861.html.

[28] Gurmeet Kanwal, "Taming the Dragon: U.S. Policy on China," *Deccan Herald*, January 26, 2012, http://www.deccanherald.com/content/222303/taming-dragon.html.

[29] Remarks to the author by senior opposition politician Seshadri Chari of the Bhartiya Janta Party, Foreign Affairs Cell, on August 10, 2012.

achieved. An even greater concern is that the proposal to settle the boundary dispute by simply swapping territory that is already under the de facto control of each side—with India to be accorded control of Arunachal Pradesh and China to be granted Aksai Chin opposite the Ladakh sector—has been hijacked by broader strategic considerations.[30] For China, Tibet has emerged as an issue of renewed sensitivity following recent ethnic riots and activism. The Dalai Lama's poor health has also stoked fears over the emergence of more radical Tibetan leaders less conciliatory toward Beijing.[31]

Possible Causes of Tensions

The manner in which the India-China matrix plays out over the next few decades will be dictated by perceptions of relative power and the policies each side is pursuing alongside wider political and security developments. Given that both countries at this juncture are involved in the arduous task of nation-building and addressing economic, socioeconomic, and security challenges, they can be expected to remain cooperatively engaged in the short term in pursuing peaceful ties while managing their respective military modernizations. The broader question, however, is under what circumstances could India-China relations become competitive or even confrontational.

China is not a status quo power and will doubtlessly react politically and militarily should it feel threatened by inimical strategic shifts across Asia, such as India's economic and military rise and changing relations with the United States, Japan, and Southeast Asian countries. India, on the other hand, is an equally proud civilizational power with an umbilical attachment to Tibet, besides being home to the Dalai Lama and some 150,000–200,000 Tibetan exiles. Therefore, it will not be easy for India to fully concur with China's claims to sovereignty over Tibet, even though New Delhi has politically accepted Tibet as Chinese territory.

The geographical importance of Tibet to both countries renders it more than possible that the undercurrents of hostility over the area will prevail at least in the short to medium term. Tensions between the two sides could be aggravated by Chinese intrusions and aggression, such as pushing for new claim lines or asserting old claims with greater stridency. Tensions would also likely rise above currents levels if China were to enhance its activities

---

[30] Chinese premier Deng Xiaoping proposed recognition of the status quo in 1988, and the 2005 guiding principles committed both countries to recognize the interests of settled populations. See S.N.M. Abdi, "Standing Their Ground," *South China Morning Post*, August 7, 2009, as cited in Chieitgj Bajpaee, "China-India Relations: Regional Rivalry Takes the World Stage," *China Security* 6, no. 2 (2010): 41–58.

[31] Such groups include the Tibetan Youth Congress, the Tibetan Uprising Organization, the National Democratic Party of Tibet, and Students for a Free Tibet.

in Pakistan-occupied Kashmir, upgrade military and nuclear relations with Pakistan, or attempt to make Nepal a third pressure point against India by building wider road and rail infrastructure and providing materiel military assistance. An imminent cause for tension could be events following the death of the Dalai Lama and attempts by Beijing to replace him with its own nominee, which would elicit protests from Tibetan émigrés in India and across the world.

Yet another possible trigger for conflict, and one not fully appreciated by the Indian strategic community, would be a stand-off in the Bay of Bengal caused by China's attempts to secure its growing assets in Myanmar—namely oil and gas pipelines running from the deepwater port of Kyaukpyu on Ramree Island—through naval deployments. Under such circumstances, China's principal aim would be to gain a strategic or at the very least tactical advantage commensurate with its political interests by "teaching India a lesson" or, worse, capturing territory in disputed areas. Such an option remains on the table, despite the winds of change in Myanmar and upbeat India-Myanmar relations. China retains the potential to coerce Myanmar's regime, which is still dominated by the military.

The Nature of Conflict

There are potentially four theaters for conflict: Ladakh in northern India, the central theater in Uttar Pradesh Province, Sikkim, and finally along the McMahon Line in India's northeast. The latter was agreed to by the British colonial administration and Tibet in 1914 as the boundary between China and India but later rejected outright by the Communist Chinese government.[32] An all-out conflict, although possible, appears highly improbable because it could spiral into nuclear war and would upset the prevailing harmonious development model adopted by both sides. Hence, it is more likely that military conflict between the two states would be marked by a calibrated use of force and careful management of escalation.

Degeneration of Indian-Chinese friction into a conflict would be an incremental process that would pass through various stages of escalation, which will be discussed below. Indian analysts have also considered a scenario in which China resorts to hostilities under the garb of training exercises, an old and tried method. The use of force and the nature of escalation would be driven largely by relative conventional and strategic balance, the perception of a "quick victory," and the political and military payoffs. A large perceived asymmetry in the military balance could embolden China to act unilaterally

---

[32] Ali Ahmed, "Consideration of Sino-Indian Conflict," Institute for Defence Studies and Analyses, Issue Brief, October 24, 2011.

in the hope of forcing India to accede to Beijing's terms on the boundary issue or sending New Delhi a broader strategic message about Chinese regional military preeminence. Nonetheless, the threat of nuclear war and the likelihood of disruptions to the global order are perceived as restraining factors on China.

Coercive muscle-flexing or intimidation. In one scenario, China could use force posturing or a calibrated display of force to induce Indian compliance through coercive muscle-flexing, without resorting to the application of major force. Chinese intimidation could take one or more of the following forms:

- Targeted cyberattacks against India's command and control facilities and commercial entities
- Partial PLA mobilization to change the balance in the disputed areas, backed by the PLAAF and missile deployment
- Aggressive patrolling (both on land and at sea) and encroachments in selected areas as a show of strength
- Increased support to the numerous insurgencies in India's northeast and to Pakistan in J&K, backed by overt military operations
- Support to Indian Maoist insurgents through proxies to foment unrest in the border regions
- Increased PLAN presence in the IOR, Bay of Bengal, and Arabian Sea as part of an intimidation strategy
- The degrading of India's satellite-based communications systems, including through a show of force by testing an improved version of its anti-satellite weaponry
- Attacks on preselected, politically sensitive economic and military targets to coerce India's political leadership and convey the price of any reactive escalation

Intermediate-level conflict: A limited war of high intensity. China could launch a limited war confined to a specific area of interest that is bounded in duration and amenable to a negotiated termination. Alternatively, the PLA could take over selected places such as Tawang to drive a partial victor's bargain. Resorting to either of these two actions has the potential of escalating a limited conflict into a broader one encompassing both the northeastern region and Ladakh, and possibly drawing in Bhutan and Nepal as well. For Beijing, this could be a stand-alone tactic driven by larger political and strategic considerations or an extension of coercive muscle-flexing. However, a high-intensity limited war under "informationized" conditions remains China's basic military doctrine and its decision to escalate will be a calculated one.

China could also initiate hostilities in the belief that it could successfully fight a short punitive campaign. The PLA could attempt to rapidly and clandestinely change the force balance in the border areas to catch India off guard. Such an option would largely be driven by India's sketchy ISR (intelligence, surveillance, and reconnaissance) cover over Tibet and its force mobilization and firepower disadvantages along the LAC. This could take the form of a punitive Cold Start–type operational model to teach India a lesson.

India Responds to the Chinese Challenge

India faces a unique security scenario involving two nuclear-armed neighbors with whom it has not only been to war but who together pose a collusive threat that forces India to prepare for a two-front war.[33] Such preparation is easier said than done, given that two-front wars essentially entail maintaining twin sets of forces. This creates an economic challenge because the cost of conventional deterrence is largely unaffordable for a developing country such as India that depends largely on imported weapon systems. To highlight the wide gap in military spending, **Figure 1** shows the comparative differences in the Indian and Chinese defense budgets.

This perspective has forced India's national security establishment and successive administrations to politically and diplomatically respond to the threat posed by China and Pakistan. Nuclear weapons factored into the policy discourse of mutually assured destruction also help keep the conventional threat within manageable limits. Yet it is not possible for India to ignore that the challenge from China has the potential to escalate to threatening levels if not managed adequately.

During the 2004 Combined Commanders Conference, the issue of augmenting India's defensive capability against China was seriously discussed with the prime minister in response to the mounting military challenge in Tibet, increased PLA incursions across the LAC, and growing Chinese belligerence. The conference stressed the need to initiate early steps to upgrade India's military profile and capability and set the target date of 2010 for India to adequately prepare to meet the Chinese challenge. The underlying

---

[33] Pandit, "Army Reworks War Doctrine."

FIGURE 1   Defense budgets of China and India, 2002–11

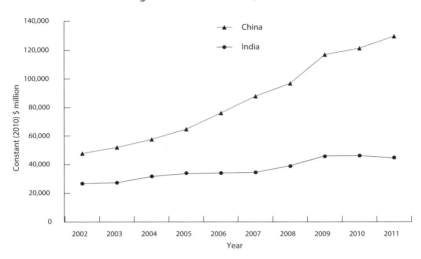

SOURCE: Stockholm International Peace Research Institute (SIPRI), SIPRI Military Expenditure Database, 2012.

message was that the military asymmetry could become too pronounced to be manageable if this deadline were not met.[34]

The seriousness of the situation was once again highlighted recently when India's normally reticent defense minister, A.K. Antony, demanded an increase from parliament in the country's defense budget for FY 2012–13 of 1,934.08 billion rupees ($38.68 billion). Antony told parliament on May 7, 2012, that the "growing proximity of China and Pakistan is a cause of worry….The defense budget has to be enhanced to deal with these new emerging challenges."[35] He reiterated his fears over India being confronted with a two-front war with its nuclear-armed neighbors. Antony added that if China can increase its strength in Tibet, India can do the same in its frontier areas of Sikkim and nearby Arunachal Pradesh.[36]

---

[34] Author's interview with the former Indian chief of army staff, General N.C. Vij, at Vivekananda Foundation International, New Delhi, May 18, 2012.

[35] Rajat Pandit, "Antony to Seek Hike in Defence Outlay to Counter Twin Threats from Pakistan, China," *Times of India*, May 9, 2012, http://articles.timesofindia.indiatimes.com/2012-05-09/india/31640475_1_defence-outlay-defence-budget-zakama.

[36] Pandit, "Antony to Seek Hike in Defence Outlay." See also Rajya Sabha, "Synopsis of Debate," May 8, 2012, http://164.100.47.5/newsynopsis1/Englishsessionno/225/Synopsis%20dated%2008.05.pdf.

Opportunely, this period of military consolidation with regard to China came at a time when the threat posed by Pakistan was easing. India's new preemptive doctrine reassured its military planners that any conventional challenge from Pakistan could be effectively managed. India had also largely controlled the Islamist insurgency in J&K, bringing it down to manageable levels, and the only overriding concern was that a major terrorist attack similar to the November 2008 siege of Mumbai would force New Delhi to respond militarily, leading in all probability to a nuclear stand-off. Developments in the Afghanistan-Pakistan imbroglio, where Pakistan's military was for the first time embroiled in counterinsurgency operations in the tribal regions across the border, also provided India with breathing space to augment its military capability to counter China.

A three-tier strategy is presently being planned based on India's overall operational philosophy predicated on a credible dissuasive defensive posture. It encompasses a quid pro quo strategy by which any intrusion into Indian territory would be answered with similar, limited offensive operations in preselected areas. Developing such a capability will require intra-theater force rationalization to create a quick response capability and include redeployment of forces presently deployed against Pakistan to the Chinese border. To execute this strategy, the infrastructure to perpetuate rapid mobility is being created.

The capacity to interdict Chinese operational and logistic infrastructure in Tibet is the key to India's operational plans. In 2009 the Indian Army undertook a major transformational study that focused on growing concerns regarding the PLA's military modernization, particularly with respect to the networking of its command and control systems, its ability to field effective and near real-time command, control, communications, computers, intelligence, surveillance, and reconnaissance (C4ISR), and growing cyberwarfare capabilities.[37] The study revealed the following critical weaknesses: unfavorable combat ratios against China, constraints in the overall capability of Indian forces to meet two-front scenarios, poor logistics infrastructure that would prevent mobilization and redeployment of additional forces within acceptable time frames, and important technological gaps in ground-, air-, and space-based systems, particularly ISR and cyberwarfare capabilities.

Building Capacities and Capabilities

To address these imbalances, the first phase of India's strategy has been to close the wide gap in the two countries' prevailing defensive postures.

---

[37] The author's understanding is based on formal and informal interactions with Indian military officers during lecture tours to various institutions.

Under the Indian Army's eleventh five-year defense plan (2006–11), two mountain divisions and an artillery brigade totaling 1,260 officers and nearly 35,011 soldiers were raised.[38] Importantly, these increases are in addition to the army's sanctioned manpower of 1.2 million personnel and are intended for exclusive employment along India's eastern border with China. The new formations are to be equipped with ultra-light, easily transportable M777 155-mm, 39-caliber howitzers from BAE Systems. The Indian Ministry of Defence has recently cleared the acquisition of 145 howitzers via U.S. foreign military sales, with the possible addition of 300–400 at a later stage under licensed production.[39]

Defensive formations in the eastern theater and in Ladakh are being provided with built-in rapid-reaction capabilities, including helicopter-lift capacity, aimed at facilitating a quick response to local contingencies by acquiring attack and heavy-lift helicopters, the procurement of which is in an advanced stage of negotiation. New medium- and heavy-transport aircraft using renovated airfields along the border will also sustain these formations.

Second, to provide an independent limited offensive capability, permission has been accorded in the army's recently approved twelfth five-year defense plan (2012–17) to raise a mountain-strike corps comprising two light mountain divisions and an artillery division armed with lightweight howitzers and BrahMos, a cruise missile having a 292-km range that India developed jointly with Russia.

The earlier so-called scorched-earth policy of leaving the border regions underdeveloped has been revised because it seriously handicapped the military's mobilization and tactical movements in Arunachal and Ladakh and left troops exclusively dependent on air drops and mule trains. In all likelihood, by 2016–17, ongoing infrastructure projects—including 6,000 km of border roads, bridges, and helipads built for an estimated 92.43 billion rupees under the Special Accelerated Road Development Programme for North East (SARDP-NE)—will be completed.[40] Additionally, some fourteen rail lines feeding into this network are planned by 2021 at a cost

---

[38] "Modernisation of Chinese Armed Forces a Serious Concern," Indian Military, February 17, 2011, http://www.indian-military.org/news-archives/indian-navy-news/1382-modernisation-of-chinese-armed-forces-a-serious-concern-antony.html.

[39] The Indian Ministry of Defence has cleared the long-pending deal worth 30 billion rupees ($560 million) for the acquisition of 145 M777 ultra-light howitzer guns from BAE Systems to accelerate the Indian Army's modernization process. The deal was cleared by the Defence Acquisition Council, following a favorable report submitted by the head of the Defence Research and Development Organization (DRDO) committee that studied the suitability of the weapon system. See "Indian Army to Acquire M777 Howitzers from BAE," Army-Technology.com, May 14, 2012, http://www.army-technology.com/news/newsindian-army-to-acquire-m777-howitzers-from-bae.

[40] Government of India, "Special Accelerated Road Development Programme for North-East Region," Press Information Bureau, Backgrounder, January 25, 2012, http://www.pib.nic.in/newsite/erelease.aspx?relid=79886.

of 261.55 billion rupees ($5.12 billion). This infrastructure upgrade would facilitate the deployment of long-range assets such as the Smerch multi-barrel rocket launcher (MBRL) system with a 90-km range and the indigenously produced Pinaka MBRL system with a range of 40–45 km. These systems would provide the capability to neutralize China's forward deployments. Infrastructural development would also facilitate improved logistics.

To further enhance the Indian Army's preparedness in the eastern sector, the government has approved the induction of the BrahMos Block III steep-dive variant, raising the number of cruise-missile regiments deployed along the Chinese border to four.[41] Also proposed is the induction of Prahar, the short-range battlefield missile with a 150-km range.[42] This missile is part of the Indian Army's quest to acquire precision-guided munitions to augment its long-range lateral fire support.

To enhance its ISR capabilities, India has embarked on developing an indigenous satellite-based global-positioning capability called the GPS-Aided Geo-Augmented Navigation (GAGAN) system. The experience gained in creating GAGAN will in turn be harnessed to build an autonomous regional navigation system called the Indian Regional Navigational Satellite System (IRNSS). These collaborative technologies will provide India's military high positional accuracy for its weapon systems. To further increase its ISR capacity, the army is also inducting three additional troops of Heron unmanned aerial vehicles (UAV) apart from the satellite-based information systems. Similarly, to ensure a high degree of communication security and connectivity, the military is planning a dedicated satellite-based defense network for the armed forces. Tactical air-defense cover is also being improved with the induction of newly acquired Israeli low-level quick-reaction missiles to replace existing outdated systems.

Air Force Modernization

The Indian Air Force (IAF) is upgrading its assets at a rapid pace and is expected to operate 42 combat squadrons by 2022 (up from 32) by acquiring varied platforms, such as SU-30MKI multirole fighters; importing medium multirole combat aircraft (MMRCA); and inducting locally designed light-combat aircraft alongside mid-air refuelers. By 2020, the IAF plans to induct a fifth-generation fighter aircraft developed jointly with Russia. Such

---

[41] "Army to Have Another BrahMos Missile Regiment," Press Trust of India, September 23, 2011, http://zeenews.india.com/news/nation/army-to-have-another-brahmos-missile-regiment_733222.html.

[42] Prasun K. Sengupta, "'Prahaar' NLOS-BMS Explained," Trishul web log, September 17, 2011, http://trishul-trident.blogspot.in/2011/09/prahaar-nlos-bsm-explained.html.

acquisitions will transform the IAF into a long-range strike force that is capable of addressing out-of-area contingencies.[43]

A large part of the IAF's modernization plans is China-centric and includes revamping advance landing grounds in Ladakh and the eastern sector to support SU-30MKIs and the under-acquisition MMRCA. The IAF has already deployed SU-30MKIs at Tezpur and Chabua in the east to provide greater depth and radius of action to meet the challenges posed by the PLAAF operating from Tibet and the nearby Chengdu Military Region.

Tezpur's runway has been renovated and its infrastructure upgraded to house the "air dominant" SU-30MKIs capable of striking targets deep inside China. Their radius of operation can be further enhanced to around 5,000–8,000 km with air-to-air refueling by the IAF's recently acquired IL-78 tankers. Conversely, the PLAAF has established at least four airbases in Tibet and three in southern China that could mount operations against India. But since these bases are located at average heights of around 10,000 feet, the weapon-carrying capacity of PLAAF fighters is restricted, a handicap that the IAF does not face in operating from Tezpur and Chabua. By 2020, however, the PLAAF's profile will begin changing when it fields larger numbers of third- and fourth-generation fighters, as well as some fifth-generation fighters. In comparison, the IAF's air power assets will suffer from increasing obsolescence and a slow rate of replacement.

In addition, China's air-defense capability is likely to improve and over time could shift the advantage in the PLAAF's favor. Fielding a real-time battle management system could provide China with a deep-strike capability that would force the IAF to defend in depth. However, the IAF is also developing a layered, hardened, and in-depth air-defense command, control, and communications network, called the Integrated Air Command, Control, and Communications System (IACCCS). The IACCCS is being established through a two-phase program costing approximately $3 billion, with phase one scheduled to be completed by the end of 2012. The complete system is being designed as the following:

> a robust, survivable network-centric C4ISR infrastructure that will receive direct real-time feeds from existing space-based overhead reconnaissance satellites, ground-based and aerostat-mounted ballistic missile early-warning radars and high-altitude-long-endurance unmanned aerial vehicles, and manned airborne

---

[43] "Air Chief Sounds Caution on Afghan Scenario," *Hindu*, April 28, 2012.

early warning & control (AEW&C) platforms. The IACCCS will also coordinate the early-warning and response aspects of a layered, ground-based, two-tier ballistic missile defence (BMD) network that is now at an advanced stage of development.[44]

Maritime Perspective

Operationally and doctrinally, the Indian Navy (IN) is perhaps the fastest evolving of the country's three services, despite being the smallest and for years the most financially deprived. Three primary considerations shape this evolution: dominating the IOR, exploiting the full potential of India's exclusive economic zone, and creating robust infrastructure at offshore island chains such as the Andaman and Nicobar archipelago, as well as the need to develop amphibious capabilities. The IN is clearly concerned with the PLAN's expansion into what India considers its own geopolitical space.[45]

Structurally, the Indian Navy's current and planned assets by 2025 could consist of 162 imported and locally designed network-centric platforms, including two aircraft carriers and both conventional and nuclear-powered submarines (SSN and SSBN) backed by cruise missiles and smart mines. Defense Minister Antony recently told parliament that the IN would annually induct five new warships, beginning in 2012. The platforms that the navy is acquiring will considerably expand its maritime domain awareness and reach and will provide limited capability for expeditionary and intervention operations.

The recently inducted INS *Chakra*, which is the Russian Project 971 (Akula-I) SSN that the IN has leased for ten years, together with induction of the INS *Arihant*, the first of four locally developed SSBNs, by 2013–14 will provide the IN with fledgling tactical deterrence against the PLAN's three SSBNs and seven SSNs. More importantly, these submarines will complete India's development of retaliatory, strategic deterrence based on a mix of nuclear weapons that are deliverable by air, mobile land-based platforms, and sea-based assets.

Shore-based naval fighters, such as Russian Mig-29Ks, supported by at least twelve Boeing P-8 maritime reconnaissance aircraft (MRA) and additional medium-range MRAs, will form part of the IN's maritime domain awareness envelope and provide anti-access/area-denial (A2/AD) capabilities. Additionally, India's island territories provide strategic vantage points along key waterways and chokepoints that could be exploited for A2/AD ends.

[44] Prasun K. Sengupta, "IAF's Multi-Phase IACCCS Being Enhanced," Trishul web log, January 22, 2012, http://trishul-trident.blogspot.in/2012/01/iafs-multi-phase-iacccs-being-enhanced.html.

[45] "Navy Plans Major Expansion in Manpower, Shore-Based Infrastructure," *Times of India*, October 15, 2011, http://articles.timesofindia.indiatimes.com/2011-10-15/india/30283327_1_karwar-naval-base-major-warships-admiral-nirmal-verma.

The tri-service command located on the Andaman and Nicobar archipelago of some seven hundred islands, located midway between the Bay of Bengal and the Malacca Strait and astride major sea lanes linking the Indian and Pacific oceans, likewise provides an ideal launch pad for India to implement an A2/AD strategy.[46]

The IN gains further tactical traction from geography that permits the IAF's ground-based strike and surveillance systems to operate seamlessly in tandem with fleet operations. Thus, any opponent attempting to invade India's littoral waters would have to contend with both naval and air power. The IAF also has assets based on the Andaman and Nicobar island chain and over the years has developed all-weather airstrips to support its multirole Su-30MKI combat aircraft.

In addition to conventional deterrence measures, India in a calibrated manner is ratcheting up its strategic deterrence through the successful launch of a 3,500-km Agni 4 IRBM and the much-publicized 5,000-km Agni 5, whose range has been carefully calibrated to reach targets anywhere except for the United States and Australia. Purely from a capabilities perspective, this IRBM provides India with the capacity to target most of the Chinese heartland in response to the Chinese MRBM threat to the populated heartland of central Indian states.

India is developing such capabilities in order to deter China from taking any preemptive steps toward armed conflict. For this strategy to be successful, however, India must acquire capabilities in an acceptable time frame and at an affordable cost. The issue gains salience against the backdrop of a poor defense industrial base, which has forced India to import systems from abroad. This process is both time consuming and leaves India operationally vulnerable. The much-vaunted "transfer of technology," either as direct transfers or part of offsets, has not worked well for India. The route to public-private partnership has also been slow to develop, being constrained by scales of equity participation and a limited indigenous vendor base. If India and the United States choose to upgrade their strategic partnership, this is one area that will need to be given serious consideration and will require establishing acceptable terms for technology transfer and joint development.

In addition to capability-building, the IN has embarked on trust- and relationship-building among the IOR littoral states and taken a number of initiatives including exercises such as Milan ("togetherness") and the Malabar maneuvers with the U.S. Navy and the navies of Japan and Singapore, among others. The importance of these initiatives is to reassure friends and allies about the IN's ability to play a role in regional balancing, something which the

---

[46] Walter Ludwig, "Indian Navy Anti Access" (paper presented at Observer Research Foundation, New Delhi, January 21, 2012).

navy demonstrated clearly during the 2004 tsunami. However, developments in the South China Sea and the growing capabilities of the PLAN have highlighted the need to build a much wider maritime security initiative. "Rimland security" is one concept that would unite all Asian littorals in a common architecture for securing commerce, trade, and resources in the sea lanes of the Indian and Pacific oceans.

The rimland security initiative was originally conceived at a Track II trilateral dialogue between India, Japan, and Taiwan in 2006. The initiative aims to foster maritime cooperation among the Asian littorals, focusing on freedom of the seas, nontraditional security threats, and peaceful resolution of bilateral and multilateral disputes. The idea found traction during subsequent Track II meetings wherein the dialogue process was enlarged to include representatives of Singapore and Australia. In recent studies undertaken by the author on regional dynamics of the Asia-Pacific, the concept has been recommended for consideration as a wider regional maritime security initiative. The Track I trilateral dialogue recently held in Washington between India, the United States, and Japan, which focused on maritime cooperation, provided further impetus for rimland security.[47]

External Balancing: India's Options

The capabilities and capacities outlined above are either already under development or part of projections from the Indian military to upgrade its overall posture to deal with threats from China and Pakistan. These capacities are likely to bear fruit over the next fifteen years as part of India's long-term integrated perspective plan that runs from 2012 to 2027. Given India's inability to develop a credible defense industrial base, equipment gains will largely be met through acquisitions, direct imports, or transfers of technology. While a number of projects are already in the pipeline to address the challenges India faces, New Delhi will need to take a number of steps in a timely manner to ensure that asymmetry with China remains manageable:

- Improve acquisition procedures, including norms of technology transfer
- Create an indigenous industrial base through credible and workable public-private partnership models

---

[47] Josh Rogin, "Inside the First Ever U.S.-Japan-India Trilateral Meeting," *Foreign Policy*, Cable web log, December 23, 2011, http://thecable.foreignpolicy.com/posts/2011/12/23/inside_the_first_ever_us_japan_india_trilateral_meeting.

- Create norms and standards for the contribution of "make India" procurement procedures to aid foreign collaboration and support overall efforts to build defense infrastructure

- Address the shortage of both indigenous capacity and technical manpower that prevents India from becoming a technology hub

- Revamp India's defense industrial base through the task force on defense modernization established by the country's National Security Council

- Fast-track domain awareness and C4ISR capabilities and create separate military space infrastructure

- Improve infrastructure development in the border areas to ensure both operational and strategic mobility

These tasks are indicators of efficient and timely capability development based on blueprints that are very much in place. The next fifteen years will be a period of strategic vulnerability, which New Delhi will need to manage deftly through diplomacy and political foresight. Any delays on account of political inertia could expose India to coercion from China, given that by the end of this period the PLA is likely to have emerged as a high-tech, network-centric, and regionally predominant military power.

Setting aside for the moment specific issues such as the border dispute, trade, and energy, future Sino-Indian relations—from a macro-level perspective—will likely be characterized by an aggressive competition between the two states for strategic influence across Asia. Whereas the contours of this struggle may not be entirely clear today, restrained by India's limited strategic perspective that is essentially driven by its "look east" policy, over the next few decades the shape of the rivalry could become increasingly sharp and focused.

As already highlighted, China's growing influence has spread far beyond its immediate periphery into the Indian Ocean, Central Asia, West Asia, Africa, and even Latin America. Its activities across Eurasia, particularly in South Asia, suggest that China's definition of its strategic neighborhood is increasingly overlapping with India's. On the other hand, China's self-defined area of strategic interest includes Japan, the Korean Peninsula, Taiwan, Southeast Asia, Iran, the Arab Gulf states, and Central Asia. In this overlap between the two countries' areas of interest, several pivotal states and regions are likely to become arenas of future competition.

The question is how China will react to India's strategic assertion through its look east policy and developing bilateral and multilateral relations with major actors in the Asia-Pacific. China increasingly sees Indian initiatives, both in regional forums and in the South China Sea, as attempts to carve out a military and security role in concert with the United States, Japan, and Vietnam as part of a U.S. strategy of containing China. Some Chinese observers have viewed India's look east policy toward ASEAN as having maritime implications. They believe that in the second stage of the policy New Delhi will expand its scope into the political and security realms in order to bring cooperation on counterterrorism and maritime security, among other issues, under India's grand strategy. These observers believe that this strategy is aimed at controlling the Indian Ocean, particularly the Malacca Strait.[48]

The United States, for its part, increasingly sees India as an alternative to Chinese hegemony in the region. While countries such as Australia, Japan, and the smaller Southeast Asian countries are also relevant to the United States' Asia-Pacific strategy, India—as a nuclear power and with a growing economy that is destined to leapfrog in the next two decades or so as an important regional power—currently tops the U.S. priority list. Despite some hiccups, the Indo-U.S. relationship has improved in every respect: economically, militarily, strategically, and so on.

The importance of the bilateral relationship was underscored during the recent visit of U.S. defense secretary Leon Panetta to New Delhi and in the following Indo-U.S. strategic dialogue, at which the United States outlined its vision for bilateral defense cooperation. Commenting on the U.S. rebalancing strategy toward Asia, Secretary Panetta explained that the U.S. military will look to expand its partnerships and presence in the arc extending from the western Pacific to East Asia and into the IOR and South Asia. By 2020, Washington plans to redeploy the bulk of its naval forces, including as many as six aircraft carriers, within this area. Other issues outlined during the visit included the shared challenges of ensuring open access to the maritime, air, space, and cyberspace domains, as well as the challenges posed by radical ideologies, piracy, and the proliferation of WMDs.[49]

The fundamental thrust of the secretary's discourse was that in addition to an upgraded military presence in the Asia-Pacific, the United States is keen to encourage and assist regional states in developing capabilities to deal with these challenges. He described India—being the biggest and most dynamic country in South Asia—as the linchpin of this U.S. strategy. In order to achieve these objectives, Secretary Panetta committed to upgrading the current level of bilateral defense cooperation in the field of arms sales and technology transfers from a "buyer and seller" arrangement to a more substantial one.

---

[48] "India's 'Look East Policy,'" *People's Daily*, April 6, 2012, http://www.china.org.cn/opinion/2012-04/06/content_25075354.htm. Also see "India's Look East Policy Should Not Mean Encircle China," *People's Daily*, October 28, 2010.

[49] Leon E. Panetta, "Partners in the 21st Century" (address delivered at Institute for Defence Studies and Analyses, New Delhi, June 6, 2012).

The United States would share important, cutting-edge technologies and enter into a substantial coproduction relationship that would eventually expand to include joint high-tech research and development. It is apparent that the United States is keen to draw India into a much stronger strategic partnership and provide technologies and equipment that would enhance India's overall defense capacities and preparedness, apart from enhanced intelligence-sharing and cooperation in the space and cyber domains.

Yet these U.S. overtures, significant as they are, put India in a difficult position. There is no doubt that India needs U.S. technological and military hardware support for building both its military capacity and its own military industrial complex. Nonetheless, New Delhi must consider the larger geostrategic calculation of such an embrace. Within India there are two schools of thought on the future course of the Indo-U.S. bilateral relationship. There are those within the policy establishment and among policy elites who believe that, in the prevailing geostrategic environment, building a strong political-military relationship with the United States is imperative. This group largely comprises senior policymakers from both the civilian and military bureaucracies. In this view, growing engagement with the United States in diverse domains is to India's advantage. Proponents of this view argue that there is already growing strategic congruence between the two countries on a host of issues, including freedom of the seas, China's rise, Beijing's growing assertiveness, Chinese claims in the South China Sea, and Afghanistan-Pakistan relations. They also see defense cooperation as an opportunity to close the technology gap with China, particularly in critical areas such as C4ISR, space, IT, and cyber domains. On this view, India needs to leverage its relationship with the United States to its geopolitical advantage, with a caveat that building up the relationship must be premised on shared values and interests without compromising core national interests.

There are others groups, however, who remain skeptical of U.S. intentions and warn that India could become a pawn in the United States' China containment strategy. These observers look on U.S. attempts to enlist India in Washington's new rebalancing strategy as essentially driven by self-interest. In their view, open endorsement of U.S. strategy would harm India's relations with China. This school of thought, while endorsing a strong bilateral relationship, would like India to follow an independent course of strategic autonomy. The thinking within this circle is that the balancing factors that existed before are no longer available, with Russia, the European Union, and the United States losing prominence in the world economy. The close U.S. economic relationship with China, exemplified by the proposed group of two (G-2), continues to provoke these skeptics. They opine that to expect the United States, or another third party, to defend India is misguided.[50] Instead, this group is keen to charter a course driven by self-interest and build a bilateral relationship with the United States on the broader congruence of interests and shared values, without fully acquiescing to U.S. perceptions and regional policy.

Given the foregoing differences in perceptions of the two schools of thought, India is unlikely to fully endorse the U.S. rebalancing strategy because of its probable impact on the balance of power in Asia. In his bilateral discussion with the U.S. defense secretary, the Indian defense minister cautioned his counterpart against hastening efforts to strengthen the multilateral security architecture in the Asia-Pacific, suggesting instead that the process be allowed to develop at its own pace.[51]

India can thus be expected to adopt a cautious and calculated policy posture. The nature of Indo-U.S. bilateral ties will be marked by an incremental buildup of trust as the relationship slowly transcends what can be termed "cooperative aloofness." India's actions and level of engagement will be dictated by how policy elites perceive their country's role in the region and its impact on India's overall China policy. The basic dilemma for India within the emerging order in Asia is how to promote its own interests in the face of the preeminence of Chinese power and growing U.S. regional engagement. Will India, as a swing state, attempt to balance Chinese assertions with those of the United States, while continuing to engage with both countries? Will India bandwagon with Southeast and East Asian states, such as Japan and South Korea, to balance Chinese power? There are several different paths that New Delhi could follow over the next few decades that will shape its policy options.

First, India's geopolitical, energy, economic, and maritime interests could force it into a security understanding with U.S. allies and partners such as Vietnam, Japan, South Korea, and Australia. There would be a marked enhancement in the self-reliance of India's capabilities, which could be boosted by U.S. technology transfers and military hardware support. The Indian military would develop a strong maritime capability and nuclear triad that would be backed by significant space and cyber capacities with a large C4ISR footprint over its region of strategic interest. The Andaman and Nicobar islands would become a strong "iron choke" to counter the Chinese

---

[50] "'Handle China Like a Test Match.'"

[51] P.R. Chari, "Antony and Panetta: A Shakespearean Drama?" Institute of Peace and Conflict Studies, June 12, 2012, http://www.ipcs.org/article/india/antony-and-panetta-a-shakespearean-drama-3634. html. Chari notes that the Indian defence minister appeared to have adopted a cautious approach while endorsing the broad principles of strengthening partnerships in the Asia-Pacific region and resolution of bilateral disputes.

string of pearls. India could also put into place an effective A2/AD strategy in the Indian Ocean and along its land borders.

Second, India could play the role of a swing state and attempt to balance Chinese assertiveness and U.S. interests. Toward this end, India would boost its economic relationship with China while simultaneously developing close political and economic linkages with the United States, though without any overt security understanding. Some commentators are already highlighting that India is in the unique position of being wooed by both the United States and China.[52] In this scenario, New Delhi would foster its regional economic interests and boost trade and economic relationships with ASEAN, Japan, the Republic of Korea, and Australia, among others. It could buttress these initiatives through forging close strategic relationships with Russia and Central Asian states, while also taking effective steps to improve bilateral relations in South Asia, including with Pakistan. India could use this period to build its comprehensive national power while ensuring economic progress.

A third path is sustained economic development and military modernization to build a credible dissuasive capability. To buy time and foster regional peace and stability, India would need to reach a political and economic understanding with Beijing through conciliatory measures on issues such as the South China Sea, membership in the Shanghai Cooperation Organisation, and joint development projects in South and Southeast Asia. Such actions would help initiate a dialogue to address Chinese fears in the IOR. In short, on this third path, India would attempt to build a peaceful periphery without being a so-called swing state or falling into a China containment trap.

Conclusion

China's military modernization, persistent adversarial stances, and increasing forays along India's borders and in the Indian Ocean are not only matters for deep concern but pose serious political and military challenges. India has tried to downplay the China threat in a bid to seek political accommodation and cooperation. Nonetheless, there are deep suspicions in New Delhi about Chinese behavior and Beijing's attempts to carve out strategic space both in South and Southeast Asia and in the IOR. What India is attempting to achieve is a balancing act in which a judicious mix of

---

[52] Sandy Gordon argues that India has "found itself in the enviable position of being courted by both the U.S. and China, thus confirming its status as the 'swing state' of Asia." See Sandy Gordon, "India: Which Way Will the 'Swing State' Swing?" East Asia Forum, June 24, 2012, http://www.eastasiaforum. org/2012/06/24/india-which-way-will-the-swing-state-swing/.

pragmatism and nationalism pushes Sino-Indian relations forward without in any way compromising the country's core interests.

There is a growing understanding within the country that India needs to hedge its bets against China through strategic partnerships with the United States and other major actors in Asia, notably Japan, South Korea, and important ASEAN countries such as Vietnam and Indonesia. At the same time, India must build a strong dissuasive capability to deal with the challenges posed by China's military, which could become increasingly unmanageable if the growing strategic asymmetry remains unaddressed.

In meeting these challenges, a strong bilateral relationship with the United States, based on a congruence of strategic interests, is important not only as a hedge against China but also to build indigenous defense capabilities and an industrial base. The United States has promised cooperation on both these counts. India's dilemma is how to balance this strategic partnership with its broader regional concerns.

Three possible paths have been outlined for India's Asia-Pacific strategy: (1) developing a close political and strategic relationship with the United States to build comprehensive national power, (2) assuming the role of a swing state to balance relations with China and the United States, and (3) accommodating China to buy time to build India's own dissuasive power. The Indian leadership will need to walk a fine line to build an economic and military relationship with the United States that serves the common aim of maintaining strategic stability in Asia while at the same time ensuring good cooperative relations with China. The main challenge for India is that its strategic vulnerability will increase by 2020–25. In other words, New Delhi does not have time on its side and must get its act together now.

STRATEGIC ASIA 2012–13

U.S. RESPONSES

EXECUTIVE SUMMARY

This chapter will argue that the U.S. must protect its primacy in the Asia-Pacific in order to advance its strategic goals in the face of China's military modernization.

MAIN ARGUMENT:
Since the end of World War II, U.S. strategic aims in the Asia-Pacific have included maintaining a forward defense of the homeland, enforcing a great-power peace, stemming the tide of WMDs, and creating a liberal political and economic order. The U.S. has accomplished these goals through a strategy of primacy that is underpinned by the U.S. military's preeminence. However, the rise of China and its increasing military capacity are undermining American primacy and thereby the broader Asian order. The current U.S. response to this strategic problem, manifested in part by the operational concept called air-sea battle (ASB), is inadequate in several respects. First, cuts to the defense budget will make it difficult to resource ASB. Second, ASB is an operational concept detached from a strategy. Finally, the concept underemphasizes the need for nuclear deterrence. As a result, the U.S. is both making commitments to Asia that it may not be able to afford and articulating a high-risk operational doctrine that does not answer basic strategic questions.

POLICY IMPLICATIONS:
- The president should have a range of options to control the escalation of conflict.

- The U.S. military must be able to master the main military domains—air, sea, and space—should they come under threat.

- The U.S. should be able to wrest back control of contested zones that China sets up closer to its shores.

- The U.S. must have the capacity to punish and weaken any aggressor that challenges U.S. primacy.

The U.S. Response to China's Military Modernization

Dan Blumenthal

The idea of extended deterrence is a product of the nuclear age. From the perspective of the deterrence guarantor, the purposes of such a policy are threefold: to deter an attack on an ally, to deter the use of nuclear weapons against an ally, and to deter nuclear war altogether. Because nuclear weapons cause unthinkable destruction, statesmen strive to deter their use entirely. As a result, debates about deterrence are largely "astrategic": they are fundamentally about how not to use a particular kind of weapon rather than how a capability may further political goals. As Henry Kissinger has written, the crafting of deterrence policy can quickly become an intellectual exercise: the effectiveness of deterrence can be proved only by events that do not occur, and it is impossible to prove why something never happened.[1] Did the defender prevent an impending attack? Or did a potential adversary never in fact desire to launch an attack in the first place? These questions can quickly become esoteric. To avoid such an outcome, this chapter seeks to put the United States' guarantee of extended deterrence into the broader context of the U.S. strategy of maintaining primacy in Asia.

Since the end of World War II, the United States first won and then maintained its primacy in Asia. A grand strategy of primacy was (and is) but one of several strategic options available to U.S. statesmen. Others

Dan Blumenthal is the Director of Asian Studies and a Resident Fellow at the American Enterprise Institute. He can be reached at <dblumenthal@aei.org>.

The author would like to thank Lara Crouch for her exceptional research and editorial assistance.

[1] Henry Kissinger, *Diplomacy* (New York: Simon & Schuster, 1994), 608.

include "offshore balancing" and "selective engagement."[2] But the United States chose and has heretofore remained committed to primacy—defined as a preponderance of power over all extant and potential great powers. In Asia, U.S. grand strategy has benefited both the United States and its regional allies. The leaders of Asian nations who chose prosperity and liberal economic policies after the war did so in a system fortified by U.S. presence and power. However, this peaceful Asian order is now challenged by the rise of China, and the United States must maintain a strategy of primacy to protect it.

This chapter concerns itself with the military underpinnings of U.S. primacy—the strategy that has provided for great-power peace, the prosperity of Asia, and the minimal spread of WMDs. The chapter will analyze the elements of U.S. military primacy and demonstrate how primacy has allowed the United States to guarantee an extended deterrent and helped Washington achieve its objectives of homeland defense, great-power peace, and Asian economic and political development. Next, the chapter will show how the troubling course of China's rise is undermining U.S. primacy.

Following this discussion, the chapter will then argue that the apparent response to China's challenge, articulated in the new operational concept of air-sea battle (ASB), suffers from three deficiencies. First, resources devoted to ASB are insufficient to meet the challenge of China's growing military might because of the United States' shrinking defense budget. Second, ASB does not seem to be tied to a larger strategic concept for Asia. It thus raises a number of questions, including whether the doctrine is meant to underpin primacy or some other strategy, such as U.S. strategic thinking about punishment of aggression. Third, ASB underestimates the value of a robust nuclear force required to maintain great-power peace, nonproliferation, and a credible threat to escalate a conflict beyond the enemy's capability to respond in kind.

U.S. Strategy in Asia: How It Got There and Why It Remains

The Pacific War ravaged Asia and decimated the old colonial order. Rather than leave Asia in chaos and risk a Soviet or Chinese Communist takeover, the United States created a new Asian political-economic order. Washington hoped to bring Asia into the liberal global system it was creating to both protect U.S. interests and, as Paul Nitze put it in his famous

---

[2] See Richard Fontaine and Kristin M. Lord, eds., "America's Path: Grand Strategy for the Next Administration," Center for New American Security, May 2012, http://www.cnas.org/files/documents/publications/CNAS_AmericasPath_FontaineAndLord.pdf.

National Security Council report "NSC 68," shape the world in a way that was conducive to American principles.[3]

The prewar European experience was instructive for U.S. strategy in Asia. Europe tried unsuccessfully to achieve a stable balance of power throughout the first part of the twentieth century. Ultimately, however, European powers had neither the will nor the wherewithal to enforce the peace, and Europe descended into two of the bloodiest wars in human history. Given this history, U.S. leaders thought it too risky to leave a war-torn Asia to its own devices following World War II. Rather, the United States would act as a benign hegemon to build a political order and enforce the new peace. The United States calculated that Asian conflicts would inevitably draw it back to the region and that the rise of a hostile hegemon would deny the United States open access to Asia and defense of the homeland from Pacific approaches. The Pacific War no doubt had a profound psychological impact on U.S. statesmen and thus on U.S. strategic thinking. All agreed that the United States would do what was necessary to avoid another horrifying slog through the Pacific.

With all other great powers themselves devastated by the war, U.S. leaders settled on a strategy of primacy in the Asia-Pacific. They saw no other means to accomplish the United States' key strategic objectives. The regional countries were too weak to establish order and keep the peace by themselves, and the other great powers either did not have the same interests as Washington or were too damaged by the war to help provide global public goods.[4] Washington feared that if another hegemon did arise, it would dominate Asia in ways threatening to U.S. purposes. None of its strategic aims could be achieved if Asia once again fell under the rule of a hegemon capable of dividing the region into military spheres of influence and exclusive trading blocs—a scenario that would likely lead wary regional powers to adopt self-help military strategies and possibly acquire WMDs.

While the U.S.-created order is far from perfect, by the 21st century it had achieved its most important objectives. No single power has been able to dominate Asia. Additionally, those countries allied with the United States have not engaged in enervating security competitions that could have included nuclear competition.[5] Finally, most of Asia has become part of the

---

[3] See National Security Council, "NSC 68: United States Objectives and Programs for National Security," Report, April 14, 1950, http://www.fas.org/irp/offdocs/nsc-hst/nsc-68.htm.

[4] For international stability, one dominant power or group of powers must provide public goods such as freedom of navigation, security of supply lines, and great-power peace. See Ashley J. Tellis, "Preserving Hegemony: The Strategic Tasks Facing the United States," in *Strategic Asia 2008–09: Challenges and Choices*, ed. Ashley J. Tellis, Mercy Kuo, and Andrew Marble (Seattle: National Bureau of Asian Research, 2008), 3–37.

[5] It is easy to overlook the stunning success of the U.S. strategy of primacy in Asia and the nuclear umbrella it provided. Advanced industrial countries that were capable of acquiring nuclear weapons—such as Australia, South Korea, Japan, and Taiwan—did not do so.

liberal trading and political order. In short, U.S. strategy set the conditions for Asian elites to make strategic choices for economic growth and political modernization—what has come to be called the "Asian miracle."[6]

The primary exception to undiluted success is the increasing uncertainties attendant to China's rise. As a nuclear-armed great power, the People's Republic of China (PRC) poses the most consequential challenge to continued peace, a condition largely secured by the nuclear umbrella the United States provides to the other great powers. If major U.S. allies and partners were less secure in the U.S. "extended deterrent," a resulting security competition could get out of control and would be more likely to lead to conflict. As China began to rise in both economic and great-power terms, Washington's leaders were faced with a tough choice: contain China by trying to weaken and slow its rise, or welcome it into the U.S.-made system. The United States chose the latter. Just as it had done with the "Asian tigers," the United States sought to encourage China to join international and political institutions and to enrich itself. Meanwhile, Washington would patiently wait for Beijing to liberalize its political system. Political liberalization, it was hoped, would tame China's ambitions and gradually lead to a convergence of Sino-U.S. views on security matters.

For its part, China decided to accept part of the international order. Beijing has embraced the opportunity for economic growth with great gusto and has seen its economy quadruple in size over the last 30 years. But Chinese leaders had other plans for domestic politics and foreign policy. Indeed, the PRC increased and modernized its military power. Yet more power has meant greater ambition. Thus, the very Chinese success hoped for by U.S. strategists now poses a new strategic challenge. That is, the United States now faces a dynamic, high-growth economy that is tempted to change the Asian order coercively.

Additionally, China is a nuclear weapons state. The massive extent of the U.S. power differential has been such that the use of coercive force with nuclear weapons by any country against a U.S. ally has been unthinkable. However, that might no longer be the case. Because there is still no concert of powers lying in wait to share in system maintenance, once again the only credible strategic choice for Washington is primacy.

---

[6] As Ashley Tellis explains, the first wave of Asian miracles was made up of U.S. friends and allies and the second of neutral countries or potential adversaries. The fact that potential adversaries followed the path of the Asian tigers complicated U.S. strategy in the region. See Ashley J. Tellis, "Power Shift: How the West Can Adapt and Thrive in an Asian Century," German Marshall Fund, Asia Paper Series, January 2010, http://www.gmfus.org/galleries/pdf/GMFPower20Shift20Asia20Paper_for_web200128.pdf.

The Military Underpinnings of Primacy

The military underpinnings of the strategy of primacy are best described by Barry Posen. What some call military preeminence or mastery, Posen describes as command of the commons.[7] Command of the commons is a far different concept than "access to the commons," a phrase that sacrifices clarity and necessity for the sake of politeness. In truth, a strategy of primacy requires far more than access and equal use of the global commons: the U.S. military needs the ability to dominate them. It must plan varying force sizes for different plausible conflicts. But contingency planning for conflicts in Asia, let alone retaining a credible nuclear security guarantee, would not be possible without command of the commons. Posen describes such command as akin to Paul Kennedy's "naval mastery"[8] but argues that it goes beyond that concept:

> Command means that the United States gets vastly more use of the sea, space, and air than do others; that it can credibly threaten to deny their use to others; and that others would lose a military contest for the commons if they attempted to deny them to the United States.[9]

In other words, military preponderance means that, during a conflict, the United States will not simply prevail because of greater combat power deployed permanently in Asia. Rather, the United States can fully bring to bear extant and latent economic and military power while denying enemies the full use of their capabilities. Command of the commons means that enemy power may be neutralized before it is even usable.

A strategy of military preponderance is dependent on U.S. mastery of the main domains of warfare. For command of the sea, the foremost requirement is a nuclear-submarine attack force equipped with precision-guided munitions and antisubmarine warfare (ASW) capabilities, as well as carriers able to position fighter aircraft for land and maritime strikes. The United States achieves air supremacy by suppressing enemy air defenses and sanitizing the skies of enemy fighter aircraft. The U.S. Air Force can deliver precision-guided munitions to their targets from above fifteen thousand feet with relative impunity.[10]

---

[7] This section draws heavily from Barry Posen's influential work, "Command of the Commons: The Military Foundation of U.S. Hegemony," *International Security* 28, no. 1 (2003): 5–46.

[8] For a full discussion of this concept, see Paul Kennedy's famous book *The Rise and Fall of British Naval Mastery* (London: Allen Lane, 1976; repr., London: Macmillan, 1985).

[9] Posen, "Command of the Commons," 8.

[10] Ibid., 11–16.

Military primacy can require the use of hundreds of satellites at a time, as well as GPS and geolocation and targeting complexes that include reconnaissance aircraft and high-altitude unmanned aerial vehicles (UAV). Command of space allows the U.S. military to see enemy battlefield formations, mobilization, and movement well before joining a battle.[11] During Operation Iraqi Freedom, command of the commons allowed the United States to deny Saddam Hussein even a chance to marshal his most valuable resources: the U.S. military destroyed valuable targets from relatively far distances before even engaging his forces on the ground.[12]

U.S. military primacy is also enabled by many global access arrangements. During wartime this structure supports substantial military logistics that allow the United States to bring the full measure of its power to bear rapidly over very long distances. This capability is particularly necessary in the Asia-Pacific, where the United States has utilized this strategy of command to prosecute two wars (albeit one unsuccessfully), quiet crises in the Taiwan Strait on at least three occasions, engage in "tanker wars" as far afield as the Persian Gulf, stop a coup attempt in the Philippines, respond to various humanitarian disasters, assist in operations in East Timor, and successfully deter a now nuclear North Korea from attacking either Japan or South Korea.[13]

While the United States deploys forces forward, the key to its primacy has been the ability to utilize the full extent of its deterrent and combat power wherever and whenever it is needed without basing the bulk of its power in Asia. Equally salient is the relationship of command of the commons to nuclear deterrence and proliferation. The United States has kept the peace and dissuaded most Asian countries from acquiring nuclear weapons without much, if any, of its nuclear power resident in Asia. Indeed, this military preponderance has allowed the United States to pull all tactical nuclear weapons out of Asia and yet still demonstrate its continued deterrent strength by rotating nuclear bombers and nuclear-equipped submarines into the theater. To paraphrase former secretary of defense James Schlesinger, command of the commons enables the U.S. military to use nuclear weapons on patrol on nuclear submarines and elsewhere to maintain deterrence every day of the year.[14] Thus, while there are many reasons for Asia's long peace—foremost among them the decisions of Asian leaders to focus on stability and modernization—there is a high correlation between U.S. military primacy and the peaceful regional order.

---

[11] For Posen's description of maintaining command of space, see "Command of the Commons," 12–14.

[12] See the description in ibid., 29n69.

[13] See Dan Blumenthal et al., "Asian Alliances in the 21st Century," Project 2049 Institute, August 30, 2011.

[14] Melanie Kirkpatrick, "Why We Don't Want a Nuclear-Free World," Wall Street Journal, July 13, 2009, http://online.wsj.com/article/SB124726489588925407.html.

China and the Challenges to Primacy

China poses the most consequential challenge to U.S. command of the commons and therefore to the U.S. strategy of primacy in Asia. Like all rising great powers before it, Beijing has goals and ambitions inconsistent with those of the existing hegemon. There should be no surprise that China has great-power ambitions; it would be an historical anomaly if it did not. While the PRC's grand strategic goals are manifold, this chapter is narrowly focused on its military and national security goals, defined as the ways in which China's leaders want to defend their nation from attack and protect the Chinese Communist Party's power and prosperity.

China's leaders are at least as concerned with questions of regime survivability and internal problems as they are with strategic matters. But even a focus on domestic policy can translate into new foreign policy goals. Regime survival requires keeping the world safe for autocracy—particularly, in the eyes of Chinese leaders, from the menacing U.S. hegemon. Similarly, economic growth means gaining access to natural resources, which in turn creates military requirements. Regime survival also requires maintaining party legitimacy as the vanguard of a reversal of national humiliations.

Beijing has not yet fully worked out the ultimate goals of its grand strategy. Indeed, as China's equity in the world has grown, so have its internal debates about how to secure its position. The existence of these debates explains why China can be at once a responsible member of most economic institutions and an enabler of proliferation and other threats to regional security. But while internal debates about grand strategy continue, Chinese national security goals have become more apparent. They seem to include coercing Taiwan into unification, playing a dispositive role on the Korean Peninsula should North Korea collapse, controlling China's peripheral seas, and perhaps over time developing the ability to defend sea lines of communication (SLOC) further afield.

Chinese Military Strategy

China embarked on a major program of military modernization decades ago. But it has also watched keenly and learned from post–Cold War U.S. operations and made adjustments accordingly. The two gulf wars and operations in Kosovo made a particular impression on Chinese strategists. From a defensive standpoint, the People's Liberation Army (PLA) concluded that it needs the ability to push the U.S. precision-strike complex further away from Chinese shores. To do so, the PLA must be able to wrest away parts of the commons. From an offensive standpoint, once the PLA contests the commons, it can use military power coercively to attain its goals. The strategies of both imperial Japan and the Soviet Union provide useful if imperfect analogues for Chinese military strategy.

The main strategic aim of the imperial Japanese military was to hold onto and consolidate its continental gains, particularly in China, and Japan's leaders feared that increasing U.S. sanctions on oil exports would deprive Tokyo of the wherewithal to implement its plans. However, U.S. and allied sanctions not only failed to compel Japan to call it quits; they convinced Japan of the need to acquire more resources to further its aims. But in deciding to seize resources from Southeast Asia, Tokyo realized that U.S. intervention was inevitable.[15] Following a strategy that may be of some use to China,[16] Japan decided to preemptively attack the Pacific fleet, seize U.S.-held territory, and cut the sea lanes that the United States needed to fight its way back into Asia. Japan's strategy then turned defensive.

The Japanese leadership embarked on such a strategy for two key reasons. First, they were aware that a total military victory against the United States in the traditional sense was impossible. Second, they believed that the United States would not have the fortitude to fight its way through the Pacific. Thus, Japan would do significant damage early, followed by the establishment of dense layers of defense.

Given that the geography has not changed, Japanese strategy may have some appeal to contemporary Chinese war planners. The PLA is capable of inflicting decisive first blows to forward-based U.S. and allied forces and then creating defensive perimeters. Their hope would be that Washington would not want a repeat of the Pacific War.[17] China may calculate that it possesses two advantages not enjoyed by imperial Japan. First, it has greater strategic depth, as well as stronger interior lines of communications. Second, China possesses nuclear weapons of its own. If the PRC were to decide on war, a plan that tries to strike a decisive blow and construct dense defense perimeters in the first and second island chains to consolidate gains would be highly risky and audacious. However, China may calculate that such a strategy is the only way to defeat the U.S. military.

---

[15] This analysis draws from Scott D. Sagan, "The Origins of the Pacific War," *Journal of Interdisciplinary History* 18, no. 4 (1988): 893–922, especially 914–17. For more general overviews of Japanese strategy, see Forrest E. Morgan, *Compellence and the Strategic Culture of Imperial Japan: Implications for Coercive Diplomacy in the Twenty-First Century* (Westport: Praeger, 2003); Michael A. Barnhart, *Japan Prepares for Total War: The Search for Economic Security, 1919–1941* (Ithaca: Cornell University Press, 1987); and James B. Wood, *Japanese Military Strategy in the Pacific War: Was Defeat Inevitable?* (Lanham: Rowman & Littlefield, 2007).

[16] On Chinese interest in Japanese strategy, see Toshi Yoshihara and Jim Holmes, *Red Star over the Pacific: China's Rise and the Challenge to U.S. Maritime Strategy* (Annapolis: Naval Institute Press), 2010.

[17] See Jan van Tol, Mark Gunzinger, Andrew Krepinevich, and Jim Thomas, "AirSea Battle: A Point-of-Departure Operational Concept," Center for Strategic and Budgetary Assessments, 2010, 20–21; and Yoshihara and Holmes, *Red Star over the Pacific*.

As for lessons from the Soviet Union, Moscow also faced a predominant U.S. military, frustrating its goals in Eurasia. Soviet leaders realized that in the case of an attack on Europe, the United States would use carrier-based aircraft to strike the Soviet homeland. In response, Moscow crafted a "line in the oceans" strategy to push back U.S. carriers by establishing defensive maritime perimeters.[18] The most concentrated defenses were 200 nautical miles from Soviet coasts, but Moscow set a 1,250–nautical mile "keep out" zone as well. The strategy was resourced with hundreds of attack submarines, hundreds of surface combatants, and over one thousand naval-based fighter aircraft. These capabilities were knit together with open-ocean surveillance systems and carried cruise missiles of different classes.[19] It is noteworthy that these maritime defensive perimeters were necessary for the Soviet Union to conduct offensive operations in continental Europe. The threat to the United States was not that the Soviet Union had constructed punishing maritime defenses (or anti-access strategies). Rather, the threat was that the Soviet military could meet its offensive goals in Europe by deterring U.S. intervention.

From the Soviet strategy, China seems to have adopted the lines-in-the-ocean approach. The 2004 Chinese defense white paper calls for the construction of its navy, air force, and Second Artillery Corps "in order to strengthen the capabilities for winning both *command* of the sea and *command* of the air and conducting strategic counter-strikes" (emphasis added).[20] Indeed, Chinese strategists never mention the fashionable U.S. terminology of "anti-access/area denial capabilities." Rather, Chinese defense white papers refer to such traditional military goals as regional command of military domains to achieve strategic goals, followed by "counter-intervention."

China has its eyes on territories that would need to be defended if it came to control them. According to Gabe Collins and Andrew Erickson, the concept of the "near seas" (sometimes referred to as the "first island chain") was originally developed by Admiral Liu Huaqing as the main force behind the early stages of China's naval modernization.[21] The near seas contain the

---

[18] Michael McDevitt explains the Soviet experience in warfare at sea and demonstrates its influence on Chinese maritime strategy in "The PLA Navy's Antiaccess Role in a Taiwan Contingency," in *The Chinese Navy: Expanding Capabilities, Evolving Roles*, ed. Phillip C. Saunders et al. (Washington, D.C.: National Defense University, 2011), 191–214.

[19] Ibid, 196.

[20] Information Office of the State Council of the People's Republic of China, *China's National Defense in 2004* (Beijing, December 27, 2004), http://www.fas.org/nuke/guide/china/doctrine/natdef2004.html.

[21] Andrew Erickson and Gabe Collins, "Near Seas 'Anti-Navy' Capabilities, Not Nascent Blue Water Fleet, Constitute China's Core Challenge to U.S. and Regional Militaries," *China SignPost*, March 6, 2012, http://www.chinasignpost.com/2012/03/near-seas-%E2%80%9Canti-navy%E2%80%9D-capabilities-not-nascent-blue-water-fleet-constitute-china%E2%80%99s-core-challenge-to-u-s-and-regional-militaries/.

vast majority of China's outstanding territorial and maritime claims, including Taiwan, the Senkaku/Diaoyu Islands in the East China Sea, and the Spratlys, Paracels, and other islands and reefs in the South China Sea. This geographical area contains the densest layer of Chinese coercive power. Since all of those claims are contested by U.S. allies and partners, and the United States itself has stated that China's control of these seas is not in U.S. interests, the PLA is prudently planning to defeat U.S. intervention in this area.

More specifically, to coerce Taiwan, the PLA is developing capabilities to conduct mass precision-guided strikes against Taiwan, Japan, and elsewhere that would deal a quick and decisive blow both to the island and to U.S. and Japanese military assets in Japan.[22] In turn, China could dare the United States to enter back into the first island chain. If the United States were to decide to do so, it would face sharp attacks on what Posen has described as its "infrastructure of command"—the logistics, access points, cyber networks, and space assets that the U.S. military needs to fully bring to bear its combat power.[23]

Chinese Capabilities and Their Utility in Possible Military Scenarios

A Chinese campaign utilizing coercive force could begin with an initial strike on a large scale that involves the use of massive ballistic-missile and cruise-missile attacks launched from various platforms against U.S. and Japanese air and naval bases. Forward airbases such as Andersen, Kadena, and Misawa may be especially vulnerable. The PLA is also developing capabilities to strike major U.S. Pacific logistical hubs such as airfields and runways, ports, refueling stations, and facilities for holding and transporting cargo.

After an initial attack, it is plausible that the PLA's next military objective would be to deny U.S. forces the ability to generate combat power from its bases, ports, and surface vessels in the western Pacific in order to preclude adequate intervention. China could use its land-based antiship ballistic missiles as well as antiship cruise missiles launched from submarines and destroyers to target U.S. naval forces. These kinds of strikes could be followed by interdiction of U.S. and allied SLOCs throughout Southeast Asia and the western Pacific.[24]

---

[22] See Roger Cliff et al., *Entering the Dragon's Lair: Chinese Antiaccess Strategies and Their Implications for the United States* (Santa Monica: RAND, 2007), http://www.rand.org/pubs/monographs/2007/RAND_MG524.pdf; and David Shlapak et al., *A Question of Balance: Political Context and Military Aspects of the China-Taiwan Dispute* (Santa Monica: RAND, 2009), http://www.rand.org/pubs/monographs/2009/RAND_MG888.pdf.

[23] Posen, "Command of the Commons," 16–19.

[24] The scenario above is drawn from van Tol et al., "AirSea Battle," 21. On Chinese military strategy more broadly, refer to Yoshihara and Holmes, *Red Star over the Pacific*; Cliff et al., *Entering the Dragon's Lair*; and Shlapak et al., *A Question of Balance*.

Chinese capabilities would render it difficult for the United States to come to the aid of its allies in the near seas. For example, the Chinese integrated air defense system (IADS) could put at risk U.S. air power strategy. In turn, the IADS would protect Chinese missile launchers, space launchers, over-the-horizon radars, airbases, and ports. Regarding sea command, the United States may find it deadly to enter contested zones to come to the defense of any ally: "China's sea-denial capability in the littoral combines most of the elements that Posen describes as necessary for the creation of a 'contested zone': bottom mines; diesel electric submarines; small, fast, surface attack craft; surveillance radars; electronic intelligence; long-range mobile land-based SAMs; and long-range, mobile, land-based antiship missiles as well as aircraft and helicopters."[25]

In addition, the PLA may have the most active cruise- and ballistic-missile programs in the world.[26] Mobile land-based antiship missiles will be very difficult to find and target. The PLA is certainly also well aware that antiship missiles have damaged or sunk large naval vessels in previous conflicts. The PLA has also watched smaller boats successfully attack U.S. surface combatants, such as the attack by a small motorboat on the USS *Cole* in 2000.[27] Similarly, China has obtained highly sophisticated fast-attack craft such as new Houbei-class vessels that can be deployed with similar lethality. Finally, China possesses a growing fleet of increasingly quiet submarines, both nuclear-powered and diesel-electric. This is important because diesel-electric submarines are very difficult to track.[28]

The PLA has thus been very wise to focus on acquiring conventional submarines, ship- and land-based cruise and ballistic missiles, mining, and an IADS that are all knitted together with a sophisticated C4ISR (command, control, communications, computers, intelligence, surveillance, and reconnaissance) system. In addition, the PLA's focus on cyber and electronic

---

[25] Blumenthal et al., "Asian Alliances," 12–13. For an excellent overview of the impact of missile capabilities on what the authors call "Sino-U.S. maritime interactions," see Yoshihara and Holmes, *Red Star over the Pacific*, 101–24.

[26] The Project 2049 Institute has done extensive work on China's cruise- and ballistic-missile programs. See, for example, Mark Stokes on the development of the antiship ballistic missile in "China's Evolving Conventional Strategic Strike Capability: The Anti-Ship Ballistic Missile Challenge to U.S. Maritime Operations in the Western Pacific and Beyond," Project 2049 Institute, September 14, 2009, http://project2049.net/documents/chinese_anti_ship_ballistic_missile_asbm.pdf. For an explanation of the lethality of China's cruise missiles for U.S. military presence in Asia, see Ian Easton's primer on the DH-10 cruise missile, "The Assassin under the Radar: China's DH-10 Cruise Missile Program," Project 2049 Institute, Futuregram, no. 09-005, October 1, 2009, http://project2049.net/documents/assassin_under_radar_china_cruise_missile.pdf.

[27] Posen, "Command of the Commons," 37.

[28] Ibid., 40. On China's submarine force more specifically, see Lyle Goldstein and William Murray, "Undersea Dragons: China's Maturing Submarine Force," *International Security* 28, no. 4 (2004): 161–96.

warfare enables it to potentially impede a U.S. response, given the United States' reliance on battle networks to optimize its considerable conventional firepower. The Chinese fleet of submarines, cruise and ballistic missiles, space- and land-based ISR (intelligence, surveillance, and reconnaissance), mines, and air power has provided it with the ability to undo the military underpinnings of U.S. grand strategy. Should China successfully create impenetrable contested zones, the United States' ability to meet the strategic requirements of primacy will be impaired severely.

China may want to force a choice on Washington: sue for peace or fight a bloody war in Asia. Striking Japan even with conventional assets is indeed a high risk for China. But the point is not that China wants to embark on such a course, but rather that should it decide to use force, it may not have another choice.

Chinese strategy poses high risks for the United States as well. Since Japan is not a nuclear power, it is limited in its ability to retaliate. The onus for retaliation is on Washington. A U.S. president may face a number of very unattractive choices: negotiate a settlement, fight a long conventional war, or consider the use of nuclear weapons if conventional forces are wiped out. These dilemmas would be familiar to Cold War presidents Dwight D. Eisenhower and John F. Kennedy. Indeed, much of U.S. Cold War history is the story of wrestling with these dilemmas and often arriving at less than satisfactory answers. Given these choices in the present day, how has the United States chosen to respond? How adequate is that response?

The U.S. Response: Rebalancing and Air-Sea Battle

The United States has embarked on a policy of what it calls "strategic rebalancing." Strategic rebalancing includes economic statecraft through the use of the Millennium Challenge Compact and free trade agreements, intense diplomatic engagement in order to create new security ties, maintaining a forward military presence, and building partnership capacity to modernize allied militaries. The genesis of rebalancing is the Obama administration's realization that Chinese dominance in the region represents a potential threat to Asia's peace.

To put the military aspect of rebalancing into context, it is important to remember that the Department of Defense has been conceptualizing responses to Chinese coercive power since at least the publication of the 2006 *Quadrennial Defense Review Report*.[29] More recently, the United States

---

[29] U.S. Department of Defense, *Quadrennial Defense Review Report* (Washington, D.C., February 6, 2006), http://www.defense.gov/qdr/report/report20060203.pdf.

has begun to articulate some of its warfighting concepts. The military has seemingly coalesced around the term "air-sea battle," a deliberate nod to the air-land battle concept developed during the Cold War and designed to halt a Soviet conventional onslaught on Western Europe. Elements of the ASB concept were articulated by a number of administration and senior military officials at around the same time "strategic rebalancing" was announced. Whether or not by design, the two concepts have become somewhat synonymous.

Not much information is available to analysts about the content of ASB. However, a close parsing of the limited statements and documents available hint that it is a "conventional deterrence by denial" approach. In the case of China, the U.S. military's response is to demonstrate that it can operate in Chinese-created "contested zones" and deny China its strategic objectives through defensive means. The major operational goal of ASB is to slow or stop Chinese missile and air forces rather than punish or retaliate against China for its aggression.

While the operational concept may be sound, ASB is still an operational approach to a strategic problem: it gives no indications about what U.S. political goals would be should war arise. That is, both the defense strategic guidance released in January 2012 and related statements on ASB focus on possessing the means to continue operating in contested zones but do not explain the ends of these operational aspirations. For example, if China initiated a conflict, the United States would respond to a military provocation with some political purpose in mind. Would the United States be satisfied with the re-establishment of the status quo ante? Is there no punishment for aggression? Are there ways to employ U.S. military force during peacetime to weaken the adversary so as to tame a longer-term strategic competition or enhance deterrence?

Strategic Rebalancing

Strategic rebalancing was first discussed in an October 2010 speech by Secretary of State Hillary Clinton.[30] In an essay the following year, Secretary Clinton characterized the strategy as a "pivot" to Asia, with the implication that the United States was returning to a region that had not been receiving sufficient attention.[31] This pivot would occur as the United States wound down its military commitments in the Middle East and South Asia and reduced its

---

[30] Hillary Clinton, "America's Engagement in the Asia-Pacific" (remarks in Honolulu, October 28, 2010), http://www.state.gov/secretary/rm/2010/10/150141.htm.

[31] Hillary Clinton, "America's Pacific Century," *Foreign Policy*, October 11, 2011, http://www.foreignpolicy.com/articles/2011/10/11/americas_pacific_century.

focus in Europe. The administration has since moved away from the term "pivot," which mischaracterized the United States' role and presence in Asia throughout the post–Cold War period. It also overstated the feasibility of the United States turning its back on other critical regions.

In Secretary Clinton's words, the major elements of the strategy are as follows:

> [O]ur work will proceed along six key lines of action: strengthening bilateral security alliances; deepening our working relationships with emerging powers, including with China; engaging with regional multilateral institutions; expanding trade and investment; forging a broad-based military presence; and advancing democracy and human rights.[32]

Similarly, in a speech at this year's Shangri-La Dialogue, Secretary of Defense Leon Panetta outlined several key principles consistent with Secretary Clinton's list of objectives, such as aligning with "international rules and order," building partnerships, maintaining "presence," and "force projection."[33] Secretary Panetta naturally focused on the military dimension of the strategy.

Thus far, the strategy has manifested itself in several other respects. The Obama administration has built on its predecessors' accomplishments by continuing to tighten alliance cooperation with Japan and utilizing a set of "mini-laterals" (for example, Japan, Australia, and the United States, or India, Japan, and the United States). In addition to using already long-standing diplomatic forums, the administration has established relations with Burma, intensified engagement with ASEAN nations, and led the efforts to negotiate the multilateral Trans-Pacific Partnership.

The administration is also deepening relations with Vietnam, Singapore, and the Philippines as part of its efforts to increase U.S. presence diplomatically and militarily in Southeast Asia. The U.S. Navy has deployed a littoral combat ship in Singapore.[34] The military has also begun rotational deployment of 2,500 U.S. Marines in Darwin, Australia, while bases in the Philippines have been reopened for limited use by U.S. forces.[35] Additionally, Secretary Panetta has stated that 60% of the navy's forces will be deployed in the Asia-Pacific theater.

---

[32] Clinton, "America's Pacific Century."

[33] Leon Panetta, "The U.S. Rebalance Towards the Asia-Pacific" (speech at the Shangri-La Dialogue, Singapore, June 2, 2012), http://www.iiss.org/conferences/the-shangri-la-dialogue/shangri-la-dialogue-2012/speeches/first-plenary-session/leon-panetta/.

[34] During the Shangri-La Dialogue, reports emerged that Singapore had agreed in principle to host up to four of these vessels. See Marcus Weisgerber, "Singapore Will Now Host 4 Littoral Combat Ships," *Navy Times*, June 2, 2012.

[35] Carlo Munoz, "The Philippines Re-opens Military Bases to U.S. Forces," *Hill*, DEFCON Hill web log, June 6, 2012, http://thehill.com/blogs/defcon-hill/operations/231257-philippines-re-opens-military-bases-to-us-forces-.

But how effective implementation will be is an open question. Although a stated goal of this strategy is to reassure U.S. allies and partners of the United States' sustained presence in Asia, Washington has not done so entirely. The United States is edging close to a dangerous gap between stated objectives and resources—a condition that will send the wrong signal to allies and adversaries alike. This leads to other questions alluded to earlier and expanded upon below. That is, is ASB sufficient to securing the military objectives within the strategy? Will this strategy be resourced adequately? And most importantly, is the strategy meant to maintain American primacy?

What Is Air-Sea Battle?

Randy Forbes, a congressional leader on the House Armed Services Committee, has articulated his understanding of ASB based on Department of Defense writings and presumably briefings.[36] Congressman Forbes writes:

> Air-Sea Battle seeks to use "Networked, Integrated Attack-in-Depth" to "disrupt, destroy, and defeat" (NIA-D3) adversary capabilities. More specifically, the joint force (integrated air, ground, and naval forces) armed with resilient communications (networked) aims to strike at multiple nodes of an enemy's system (attack-in-depth) along three lines of effort. If we can consider these lines in terms of an enemy archer, one could choose to blind the archer (disrupt), kill the archer (destroy), or stop his arrow (defeat).[37]

Likewise, General Martin Dempsey, the chairman of the Joint Chiefs of Staff, wrote: "The essential access challenge for future joint forces is to be able to project military force into an operational area and sustain it in the face of armed opposition by increasingly capable enemies when U.S. overseas defense posture is changing and space and cyberspace are becoming increasingly important and contested domains."[38]

These statements point to three animating ideas behind ASB. First, the U.S. military needs the capacity and capability to sustain operations in contested areas. For example, it must be able to survive the onslaught of Chinese aerospace and undersea power by hardening and dispersing its high-value assets while protecting its space and information assets. Second, achieving the first objective would provide U.S. forces with an opening to attack the PLA's corresponding high-value assets in depth and thereby degrade

---

[36] Norton A. Schwartz and Jonathan Greenert, "Air-Sea Battle: Promoting Stability in an Era of Uncertainty," *American Interest*, February 20, 2012, http://www.the-american-interest.com/article.cfm?piece=1212.

[37] Randy Forbes, "America's Pacific Air-Sea Battle Vision," *Diplomat*, March 8, 2012, http://the-diplomat.com/2012/03/08/americas-pacific-air-sea-battle-vision/.

[38] U.S. Department of Defense, *Joint Operational Access Concept (JOAC)* (Washington, D.C., January 17, 2012), http://www.defense.gov/pubs/pdfs/JOAC_Jan%202012_Signed.pdf.

the capacity of its multifaceted precision-strike complex. Third, the U.S Air Force and Navy in particular need greater battle networks of coordinated ISR and strike capabilities.

The Shortcomings of the U.S. Response

Rebalancing Meets the Budget

By any measure, what the U.S. military hopes to do in Asia will require large numbers of expensive capabilities. The immediate question is, will the ASB concept be resourced adequately? The defense budget is undergoing deep cuts that call the viability of ASB into question.[39] While the United States has not made public the kinds and numbers of capabilities needed for ASB, piecing together statements by defense leaders can help build the puzzle. Several leaders have identified key vulnerabilities in current U.S. military posture in Asia. For example, then Pacific commander Admiral Robert Willard testified before Congress that missile defense in Northeast Asia may not be adequate to respond to a "large-scale attack."[40] Willard identified two other weaknesses in current U.S. force posture: an insufficient focus on the cyber and space domains and an overreliance on deployed (versus stationed) forces in Southeast Asia.[41]

According to the chief of naval operations, Admiral Jonathan Greenert, and the chief of staff of the Air Force, General Norton Schwartz:

> Having a strong Air Force no longer guarantees control of the air, and having a strong Navy no longer guarantees control of the seas. Our respective warfighting domains have become intertwined such that the ability to control and exploit one increasingly depends on control in the others. We have already begun this collaboration with our work on the Global Hawk and Broad Area Maritime Surveillance aircraft, the F-35 Lightning II, and a range of sensor, network and weapon systems.[42]

An operational concept that disrupts, destroys, and defeats Chinese forces would require a very capable attack submarine force; stealthy aircraft that can attack in-depth, long-range bombers; redundant cyber, space, and

---

[39] Like all legislation, the defense budget is a process. Therefore, it should be made clear that the current numbers are not law and not set in stone. However, they do represent the broad direction in which U.S. defense spending is headed. The information on the fiscal year 2013 budget is current as of June 10, 2012.

[40] Robert F. Willard, testimony before the House Appropriations Committee (Subcommittee on Defense), April 14, 2011, 12, http://www.pacom.mil/web/PACOM_Resources/pdf/TestimonyofA dmRobertWillardUSNavy-14April2011.pdf.

[41] Ibid., 12–13.

[42] Schwartz and Greenert, "Air-Sea Battle."

other ISR assets; ships capable of defending against ballistic missiles; offensive mining and anti-mining; and antisubmarine warfare (ASW). They all must be tightly networked for maximum strategic impact. Likewise, high-value assets at bases and ports in Japan need to be protected through passive and active measures. ASW is needed to ensure that long logistical lines can be secured from the homeland to Japan. Finally, U.S. and allied militaries must regain command of the littorals and the air by sanitizing the skies, suppressing IADS assets, and neutralizing nodes in the air and missile-launch kill chain.

However, ASB is colliding with the realities of the defense budget (see **Table 1**). Even before the passage of the Budget Control Act (BCA) in August 2011, the Obama administration had reduced defense spending by almost $400 billion since 2009, which canceled more than $300 billion in programs.[43] The BCA then reduced the dollars that then secretary of defense Robert Gates had requested in his final future years defense program (FYDP). The final Gates request in the fiscal year (FY) 2012 president's budget (PB) included $570.7 billion in 2013, $586.4 billion in 2014, $598.2 billion in 2015, $610.6 billion in 2016, and $621.6 billion in 2017. The BCA, as reflected by cuts in the FY 2013 PB, has reduced those numbers in billions through FY 2017 to

TABLE 1   Department of Defense toplines (subset of 051), in billions of dollars

	FY 2013	FY 2014	FY 2015	FY 2016	FY 2017	Total
2012 PB	570.7	586.4	598.2	610.6	621.6	2,987.5
2013 PB	525.4	533.6	545.9	555.9	567.3	2,728.0
Real growth (without sequestration)	-2.5%	0.0%	+0.8%	+0.2%	+0.2%	-0.3%

SOURCE: FY 2013 Budget Request Overview, 9.

NOTE: The figure of -2.5% real growth was calculated based on the actual FY 2012 appropriation ($530.6 billion). The total growth of -0.3% is the average real growth of the budget over the course of the FY 2013 Future Years Defense Program. FY = fiscal year. PB = president's budget.

---

[43] Mackenzie Eaglen and Diem Nguyen, "Super Committee Failure and Sequestration Put at Risk Ever More Military Plans and Programs," Heritage Foundation, Backgrounder, no. 2625, December 5, 2011, http://www.heritage.org/research/reports/2011/12/debt-ceiling-deal-puts-at-risk-ever-more-military-plans-and-programs; and "Statement on Department Budget and Efficiencies, as Delivered by Secretary of Defense Robert M. Gates," U.S. Department of Defense website, http://www.defense.gov/speeches/speech.aspx?speechid=1527.

$525.4 billion in 2013, $533.6 billion in 2014, $545.9 billion in 2015, $555.9 billion in 2016, and $567.3 billion in 2017.[44] These cuts will have a great impact on the capabilities needed for ASB.[45] The following is an analysis of the state of relevant programs.

Shipbuilding and conversion. The future of shipbuilding is uncertain.[46] A major source of uncertainty is the frequent revisions to the navy's stated requirements. In September 2011 the navy published a shipbuilding plan that would provide for a total force of 313 ships. However, the newest shipbuilding plan, published in April 2012, has revised this number down to

---

[44] U.S. Department of Defense, *Overview: Fiscal Year 2013 Budget Request*, prepared by the Office of the Under Secretary of Defense (Comptroller)/Chief Financial Officer (Washington, D.C., February 2012), 9, http://comptroller.defense.gov/defbudget/fy2013/FY2013_Budget_Request_Overview_Book.pdf. These numbers are taken directly from Figure 1-3. Please note that these numbers as expressed in current dollars (adjusted for inflation) represent the requested budget appropriation numbers of the discretionary portion of Department of Defense (DoD) toplines (budget function 051). They do not include the other agencies covered under the National Defense budget function (050), a few of which are involved in U.S. nuclear policy and R&D. According to Eaglen and Nguyen, the DoD budget represents approximately 95% of 050 spending. It thus represents the vast majority of defense spending relevant to the trend lines discussed in this chapter. See Eaglen and Nguyen, "Super Committee Failure and Sequestration." For a table breaking down defense spending that includes the other agencies, see U.S. Department of Defense, *National Defense Budget Estimates for FY 2013*, prepared by the Office of the Under Secretary of Defense (Comptroller) (Washington, D.C., March 2012), http://comptroller.defense.gov/defbudget/fy2013/FY13_Green_Book.pdf.

[45] Both houses of Congress are now attempting to mitigate the effects of the BCA by restoring funding for certain programs. Since the release of the FY 2013 PB, the armed services committees in both houses have put forth their own versions of the FY 2013 National Defense Authorization Act. These bills have sought to restore some of the capabilities cited in this chapter. For example, HR 4310, which passed the full House on May 18, 2012, and the Senate Armed Services Committee bill (S 3254), which passed the committee only on June 4, 2012, both provide advanced procurement funding for the Virginia-class nuclear-powered attack submarine (SSN) so that one of the hulls intended for procurement in 2014 does not slip outside the FYDP. While the bills show congressional agreement in some areas, their differences highlight the fact that the budget battle is far from over. For example, HR 4310 restores operations and maintenance funding for the Block 30 Global Hawks, whereas the Senate bill does not. The debate could take any number of paths between now and the end of the year, but every policymaker is operating under the same constraints imposed by the BCA. Any outcome will involve difficult funding choices and fewer funds for important capabilities. For an overview of HR 4310, see "The National Defense Authorization Act for Fiscal Year 2013: Highlights of H.R. 4310," House Armed Services Committee Communications Office, May 14, 2012, http://armedservices.house.gov/index.cfm/files/serve?File_id=2a2e1b35-2fdc-404b-ab42-f929c34ca273. See also the Senate Committee on Armed Services fact sheet for S 3254, "Senate Committee on Armed Services Completes Markup of the National Defense Authorization Act for Fiscal Year 2013," Senate Committee on Armed Services, Press Release, May 24, 2012, http://hss-prod.hss.aol.com/hss/storage/industry/7841819d2535d87055d8da57ea267ed/SASC%20NDAA%20press%20release%20-%202012-05-24.pdf.

[46] For an excellent and user-friendly overview of the major cuts from the Department of the Navy set to begin in FY 2013, see "FY 2013 Department of the Navy (DON) President's Budget Summary," Department of the Navy, Financial Management and Comptroller Information Paper, February 13, 2012, http://www.finance.hq.navy.mil/fmb/13pres/FY_2013_PB_Overview.pdf.

an interim figure of 300.[47] The navy is currently conducting a force structure and requirements assessment that may cause these numbers to change again. But prior to the publication of the April 2012 plan, the deputy chief of naval operations for warfare systems, Vice Admiral William Burke, told the House Armed Services Committee that ideally the navy needs at least 500 ships and that the current long-term plan would result in serious shortfalls.[48]

If current trends continue, the overall number of ships in the fleet will remain at 285 or below through the end of the current FYDP.[49] Total force levels are projected to reach 300 in 2019, but only stay at or exceed that number in 16 of the remaining years in the plan (FY 2019–42). The navy planned to build 57 ships during FY 2012–16. Now it is only planning to build 41 during FY 2013–17.[50] These cuts will affect specific navy programs over the next five years. An analysis by the International Institute for Strategic Studies (IISS) highlights some of the most significant cuts and delays in procurement for shipbuilding:

> Some ship-building programs will be delayed: construction of the second Ford-class aircraft carrier will now take six years rather than four; the second America-class amphibious assault ship will be delayed by one year; and the Ohio-class submarine replacement—the SSBN(X)—will be delayed by two years.[51]

The future of another essential platform, the Virginia-class submarine program, deserves attention. In the FY 2013 budget request, the navy deferred one unit that was supposed to be procured in FY 2014 to FY 2018, outside the current FYDP. The armed services committees in both houses of Congress have approved advanced procurement to restore it to FY 2014. Even so, over the long term the Virginia-class is one of the many platforms that will experience shortfalls over the next 30 years.

---

[47] U.S. Department of Defense, *Annual Report to Congress on Long-Range Plan for Construction of Naval Vessels for FY 2013*, report prepared by the Office of the Chief of Naval Operations (Washington, D.C., April 2012). The FY 2013 30-year shipbuilding plan states that it aims for a total force of about 300 ships, but Ronald O'Rourke's most recent report on trends in shipbuilding and conversion notes that the number of assets adds up to 310–16 ships. See Ronald O'Rourke, "Navy Force Structure and Shipbuilding Plans: Background and Issues for Congress," Congressional Research Service, CRS Report for Congress, RL32665, June 14, 2012.

[48] Carlo Munoz, "Shipbuilding Budget Falls Short of Navy's Needs, Says Top Admiral," *Hill*, DEFCON Hill web log, March 22, 2012, http://thehill.com/blogs/defcon-hill/navy/217687-navy-shipbuilding-plan-wont-meet-commanders-needs-admiral-says.

[49] The current number of warships is 282, as cited in the newest shipbuilding plan (as of March 19, 2012).

[50] See O'Rourke, "Navy Force Structure and Shipbuilding Plans," 4. See also U.S. Department of Defense, *Plan for Construction of Naval Vessels*.

[51] "Streamlined Military Looks towards Asia," International Institute for Strategic Studies (IISS), Strategic Comments, no. 5, February 2012, http://www.iiss.org/publications/strategic-comments/past-issues/volume-18-2012/february/streamlined-us-military-looks-towards-asia/.

The latest shipbuilding plan has attempted to remediate these attack submarine (SSN) shortfalls: the SSN force falls below the 48 ships that the navy wants for a shorter period of time than in last year's plan (FY 2022–34 compared with FY 2023–41). Additionally, the FY 2013 plan adds the procurement of two additional units for a total of 46 rather than 44 SSNs.[52] But given the overall budget trends and ever-changing shipbuilding plans, it is likely that these numbers could be revised downward again.

Ballistic-missile defense. From FY 2012 to 2013, total funding for general ballistic-missile defense (BMD)—for procurement as well as research, development, testing, and evaluation (RDTE)—was cut by approximately 7%. Within that program, Aegis BMD, especially important for the Pacific region, was cut by slightly over 11%, 31% of which came from the procurement account.[53] The president's budget proposes early retirement in FY 2013 for four Ticonderoga-class Aegis-equipped vessels: the USS *Cowpens*, USS *Anzio*, USS *Vicksburg*, and the BMD-capable USS *Port Royal*. Cuts to all missile-defense activities totaled about $700 million.[54]

Next-generation fighters. The F-35 Joint Strike Fighter stealthy aircraft program is also taking a budgetary hit. Overall reductions in the program amount to roughly $75 million.[55] A comparison between last year's and this year's FYDP of planned buys by both the air force and navy shows that the U.S. military will end up with a smaller force of fifth-generation fighters (which will drive up per-unit costs).[56] For the F-35A, the military had planned to buy

---

[52] O'Rourke, "Navy Force Structure and Shipbuilding Plans," 10.

[53] The major programs that make up this line item are patriot advanced capability-3 (PAC-3), Aegis BMD, PAC-3 missile segment enhancement (MSE), ground-based midcourse defense (GMD), and terminal high-altitude area defense (THAAD). See U.S. Department of Defense, *Program Acquisition Costs by Weapons System*, budget report prepared by Office of the Under Secretary of Defense Comptroller/Chief Financial Officer (Washington, D.C., February 2012), section 4-2, http://comptroller.defense.gov/defbudget/fy2013/FY2013_Weapons.pdf.

[54] See U.S. Department of Defense, *Program Acquisition Costs*, section 4-2; and "White House Seeks Cut in Ballistic Missile Defense Spending," *Global Security Newswire*, February 14, 2012, http://www.nti.org/gsn/article/white-house-seeks-cut-ballistic-antimissile-spending/.

[55] See Department of Defense, *Program Acquisition Costs*, section 1-6.

[56] The data in this paragraph comes from the FY 2012 and FY 2013 budget justifications for the Navy and the Air Force. See U.S. Department of Defense, *Fiscal Year (FY) 2012 Budget Estimates: Air Force, Justification Book Volume I*, prepared by the Department of the Air Force Financial Management and Comptroller (Washington, D.C., February 2011), http://www.saffm.hq.af.mil/shared/media/document/AFD-110211-038.pdf; U.S. Department of Defense, *Fiscal Year (FY) 2013 President's Budget Submission: Air Force, Justification Book Volume 1*, prepared by Department of the Air Force Financial Management and Comptroller (Washington, D.C., February 2012), http://www.saffm.hq.af.mil/shared/media/document/AFD-120210-115.pdf; U.S. Department of Defense, *Fiscal Year (FY) 2012 Budget Estimates: Justification of Estimates, Aircraft Procurement*, prepared by Department of the Navy Financial Management and Comptroller (Washington, D.C., February 2011), http://www.finance.hq.navy.mil/FMB/12pres/APN_BA1-4_BOOK.pdf; and U.S. Department of Defense, *Fiscal Year (FY) 2013 President's Budget Submission, Justification Book Volume 1, Aircraft Procurement*, prepared by Department of the Navy Financial Management and Comptroller (Washington, D.C., February 2012), http://www.finance.hq.navy.mil/fmb/13pres/APN_BA1-4_BOOK.pdf.

203 from 2012 to 2016 but now only plans to buy 166 from 2013 to 2017. For the F-35B, last year's planned buy was 50, but that has been reduced to 41 (see **Table 2**). The planned procurement quantities for F-35Cs dropped sharply

TABLE 2   Funding for equipment relevant to air-sea battle, by number scheduled for procurement before and after the Budget Control Act

Program	Budget year	FY 2012	FY 2013	FY 2014	FY 2015	FY 2016	FY 2017	FYDP totals
F-35A	FY 2012 PB	19	24	40	50	70	–	203
	FY 2013 PB	18	19	19	32	48	48	166
F-35B STOVL	FY 2012 PB	6	6	8	12	18	–	50
	FY 2013 PB	6	6	6	6	9	14	41
F-35C CVN	FY 2012 PB	7	12	14	19	20	–	72
	FY 2013 PB	7	4	4	6	9	14	37
Virginia-class SSN	FY 2012 PB	2	2	2	2	2	–	10
	FY 2013 PB	2	2	1	2	2	2	9
DDG-51 Aegis destroyer	FY 2012 PB	1	2	2	2	1	–	8
	FY 2013 PB	1	2	1	2	2	2	9
Aegis ballistic-missile defense (SM-3 interceptors)*	FY 2012 PB	129	155	201	263	341	–	341
	FY 2013 PB	129	138	200	239	308	397	397
Global Hawk RQ-4	FY 2012 PB	3	3	3	1	1	–	11
	FY 2013 PB	3	0	0	0	0	0	0
Standard missiles for Aegis platforms	FY 2012 PB	89	121	129	152	168	–	659
	FY 2013 PB	89	94	115	157	168	204	738
Advanced mid-range air-to-air missiles	FY 2012 PB	161	210	216	244	232	–	1,063
	FY 2013 PB	67	67	105	113	120	120	525

SOURCE: Department of the Navy and Department of the Air Force justification books for FY 2012 and FY 2013.

NOTE: Round 1 of the Budget Control Act cut $259.4 billion from FY 2013–17 of the FYDP. FYDP totals for FY 2013 PB do not include FY 2012. Asterisk indicates that Aegis SM-3 totals are calculated cumulatively year to year. FY = fiscal year. PB = president's budget. FYDP = Future Years Defense Program, a five-year plan projecting future U.S. defense spending.

from 72 to 37. As the F-35 program keeps taking blows, it is important to remember the limited number of stealthy aircraft in the U.S. arsenal today. Maintaining an edge in stealth is especially important as China moves closer to producing its own next-generation fighter.

Additionally, high numbers of cutting-edge tactical fighters would be necessary for a campaign in a contested air environment. According to Mackenzie Eaglen and Douglas Birkey, an average theater campaign has about 30,000 targets.[57] In the very small-scale operation in Libya—a country with no modern air-defense system—NATO flew 26,000 sorties against 6,000 targets.[58] Given China's size, the number of valuable targets would be orders of magnitude higher.

Some critics of the short-range tactical F-35B may be satisfied with these numbers, claiming that there are not enough safe places from which the short-range F-35 can fly. There are two responses to this claim. The first is that the F-35 is still a highly capable stealthy aircraft that has received much money, time, and effort. It may grow in importance as China is committed to acquiring stealthy aircraft of its own. Fixed-wing tactical aircraft have always been vulnerable to airbase attacks. But the answer has always been dispersal, diversification, and hardening of bases. The second response is that the proposed solution—a long-range bomber—is not a silver bullet either. Overreliance on striking power launched from outside Asia entails strategic risk: it can undercut reassurance to allies with which the United States will remain coupled in Asia. Furthermore, as will be expanded on below, even under optimistic scenarios the bomber is still a decade away. Deterrence in Asia is needed today.

Long-range bomber program. ASB requires long-range strike capabilities, including a next-generation bomber. This year's budget request allocated $6.3 billion through 2017 for the manned and unmanned iterations of a new bomber, which is a small amount for such a badly needed capability (see **Table 3**).[59] Furthermore, initial operational capability is tentatively projected for the mid-2020s. At the same time, the Department of Defense is cutting the current bomber fleet of B-1s, B-2s, and B-52s. RDTE funding was cut from all three programs, with the decline in B-2 squadrons amounting to almost 90%. Today, the air force has far fewer bombers than it had at any point during the

---

[57] Mackenzie Eaglen and Douglas Birkey, "Nearing Coffin Corner: U.S. Air Power on the Edge," American Enterprise Institute (AEI), National Security Outlook, no. 1, March 2012, 4.

[58] Ibid., 4.

[59] See Philip Ewing, "The Air Force's Simple, No-Frills, Advanced New Bomber," *DoD Buzz*, February 13, 2012, http://www.dodbuzz.com/2012/02/13/the-air-forces-simple-no-frills-advanced-new-bomber/.

TABLE 3   Funding for research, development, testing, and evaluation relevant to air-sea battle, in millions of dollars

Program	Budget year	FY 2012	FY 2013	FY 2014	FY 2015	FY 2016	FY 2017
Long-range strike/ next-generation bomber	FY 2012 PB	197	294	550	1,000	1,700	–
	FY 2013 PB	295	292	550	1,045	1,727	2,707
Joint dual-role air-dominance missile	FY 2012 PB	30	48	78	146	188	–
	FY 2013 PB	30	0	0	0	0	0
KC-46A tanker (aerial refueling)	FY 2012 PB	877	1,150	817	384	48	–
	FY 2013 PB	877	1,816	1,576	1,100	567	345
Undersea warfare applied research	FY 2012 PB	109	113	116	122	125	–
	FY 2013 PB	109	97	98	101	101	100
Future naval capabilities applied research	FY 2012 PB	–	–	–	–	–	–
	FY 2013 PB	–	162	164	180	194	189
Surface- and shallow-water mine countermeasures	FY 2012 PB	143	150	128	79	59	–
	FY 2013 PB	128	191	147	121	80	70

SOURCE: Department of the Navy and Department of the Air Force justification books for FY 2012 and FY 2013.

NOTE: Undersea warfare applied research and future naval capabilities applied research are both large programs that include several elements. They are included here because both include antisubmarine warfare research. FY = fiscal year. PB = president's budget.

Cold War. Whereas the United States had over 500 B-52s alone during the Vietnam War, the air force currently has only 134 total bombers.[60]

Additionally, General Schwartz has said that the per-unit cost of the bomber must stay at $550 million per plane in order for the program to keep moving forward.[61] Historically, program costs increase substantially, especially in the face of shortsighted cuts. For the B-2, instead of spending $58.2 billion (1986 dollars) for 133 aircraft, the air force spent $44.3 billion

---

[60] Eaglen and Birkey, "Nearing Coffin Corner," 3.

[61] Jeff Schogol, "Schwartz Defends Cost of Next-Gen Bomber," *Air Force Times*, February 29, 2012, http://www.airforcetimes.com/news/2012/02/airforce-schwartz-defends-cost-of-next-gen-bomber-022912w/.

(1998 dollars) on just 21, with costs skyrocketing to $2.2 billion per plane. It is only prudent to assume that the new bomber could suffer a similar fate. The figure $44.3 billion in 1998 dollars is about $62 billion in 2012 dollars, but the current bomber program envisions a less-than-realistic figure of $55 billion in total costs.[62]

Thus, the capability that military and defense officials have been talking about for over a decade as one of the main answers to the China challenge may take another decade to deploy, and considering budget uncertainties, even that time frame may be extended. Given the history of the B-2 program described above, as well as both the F-22 and F-35 programs, a new bomber could be vulnerable to expensive additional requirements that Congress and new administrations may place on the program over its lifespan. This would result in cost overruns.[63]

Army and Marine Corps. Army regulars will be reduced from 570,000 to 490,000 regulars, with cuts to the Marine Corps totaling 20,000 active duty troops.[64] In addition, at least eight, but as many as thirteen, of the army's regular brigade combat teams will be cut for the purpose of reorganization,[65] and four marine infantry battalions will be disbanded. This reorganization will occur despite the fact that the army has historically played a major role in the Asia-Pacific, including training allied armies and fighting on the Korean Peninsula and in the Philippines. Bruce Bennett of the RAND Corporation paints a daunting picture of what it would take to stabilize a collapsing North Korea. He estimates that operations to mop up North Korean units left fighting, maintain stability, execute humanitarian relief, deter a conflict with China, and clear WMDs could require more than the roughly 750,000 Iraqi and U.S. ground troops that were needed for stability operations in Iraq.[66]

---

[62] The figures for the B-2 were found in the following U.S. Government Accountability Office reports: *B-2 Bomber Costs and Operational Issues* (Washington, D.C., August 1997), http://www.gao.gov/ archive/1997/ns97181.pdf; and *B-2 Bomber Additional Costs to Correct Deficiencies and Make Improvements* (Washington, D.C., June 1998), http://www.gao.gov/assets/230/225819.pdf. The conversion from 1998 to 2012 dollars was achieved using approximations based on the official Consumer Price Index calculator.

[63] For a brief history of the F-22 Raptor program, including procurement trends, cost, and issues for Congress, see Jeremiah Gertler, "Air Force F-22 Fighter Program: Background and Issues for Congress," Congressional Research Service, CRS Report for Congress, RL31673, December 22, 2009, http://www.au.af.mil/au/awc/awcgate/crs/rl31673.pdf.

[64] "Streamlined Military Looks towards Asia."

[65] Lance M. Bacon, "Odierno: Brigade Cuts Needed to Reorganize," *Army Times*, March 3, 2012, http://www.armytimes.com/news/2012/03/army-ray-odierno-says-brigade-combat-team-cuts-needed-reorganize-030312w/.

[66] Bruce Bennett, "Managing Catastrophic North Korea Risks," *Korea Herald*, January 21, 2010, available at http://www.rand.org/commentary/2010/01/21/KH.html.

A cursory glance at Marine Corps history in the Pacific demonstrates how important that force will be in a high-intensity conflict.[67] With forward-operating bases under threat, the marines could be called on to secure airbases, grab and seize land for the air force to use, and carry out other traditional missions such as noncombatant evacuation operations. Given that the Korean Peninsula may well be an area of contention between the United States and China, analysis of how such a conflict would play out shows that it is not prudent to assume that the air force and navy will be able to meet the challenges of China on their own.

Other cuts relevant to ASB. In the realm of ISR, three important programs that have already produced platforms—eleven RC-26s, one E-8 joint surveillance target and attack radar system, and eighteen RQ-4 Block-30 Global Hawk UAVs—are being retired or terminated.[68] In particular, the Block-30 Global Hawk program is in peril. The air force has requested early retirement for the eighteen units already procured, has approved no new funding for future procurement, and will rely solely on the U-2 to fulfill relevant ISR missions. Because of its endurance and range, the Block-30 would be more survivable than the U-2 in the vast geography of Asia. Procurement of munitions is also under the knife. The joint dual-role air-dominance missile, designed as a replacement for both the AIM-120 advanced medium-range air-to-air missile (AMRAAM) and the AGM-88 high-speed anti-radiation missile, has been terminated.[69] At the same time, AMRAAM procurement quantities are lower in this year's budget than in last year's.

The above analysis provides a very rough sketch of why the quantities of certain capabilities matter, as well as of the effects of the recent budget cuts on those numbers. The bottom line is that the budget is dictating something less than a "rebalancing" to Asia. As the authors of the recent IISS report put it, "Steps taken towards this [military rebalancing to Asia] in the FY 2013 budget are quite modest."[70] Marines are to be deployed to Australia, up to four littoral combat ships will go to Singapore, and ties between the U.S. and Philippine militaries are tightening. ASB and talk of rebalancing are supposed to provide a message of reassurance to Asian allies and a deterrent message

---

[67] See, for example, William B. Hopkins, *The Pacific War: The Strategy, Politics, and Players That Won the War* (Minneapolis: Zenith Press, 2008).

[68] "Streamlined Military Looks towards Asia."

[69] Ibid.

[70] Ibid.

to China, but the budget undercuts these critical messages.[71] U.S. allies are in a unique position to measure how much actual power the U.S. military can project into Asia at any given time and thereby make comparisons to China. As China increases its display of strength, the relative decline of the U.S. response will become apparent.

Air-Sea Battle and the Strategy of Primacy

Resource trends are an immediate concern that arises but the larger questions that should preoccupy policymakers have to do with the United States' strategic aims. If developing the capabilities to "disrupt, destroy, and defeat" Chinese attempts to coerce Asian powers or to defend a forward presence in Asia is not enough, then how do we know what is? All operational concepts must further a U.S. strategy of primacy. Does ASB fit that category? Related to this question, is a strategy of deterrence by denial sufficient to retain U.S. primacy and assure U.S. allies?

The United States was willing to assume major risks, including the possibility of a nuclear attack on the Soviet Union, to keep continental Europe out of Soviet hands. Is the United States prepared to assume similar risks in Asia today, particularly to defend Taiwan, Japan, South Korea, and the nations of Southeast Asia? Is the possibility of a China that controls or neutralizes these countries as threatening to U.S. interests as was the prospect of Soviet control over Europe? Given the aims declared by U.S. leaders, the answer is probably yes. Over the long term, it is more likely than not that the United States will have to contemplate the threat or use of nuclear weapons. So far, however, the United States has put the operational cart before the strategic horse. Before contemplating an attack on a nuclear-armed country in depth,

---

[71] As of June 10, 2012, the specter of sequestration looms large. The cuts outlined above are significant, and yet they do not even take into account another $500 billion in cuts mandated by the BCA in the form of automatic sequestration. Administration officials have described the specter of sequestration in harsh terms. Deputy Secretary of Defense Ashton Carter recently termed it an "irrational" way to plan and manage strategy. Secretary of Defense Leon Panetta said in January 2012 that the newly published strategic guidance would have to be thrown "out the window," should sequestration come into effect in early 2013. Sequestration would have a severe impact on the DoD's ability to provide for the programs that support the ASB concept of operations. At this juncture, it is impossible to know how exactly sequestration would affect ASB and what programs would be cut or even canceled, especially because DoD officials have stated publicly that they are not yet planning for this possibility. However, as Deputy Secretary Carter stated in May 2012, echoing similar warnings from Secretary Panetta, "A sequester would have devastating effects on our readiness and our workforce, and disrupt thousands of contracts and programs." See Todd Harrison, "The Fiscal Year 2013 Defense Budget: Continuity or Change?" Center for Strategic and Budgetary Assessments, Backgrounder, February 2012, 3, http://www.csbaonline.org/publications/2012/02/the-fiscal-year-2013-defense-budget-continuity-or-change; and "Deputy Secretary of Defense Carter Speech to the American Enterprise Institute, Washington, D.C.," U.S. Department of Defense, http://www.defense.gov/transcripts/transcript.aspx?transcriptid=5044.

it would be wise to know for what purposes the United States would take such risks.

The Need for Nuclear Deterrence

The debate about whether conventional deterrence is sufficient was never resolved, and mercifully never really put to the test, during the Cold War.[72] But one can conclude fairly that a robust nuclear arsenal and the ability to dominate escalation played a substantial role in advancing U.S. Cold War objectives. U.S. allies certainly thought so, which is why they wanted both to tie conventional defenses to U.S. nuclear responses and, for the most part, keep U.S. nuclear forces in Europe. The extended deterrent in Europe and Asia needed both forward-deployed forces and a variety of nuclear capabilities that reassured allies of the United States' willingness to risk war to stop a Soviet onslaught. The grave fear among the allies was the possibility of the Soviet Union gaining a large and survivable force that could credibly threaten the U.S. homeland, which would serve as a deterrent to a conventional defense of Europe.

These strategic problems have remained fairly constant. As the Chinese build a second-strike nuclear capability and a more robust intercontinental nuclear force,[73] allies in Asia will have the same fears of decoupling. The logic of self-deterrence by the United States is even stronger considering the uncertainties of Chinese nuclear doctrine and force structure. While China does have a "no first use" policy, it would be imprudent to take the policy at face value given the country's changing strategic circumstances. In particular, it would be unwise to assume that China will hold back a nuclear response if its forces are devastated by U.S. conventional strikes. The United States attacking in depth could cause China to escalate conflict quickly.

In such a scenario, the United States could choose not to roll back China's air and missile power or sea-denial capabilities. But even if Washington decides against striking the Chinese mainland, other strategies such as economic strangulation could escalate. In the Sino-U.S. competition, a strategy that includes nuclear weapons could provide the United States with two advantages. First, it would add a degree of uncertainty in the minds of

---

[72] On the debate, see, for example, Richard K. Betts, "Conventional Deterrence: Predictive Uncertainty and Policy Confidence," *World Politics* 37, no. 2 (1985): 153–79; and Samuel P. Huntington, "Conventional Deterrence and Conventional Retaliation in Europe," *International Security* 8, no. 3 (1983–84): 32–56.

[73] For brief overviews of Chinese nuclear strategy, see Dan Blumenthal and Michael Mazza, "Why China May Want More Nuclear Weapons," AEI, April 6, 2011, http://www.aei.org/article/foreign-and-defense-policy/regional/asia/why-china-may-want-more-nuclear-weapons/; and Yao Yunzhu, "China's Perspective on Nuclear Deterrence," *Air & Space Power Journal* 24, no. 1 (2010), http://www.airpower.au.af.mil/airchronicles/apj/apj10/spr10/yao.html.

Chinese planners, which would increase the strength of deterrence. Second, such a strategy could allow Washington to control escalation. If a U.S. president decides to attack China in depth, he or she will also need to deter a nuclear response by China. This can only be done with nuclear weapons.

Toward a Force Structure for Asia

A force structure that underpins U.S. primacy in Asia should provide the U.S. president with a diverse set of options to control escalation should China initiate a conflict. This overarching requirement, in turn, necessitates three interrelated strategic military objectives that involve a variety of platforms and capabilities.

First, the force structure must permit U.S. forces to maintain command of the commons by mastering (or remastering) the seas, air, and space.[74] This requires the United States to maintain a fortified military presence in the Asia-Pacific while demonstrating an ability to bring additional power to bear from afar.

Linked to this objective, a second goal is for U.S. forces to wrest back control of the commons closer to Chinese shores should China succeed in establishing "contested zones." Parts of the ASB concept, if resourced properly, could help U.S. forces carry out this mission. With its focus on survivability in the face of electronic, space, and missile attack, along with joint C4ISR, ASB could help build air and naval forces that can operate within China's most dense "kill zones."

Third, the U.S. force structure should enable the United States to advance its strategy of primacy following a conflict. In other words, U.S. forces should be capable of not only defeating Chinese forces but also doing so in a way that shifts the Asian balance of power decisively in the United States' favor. Accomplishment of this mission will require capabilities and platforms that can be utilized to punish an adversary and degrade its forces such that future challenges to U.S. primacy are simultaneously more difficult and less appealing. The following sections describe the capabilities necessary to fulfill these three force-structure criteria. Implicit is the development of a host of options for a president to control escalation.

Capabilities Needed for All Three Tasks

All of the aforementioned tasks require a robust attack-submarine fleet with wide area surveillance and large stocks of munitions. SSNs would be

---

[74] This analysis omits any discussion of cyberspace because it is unclear whether the U.S. military ever dominated or could dominate this area.

needed to re-establish command of the sea, operate in the contested zone, and implement a strategy of punishment. In the short run, Washington should restore the FY 2014 submarine budget to ensure that a steady building schedule of two hulls per year is maintained. Over the next 30 years, the navy should revise its shipbuilding plan to build at least two hulls per year to prevent or at least ameliorate the currently projected shortfalls in FY 2022–34.

All the major tasks also require carrier strike groups (CSG) with robust anti-missile countermeasures and the full complement of accompanying ships stocked with precision-guided munitions. While CSGs may not be the first set of capabilities to join a close-in East Asian fight, they will be needed to re-establish air supremacy in Northeast and Southeast Asia, reinforce defenses in the first island chain, and possibly create a blockade and maritime and exclusion zone in both the first and second island chains.[75] Finally, CSGs to the west of the Malacca Strait in the Indian Ocean could be used for maritime interdiction or distant blockade operations of Chinese commerce. As a baseline, it is worth noting that during Operation Iraqi Freedom, the navy provided five to seven CSGs throughout the course of the war.[76]

The president and combatant commanders could also require that marine and navy expeditionary strike groups (ESG) be available on short notice. Accelerating the purchase of the F-35B could prove very useful, as this aircraft is both versatile and survivable in less than ideal conditions. In addition to flying off amphibious ships, F-35Bs can fly off bases that are constructed quickly in a conflict. With vulnerable runways enduring continued Chinese missile and air strikes, F-35Bs flying off amphibious ships could be an attractive means to both establish air supremacy and provide a strike option. Operation Iraqi Freedom, during which the marines deployed four amphibious ready groups to the area of operation, demonstrates the combined effectiveness of this system of capabilities.[77]

All three strategic tasks also require a strong and survivable joint C4ISR system, such as the air force's UAVs and the navy's broad area maritime surveillance (BAMS) systems working together with space assets. Given China's burgeoning space capabilities, the ability to defend space assets and reconstitute them will be imperative.

---

[75] See T.X. Hammes, "Offshore Control: A Proposed Strategy," *Infinity Journal* 2, no. 2 (2012): 10–14. Elements of Hammes's proposed strategy should be available to the U.S. president. Although Hammes makes a very provocative case, it is unclear how the United States can defend Taiwan without entering the contested zone and establishing air supremacy close to China's shores.

[76] Raymond Keledei, "Naval Forward Presence," Naval War College, October 23, 2006, 1, http://www.dtic.mil/cgi-bin/GetTRDoc?AD=ADA463587.

[77] "U.S. Navy Order of Battle: Operation Iraqi Freedom," Unofficial U.S. Navy Site, webpage, http://navysite.de/navy/iraqi-freedom.htm.

Capabilities for Wresting Control of the Contested Zone

For this task, many of the capabilities and concepts espoused in ASB would be necessary. Because of the kill zones that China may create around the Taiwan Strait and its surrounding seas, emphasis should be placed on survivable platforms, including SSNs, long-range bombers, undersea and surface ships with ballistic-missile defenses, ASW and mine-laying capabilities, and F-35s (again, primarily the B variant). These should be supplemented with capabilities that disrupt the enemy and its battle networks, such as electronic warfare assets for jamming ISR and cyber capabilities for disrupting operations.

In addition, the president should have the option to degrade Chinese air and missile strikes by rolling back China's IADS and destroying C4ISR assets, bases, and ports. For these purposes, the long-range bomber should be allocated sufficient funding to at least develop into a prototype by the end of the current FDYP in 2017. The United States should also consider exiting the Intermediate-Range Nuclear Forces Treaty with Russia in the event that China elects not to enter it. If such a geopolitical decision is made, the U.S. military could deploy shorter-range ground-launched cruise and ballistic missiles. This capability would provide the military with a survivable, mobile-strike option that puts China in a more defensive crouch.

Capabilities for Punishment and Retaliation

For a strategy of primacy to ultimately be successful, any challenger must be weakened and punished. This task requires the capabilities to offensively strike to destroy and degrade military assets and to use military power to cause sustained economic strangulation. To ensure such capabilities, the navy needs at least the 313 ships it had requested previously. The navy deployed around 115 ships during Operation Desert Storm for sea-based and air-strike missions, mine countermeasures, surface warfare, and blockades.[78] It is hard to imagine even a limited war with China requiring fewer U.S. ships than that figure, let alone a war that seeks to achieve a long-term weakening of China's military capability.

Additionally, punishment and retaliation capabilities would almost certainly require a strike campaign larger than the average theater campaign of 30,000 targets. Should the president choose that option, the full nuclear triad would need to be available for robust counterforce capabilities. As Tom Donnelly and David Trachtenberg have written:

---

[78] "U.S. Navy in Desert Shield/Desert Storm," Naval History and Heritage Command, webpage, http://www.history.navy.mil/wars/dstorm/ds5.htm.

> U.S. nuclear weapons must be tailored to meet new security requirements. This includes the development of low-yield nuclear weapons that can strike hard and deeply buried targets with minimal collateral damage. Targets that are deep underground or in protected environments are difficult to hold at risk with existing nuclear forces, whose yields would ensure high levels of collateral damage. The technology exists to improve the accuracy and lower the yields of nuclear weapons in ways that would enhance their effectiveness against hard and deeply buried targets while minimizing collateral damage. But the United States has been prevented from developing these capabilities because they are seen as new types of nuclear weapons…[T]he continued credibility of U.S. nuclear deterrence relies on the ability to adapt U.S. nuclear weapons capabilities in ways that can effectively hold those targets at risk.[79]

The credibility of a contemporary nuclear deterrent requires not only large numbers of nuclear forces delivered from the triad but also weapons that can hit their targets with minimum collateral damage. If weapons are not survivable and discriminating, both allies and adversaries will doubt their utility.

War with China is a horrifying prospect. Yet planning for contingencies up the escalation ladder is just as prudent as it was when the United States faced the nuclear-armed Soviet Union. It would be reasonable to assume that China is developing similar war plans, just in case.

Conclusion

The United States has employed a strategy of primacy in Asia since the end of the Cold War. The ends of this strategy include a forward defense of the homeland, upholding peace among the regional powers, preventing nuclear proliferation, fostering an open trading system that demands access to sea lanes and waterways connecting Asia with the rest of the world, and promoting continued liberalization in the world's most dynamic region. The military underpinning of this strategy is command of the commons. The ability to master the air, sea, and space domains has enabled the United States to exert the full force of its power in places and at times of its choosing, while denying adversaries the ability to do the same. This ability has thus been the key to extended and general deterrence, allowing the United States to move nuclear and conventional capabilities in and out of Asia with ease. But Washington now faces a monumental challenge. China has developed many of the capabilities necessary to construct contested zones during a conflict, which would allow it to challenge and then employ coercive power.

---

[79] Thomas Donnelly and David Trachtenberg, "Toward a New 'New Look': U.S. Nuclear Strategy and Forces in the Third Atomic Age," AEI, Center for Defense Studies, Working Paper, March 2010, 35, http://www.aei.org/files/2010/03/01/Toward-a-New-New-Look-final.pdf.

The United States has begun to respond through the ASB operational concept, the animating idea of which is to demonstrate that the United States can operate in the contested commons and slow or halt a Chinese attack on an ally or strategic partner. However, ASB suffers from three problems. First, current trends in the defense budget are undercutting the viability of the concept. Second, ASB is a high-risk operational doctrine that could entail deep strikes on nuclear-armed China; however, unlike air-land battle, ASB is not tied to a greater strategic purpose. This doctrine should be tied to a strategy of primacy, which is the only realistic U.S. approach in Asia. Third, ASB underemphasizes the need for a nuclear deterrent. If the United States is contemplating defense in-depth, it would be wise to have a demonstrated nuclear retaliatory capacity that can determine the pace of escalation.

Current strategic debates are far from reaching a consensus on which Chinese actions could threaten U.S. grand strategy and thus merit a military response. It may be that, as during the Cold War, the United States will not know when its primacy is under threat until it is actually challenged.[80] In the meantime, Washington must maintain the strategy that has upheld its long-standing goals in Asia.

---

[80] The United States did not predict that it would go toe to toe with the Soviet Union in Berlin, Cuba, or Korea.

STRATEGIC ASIA 2012–13

SPECIAL STUDY

EXECUTIVE SUMMARY

This chapter examines three sets of factors that shape Chinese thinking and actions with respect to world order and examines the possible contours and implications of the order China may seek.

MAIN ARGUMENT:

China has benefited from the liberal international order led by the U.S. However, China is uncomfortable with aspects of the current system and will seek to change them as part of a broader effort to reform global institutions to reflect its perception of 21st-century realities. One set of shaping factors— China's assessment of the current world order—identifies much that Chinese leaders would be reluctant to change because they want to continue to reap benefits without assuming greater burdens. A second set of factors includes traditional Chinese or Confucian concepts of world order. A third set of factors comprises the attitudes and actions of other countries. China's rise has been achieved by accepting greater interdependence, and its ability to exert influence depends on the responses of other nations.

POLICY IMPLICATIONS:

- China appears to want to maintain most elements of the current global order, including U.S. leadership. But it also wants the U.S. to allow other nations, specifically China, to have a greater voice in decisions affecting the international system.

- China is more interested in improving and establishing rules and institutions needed to meet 21st-century challenges than in wholesale replacement of existing mechanisms. This makes China a willing as well as necessary partner in the remaking of institutions to meet shared international challenges.

- Despite incurring Beijing's disapproval, the U.S. must continue to hedge against uncertainties by maintaining the collective security arrangements and institutions that have contributed to global stability and the security of individual nations.

China's Vision of World Order

Thomas Fingar

If China had an opportunity to refashion the global order, what would it change and what would it seek to accomplish? The question is certainly premature because it will be a long time, if ever, before China has an opportunity to replace or restructure the liberal world order that has been established and led by the United States during the decades since World War II.[1] But many, inside and outside China, recognize that the current system is increasingly ill-suited for the challenges of today and tomorrow, and that China will have an important voice in deciding what to keep, what to replace, and what to reengineer.[2] That being the case, it is not at all premature to begin asking about China's objectives and expectations with respect to a post-American world.

This chapter relies more on inference and imagination than on discovery and analysis. Beijing has not published or even hinted at the existence of a

---

Thomas Fingar is the inaugural Oksenberg-Rohlen Distinguished Fellow in the Freeman Spogli Institute for International Studies at Stanford University. He can be reached at <tfingar@stanford.edu>.

[1] Stimulating recent works on the origins, character, and possible futures of the global order led and maintained by the United States include G. John Ikenberry, *Liberal Leviathan: The Origins, Crisis, and Transformation of the American World Order* (Princeton: Princeton University Press, 2011); Robert Kagan, *The World America Made* (New York: Alfred A. Knopf, 2012); and Charles A. Kupchan, *No One's World: The West, the Rising Rest, and the Coming Global Tumult* (New York: Oxford University Press, 2012).

[2] See, for example, Kupchan, *No One's World*, chapter 5; National Intelligence Council, *Global Trends 2025: A Transformed World*, November 2008, http://www.dni.gov/nic/PDF_2025/2025_Global_Trends_Final_Report.pdf; and National Intelligence Council, *Global Governance 2025: At a Critical Juncture*, September 2010, http://www.dni.gov/nic/PDF_2025/2025_Global_Governance.pdf. China's interest in changing the existing system appears to be motivated by the recognition (shared with the United States and many other countries) that old arrangements are no longer adequate to manage the world they helped to create, by a desire to increase China's influence in the system, and by an ability to use this influence to achieve Chinese objectives.

vision statement, blueprint, or grand strategy for remaking the global order.[3] Desire to keep the plan secret probably is not the reason. A far more likely explanation is that there is no single specific Chinese plan or vision. Party, state, and military leaders, not to mention academics and "netizens," appear to have significantly different views on what is desirable, what is possible, and how best to pursue particular objectives.[4] Views range from very cautious and pragmatic admonitions to eschew statements or actions that might jeopardize China's ability to sustain rapid growth through participation in the existing world order, to jingoistic calls for China to speed the inevitable power transition to a Chinese-led world.[5] Rather than attempt to catalog, compare, and assess the relative strength of the various visions of world order discernible in the Chinese media and scholarly publications, the goal in this chapter is to explore factors that will shape Chinese views with respect to world order and the efforts China will make to change the existing system.[6]

The chapter first examines Chinese assessments of the current world order, focusing on its importance to China's "rise" and on attributes that please and displease Chinese geopolitical thinkers. The next section speculates on

---

[3] See, for example, Wang Jisi, "China's Search for a Grand Strategy: A Rising Great Power Finds Its Way," *Foreign Affairs* 90, no. 2 (2011): 68–79; Aaron L. Friedberg, *A Contest for Supremacy: China, America, and the Struggle for Mastery in Asia* (New York: W.W. Norton, 2011); and Thomas Fingar, "China's Rise: Contingency, Constraints, and Concerns," *Survival* 54, no. 1 (2012): 195–204.

[4] See, for example, Linda Jakobson and Dean Knox, *New Foreign Policy Actors in China* (Solna: Stockholm International Peace Research Institute, 2010), http://books.sipri.org/files/PP/SIPRIPP26.pdf; and Chin-Hao Huang, "Assessing the Role of Foreign Policy Elites in China: Impact on Chinese Foreign Policy Formulation," University of Southern California U.S.-China Institute, September 12, 2011, http://china.usc.edu/ShowArticle.aspx?articleID=2569.

[5] On power transitions, see, for example, Jack S. Levy, "Power Transition Theory and the Rise of China," in *China's Ascent: Power, Security, and the Future of International Politics*, ed. Robert Ross and Zhu Feng (Ithaca: Cornell University Press, 2008), 11–33. See also Zhu Liqun, *China's Foreign Policy Debates* (Paris: Institute for Security Studies, 2010), http://www.iss.europa.eu/publications/detail/article/chinas-foreign-policy-debates/.

[6] The existing global order is the product of both conscious design and decades of evolutionary adjustment. It has three principal subsystems: trade and finance, stability and security, and leadership and management. The subsystems are interconnected and, to a degree, interdependent. They and the operation of the system are characterized by John Ikenberry and others as "liberal" primarily because the trade and finance components seek to promote open markets and are relatively easy to join, and because U.S. leadership and management of the system allows for considerable diversity and independence. China, and now most other nations, likes the benefits and relatively low costs of participation in the trade and finance subsystem. Beijing understood when it decided to take advantage of the U.S.-led system that China's ability to achieve rapid and sustained economic growth and modernization of the country was dependent on the maintenance of peace and stability. Beijing also recognized that its own security required acceptance, at least temporarily, of U.S. alliances, military deployments, and other arrangements considered important to the maintenance of peace and stability. The demise of the Soviet Union, however, reduced the perceived importance of the United States and its security arrangements and made them more objectionable to China. To take advantage of the trade-finance and peace-stability opportunities of participation in the international system, China also had to temporarily accept U.S. leadership and provision of services to maintain the system as a whole. In other words, China accepted the system as a whole because it wanted to take advantage of specific subsystems and opportunities. Changes in the world and in Chinese capabilities have caused some in China to demand—and many outside China to expect—Beijing to seek reforms to the stability and leadership subsystems.

the possible influence of traditional Chinese concepts of world order and preferences inferred from the nature of China's political system and the interests of its ruling elite. The third section explores how other nations might perceive and respond to a China-dominant world order by examining China's relations with its closest partners and Chinese foreign policy actions during 2010. The final two sections speculate about what to expect and the type of world order China is likely to seek in the foreseeable future.

Chinese Views of the Current World Order

The existing world order shapes Chinese thinking in at least four ways. One is its importance to China's rise and prospects for continued growth and security. China benefits greatly from existing institutions and arrangements that preserve stability, facilitate trade, and constrain potential rivals. Stated another way, China's continued economic growth, internal order, and political legitimacy are heavily dependent on the existing international system.[7] Any changes to that system, whether proposed by China or by other nations, entail at least some risk of disruption and domestic disorder. A second dimension of the existing system affecting Chinese thinking is the preeminent position of the United States. China benefits from the public goods provided by the United States but, in the view of many Chinese, the system is rigged in ways that favor the United States and disadvantage others, especially China.

The third way in which the existing order shapes Chinese thinking derives from the first two. China's dependence on the global system makes it dependent on the United States, which it sees as determined to constrain China's ability to challenge U.S. preeminence and to prevent China from assuming its "proper" place in the global order.[8]

The fact that all but a handful of countries now benefit significantly from their participation in the U.S.-led global system is the fourth way in which the system influences Chinese thinking and options.[9] Like China, the growth, prosperity, and internal stability of countries in the global system are increasingly dependent on the existing order. Unlike China, however, most of them did not begin to take advantage of the U.S.-led system until a decade

---

[7] See, for example, Edward S. Steinfeld, *Playing Our Game: Why China's Rise Doesn't Threaten the West* (New York: Oxford University Press, 2010).

[8] See, for example, Kenneth Lieberthal and Wang Jisi, "Addressing U.S.-China Strategic Distrust," John L. Thornton Center Monograph Series, no. 4, March 2012, especially 7–19, http://www.brookings.edu/~/media/research/files/papers/2012/3/30%20us%20china%20lieberthal/0330_china_lieberthal.pdf.

[9] Countries that have opted out or been precluded from taking full advantage of the system include North Korea, Iran, Sudan, Cuba, and until recently, Myanmar and Libya.

or more after China was enabled to do so by the Carter administration.[10] This makes these countries particularly sensitive to the prospect of Chinese efforts to change the existing order because many would regard such efforts as reckless actions endangering their own ability to achieve sustained growth. Some would see such attempts to change the system as intended to limit their own ability to challenge China's position in global production chains and the system more generally.

Chinese views of the existing world order can be described as pragmatic, inconsistent, and somewhat paranoid. They clearly value what the U.S.-led liberal order has allowed China to accomplish over the last 33 years, but many in China are also uncomfortable with the fact that the global system is led by the United States.[11] This discomfort seems to stem primarily from concern, bordering on conviction, that the United States is determined to do whatever it considers necessary to preserve its preeminent or "hegemonic" position, including containing or thwarting China's rise and resumption of its rightful place in the world order.[12] In other words, Chinese concerns may have less to do with the unipolar character of the global order than with the fact that it is the United States, not China, that is the preeminent power.

When Deng Xiaoping launched the "reform and opening" policy in 1978, he abandoned the quest for a uniquely Chinese path to wealth and power that his predecessors had sought for more than a century. Three decades of Maoist experimentation had left the country almost as poor and backward as it had been in 1949. During the same period, countries that China feared were pulling ahead at an accelerating rate. The decision to abandon experimentation in favor of emulation—following the path that had enabled Japan and other Asian "tigers" to become prosperous, more capable, and more influential—was a decision to tie China's fate to the system that had enabled the "free world" to develop much more rapidly than its Cold War rivals and the nonaligned countries that had eschewed membership in either camp. That free world system eventually became the global system after the demise of the Soviet Union and now includes all but a handful of nations.[13]

Deng and other Chinese leaders justified the decision to seek development through cooperation with the U.S.-led order by arguing that

---

[10] See, for example, Thomas Fingar, "Global Implications of China's Challenges," *YaleGlobal Online*, January 16, 2012, http://yaleglobal.yale.edu/content/global-implications-china%E2%80%99s-challenges-%E2%80%93-part-i.

[11] See, for example, Robert G. Sutter, *Chinese Foreign Relations: Power and Policy Since the Cold War*, 3rd ed. (Lanham: Rowman and Littlefield, 2012), chapter 6.

[12] See Lieberthal and Wang, "Addressing U.S.-China Strategic Distrust"; and David M. Lampton, "Power Constrained: Sources of Mutual Strategic Suspicion in U.S.-China Relations," *NBR Analysis*, June 2010.

[13] Ikenberry, *Liberal Leviathan*, chapter 6.

doing so would make China richer, stronger, and better able to reduce its dependence on what some considered imperialist powers. Participation in the liberal order was acknowledged to entail short-term risks and dependencies (e.g., for technology, capital, and markets), but the resultant self-strengthening, advocates argued, would soon enable China to become steadily less dependent on the more developed countries and "their" system. Advocates of "engagement" in the United States and elsewhere predicted a different outcome, namely, that development would lead to greater, not diminished, dependence on the international system China had joined for expedient and instrumental reasons.[14]

Three decades later, China has reaped enormous benefits and changed dramatically. The changes—double-digit economic growth, breakneck urbanization, hundreds of millions lifted out of abject poverty and hundreds of millions more moving into cities and the middle class—and other successes of the reform and opening policy have made the country more, not less, dependent on the liberal order. Just as importantly, they have increased the potential for—and potential costs of—social and political discontent if growth rates slow and citizens lose confidence in the Chinese Communist Party's ability to alleviate worsening social problems such as corruption and inequality. China and the party are more dependent on the continued viability of the global system than at any time in the past, and the clear trajectory is toward even greater dependence.[15] The policy of reform and opening effectively subordinated ideology to the requisites of sustained economic growth. In conjunction with the decision to eschew charismatic authority in order to prevent the excesses of another Mao Zedong (i.e., to deal with the "bad emperor" problem) and the waning efficacy of claims to have "liberated" the Chinese people, enacting the reform and opening policy reduced the number of pillars supporting regime legitimacy to two: economic performance and nationalism.

Despite China's growing dependence on the liberal world order, official statements and China's international behavior indicate that the benefits of participation are judged to outweigh the costs of dependency, at least for the time being. Regardless of what else they may think about the current world order, most Chinese commentators on the matter acknowledge that its institutions and procedures have enabled China to develop more rapidly and to become stronger and more prosperous than any of its previously attempted

---

[14] See, for example, Li Lanqing, *Breaking Through: The Birth of China's Opening-Up Policy* (New York: Oxford University Press, 2009); and Ezra F. Vogel, *Deng Xiaoping and the Transformation of China* (Cambridge: Harvard University Press, 2011), chapter 7.

[15] See, for example, Jianyong Yue, "Peaceful Rise of China: Myth or Reality?" *International Politics* 45 (2008): 439–56.

paths to modernity.[16] For economic, social, military, and political reasons, the majority in China want to preserve most attributes of the existing system. Many want to make it more equitable or more efficient; none want to destroy it or to do anything that might jeopardize China's ability to derive current and future benefits. This suggests that if China had an opportunity to replace or radically transform the existing liberal order, it would be reluctant to do so and probably would leave most current features intact.

A second feature of the existing order that Chinese analysts seem to like is the fact that it is a rule-based system. In the early years of the reform and opening era, Chinese officials often professed reluctance to be bound by rules that they had not made, and sometimes demanded that rules, norms, and procedures be renegotiated to accommodate China's entry into the system. That seldom happened, and over time China's behavior evinced a recurring pattern that can be summarized as refusal to be bound by rules imposed by others, followed by reluctant willingness to accede to such rules on a case-by-case basis, followed by agreement to adhere to relevant principles and guidelines, and eventual accession to relevant conventions and control regimes. The process continued with the adoption of domestic legislation consistent with the new commitments, eventual enforcement of the legislation, and, in a small but growing number of cases, becoming an active champion of the rules.[17]

Among the reasons Chinese analysts like the rule-based character of the existing order is that, at least much of the time and on most issues, the leading/hegemonic/imperial power—the United States—has operated within the rules that it imposed or orchestrated for the system as a whole.[18] During a series of five workshops in May 2012, Chinese analysts and officials from party, state, military, educational, and research organizations commented favorably on the fact that the current system is rule-based and on the willingness of

---

[16] See, for example, Loren Brandt and Thomas G. Rawski, eds., *China's Great Economic Transformation* (New York: Cambridge University Press, 2008).

[17] See, for example, Bates Gill, *Rising Star: China's New Security Diplomacy*, rev. ed. (Washington, D.C.: Brookings Institution, 2010); and Evan S. Medeiros, *Reluctant Restraint: The Evolution of China's Nonproliferation Policies and Practices, 1980–2004* (Stanford: Stanford University Press, 2007).

[18] On U.S. willingness to be bound by rules of the liberal global order, see Ikenberry, *Liberal Leviathan*. For representative Chinese statements on the rule of law, see Duan Jielong, "Statement on the Rule of Law at the National and International Levels," *Chinese Journal of International Law* 6, no. 1 (2007): 185–88, http://chinesejil.oxfordjournals.org/content/6/1/185.full.pdf+html; and State Council Information Office, "China's Efforts and Achievements in Promoting the Rule of Law," *Chinese Journal of International Law* 7, no. 2 (2008): 513–55, http://chinesejil.oxfordjournals.org/content/7/2/513.full.pdf+html.

the preeminent power to follow those rules.[19] This was also identified by a number of participants as a factor mitigating Chinese discomfort with U.S. leadership and a reason why China is not eager to displace the United States from its leadership role.

The aspect of the existing order that Chinese participants found most in need of reform during the May 2012 workshops was its highly unipolar quality. Chinese participants argued that the current system was insufficiently democratic insofar as it accorded too little weight to the views and interests of emerging powers (interestingly, there were no complaints that it gave either too much or too little weight to members of the Organisation for Economic Co-operation and Development other than the United States). A related criticism was that the United States built and led the system in ways that gave itself disproportionate and unfair advantages. The discussions in May did not explore this point in detail, and it was impossible to determine whether those who mentioned the unfair U.S. advantage thought that it was simply a natural, expected consequence of the leading role played by the United States or a serious and no longer acceptable defect of the current world order that had to be corrected in some way. From the fact that more attention was devoted to calls to make the system more democratic, one could infer that Chinese observers who thought about the situation considered it desirable to reduce or eliminate U.S. advantages and to level the playing field, but no one specifically stated that doing so was desirable or necessary.[20]

Although uncomfortable with and somewhat critical of the U.S. role in the existing world order, many of the Chinese participants in the five workshops stated explicitly that the United States would remain the preeminent power for a very long time. Factors cited to explain this judgment included the size and quality of the U.S. economy (in contrast to China's economy, which was described as big but simple), U.S. innovative and entrepreneurial capabilities, its unrivaled and growing military power, and its prospect of becoming far

---

[19] The purpose of the workshops was to review a draft of the National Intelligence Council's forthcoming report entitled *Global Trends 2030: Alternative Worlds,* and assess the implications of those trends for U.S.-China relations. Separate workshops were organized by the China Institutes of Contemporary International Relations, the Ministry of Foreign Affairs' China Institute of International Studies, the International Liaison Department of the Chinese Communist Party, the Foundation for International Strategic Studies, and the Shanghai Institutes for International Studies. The National Intelligence Council and the Atlantic Council were the U.S. co-sponsors. Each workshop included participants from multiple Chinese organizations.

[20] This assessment is based on what this author heard during the May 2012 workshops. See also Niu Xinchun, "Eight Myths About Sino-U.S. Relations," *Contemporary International Relations* 21, no. 4 (2011), http://www.cicir.ac.cn/english/ArticleView.aspx?nid=2935; and Stewart M. Patrick and Farah Faisal Thaler, "China, the United States, and Global Governance: Shifting Foundations of World Order" (summary report of workshop, hosted by China Institutes of Contemporary Relations and Council on Foreign Relations, Beijing, March 15–17, 2010), http://www.cfr.org/content/thinktank/ CFR_CICIR_MeetingNote.pdf. The latter piece is notable because the workshop was held during a period when China was more assertive.

more "energy independent."[21] No one challenged this prediction or the reasons adduced to explain it. Most of the time, U.S. preeminence was discussed as a fact of life rather than as a problem or intolerable situation requiring action by China or a coalition of nations.[22] Indeed, far more time was devoted to comments on what the participants seemed to regard as fortunate and positive attributes of U.S. leadership.

Two specific positive attributes of U.S. leadership cited by participants, but mostly absent from Chinese media commentary on the U.S. global role, are the way in which the United States exercises its unrivaled hegemony and its willingness to provide public goods. The Chinese did not use the term "liberal hegemon," but what they described was consistent with the way John Ikenberry uses the term in his superb analysis of the liberal world order.[23] Examples of positive behavior by the United States include restraint in taking advantage of its preeminent position, support for—indeed, insistence on— rule-based relationships and transactions, and willingness to be bound by the rules it advocated or acceded to in response to pressure from other countries.

On the first point, namely, self-imposed restraint, some of the commentary suggested an element of respect as well as mystification that the United States had not exacted more advantages from the system it led. When pointing to examples—such as the real and imputed advantages that flow from the dollar's status as the principal global reserve currency, and the ability to set technical and other standards for products destined for the U.S. market—the workshop's Chinese participants acknowledged, albeit sometimes grudgingly, that the United States had not tipped the playing field as far in its favor as it could have. The resultant global system is not completely fair, but it is much more equitable than it might have been and, by implication, more equitable than it would have been under a different hegemon. This line of analysis suggests more than just a desire to avoid jeopardizing China's continued rapid growth by tampering with the status quo. Instead, it seemed to reveal a preference for continued reliance on the current order and also for continued U.S. leadership of that system. Here too, the rationale seemed to be more than "stick with the devil you know" and closer to a judgment that, for the foreseeable future, U.S. leadership would be preferable to that of any other individual country or group of countries that did not include the United States.

---

[21] When asked the meaning of their statements asserting the superior quality of the U.S. economy, participants in the May 2012 workshops said they referred to its ability to innovate, its entrepreneurial character, and the sophistication of both its products and its processes. Some linked this to the quality of higher education and to competition among firms in the United States.

[22] See, for example, Liu Liping, "China Can Hardly Rule the World," *Contemporary International Relations* 21, no. 1 (2011), http://www.cicir.ac.cn/english/ArticleView.aspx?nid=1965.

[23] Ikenberry, *Liberal Leviathan*, 66–77.

The discussion of what the Chinese workshop participants saw as defects in the current system and attributes that should be changed to accommodate the rise of additional powers and other realities of the 21st century often focused on specific actions or patterns of behavior by the United States that seemed to depart from its past restraint by exempting itself from rules and norms that were supposed to apply equally to all participants in the global order.[24] In other words, they were troubled by evidence that the United States was behaving as an "imperial hegemon" rather than as the "liberal hegemon" it had been for decades.[25] The implicit—and sometimes explicit—correction advocated by the Chinese participants was to persuade the United States to return to behaviors that largely conformed to the rules and norms of the system.[26] They did not advocate replacing the United States at the helm of the global order.

Continued U.S. leadership was given a positive spin not just because it was thought to be better than potential replacements, but also, and more importantly in these discussions, because of the type of leadership it has provided to the global order. One attribute of that leadership has been the ability and willingness of the United States to adapt and adjust to changing circumstances—such as the "rise of Japan" in the 1980s and 1990s and the end of the Cold War—rather than seek to enforce a rigid version of the order extant at any point in time. Another characteristic is U.S. willingness to expend political capital in order to propose and promote adjustments to the status quo. Such proposals often required changes in other countries and in the way the system as a whole functions. They were made more acceptable by the magnitude and legitimacy of U.S. soft power. Given the history of success and the benign-to-beneficial character of U.S. leadership and the changes it has engineered or enforced, participants in the free world and current global order are willing to accept U.S.-proposed changes more readily than if they had been proposed by a state with less soft power.[27] Many of the Chinese

---

[24] Examples cited by the Chinese to criticize what they regard as U.S. violations of international law often cite what they claim are violations of China's sovereignty or sovereign territory. See, for example, "U.S. Seriously Violates International Law," Embassy of the People's Republic of China in the United States of America, April 15, 2001, http://www.china-embassy.org/eng/zt/zjsj/t36383.htm; and "China Says U.S. Naval Ship Breaks International, Chinese Law," Xinhua, March 10, 2009, http://news.xinhuanet.com/english/2009-03/10/content_10983647.htm.

[25] Chinese workshop participants did not use the terms "imperial hegemon" or "liberal hegemon," which are described by Ikenberry in *Liberal Leviathan*, but they did note and comment on the change in U.S. behavior within the global system.

[26] These points were not explicated during the May 2012 workshops, but previous conferences and discussions have expressed concern about U.S. unilateral actions, such as the decision to invade Iraq without UN Security Council (UNSC) endorsement and the imposition of U.S. sanctions on third countries that trade with Iran or the Democratic People's Republic of Korea (DPRK).

[27] This assessment is based on discussion during the May 2012 workshops. On soft power, see Joseph S. Nye, *Soft Power: The Means to Success in World Politics* (New York: Public Affairs, 2004).

participants acknowledged that China does not have—and will not have for a long time—anything approaching the soft power of the United States.

Thus, Chinese assessments of the existing global order and the role of the United States are mostly positive, but the relatively few attributes that they do not like are viewed so negatively that, for some individuals and groups, they far outweigh the positive features. Three of the most often cited—but notably not often by participants at the May 2012 workshops—are U.S. alliances and global military presence; assessed or imputed U.S. ideological antipathy toward China and determination to achieve regime change; and suspicion, if not conviction, that the United States is determined to prevent China from becoming a peer competitor and is already taking steps to thwart China's rise and resumption of its rightful place in the global order. The chapter will later return to the problem of mutual suspicion and strategic distrust; it is noted here because the complaints and concerns have more to do with imputed U.S. motivations and specific actions than with the structure and operation of the global order.[28]

The purpose of this section has been to identify attributes of the current world order that influence Chinese analysts to advocate preserving and prolonging the basic character of the U.S.-led system. It has also sought to identify attributes that Chinese assessments evaluate positively and would probably seek to incorporate into a successor order and features they do not like and would probably attempt to change should they have an opportunity to reform or remake the global order. The status quo order provides the starting point and frame of reference, but it is not the only influence on Chinese thinking.

Chinese Conceptions of World Order

The most authoritative description of China's vision for a future global order is that sketched out by President and Party General Secretary Hu Jintao at the 17th Party Congress in October 2007. According to Hu, people of all countries should join hands and work for lasting peace and common prosperity. To this end, all countries should uphold the purposes and principles of the United Nations Charter, observe international law and universally recognized norms of international relations, and promote democracy, harmony, collaboration, and win-win solutions in international relations. All countries should respect one another and conduct consultations

---

[28] Chinese commentaries on the nature of U.S. hegemony sometimes focus on behaviors ascribed to status quo powers by realist theory, as when they assert the United States' determination to contain China's rise. Others—a minority overall but the dominant view expressed in the May 2012 workshops—focus more on behaviors that Ikenberry ascribes to liberal hegemons.

on an equal footing, cooperate economically, and work together to advance economic globalization. In the area of security, countries should trust each other, strengthen cooperation, settle international disputes by peaceful means, and work for peace and stability.[29] These themes have been reiterated many times, and many commentators have written about them in the years since, but they have not moved much beyond platitudes and none have said anything about how these conditions are to be achieved, monitored, or enforced.[30]

In the absence of authoritative or detailed Chinese explanations or descriptions of how a harmonious world would come into being, what role China would play in such a global order, or what existing or new institutions would be used to regulate international dealings, commentators outside China have tended to dismiss Hu's rhetoric as vacuous political cant intended to obscure hard-nosed realism and a determination to displace the United States as the world's preeminent power.[31] Others, until 2010, merely repeated his words as if doing so reflected a meaningful understanding of Beijing's aspirations and intentions.[32] Neither the pessimistic nor Pollyannaish interpretation is very helpful for understanding or anticipating Chinese behavior on the world stage. We need a better model or theory of China's global vision. What follows may be lacking in important respects. But, hopefully, it will elicit corrections and clarifications from Chinese colleagues and constructive comments from others who wrestle with the challenges of explaining and predicting Chinese foreign policy.

One way to construct a framework for anticipating future Chinese actions is to begin from the proposition that the People's Republic of China (PRC) is, first and foremost, the contemporary incarnation of the Middle Kingdom. Among the reasons this seems a reasonable approach is that Hu's call for a "harmonious world" appears to be an extension into the international arena of concepts discussed in his speech a year earlier at the sixth plenum of the 16th Party Congress in which he called for the creation of a "harmonious society" in China.[33] Although that speech was also quite vague, it seemed to signal a

---

[29] "Hu Jintao Calls for Building Harmonious World," Xinhua, October 15, 2007, http://news.xinhuanet.com/english/2007-10/15/content_6884160.htm.

[30] Examples include "President Hu Elaborates the Theory of Harmonious World," *People's Daily Online*, November 26, 2009, http://english.peopledaily.com.cn/90001/90780/91342/6824821.html; and Liu Liping and Zhang Yimeng, "Harmonious World and Neo-idealism," *Contemporary International Relations* 19, no. 2 (2009): 82–87.

[31] See, for example, Yu Bin, "China's Harmonious World: Beyond Cultural Interpretations," *Journal of Chinese Political Science* 13, no. 2 (2008): 119–41.

[32] See, for example, Huang Deming, Kong Yuan, and Zhang Hua, "Symposium on China's Peaceful Development and International Law," *Chinese Journal of International Law* 5, no. 1 (2006): 261–68, http://chinesejil.oxfordjournals.org/content/5/1/261.full.pdf+html.

[33] "Communiqué of the Sixth Plenum of the 16th CPC Central Committee," Xinhua, October 12, 2006, http://www.china.org.cn/english/congress/226989.htm.

shift in priority from maximum efforts to promote rapid economic growth to greater concern for the social consequences of breakneck development.[34]

China's internal system is a hybrid that combines elements of Confucian philosophy, Communist ideology, and elite self-interest. Confucianism has deep roots and retains considerable influence on Chinese thinking, despite official efforts to discredit and extirpate Confucian philosophy and all other vestiges of "feudal" society. Those efforts largely ended with the death of Mao Zedong in 1976, but the ancient sage and his ethical teachings were not formally rehabilitated until 2004 when they were pressed into service to provide moral and ethical underpinnings to replace the discredited or discarded ethics of Marx and Mao.[35] Confucian advocacy of social harmony and putting people first was seen as an antidote to increasing greed, amorality, and disregard for the rights and well-being of fellow citizens.

The persistent, and now resurgent, influence of Confucianism almost certainly helps shape Chinese thinking on proper relationships among people inside China and among countries in the international system. It certainly did so in the past, and it is difficult to believe that it is without influence in the current era.[36] Selected elements of the Confucian system that seem relevant to our effort to imagine China's vision of world order include the central importance of hierarchical relationships (e.g., those between emperor and subject, husband and wife, and parent and child) and acceptance of one's "assigned" role in the social order. The emperor is assumed to rule in the interest of the nation and populace as a whole (i.e., the individual is subordinate to the collective), and officials are to be wise, honest, and loyal.

Contemporary China is not a reincarnation of an ancient ideal; it is an authoritarian state with both Chinese and Communist characteristics. Communist ideology has been reduced to little more than a convenient rationalization for continued Communist Party rule, specifically the leadership's self-proclaimed ability to speak for and balance (in the style of Confucian officials) the interests of all people in China. This ability is possible because the party alone has a "scientific" understanding of the forces

---

[34] See, for example, Alice Miller, "Hu Jintao and the Sixth Plenum," Hoover Institution, China Leadership Monitor, no. 20, February 2007, http://media.hoover.org/sites/default/files/documents/clm20am.pdf; and "CPC Seeks Advice on Building Harmonious Society," Xinhua, October 13, 2006, http://www.china.org.cn/english/government/183853.htm.

[35] See John Dotson, "The Confucian Revival in the Propaganda Narratives of the Chinese Government," U.S.-China Economic and Security Review Commission, July 20, 2011, http://www.uscc.gov/researchpapers/2011/Confucian_Revival_Paper.pdf.

[36] See, for example, John King Fairbank, ed., *The Chinese World Order: Traditional China's Foreign Relations* (Cambridge: Harvard University Press, 1968); Li Zhaojie, "Traditional Chinese World Order," *Chinese Journal of International Law* 1, no. 1 (2002): 20–58, http://chinesejil.oxfordjournals.org/content/1/1/20.full.pdf; and Yuan-kang Wang, *Harmony and War: Confucian Culture and Chinese Power Politics* (New York: Columbia University Press, 2011).

that drive economic development and can ensure that threats to sustained growth or social harmony are addressed before the situation deteriorates into chaos and renewed victimization at the hands of imperialists and other enemies of China.[37]

The third component of the contemporary hybrid system is elite self-interest. In both the Confucian and the Communist ideal, upright officials are expected to put national (or party) interests ahead of personal gain. Innumerable examples and the frequency of public complaints about corrupt officials indicate that the conduct of many officials falls considerably short of this ideal. Indeed, it seems reasonable to assert that China's Communist elite acts more like elites in other modernizing systems than like Communist or Confucian paragons of virtue.

The hybrid system outlined above has three bases of legitimacy—ethics, nationalism, and performance. Leaders are entitled to respect and obedience, in part because they are supposed to be honest, modest, and fair. This ethical basis of their legitimacy is reinforced by their presumed or proclaimed commitment to defend the nation (its sovereignty, territory, people, culture, etc.) against all enemies, real and imagined. Both of these sources of legitimacy pale in comparison to the importance of performance. The system and its rulers retain legitimacy in direct proportion to their ability to deliver steady, if modest, improvements in living standards, education, healthcare, job security, and other tangible benefits of economic growth.[38]

Before examining how these characteristics of China's domestic system might influence or transfer to the international arena, it will be useful to comment briefly on two additional characteristics. One is that both the Confucian and the Communist "models" or ideal systems are inherently unipolar. There can be only one emperor, who has no peers, and the party's role is certainly considerably more than *primus inter pares*. Other political parties exist and have subordinate roles in the political system, but maintenance of the Chinese Communist Party's monopoly of power is a fundamental principle of the system. Stated another way, these two strands of Chinese political thinking—not to mention elite self-interest—are not compatible with the notion of a loyal opposition, coalitions, or other multipolar arrangements comprised of groups (or nations) with equal rights and responsibilities.

---

[37] See, for example, the "General Program" section of the Constitution of the Communist Party of China (as amended in 2007), http://www.china.org.cn/english/congress/229722.htm#1.

[38] See, for example, Zhengxu Wang, "Before the Emergence of Critical Citizens: Economic Development and Political Trust in China," *International Review of Sociology* 15, no. 1 (2005): 155–171; and Bruce Gilley and Heike Holbig, "In Search of Legitimacy in Post-Revolutionary China: Bringing Ideology and Governance Back," German Institute of Global Area Studies, Working Paper, no. 127, March 2010, http://papers.ssrn.com/sol3/papers.cfm?abstract_id=1586310.

The second additional characteristic, greater emphasis on relationships (*guanxi*) than on rules (*juhuo*), reflects current dominance of the Confucian tradition over the legalist tradition of Chinese political and ethical thinking. In rule-based systems, all parties, at least in theory, are bound by the same rules and regulations. Rule-based systems are supposed to be egalitarian, treating all parties equally and according no special dispensation to those with higher positions or greater wealth. In relationship-based systems, however, there is no presumption of equality or accountability to a single set of rules.[39] What any one player is allowed or expected to do is a function of relative position in social or political hierarchies. There appears to be a trend toward greater reliance on rules, but those in the current system in China know instinctively that more elaborate rules do not ensure more equal treatment. Positions and relationships still matter a great deal.

For centuries, China's view of world order evinced clear parallels with the Confucian concept of domestic order summarized above. Indeed, it is not too much of an exaggeration or mischaracterization to say that China's place and role in the global order was closely modeled on that of the emperor inside the Middle Kingdom.[40] Relations between emperor and subject were governed by both relationships and rules. The emperor's legitimacy derived from the "mandate of heaven" (similar to the "divine right" legitimacy of kings in the West) and from bureaucratic rules backed by military power. When dynasties were strong, they could exert power to control or influence their external vassals; when they were weak, China's exercise of suzerainty was more nominal than real.[41] The reality, if not the underlying theory, became very different during what is referred to in China as the century of humiliation (roughly 1840–1949), when China was victimized by stronger and more modern imperialist powers. The breakdown of the proper world order both reflected and facilitated China's descent into disorder and national decline. Mao's October 1949 proclamation that "the Chinese people have stood up" marked the end of the long slide and the beginning of the country's return to its rightful place in the world.

But what, exactly, did that mean? The world that China was about to rejoin was vastly different than the one that existed before China's long period of decline and weakness. The Cold War had begun and Mao made the fateful decision to lean to the side of the Soviet Union. That decision, and

---

[39] Ikenberry, *Liberal Leviathan*, chapter 3.

[40] See, for example, Fairbank, *Chinese World Order*, 7–11.

[41] Fairbank, *Chinese World Order*; and Benjamin I. Schwartz, "The Chinese Perception of World Order, Past and Present," in Ibid., 276–88.

the temporary high tide of Communist internationalism in China, shaped Chinese statements and behavior in the early years of the PRC.[42]

During the first decades of the People's Republic, Chinese officials proclaimed policies and called for the creation of a global order very different from the Confucian system outlined above. Examples included declarations that all nations, large and small, are equal and should be treated on that basis (i.e., no big-power chauvinism); incantation of the five principles of peaceful coexistence first articulated at the Bandung Conference in 1955; denunciation of hegemonic behavior and declarations that China would never seek hegemony; and regular expressions of preference for a multipolar world.[43] Hu Jintao's vague descriptions of the "harmonious world" China desires are consistent with and build upon these long-standing principles of Chinese diplomacy.[44]

What are we then to make of such differences between what is said to be desirable in the international arena and what is declared and done domestically? Should we interpret the differences between statement and action as reflecting the view that there is a sharp divide between the internal affairs of a nation, which should be of no concern to outsiders, and the requirements of a smoothly functioning and peaceful international system? Or should we ask whether China's prescription for global order is a function of its relative power at a particular point in time and might change as China's relative power changes? Indeed, that is precisely the question that an increasing number of people and foreign ministries have been asking since China began to proclaim its rise and become more active in the international arena.[45]

One way to explore this question is to examine the extent to which China's actions have been consistent with its rhetoric and whether the degree or nature of consistencies and inconsistencies has changed over time or in patterned ways. Such an investigation is beyond the scope of this chapter, but what I have examined suggests that the picture is a mixed one. As one would

---

[42] See, for example, Thomas W. Robinson, "Chinese Foreign Policy from the 1940s to the 1990s," in *Chinese Foreign Policy: Theory and Practice*, Thomas W. Robinson and David Shambaugh, eds. (New York: Oxford University Press, 1994), 555–602.

[43] See, for example, Christopher R. Hughes, *Chinese Nationalism in the Global Era* (New York: Routledge, 2006).

[44] See, for example, Hu Jintao, "Report to the Seventeenth National Congress of the Communist Party of China," Xinhua, October 15, 2007, http://www.china.org.cn/english/congress/229611.htm#11; Liu and Zhang, "Harmonious World and Neo-idealism"; and Yu Xintian, "Harmonious World and China's Path for Peaceful Development," *International Review* 45, (2006): 1–21, http://www.siis.org.cn/Sh_Yj_Cms/Mgz/200604/20087242316271Q7X.PDF.

[45] See, for example, Bonnie S. Glaser and Evan S. Medeiros, "The Changing Ecology of Foreign Policy–Making in China: The Ascension and Demise of the Theory of 'Peaceful Rise,'" *China Quarterly*, no. 190 (2007): 291–310.

expect of any country, China's behavior conforms to its political rhetoric when doing so seems to advance its national interests and the priorities of its political elite, and departs from the rhetoric when adherence would jeopardize attainment of higher priority objectives. Others can decide whether this makes China more or less hypocritical than other nations. The point I want to explore and emphasize here—and will examine in greater detail below—is that China's behavior on specific issues, and with respect to its specific policy principles, has changed over the last three decades as it has become more active on more issues in more parts of the world. For example, Beijing's position on the rights of sovereign nations and condemnation of imperialist, Soviet, and Western interference in the internal affairs of other countries was more absolute when China had little involvement in other parts of the world. Beijing's position changed as the PRC began to have significant investments and contingents of Chinese workers in countries with pernicious or dysfunctional legal systems.

China's Self-Proclaimed Closest Relationships

Another way to infer China's vision of world order is to examine Beijing's relationships with countries that, at least at a particular time in history, were described as China's closest or most important friends. This list includes the Soviet Union (in the 1950s), Vietnam (in the 1960s and 1970s), North Korea (1950–present), Pakistan (1960s–present), and Myanmar (1989–presemt). All are neighbors. In the case of the Soviet Union, China was by far the weaker partner; in all other cases, China was and is much stronger. All have been multifaceted relationships, and what follows is only an abbreviated analysis. Nevertheless, a brief look at what appear to be China's closest relationships may indicate how China will act and be perceived by other states as it seeks a larger role on the world stage.

The relationship with the Soviet Union during the first decade of the PRC was inherently unequal. China leaned to the side of the Soviet Union for protection, security, and development. Moscow was very supportive, and Beijing embraced most aspects of the Soviet model of development and view of the international system. But Mao, and presumably other Chinese leaders, were never comfortable with China's "little brother" relationship with Moscow. Relations deteriorated when China sought greater equality and plummeted after Mao claimed that China had surpassed the Soviet Union in the transition to a fully Communist system. Relations went into the deep freeze for two decades before thawing to a condition that was still far short of warm.[46] Thanks to its superior economic achievements, Beijing now considers its system and decisions to be more advanced than those of Moscow.

Relations between Beijing and Hanoi were said to be "as close as lips and teeth," and China provided very large amounts of assistance to the North Vietnamese during their war with the South and the United States. This relationship changed dramatically for the worse when Vietnam tilted toward Moscow and intervened in Cambodia to depose Beijing's Khmer Rouge ally. The nadir of the decline was reached in January 1979 when Deng sent the People's Liberation Army (PLA) into Vietnam to teach China's erstwhile allies a lesson: that acting counter to China's interests would not be tolerated. Relations improved subsequently but remain far from close and continue to be roiled by competing territorial claims in the South China Sea.[47]

China's relationship with the Democratic People's Republic of Korea (DPRK) continues to be of the "lips and teeth" variety, and North Korea is China's only formal alliance partner. Despite the purported closeness of the relationship, Pyongyang apparently has had insufficient confidence in the reliability or deterrent ability of the alliance to forgo acquisition of an independent nuclear weapon. Comparisons to the willingness of the Republic of Korea (ROK), as well as Japan, to rely on U.S. assurances and extended deterrence are difficult because China claims that its pledge not to be the first to use nuclear weapons precludes a policy of extended deterrence. However, it seems noteworthy that the oft-proclaimed very close relationship was insufficient to forestall Pyongyang's desire for its own nuclear weapon capability and inadequate to enable Beijing to persuade the DPRK to forgo or surrender that capability. Moreover, despite China's own success in achieving sustained economic growth through its reform and opening policy, Beijing has been unable to persuade the DPRK to adopt or adapt the Chinese path of development.[48]

Pakistan's relationship with China is described by both as "higher than the mountains and deeper than the ocean." It is unclear what that means or how it differs from a lips-and-teeth relationship, but it did not yield Chinese

---

[46] See, for example, Bobo Lo, *Axis of Convenience: Moscow, Beijing, and the New Geopolitics* (Washington, D.C.: Brookings Institution, 2008).

[47] See, for example, Brantly Womack, *China and Vietnam: The Politics of Asymmetry* (New York: Cambridge University Press, 2006); and Carlyle A. Thayer, "The Structure of Vietnam-China Relations, 1991–2008" (paper presented at the Third International Conference on Vietnamese Studies, Hanoi, Vietnam, December 4–7, 2008), http://www.viet-studies.info/kinhte/Thayer_Sino_Viet_1991_2008.pdf.

[48] See, for example, Scott Snyder and See-won Byun, "China-Korea Relations: China's Post–Kim Jong Il Debate," *Comparative Connections*, May 2012, http://www.cfr.org/north-korea/china-korea-relations-chinas-post-kim-jong-il-debate/p28282; and Christopher Twomey, "Explaining Chinese Foreign Policy toward North Korea: Navigating between the Scylla and Charybdis of Proliferation and Instability," *Journal of Contemporary China* 17, no. 56 (2008): 401–23.

assistance to Pakistan during its wars with India and did not prevent Pakistan from acquiring an independent nuclear-weapon capability. Indeed, there is evidence that China helped Pakistan acquire the bomb. Other than the ability to use Pakistan to complicate Indian defense planning—another perhaps telling indicator of China's global vision—China appears to have derived little from this relationship. Indeed, Chinese officials say that their greatest security concern is the threat of terrorist attacks by separatists associated with Islamic groups in Xinjiang, but they seem to have had no success, or perhaps have made no serious effort, to persuade Pakistan to cease training terrorists, including separatists from China. Moreover, as China's relationship with India has begun to improve, that with Pakistan appears to have become less important and more narrowly focused on economic matters.[49]

Myanmar's relationship with China was upgraded to that of a "comprehensive strategic cooperative partnership" in May 2011. Again, although not entirely clear in meaning, the declaration seems intended to signal that the relationship is special to both countries.[50] Nonetheless, Myanmar appears to have become uncomfortable with its degree of dependence on China and on specific Chinese requests or demands—at least that is the conventional explanation for the decisions to release political prisoners, hold elections, and reach out to the United States and other nations whose limited contacts with Myanmar had previously left the field to China. To the extent that the conventional wisdom is correct, one must ask why Myanmar's rulers were no longer willing to tie their country's fate so tightly to China.

The thumbnail sketches above greatly oversimplify complex relationships and treat them in isolation from other developments. Nevertheless, they raise a number of questions about how China has treated its closest partners, how those partners have perceived China's intentions and methods, and whether closer analysis of those relationships and their evolution might prove useful for inferring China's vision of how the global order should operate. For example, although it would be unwise to push the analogy too hard, there is some similarity between China's relationship with the Soviet Union and its post-1979 relationship with the United States.

---

[49] See for example, Sutter, *Chinese Foreign Relations*, 237–50; Michael Beckley, "China and Pakistan: Fair-Weather Friends," *Yale Journal of International Affairs* 7, no. 1 (2012): 9–22, http://yalejournal. org/wp-content/uploads/2012/04/Article-Michael-Beckley.pdf; and Lisa Curtis and Derek Scissors, "The Limits of the Pakistan-China Alliance," Reuters, January 20, 2012, http://blogs.reuters.com/ india-expertzone/2012/01/20/the-limits-of-the-pakistan-china-alliance/.

[50] "Newly-Forged China-Myanmar Strategic Partnership of Great Significance: Premier Wen," *People's Daily Online*, May 28, 2011, http://english.peopledaily.com.cn/90001/90776/90883/7393636.html; and "Myanmar, PRC Issue Joint Statement on Establishing Comprehensive Strategic Cooperative Partnership," *New Light of Myanmar*, May 29, 2011, 10.

China has benefited from both relationships but chafed at its inferior status. Mao wanted a larger say in the decisions of the Soviet camp than Joseph Stalin or his successors were willing to allow, and Beijing now seeks a larger role in the U.S.-led system. The world is very different now than it was during the early years of the Cold War, but in both cases, China felt constrained by its stronger partner.

China's relationships with its smaller and weaker neighbors may also be suggestive. To an extent, Beijing seems to feel that its partners have been insufficiently appreciative of China's friendship and assistance. The partners, however, seem to have been or become increasingly uncomfortable about their dependence on China and the lack of counterbalancing ties. Despite offering substantial assistance, China does not appear to have had very much influence in any of the partner states. Whether that is because of China's scrupulous respect for its neighbors' sovereignty or near-total lack of soft power is a question worthy of exploration.

What to Expect

For the time being, and probably for the indefinite future, Beijing appears content, even eager, to act as a free rider able to benefit from the liberal order without having to assume responsibility or pay the costs of system maintenance.[51] In part, this derives from a perceived need to focus on domestic challenges, which are both great and growing. But it is also because China's leaders are reluctant to be put in a position—as responsible stakeholders—in which they might feel compelled to take actions that alienate states whose continued cooperation is needed to achieve the PRC's security and development goals. Put another way, they want to be able to take advantage of the benefits made possible by U.S. management and maintenance of the global system but resent the advantages that accrue to the United States because of its status as the preeminent leader of the system.

To the extent that this analysis is correct, it poses a dilemma for China because it recognizes that the global system is not self-regulating. The global order needs a mechanism to preserve stability, manage conflicts, and resolve problems. Were China to attempt to erode U.S. preeminence, the consequences almost certainly would jeopardize the PRC's ability to continue to derive the benefits needed to sustain its peaceful rise and acquisition of the wealth and power required to deter and equal or supplant the United States. Those consequences would include alienation of both

---

[51] See, for example, Amitai Etzioni, "Is China a Responsible Stakeholder?" *International Affairs* 87, no. 3 (2011): 539–33, http://icps.gwu.edu/files/2011/05/China-Stakeholder.pdf.

the countries on which China depends and the many other countries that benefit from the U.S. willingness and ability to maintain the system. However, the longer Beijing defers predicted efforts to displace the United States from its preeminent position, the more firmly China will become enmeshed in the global system and the more dependent other nations will become on the benefits they derive from U.S. leadership.

Chinese leaders view the world through the lens of realist theory and regard power as the most important determinant of national influence and freedom of action.[52] In the Confucian order, emperors were entitled to obedience from their subjects because they ruled in a virtuous way that brought benefits in the form of peace and prosperity. But prudent emperors recognized that virtue was sometimes insufficient and that it was necessary to backstop it with hard power. Mao captured the essence of the matter with his aphorism that political power grows from the barrel of a gun.

Influenced by Confucian and Communist thinking, Chinese leaders overestimated the extent to which the so-called free world system was held together by the coercive capabilities of the United States and underestimated the extent to which the liberal democracies that comprised the system actually shared and had helped determine its norms and rules of behavior. A related misjudgment was to overestimate opportunities for China to capitalize on the imputed desire of other participants to find ways to counterbalance U.S. influence. Nations allied with the United States welcomed China into the system in the late 1970s—as the only nondemocracy invited to join—because of its importance as a counterweight to the Soviet Union and the prospective size of its market, but they did not seek an opportunity to align with China to constrain the United States. As a result, China's participation had the effect of strengthening shared commitments among the original members of the liberal order and reaffirming the importance of U.S. leadership to the continued success of the system from which all, now including China, derive substantial tangible benefits.

There were multiple reasons for this development. One was that, contrary to the prediction of the "three worlds theory" (attributed to Mao but articulated by Deng at the 1974 session of the UN General Assembly) that China could derive leverage from an imputed desire of other countries to lessen their vulnerability to U.S. pressure, the other members of the global order valued and needed the United States more than they did their new relationship with China.[53] A second reason is that the United States had a long

---

[52] See, for example, John J. Mearsheimer, *The Tragedy of Great Power Politics* (New York: Norton, 2001); and Friedberg, *Contest for Supremacy.*

[53] See, for example, Herbert S. Yee, "The Three World Theory and Post-Mao China's Global Strategy," *International Affairs* 59, no. 2 (1983): 239–49.

history and proven ability to lead the system in ways that brought benefits to all. Since the United States seemed to know what it was doing and was willing to continue to pay the price of leadership, there was no real incentive to look for a different or additional leader. Third, U.S. leadership had been mostly benign, nonaggressive, and nonthreatening to those inside the liberal order. China's rhetoric may have had a certain appeal, especially after the demise of the Soviet Union and expansion of the free world to include almost all countries (the principal exception being China's lips-and-teeth ally the DPRK), but its track record was less attractive. Even its so-called special friends were alienated or seemingly held at arm's length.

Other nations, particularly those on China's maritime periphery, have concerns about China's visions of the global order stemming from recent as well as more distant developments. For example, despite rhetoric extolling the equality of states and proclamations that the center of gravity had shifted from the West to Asia, China opposed proposals to expand the UN Security Council (UNSC), on which China is the sole Asian power, by adding Japan and India as permanent members.[54] This action suggests that China's preferred global order does not envision equal influence for even the second-most populous country (India) or the second-largest Asian economy (Japan). China's opposition to permanent membership for India and Japan could also reflect discomfort with bestowing additional power and prestige on already formidable democracies.

A number of Chinese actions in 2010 raised concern in many countries because they were interpreted as possible harbingers of how China would act if it gained regional or global preeminence. Many proclaimed that China was on the verge of attaining that status when it surpassed Japan to become the world's second-largest economy, although Chinese commentators were more cautious and tended to downplay the significance of the GDP figures. The actions summarized below are a small subset of Chinese diplomacy during this period, but they attracted a great deal of attention because they were a marked departure from China's conduct during the preceding fifteen years and were widely interpreted as possible indicators of what to expect in the future.[55]

Actions that raised questions and qualms about China's rise and possible design for a new regional or world order included the use of bullying tactics toward Japan after the arrest of a Chinese fishing boat captain who rammed

---

[54] See, for example, "China, U.S. Agree to Block G4 UNSC Expansion Plan," Xinhua, August 5, 2005, http://www.china.org.cn/english/international/137442.htm.

[55] See, for example, Li Hong, "After China Becomes 'Second' Largest Economy," *People's Daily Online*, August 16, 2010, http://english.people.com.cn/90002/96743/7106151.html; and Thomas Christensen, "The Advantages of an Assertive China: Responding to Beijing's Abrasive Diplomacy," *Foreign Affairs* 90, no. 2 (2011): 54–67.

a Japanese coast guard cutter near the Senkaku/Diaoyu Islands administered by Japan but claimed by both nations and the harassment of Vietnamese fishing and survey ships in disputed areas of the South China Sea.[56] In both cases, China's behavior seemed to suggest that Chinese claims automatically trumped those of other claimants and need not or would not be resolved using principles of equality and mutual respect.

Four actions involving Korea raised similar questions and concerns. Two were in response to incidents initiated by the DPRK, namely, the sinking of the South Korean navy ship *Cheonan* in March 2010 and the shelling of Yeonpyeong Island in November of the same year. China's calls for restraint on the part of both sides were widely interpreted as being equivalent to according equal blame to both the mugger and his victim. China clearly stood behind its lips-and-teeth ally in Pyongyang, but its primary concern was to prevent the incident from escalating in ways that might endanger regional stability and China's own security and sustained development. This looked like a "take care of China first" approach to the management of international issues involving two other countries. A related action occurred after the sinking of the *Cheonan* when an ROK newspaper announced that the United States and South Korea would conduct joint naval exercises in the West or Yellow Sea. Chinese commentators immediately denounced the reported plan to send the aircraft carrier *George Washington* into international waters east of China.[57] The fourth event was China's cavalier disregard of UNSC resolutions restricting trade with the DPRK, policies that China itself had voted for. The latter two actions both evinced China's willingness to ignore or interpret international law (customary international law and UNSC resolutions) when doing so served Beijing's interests.

Individually, each of these actions (plus others such as the warning to European governments not to attend the ceremony to award the 2010 Nobel Peace Prize to jailed Chinese dissident Liu Xiaobo) could have been explained away as policy miscalculations, clumsy overreactions, or simply the latest episode in a number of separate relationships, each with its own dynamics, that just happened to occur in the same yearlong period.[58] Whether they were independent occurrences or manifestations of a unique dynamic,

---

[56] See, for example, Satoshi Amako, "The Senkaku Islands Incident and Japan-China Relations," *East Asia Forum*, October 25, 2010, http://www.eastasiaforum.org/2010/10/25/the-senkaku-islands-incident-and-japan-china-relations/; and Carlyle A. Thayer, "South China Sea: A Commons for China Only?" *YaleGlobal Online*, July 7, 2011, http://yaleglobal.yale.edu/content/south-china-sea-commons-china-only.

[57] See, for example, Jeremy Page, Jay Solomon, and Julian E. Barnes, "China Warns U.S. as Korea Tensions Rise," *Wall Street Journal*, November 26, 2010, http://online.wsj.com/article/SB10001424052748704008704575638420698918004.html.

[58] See, for example, Michael Wines, "China Urges Europeans to Snub Nobel Ceremony," *New York Times*, November 4, 2010, http://www.nytimes.com/2010/11/05/world/asia/05china.html.

the actions were widely perceived as indicative of new and unwelcome Chinese assertiveness.[59]

Possibly by miscalculation, and certainly not by design, these behaviors had the effect of causing many states, not just the liberal democracies, to take renewed interest in shoring up their ties with the United States and talking more openly about the need to use balance-of-power methods to hedge against the possibility of objectionable Chinese behavior.[60] At a minimum, and at least for the time being, China's neighbors and many of the countries most important for the success of its effort to achieve security, prosperity, and influence through engagement in the liberal order have become more curious—and more concerned—about China's objectives and plans. This is manifest in many specific questions and general demands for greater transparency. Taken together, they signify that many people and states want to know more about China's vision of world order. The fact that they want to know this is a strong indicator that they do not—if they ever did—assume that China's vision would make the world better for them and their interests than does the current liberal order or possible modifications to that order led by the United States.

We still do not know whether China's clumsy and ultimately counter-productive foreign policy behavior in 2010 was the anomalous product of a unique concatenation of events or a trial run and forerunner of future behavior. In the near term, and possibly for a protracted period, we should anticipate additional actions that will appear—and be—more assertive and unnerving to other nations. Such actions are likely to have many causes, including determination to explore the limits of what is possible, miscalculation and overreach, inadequate coordination within an excessively centralized system, poor policy in pursuit of reasonable goals, and efforts to compensate for slower economic growth by appealing to nationalism. To the extent that the past provides a guide to the future, China will pull back when it perceives failure to do so would jeopardize its security and development objectives, and press ahead if the actions bring acceptable results. In other words, the PRC will behave like any other big player in an interdependent global system.

---

[59] See, for example, Michael D. Swaine, "Perceptions of an Assertive China," Hoover Institution, *China Leadership Monitor*, no. 32, Spring 2010, http://carnegieendowment.org/files/CLM32MS1. pdf. See also Jeffrey A. Bader, *Obama and China's Rise: An Insider's Account of America's Asia Strategy* (Washington, D.C.: Brookings Institution, 2012).

[60] See, for example, Richard Weitz, "Nervous Neighbors: China Finds a Sphere of Influence," *World Affairs*, March/April 2011, http://www.worldaffairsjournal.org/article/nervous-neighbors-china-finds-sphere-influence.

If China Could Remake the Global Order, What Would It Look Like?

Imagining or inferring China's view of world order and plans to achieve it is an artificial exercise in at least two respects. One is that it assumes that China has a clear and operational view of world order and at least a rudimentary plan or strategy to achieve it. This author doubts that Beijing does. At best, individual Chinese analyses present highly general notions of what the world should or would be like if China were able to realize its ambitions.[61] Many have tried and failed to elicit more than platitudes or unenlightening generalities when asking what a harmonious world would look like, how it would operate, and what new or transformed institutions and control regimes would be needed to preserve peace, security, and stability.[62] The most likely explanation for the lack of specificity is that China does not yet have a coherent vision, let alone a plan to achieve it.[63] Its leaders are preoccupied with day-to-day challenges and have little time to devote to grand strategies or schemes. Moreover, at least some of them probably fear that articulating any objective or arrangement that differs from the current world order (from which China and dozens of other nations derive substantial benefits at low costs to themselves) would trigger questions, fears, pressures, and other adverse reactions that, at a minimum, would be a distraction for Beijing and might impede sustained development.

If, or to the extent that, China's aspirations include diminishing or displacing U.S. preeminence, Beijing's repeated references to alleged U.S. efforts to surround, contain, or constrain China would seem to give it a strong incentive to hide or mute those aspirations lest they provoke the United States to act sooner rather than later to thwart China's rise. China needs the United States—as a market, partner, and custodian of the global order—to achieve its own strategic objectives. This requires maintaining at least reasonably good relations with Washington and U.S.-based actors. If China does harbor desires to disrupt the global order or seeks to displace the United States atop the international system, it would seem to have a strong incentive to hide those aspirations lest the United States takes preventive countermeasures and other beneficiaries of the liberal order band together to thwart China's

---

[61] Wang, "China's Search for a Grand Strategy."

[62] Yu Bin, "China's Harmonious World"; and Su Hao, "Harmonious World: The Conceived International Order in Framework of China's Foreign Affairs" in *China's Shift: Global Strategy of Rising Power*, ed. Masafumi Iida, NIDS Joint Research Series, no. 3, 29–54, http://www.nids.go.jp/english/publication/joint_research/series3/pdf/3-2.pdf.

[63] Wang, "China's Search for a Grand Strategy"; and Friedberg, *Contest for Supremacy*. For a somewhat different view, see Avery Goldstein, *Rising to the Challenge: China's Grand Strategy and International Security* (Stanford: Stanford University Press, 2005).

plans. Either outcome would be disastrous for China because the liberal democracies on which China depends for sustained growth account for the overwhelming majority of economic, military, and political power in the current world order.[64]

Though conceivable, the dynamics sketched out above are less likely and less influential than others that have been operating for more than three decades. These dynamics can be summarized as follows. The legitimacy of China's political system depends heavily on performance. Performance depends on continued ability to take advantage of the international order created and maintained by the United States. That, in turn, requires avoidance of disruptions in the global system and continued acquiescence to the rules and norms of that system.[65]

The first principle then of an imagined Chinese blueprint for a new world order is likely to be, "Do no harm." Unless the political and decision-making system put in place after Mao's death is changed to reduce or remove deliberately erected impediments to sudden or extensive departures from current policy, the bias for stability, predictability, and policy continuity engineered into the system will significantly limit the scope and extent of any changes that China attempts to make to the global order. The interests and efforts of other participants in the global system, the most important of which remains the United States, will further limit the possible space for transformation, but the focus here is on plausible Chinese desires and designs for reform.

Defense of China's sovereignty will be as important as avoidance of harm, and sometimes more so. The importance of nationalism as a source of regime legitimacy, official interpretations of why China was subjected to the century of humiliation, recognition among at least some at the top that they preside over an empire with peoples and territories that have been incompletely incorporated into the Han-dominated nation, and persistent Confucian thinking on the proper relationships between the Middle Kingdom and "vassals" on the periphery all push officials to defend vigorously any perceived threats to China's sovereignty and territorial integrity. This explains, in large part, the vehemence of China's stand on territorial disputes and the inalienability of Taiwan, Tibet, Xinjiang, or any other part of what Beijing now claims to be part of China.

China's ambitions will be shaped and constrained by domestic factors, and by its perceptions of how other nations will react to China-initiated efforts to change a system that is working reasonably well and bringing

---

[64] See, for example, G. John Ikenberry, "The Rise of China and the Future of the West," *Foreign Affairs* 87, no. 1 (2008): 23–37; and Steinfeld, *Playing Our Game*.

[65] Ikenberry, "Rise of China."

important benefits to many countries, including all the richest and most powerful nations. For example, the legitimacy of Communist Party rule and the existing system of government is heavily dependent on its ability to sustain high rates of growth and provide tangible benefits to the majority of China's more than 1.3 billion people. Rates of growth are already slowing and likely will slow further as China approaches a stage of development described as the "middle income trap."[66]

To the extent that China continues to follow the oft-traveled path of development, it will become increasingly difficult to sustain rates of growth sufficient to satisfy the rising expectations of its growing middle class and the hundreds of millions still living close to the poverty level of two dollars per day. This will make China even more dependent on the existing world order and, logically, even less willing to jeopardize the smooth functioning of the global system and China's ability to benefit from it by pushing for radical change or unilateral action in defiance of the U.S.-led system's rules and norms. This, in turn, suggests that China would adopt a cautious and conservative approach to reform of the existing order. The system needs reform and China is likely to be among the states pressing for change, but its approach is more likely to focus on fixing specific problems and correcting specific defects than on drastic overhaul. To do otherwise would entail unacceptable direct and indirect risks to the PRC's own prosperity, stability, and political order.

Domestic considerations inducing caution will be reinforced by the character and importance to China of other countries' perceptions of and responses to what China might attempt. China is not the only country that benefits from the existing global order, and its Communist Party is not the only political establishment with a stake in the predictability, open-trading system, and global stability provided by the current system. Others would not look kindly on actions by China—or any other major player—that might jeopardize the prosperity, stability, and security of their own country. Interdependence, global supply and production chains, and concern about influence and image make China (and other actors) reluctant to do anything that could trigger unhelpful or hostile reactions elsewhere in the international system. This further reinforces incentives to tread warily and eschew actions that could be construed as hazardous to the continued smooth operation of the global order.

---

[66] See, for example, Arthur R. Kroeber, "Bear in a China Shop," Brookings Institution, May 22, 2012, http://www.brookings.edu/research/opinions/2012/05/22-china-economy-kroeber; and Barry Eichengreen, Donghyun Park, and Kwanho Shin, "When Fast-Growing Economies Slow Down: International Evidence and Implications for China," *Asian Economic Papers* 11, no. 1 (2012), http://www.mitpressjournals.org/doi/pdf/10.1162/ASEP_a_00118.

The above observations do not mean that China will be content to remain a passive free rider willing to live with aspects of the global order that it dislikes or considers inimical to its interests. This author's discussions with Chinese scholars and officials over several years, especially those during the May 2012 workshops, suggest particular eagerness to change three aspects of the current system. All three of the desired changes focus on and require concurrence by the United States.

One change would be to expand the number of seats at the "high table" of global leadership to assure that China and other emerging economies have greater input into decisions affecting the procedures and performance of the global order. Different Chinese commentators use different terminology (e.g., some call for greater fairness, others refer to democratizing the system, and still others focus more specifically on reducing the ability of the United States to "run the world"), but all seem to have at least three key objectives.[67] One is to enhance and assure China's ability to influence decisions affecting its own destiny. This would entail both greater ability to block or refashion actions or proposed changes judged adverse to Beijing's interests, and, probably to a lesser extent, to advance an independent agenda.

Chinese commentators have been vague on the question of precisely what countries should gain seats and now seem more concerned about enhancing China's ability to play defense than with pushing a particular agenda of its own. Nor are they specific about whether or how to embed the additional seats in institutional structures. Raising China's profile and increasing its influence seem to be more important than assuring that all emerging economies or particular others gain seats at the table. With respect to one existing global institution, the UNSC, China has proved unenthusiastic about adding another Northeast Asian country (e.g., Japan) or other emerging nations (e.g., India and Brazil), possibly because doing so would dilute China's stature and influence.

No Chinese commentator, to this author's knowledge, has called for universal participation at the high table, probably both because they know that would be unworkable and because institutionalizing China's status as one of a small number of leading states would be an important step toward regaining what it perceives as its proper place atop (or at the center of) the world order. It would also have the symbolic and substantive effect of reducing the magnitude of U.S. preeminence. The United States would remain the most important player in the global system, but others, most importantly China, would appear to—and to some extent would actually— have diminished the power of the system hegemon.

---

[67] The observations summarized here are based on discussions during the May 2012 workshops in Beijing and Shanghai (see footnote 19).

A second objective would be to increase the likelihood that the United States will abide and be constrained by the rules and norms of the global order. One of the hallmarks of the liberal order led by the United States has been the willingness of the leading power to play by the same rules that it prescribed and enforced for other participants.[68] Washington has not always done so, but most of the time, and on most issues, it has. Or, more accurately, it did so until the first decade of the 21st century when the George W. Bush administration began to act as an "imperial hegemon."[69] China, like many other nations, was discomforted by this change in U.S. behavior and would like to engineer incentives and constraints into the system that make it less attractive and more difficult for the United States to act unilaterally and in contravention of existing rules.[70]

Both of these potential objectives would seem to be achievable by China. The United States is not adamantly opposed to expanding the number of seats at the high table, and at times appears eager to do so, provided that countries added to the decision-making and system-maintenance team are willing and able to assume some of the burdens and responsibilities that have long been borne primarily by the United States. Thus far China has been reluctant to do so, arguing that its own domestic challenges are so great that it cannot yet take on significantly greater international responsibilities.[71] It also seems reluctant to have other countries, developed or emerging, take on more responsibility or secure a larger voice in decisions than China is willing or able to assume.

Actions by the United States during the George W. Bush administration were disconcerting to many countries, in addition to China, and the Obama administration has continued the rollback of unilateral exceptionalism that began in Bush's second term. But Chinese (and other) observers remain worried that what happened once could be repeated unless preventive measures are put into place. Their concern is not limited to adherence to formal agreements, such as the ban on biological weapons. It also applies to less formal norms, such as the preservation of mutual vulnerability as a pillar of nuclear deterrence. Chinese leaders worry that U.S. missile-defense programs are intended to reduce U.S. vulnerability in ways that would enable the United States to threaten or intimidate others (i.e., China) because these programs had reduced the danger of nuclear retaliation.[72] Decisions that

---

[68] Ikenberry, *Liberal Leviathan*.

[69] Ibid.

[70] See, for example, David M. Malone and Yuen Foong Khong, eds., *Unilateralism and U.S. Foreign Policy: International Perspectives* (Boulder: Lynne Rienner, 2003); and Ikenberry, *Liberal Leviathan*, 254–77.

[71] Etzioni, "Is China a Responsible Stakeholder?"

[72] See, for example, Thomas Fingar, "Worrying about Washington: China's Views on the U.S. Nuclear Posture," *Nonproliferation Review* 18, no. 1 (2011): 51–68.

would preserve or restore U.S. willingness to abide by the same rules as others will be shaped, in part, by the actions of others, including China. China has accepted and enforced many rules and norms of the global system, but its record is far from perfect (theft of intellectual property being a case in point), and it will have difficulty persuading the United States to abide by rules while China continues to violate its own legal and political commitments.[73]

The third aspect of the existing order that China would like to change will be much more difficult for Beijing to achieve because it is a product of both perceived system-maintenance requirements and prudent hedging against uncertainty. At the core of the issue are U.S. alliance relationships, military deployments, and intelligence-gathering activities. This could be the subject of an extensive discussion, and I will simply say that China does not like U.S. security-related institutions and activities because it perceives many of them as intended to constrain China's rise and return to the apex of world power.[74] The PRC's own military modernization is designed, in part, to counter or balance U.S. capabilities and to protect its own territory, citizens, and interests. But China's own actions, like those of the United States, fuel a classic security dilemma in which each side feels compelled to counter the capabilities of the other, leading to a spiral of expenditures and increased danger of unintended conflict with higher casualties.

The root of the problem is not what either side is doing; rather, it is mutual distrust and strategic suspicion fueled by uncertainty about what the other party seeks to achieve and imputed or imagined objectives that are impossible to dismiss or disprove. Under the circumstances, it is both prudent and politically necessary for both sides to hedge against uncertainty by preparing for unlikely but not impossible developments.[75] Actions that almost certainly are undertaken to hedge are then interpreted as evidence of real and malign intent. It is a mutual problem, but one that is worse on the Chinese side. Beijing demonstrates a strong penchant to interpret any development that could entail negative consequences for China as having been adopted specifically to achieve that impact.[76] Neither side has figured out how to escape this dilemma.

---

[73] See, for example, U.S.-China Economic and Security Review Commission, "Section 3: Indigenous Innovation and Intellectual Property Rights," in *2011 Annual Report to Congress*, November 2011, 70–87.

[74] Lieberthal and Wang, "Addressing U.S.-China Strategic Distrust."

[75] See, for example, Evan S. Medeiros, "Strategic Hedging and the Future of Asia-Pacific Stability," *Washington Quarterly* 29, no. 1 (2005–6), 145–67.

[76] Fingar, "Worrying About Washington."

Prospects

Based on the analysis presented here, China will have neither the ability nor the desire to fundamentally transform the global order that exists today. Some decision-makers in China might aspire to displace the United States at the top of the system (or at the center, depending on which depiction of the world order is used), for reasons of both pride and security, but that is not going to happen for a very long time, and many Chinese geopolitical thinkers are comfortable with that. What they seek, and may achieve at least in part, are changes to the existing order that elevate China's formal and symbolic importance, preserve attributes of the system from which China and others benefit, and constrain the will and ability of the United States and others to act outside the rules of the game. These are significant but not revolutionary or dangerously destabilizing objectives, and achieving them would not necessarily be bad for world order or U.S. interests.

China's rise and size mean, among other things, that few, if any, significant international problems—for example, the need to reform and rebuild institutions of international governance, climate change, and prosperity-driven competition for energy, water, and other resources—can be solved without China's participation. They also make China an important engine of growth for later-rising states and an important provider of goods to developed states with aging populations. But they do not make China a viable near-term rival or replacement for leadership of the global order. The United States will remain the preeminent—and, in that sense, hegemonic—leader of the system for the foreseeable future, unless it stumbles badly and opens the way for China and other potential challengers.

China has a big economy, but that is only one contributor to national power, and, as Chinese commentators are quick to point out, its per capita GDP is small and its capacity to make the transition from imitation to innovation has yet to be demonstrated. Most countries have found it very difficult to make that transition, and it is not at all a certainty that China will be able to do it more quickly. It is baffling that many pundits and a surprising number of analysts seem prepared to interpret China's growing GDP as a sign of U.S. decline. When China began the policy of reform and opening in 1979, the United States accounted for roughly 26% of the world economy. Three decades later—after China's impressive accomplishments, the end of the Cold War, the subsequent entry of former Warsaw Pact states into the much stronger European Union, and the rise of India, Brazil, and dozens of other nations—the United States' share of the economy has declined only slightly to about 23%. But the world economy is much bigger, and the United States' share of the percentage of world population has declined from 6% to 5%.[77]

On other key dimensions of national power, namely military might and soft power, the gap between China and the United States remains wide. If this gap is closing, it is at a very slow rate. But perceptions are sometimes as important as reality in international politics. It is certainly the case that many people in many nations perceive the United States to be in decline and China to be on the verge of overtaking it as the most important player in the global system. Correcting this misconception is the United States' challenge. Despite unhappiness with manifestations of U.S. triumphalism during the Clinton administration and U.S. unilateralism during the administration of George W. Bush, most countries seem more eager for the United States to return to what Ikenberry calls "benign hegemony" than for another country to supplant it as leader of the global order. Many, however, would probably welcome expanding the number of countries at the high table, as the Chinese demand. The real issue for the United States is likely to be which countries join and under what terms, not whether to increase the number of seats. Working out answers to these and similar questions will require U.S.-China cooperation.

---

[77] Percentages are derived from World Bank data for 1979 and 2010 using constant U.S. dollar comparisons. Fluctuation of a percentage point or more per year is normal. Data can be found at World Bank Databank, http://databank.worldbank.org/.

STRATEGIC ASIA 2012–13

INDICATORS

Strategic Asia
by the Numbers

The following twelve pages contain tables and figures drawn from NBR's Strategic Asia database and its sources. This appendix consists of fourteen tables covering politics, economics, trade and investment, energy and the environment, security challenges, and nuclear arms and nonproliferation. The data sets presented here summarize the critical trends in the region and changes underway in the balance of power in Asia.

The Strategic Asia database contains additional data for all 37 countries in "Strategic Asia" across 70 indicators arranged in ten broad thematic areas: economy, finance, trade and investment, government spending, population, energy and the environment, communications and transportation, armed forces, nuclear arms, and politics. Hosted on the program's website (http://strategicasia.nbr.org), the database is a repository of authoritative data for 1990–2011. The database's public interface was upgraded in 2011 and now includes a mapping feature that displays current and historical Asian military developments, including international military assets, exercises, and peacekeeping operations. The Strategic Asia database was developed with .NET, Microsoft's XML-based platform, which allows users to dynamically link to all or part of the Strategic Asia data set and facilitates easy data sharing. The database also includes additional links that allow users to access related online resources seamlessly.

The information for "Strategic Asia by the Numbers" was compiled by NBR Next Generation Fellow Anton Wishik and NBR interns Naomi McMillen and Greg Chaffin.

Politics

Late 2011 and 2012 saw leadership continuity in several key actors in the region. Vladimir Putin was elected to his third term as Russia's president after a term as prime minister, Ma Ying-jeou was reelected as president of Taiwan, and Kim Jong-un became head of state in North Korea following the death of his father. The U.S. presidential election and China's leadership succession are both scheduled to occur in fall 2012.

- In September 2011, Yoshihiko Noda replaced Naoto Kan as Prime Minister of Japan. Noda is Japan's sixth prime minister in six years.

- In China, the fall of Politburo member and Chongqing party chief Bo Xilai in the run-up to the 18th Party Congress—at which time Xi Jinping was expected to succeed Hu Jintao as president of China and general secretary of the Chinese Communist Party (CCP)—called into question the unity of the top CCP leadership.

- Political liberalization in Myanmar accelerated as pro-democracy activist Aung San Suu Kyi and the National League for Democracy won 43 of the 45 parliamentary seats up for election in 2012.

TABLE 1   Political leadership

	Political leaders	Date assumed office	Next election
Australia	Prime Minister Julia Gillard	June 2010	2013
China	President Hu Jintao	March 2003	2012–13*
India	Prime Minister Manmohan Singh	May 2004	2014
Indonesia	President Susilo Bambang Yudhoyono	October 2004	2014
Japan	Prime Minister Yoshihiko Noda	August 2011	2013
Kazakhstan	President Nursultan Nazarbayev	December 1991	2016
Malaysia	Prime Minister Mohamed Najib bin Abdul Razak	April 2009	2013
Myanmar	President Thein Sein	Febuary 2011	2015
Pakistan	Prime Minister Syed Yousuf Raza Gilani	March 2008	2012
Philippines	President Benigno Simeon Cojuangco Aquino III	June 2010	2016
Russia	President Vladimir Putin	May 2012	2018
South Korea	President Lee Myung-bak	Febuary 2008	2012
Taiwan	President Ma Ying-jeou	January 2009	2016
Thailand	Prime Minister Yingluck Sinawatra	August 2011	2016
United States	President Barack Obama	January 2009	2012

SOURCE: Central Intelligence Agency (CIA), *The World Factbook*, 2012.

NOTE: Table shows the next election year in which the given leader may lose or retain his or her position. In some countries, elections may be called before these years. Asterisk indicates that although China will not hold a popular vote, a leadership transition is widely expected in 2012–13.

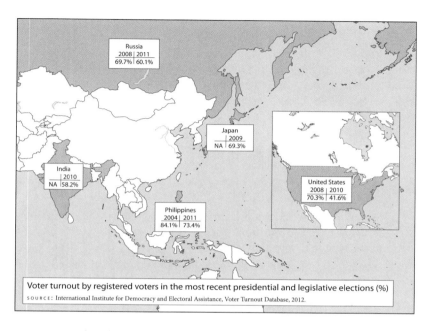

Voter turnout by registered voters in the most recent presidential and legislative elections (%)

SOURCE: International Institute for Democracy and Electoral Assistance, Voter Turnout Database, 2012.

TABLE 2 Political rights, corruption, and democracy

	Political rights score		Corruption index		Democracy index	
	2005	2011	2005	2010	2006	2011
Australia	1	1	8.8	8.8	9.1	9.2
China	7	7	3.2	3.6	3.0	3.1
India	2	2	2.9	3.1	7.7	7.3
Indonesia	2	2	2.2	3.0	6.4	6.5
Japan	1	1	7.3	8.0	8.2	8.1
Kazakhstan	6	6	2.6	2.7	3.6	3.2
Malaysia	4	4	5.1	4.3	6.0	6.2
Myanmar	7	7	1.8	1.5	1.7	1.7
Pakistan	6	4	2.1	2.5	3.9	4.6
Philippines	3	3	2.5	2.6	6.5	6.1
Russia	6	6	2.4	2.4	5.0	3.9
South Korea	1	1	5.0	5.4	7.9	8.1
Taiwan	1	1	5.9	6.1	7.8	7.5
Thailand	3	5	3.8	3.4	5.7	6.6
United States	1	1	7.6	7.1	8.2	8.1

SOURCE: Freedom House, "Freedom in the World," 2006, and 2012; Transparency International, "Corruption Perceptions Index," 2006 and 2011; and Economist Intelligence Unit, "Democracy Index," 2006 and 2011.

NOTE: Political rights score = ability of the people to participate freely in the political process (1 = most free/7 = least free). Corruption = degree to which public official corruption is perceived to exist (1 = most corrupt/10 = most open). The democracy index = level of democratization (0 = least democratic/10 = most democratic).

Economics

Amid a relatively weak global economic recovery, Asia continued to outperform other regions in GDP growth. The International Monetary Fund projected that Asia's developing economies would grow at 7.1% in 2012, below the 7.8% growth the region experienced in 2011, but still surpassing the 1.4% growth predicted for the world's advanced economies.

- GDP growth forecasts for 2012 were 8% for China, 6.1% for India, 5.4% for the ASEAN-5 economies, and 2% for the United States. Japan continued to recover from the March 2011 Tohoku earthquake, as the Japanese economy was projected to grow by 2.4% in 2012, a marked improvement from the 0.7% contraction in 2011.

- Lower non-fuel commodity prices contributed to a slower rise in inflation in Asia. Consumer prices were expected to increase by 3.9% in the region, a reduction from the 5.0% increase seen in 2011.

- Despite strong initial forecasts, China's economy appeared to be weakening. According to China's National Bureau of Statistics, China's GDP growth in the first half of 2012 fell to 7.8% while consumer prices rose by 3.3% year-on-year.

TABLE 3 Gross domestic product

	GDP ($bn)				Rank	
	1990	**2000**	**2011**	**2011 annual growth (%)**	**1990**	**2011**
United States	5,750.8	9,898.8	15,094.0	4.5%	1	1
China	356.9	1,198.5	7,298.1	23.0%	5	2
Japan	3,103.7	4,731.2	5,867.2	6.9%	2	3
Russia	516.8	259.7	1,857.0	24.8%	4	4
India	326.6	474.7	1,847.9	9.7%	6	5
Canada	582.7	724.9	1,736.0	10.0%	3	6
Australia	314.0	416.9	1,371.7	21.2%	7	7
South Korea	263.8	553.4	1,116.0	10.0%	8	8
Taiwan	150.8	386.0	885.3	7.7%	9	9
Indonesia	114.4	165.0	846.8	19.6%	10	10
Thailand	85.3	122.7	345.6	8.4%	11	11
Malaysia	44.0	93.8	278.6	17.1%	14	12
Hong Kong	76.9	169.1	243.6	8.5%	12	13
Singapore	36.1	95.9	239.7	12.4%	15	14
Philippines	44.3	81.0	224.7	12.6%	13	15
World	21,976.0	32,329.0	69,971.0	10.8%	N/A	N/A

SOURCE: World Bank, "World Development Indicators," various years; and data for Taiwan is from the CIA, *The World Factbook*, various years.

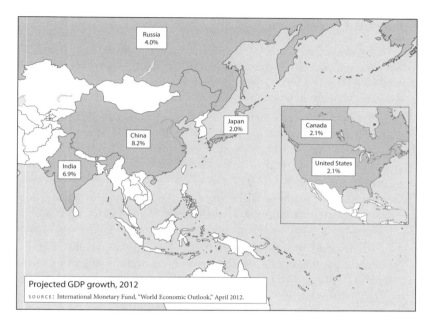

Projected GDP growth, 2012

SOURCE: International Monetary Fund, "World Economic Outlook," April 2012.

TABLE 4   GDP growth and inflation rates

	Average real GDP growth (%)			Average inflation rate (%)		
	2001–5	2006–10	2011	2001–5	2006–10	2011
United States	2.8%	1.2%	1.5%	2.4%	2.1%	3.0%
China	8.7%	10.2%	9.2%	1.8%	3.6%	5.4%
Japan	1.5%	0.4%	-0.5%	-0.4%	-0.1%	0.4%
Russia	6.0%	3.2%	4.3%	14.3%	10.3%	8.9%
India	6.1%	8.1%	7.8%	4.5%	8.6%	6.8%
Canada	2.4%	1.3%	2.2%	2.4%	1.7%	2.8%
Australia	2.9%	2.8%	1.8%	3.0%	3.0%	3.4%
South Korea	4.2%	3.7%	3.6%	3.4%	3.0%	4.0%
Taiwan	2.9%	3.3%	5.2%	0.8%	1.7%	1.6%
Indonesia	4.3%	5.7%	6.4%	9.4%	7.9%	5.7%
Thailand	4.7%	5.5%	0.1%	2.3%	3.0%	3.8%
Malaysia	4.4%	4.4%	5.2%	1.8%	2.7%	3.2%
Hong Kong	3.0%	3.5%	5.0%	-0.1%	2.1%	5.3%
Singapore	3.1%	5.8%	4.9%	0.9%	2.6%	5.2%
Philippines	4.6%	4.9%	3.7%	5.1%	5.1%	5.3%

SOURCE: CIA, *The World Factbook*, 1990–2012.

Trade and Investment

With weakening external demand, especially from the European Union, and only slightly increasing domestic demand, Asian export growth slowed in 2011. As a result, the region's trade has became more balanced, and current account balances have shrunk as a percentage of GDP.

- After posting a trade surplus of less than $1 billion in the first quarter of 2012, China's trade surplus rose to $68.92 billion in the second quarter, a 56.4% increase over the same period last year. Despite this increase, the rate of growth has slowed, reflecting decreased demand due to a weak global economy and China's own economic slowdown.

- Progress was made toward expanding the Trans-Pacific Partnership. As negotiations continued through the first half of 2012, Japan inched closer to signing on while it appeared unlikely that China would join.

- FDI inflows rose 13% across Asia while outflows from Asia fell slightly. Southeast Asia saw the greatest growth in both sectors with a 26% increase in FDI inflows and a 36% increase in outflows, primarily from Singapore, Thailand, and Indonesia.

TABLE 5   Trade flow and trade partners

	Trade flow ($bn constant 2000)		2009–10 growth (%)	Top export partner, 2010	Top import partner, 2010
	2000	**2010**			
United States	2,572.1	3,408.3	10.6%	Canada (19.4%)	China (19.3%)
China	530.2	2,551.3	19.8%	U.S. (20.0%)	Japan (12.3%)
Japan	957.6	1,308.3	15.5%	China (18.9%)	China (22.2%)
Hong Kong	475.3	917.8	14.5%	China (51.2%)	China (46.4%)
South Korea	401.6	884.2	13.3%	China (21.5%)	China (17.7%)
Canada	617.4	672.9	9.6%	U.S. (75.0%)	U.S. (51.1%)
India	130.5	451.1	12.4%	U.A.E. (12.9%)	China (10.9%)
Russia	176.8	426.4	13.7%	Netherlands (10.0%)	Germany (14.4%)
Malaysia	206.7	309.8	10.9%	Singapore (13.9%)	China (13.9%)
Australia	178.0	281.0	-12.1%	China (18.7%)	China (18.7%)
Thailand	153.3	248.5	15.4%	China (12.0%)	Japan (18.5%)
Indonesia	117.9	225.8	13.7%	Japan (16.3%)	China (15.1%)
Philippines	82.7	130.5	19.0%	China (19.0%)	Japan (14.1%)
Vietnam	35.1	116.4	12.4%	U.S. (18.0%)	China (23.8%)
New Zealand	36.6	49.6	10.8%	Australia (23.1%)	Australia (18.1%)

SOURCE: World Bank, "World Development Indicators," 1990–2012; and CIA, "The World Factbook," 2012.

NOTE: No comparable data from the "World Development Indicators" is available for Singapore or Taiwan.

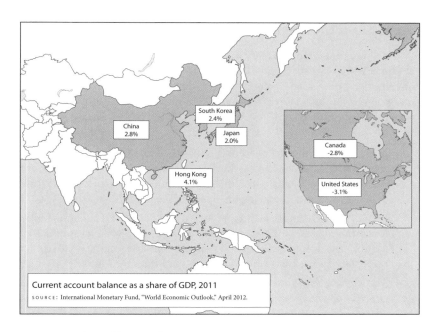

Current account balance as a share of GDP, 2011

SOURCE: International Monetary Fund, "World Economic Outlook," April 2012.

TABLE 6   Flow of foreign direct investment

	FDI inflows ($bn)			FDI outflows ($bn)		
	2000–2010 annual avg.	2010	2009–10 growth (%)	2000–2010 annual avg.	2010	2009–10 growth (%)
United States	173.5	228.2	49.3%	199.2	328.9	16.3%
China	72.0	105.7	11.3%	22.3	68.0	20.2%
Hong Kong	41.9	68.9	31.5%	42.1	76.1	18.8%
Russia	25.6	41.2	12.8%	24.1	51.7	18.3%
Singapore	18.2	38.6	152.9%	12.0	19.7	6.9%
Australia	21.9	32.5	26.3%	12.7	26.4	63.5%
India	15.9	24.6	-30.9%	8.1	14.6	-5.8%
Canada	38.9	23.4	9.4%	42.6	38.6	-7.3%
Indonesia	3.6	13.3	172.8%	2.3	2.7	18.4%
Kazakhstan	6.4	10.0	-27.7%	1.3	7.8	150.3%
Malaysia	4.6	9.1	536.6%	5.8	13.4	68.5%
South Korea	5.8	6.9	-8.4%	10.2	19.2	11.8%
Thailand	5.4	5.8	16.8%	1.7	5.1	24.4%
Pakistan	2.3	2.0	-13.8%	0.0	0.0	-35.2%
New Zealand	2.2	0.6	143.4%	0.4	0.6	201.2%
World	1,156.8	1,243.7	4.9%	1,163.7	1,323.3	13%

SOURCE: UN Conference on Trade and Development, *World Investment Report*, 2011.

Energy and the Environment

Asia accounted for 31.9% of global energy consumption, over half of which was supplied by coal. For the third time in four years, energy consumption decreased among OECD nations—led by Japan—while emerging economies, primarily in Asia, were responsible for the new growth in energy consumption in 2011. China was the leading consumer, accounting for 21.3% of global energy consumption and 71% of consumption growth.

- More than a year after the Fukushima disaster, Japan's energy outlook remained unclear. Following the disaster, Japan took all 54 of its nuclear reactors offline. In mid-2012, the Noda administration began restarting select reactors and undertook a review of the nation's energy policy.

- A 10.3% price increase was expected for oil in 2012, significantly lower than the 2011 increase of 31.6%. Oil-linked pricing for liquefied natural gas also resulted in large price discrepancies, with Asian importers facing costs several times higher than the United States.

- The United States met 81% of its energy demand through domestic sources, a level of self-sufficiency not seen since the early 1900s and a sharp turnaround from a low of 70% in 2005.

TABLE 7   Energy consumption

	Energy consumption (quadrillion Btu)				Rank	
	1990	2000	2011	2010–11 growth (%)	1990	2011
China	27.2	38.4	103.7	7.4%	2	1
United States	78.0	91.7	90.1	-0.7%	1	2
Russia	–	25.2	27.2	-0.7%	–	3
India	7.7	12.7	22.2	6.7%	5	4
Japan	17.2	20.4	17.8	-10.6%	3	5
Canada	9.8	11.5	13.1	4.0%	4	6
South Korea	3.6	7.6	10.4	3.0%	6	7
Indonesia	2.1	3.8	5.9	5.4%	8	8
Australia	3.5	4.4	4.9	4.3%	7	9
Taiwan	2.0	3.8	4.4	0.0%	9	10
Thailand	1.2	2.4	4.2	-2.3%	10	11
Malaysia	1.0	1.8	2.7	8.0%	12	12
Pakistan	1.1	1.6	2.7	0.0%	11	13
Uzbekistan	–	2.0	2.1	5.0%	–	14
Kazakhstan	–	1.6	2.0	-31.0%	–	15
World	322.7	369.4	487.1	2.2%	N/A	N/A

SOURCE: BP plc, "BP Statistical Review of World Energy," 2012.
NOTE: Dash indicates that no data is available.

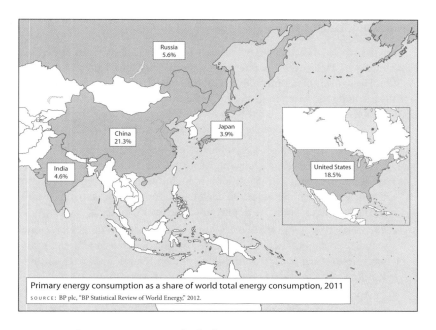

Primary energy consumption as a share of world total energy consumption, 2011

SOURCE: BP plc, "BP Statistical Review of World Energy," 2012.

TABLE 8   Energy consumption by fuel type

	2011 energy consumption by fuel type (%)					
	Oil	Gas	Coal	Nuclear	Hydro	Renewables
China	17.7%	4.5%	70.4%	0.7%	6.0%	0.7%
United States	36.7%	27.6%	22.2%	8.3%	3.3%	2.0%
Russia	19.8%	55.7%	13.3%	5.7%	5.4%	0.1%
India	29.0%	9.4%	52.9%	1.3%	5.3%	1.7%
Japan	42.2%	19.9%	24.6%	7.7%	4.0%	1.6%
Canada	31.2%	28.6%	6.6%	6.5%	25.8%	1.3%
South Korea	40.3%	15.9%	30.2%	12.9%	0.5%	0.2%
Indonesia	43.5%	23.0%	29.7%	–	2.4%	1.4%
Australia	37.2%	18.7%	40.4%	–	2.0%	1.8%
Taiwan	38.9%	12.7%	37.9%	8.6%	0.8%	1.1%
Thailand	44.2%	39.5%	13.1%	–	1.7%	1.5%
Kazakhstan	20.2%	16.4%	59.8%	–	3.6%	<
Pakistan	30.2%	52.1%	6.2%	1.2%	10.2%	<
Malaysia	38.9%	37.1%	21.7%	–	2.5%	<
Uzbekistan	8.4%	84.7%	2.5%	–	4.4%	–

SOURCE: BP plc, "BP Statistical Review of World Energy," 2012.

NOTE: Due to rounding, some totals may not add up to exactly 100%. Dash indicates that no data is available. Angle bracket indicates that value is less than 0.05%.

Security Challenges

In January 2012, the U.S. Department of Defense announced a rebalancing of U.S. forces as part of a general shift in focus to the Asia-Pacific. However, this ambitious plan was set against the backdrop of significant budget constraints, as the Department of Defense faces cutting up to $900 billion over the next ten years. Meanwhile, China announced a double-digit percentage increase in its defense spending for 2012.

- Immediate impacts of U.S. rebalancing included the arrival of U.S. marines to a base in Darwin, Australia, and the strengthening of military ties with the Philippines, including joint exercises in the South China Sea. Secretary of Defense Leon Panetta stated that 60% of the U.S. fleet would be deployed in the Pacific by 2020.

- Territorial disputes in the South China Sea continued to threaten regional stability. A standoff between Chinese surveillance ships and a Philippine warship in April 2012, with the Philippines attempting to deter Chinese fishing vessels near the Spratly Islands, lasted several months.

- In April 2012 North Korea tested a long-range missile under the guise of a satellite launch. The test, which failed, led to UN censure.

TABLE 9 Total defense expenditure

	Expenditure ($bn)				Rank	
	1990	2000	2010	2009–10 growth (%)	1990	2010
United States	293.0	300.5	693.6	4.9%	1	1
China	11.3	42.0	178.0	7.1%	3	2
Russia	–	7.3	65.2	14.0%	–	3
Japan	28.7	45.6	54.4	6.1%	2	4
India	10.1	14.7	30.9	-23.9%	6	5
South Korea	10.6	12.8	25.1	10.7%	4	6
Australia	7.3	7.1	23.6	17.3%	8	7
Canada	10.3	11.5	20.2	3.0%	5	8
Taiwan	8.7	8.9	9.0	-5.7%	7	9
Singapore	1.7	4.8	8.1	3.7%	11	10
Indonesia	1.6	1.5	7.2	33.1%	12	11
Malaysia	1.7	2.8	3.7	-6.8%	10	12
Pakistan	2.9	3.7	5.6	32.1%	9	13
Vietnam	–	1.0	2.6	18.2%	–	14
Myanmar	0.9	2.1	–	–	13	–
World	954.0	811.4	1,514.6	4.3%	N/A	N/A

SOURCE: International Institute for Strategic Studies, *The Military Balance*, various editions; SASI Group and Mark Newman, "Military Spending 1990," 2007; and data for China is based on various sources.
NOTE: Estimates for China vary widely. Dash indicates that no data is available.

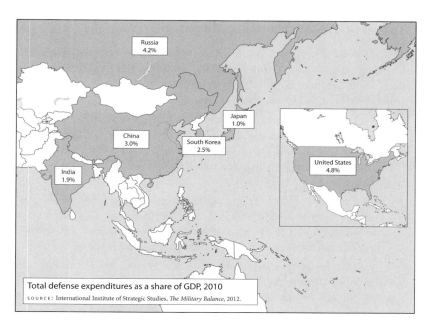

Total defense expenditures as a share of GDP, 2010
SOURCE: International Institute of Strategic Studies, *The Military Balance*, 2012.

TABLE 10   Armed forces

	Armed forces (th)				Rank	
	1990	2000	2012	2011–12 change (th)	1990	2011
China	3,030	2,470	2,285	0	2	1
United States	2,118	1,366	1,325	5	3	2
India	1,262	1,303	1,190	0	4	3
North Korea	1,111	1,082	1,159	0	5	4
Russia	3,988	1,004	956	-90	1	5
South Korea	750	683	655	0	7	6
Pakistan	550	612	642	25	8	7
Vietnam	1,052	484	482	27	6	8
Myanmar	230	344	406	0	13	9
Thailand	283	301	306	0	10	10
Indonesia	283	297	302	0	10	11
Taiwan	370	370	290	0	9	12
Japan	249	237	248	0	12	13
Sri Lanka	65	–	161	0	14	14
Bangladesh	103	137	157	0	15	15
World	26,605	22,237	20,268	-1,969	N/A	N/A

SOURCE: International Institute of Strategic Studies, *The Military Balance*, various editions.
NOTE: Active duty and military personnel only. Data value for Russia in 1990 includes all territories of the Soviet Union. Dash indicates that no data is available.

Nuclear Arms and Nonproliferation

Iran's nuclear program continued to capture the world's attention amid talk of a potential Israeli military strike on Iran's nuclear facilities. The United States maintained sanctions against Iran while pursuing diplomacy through the P5+1 meetings, which seemingly produced little progress.

- The U.S. Department of Defense's January 2012 Strategic Guidance hinted at a reduction in U.S. nuclear forces. President Obama stated that nuclear disarmament was a "moral obligation" for the United States and pledged to negotiate with Russia on further cuts to each side's arsenals.

- Following its failed long-range missile test in April, it was widely expected that Pyongyang would conduct a third nuclear test, as its second test was preceded by a similar situation in 2009. North Korea subsequently declared that it will not conduct another nuclear test for now.

- India successfully tested its Agni-5 long-range ballistic missile in April 2012, extending its nuclear deterrent reach to 3,100 miles. The test marked India's entry into the small club of nations with such a capability and brings Beijing within range of India's nuclear forces.

TABLE 11   Nuclear weapons

	Nuclear weapons possession				Total inventory	
	1990	1995	2000	2012	2011	2012
Russia	√	√	√	√	11,000	10,492
United States	√	√	√	√	8,500	8,613
China	√	√	√	√	240	240
India	√	√	√	√	80–100	<100
Pakistan	–	–	√	√	90–110	90–110
North Korea	?	?	?	√	<10	<12

SOURCE: "Status of World Nuclear Forces," Federation of American Scientists, 2011–12.
NOTE: Table shows confirmed (√) and unknown (?) possession of nuclear weapons. Dash indicates that no data is available. Total inventory includes both active and stockpiled arms.

TABLE 12   Intercontinental ballistic missiles

	Number of ICBMs			
	1990	1995	2000	2012
United States	1,000	580	550	450
Russia	1,398	930	776	292
China	8	17+	20+	66
India	–	–	–	In development
Pakistan	–	–	–	?
North Korea	–	–	–	?

SOURCE: International Institute of Strategic Studies, *The Military Balance*, various editions.
NOTE: Dash indicates that no data is available. Question mark indicates unconfirmed possession.

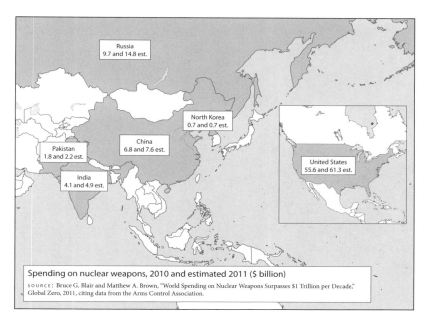

Spending on nuclear weapons, 2010 and estimated 2011 ($ billion)

SOURCE: Bruce G. Blair and Matthew A. Brown, "World Spending on Nuclear Weapons Surpasses $1 Trillion per Decade," Global Zero, 2011, citing data from the Arms Control Association.

TABLE 13   Nonproliferation treaties

	NPT	Additional Protocol	CTBT	CWC	BTWC
Russia	Ratified	Signatory	Ratified	Ratified	Ratified
United States	Ratified	Signatory	Signatory	Ratified	Ratified
China	Ratified	Ratified	Signatory	Ratified	Ratified
India	–	–	–	Ratified	Ratified
Pakistan	–	–	–	Ratified	Ratified
North Korea	Withdrew	–	–	–	Acceded

SOURCE: Nuclear Threat Initiative; and Monterey Institute for International Studies.
NOTE: NPT = Nuclear Non-proliferation Treaty. Additional Protocol = IAEA Additional Protocol. CTBT = Comprehensive Test Ban Treaty. CWC = Chemical Weapons Convention. BTWC = Biological and Toxic Weapons Convention. Dash indicates nonparticipation.

TABLE 14   WMD-export control regimes

	Nuclear Suppliers Group	Australia Group	Wassenaar Arrangement	Zangger Committee	MTCR
United States	Member	Member	Member	Member	Member
Russia	Member	–	Member	Member	Member
China	Member	–	–	Member	–
India	–	–	–	–	–
Pakistan	–	–	–	–	–
North Korea	–	–	–	–	–

SOURCE: Nuclear Threat Initiative; and Monterey Institute for International Studies.
NOTE: Dash indicates nonparticipation.

About the Contributors

Dan Blumenthal (JD, Duke University) is the Director of Asian Studies and a Resident Fellow at the American Enterprise Institute (AEI), where he focuses on East Asian security issues and Sino-American relations. Mr. Blumenthal has both served in and advised the U.S. government on China issues for over a decade. From 2001 to 2004, he served as Senior Director for China, Taiwan, and Mongolia at the Department of Defense. Additionally, he has been a commissioner on the congressionally mandated U.S.-China Economic and Security Review Commission since 2005, and held the position of Vice Chairman in 2007. He has also been on the Academic Advisory Board of the congressional U.S.-China Working Group. Mr. Blumenthal is a widely published author, with over one hundred articles and opinion pieces featured in *Newsweek*, *Foreign Policy* magazine, the *Washington Post*, the *Wall Street Journal*, the *New York Times*, the *Weekly Standard*, and *National Review*. He has also contributed chapters to numerous edited volumes. He speaks frequently on China as well as broader Asia policy issues to financial firms, academic institutions, international affairs organizations, and the U.S. government. Mr. Blumenthal is the co-author of the forthcoming book, *An Awkward Embrace: The United States and China in the 21st Century* (2012). He received a JD from Duke Law School and a MA from the Paul H. Nitze School of Advanced International Studies at the Johns Hopkins University, and studied at the Capital Normal University in Beijing.

Richard J. Ellings (PhD, University of Washington) is President and Co-founder of The National Bureau of Asian Research (NBR). Prior to serving with NBR, from 1986 to 1989 he was Assistant Director and on the faculty of the Jackson School of International Studies of the University of Washington, where he received the Distinguished Teaching Award. He served as Legislative Assistant in the U.S. Senate, office of Senator Slade Gorton, in 1984 and 1985. Dr. Ellings is the author of *Embargoes and World Power: Lessons from American Foreign Policy* (1985); co-author of *Private Property and National Security* (1991); co-editor (with Aaron Friedberg) of *Strategic Asia 2003–04: Fragility and Crisis* (2003), *Strategic Asia 2002–03: Asian Aftershocks* (2002), and *Strategic Asia 2001–02: Power and Purpose* (2001); co-editor of *Korea's Future and the Great Powers* (with Nicholas Eberstadt,

2001) and *Southeast Asian Security in the New Millennium* (with Sheldon Simon, 1996); founding editor of the *NBR Analysis* publication series; and co-chairman of the *Asia Policy* editorial board. He also established the Strategic Asia Program and AccessAsia, the national clearinghouse that tracks specialists and their research on Asia.

Andrew S. Erickson (PhD, Princeton University) is an Associate Professor in the Strategic Research Department at the U.S. Naval War College and a founding member of the department's China Maritime Studies Institute. He is also an Associate in Research at Harvard University's John King Fairbank Center for Chinese Studies and serves as an expert contributor to the *Wall Street Journal*'s China Real Time Report. Dr. Erickson has held fellowships with the Princeton-Harvard China and the World Program and with the National Committee on U.S.-China Relations' Public Intellectuals Program. He has also worked in the U.S. embassy in Beijing, the U.S. consulate in Hong Kong, the U.S. Senate, and the White House. He has lived in China, Japan, and Korea and is proficient in Mandarin and Japanese. Dr. Erickson has taught courses at the U.S. Naval War College and Yonsei University, as well as lectured at academic and government institutions throughout the United States and Asia. His work has been widely published in such journals as *Asian Security*, *Journal of Strategic Studies*, *Orbis*, *American Interest*, and *Joint Force Quarterly*. He is a co-editor of, and a contributor to, the Naval Institute Press's book series "Studies in Chinese Maritime Development," and the co-founder of China SignPost, a research newsletter and web portal that covers key developments in China, including on natural resource, trade, and security issues.

Thomas Fingar (PhD, Stanford University) is the inaugural Oksenberg-Rohlen Distinguished Fellow in the Freeman Spogli Institute for International Studies at Stanford University. He was the Payne Distinguished Lecturer at Stanford during January–December 2009. From 2005 through 2008, he served as the first Deputy Director of National Intelligence for Analysis and, concurrently, as Chairman of the National Intelligence Council. Dr. Fingar served previously as Assistant Secretary of the Bureau of Intelligence and Research (2004–5), Principal Deputy Assistant Secretary (2001–3), Deputy Assistant Secretary for Analysis (1994–2000), Director of the Office of Analysis for East Asia and the Pacific (1989–94), and Chief of the China Division (1986–89) in the U.S. Department of State. Between 1975 and 1986, he held a number of positions at Stanford, including Senior Research Associate in the Center for International Security and Arms Control. Dr. Fingar holds an AB in Government and History from Cornell

University, as well as an MA and PhD in Political Science from Stanford University. His most recent book is *Reducing Uncertainty: Intelligence Analysis and National Security* (2011).

Christopher W. Hughes (PhD, University of Sheffield) is Chair of the Department of Politics and International Studies (PAIS) at the University of Warwick, Chair of the Faculty of Social Sciences, Professor of International Politics and Japanese Studies in PAIS, and a Research Associate at the Centre for the Study of Globalisation and Regionalisation. Previously, he was Research Associate in the Institute for Peace Science at Hiroshima University and is now an honorary Research Associate. From 2000 to 2001, Professor Hughes was Visiting Associate Professor and in 2006 held the *Asahi Shimbun* Visiting Chair of Mass Media and Politics in the Faculty of Law at the University of Tokyo. He also has been a Research Associate at the International Institute for Strategic Studies and a Visiting Scholar in the East Asia Institute at the Free University of Berlin. In 2009–10, he was the Edwin O. Reischauer Visiting Professor of Japanese Studies in the Department of Government at Harvard University and is currently an Associate in Research at Harvard's Reischauer Institute of Japanese Studies. He is also co-editor of the *Pacific Review*. Professor Hughes holds degrees from the Universities of Oxford (BA and MA), Rochester (MA), and Sheffield (MA and PhD), and has received research scholarships from the Japanese Ministry of Education, the Japan Foundation Endowment Committee, the European Union, the British Council, and the British Academy.

Roy Kamphausen is a Senior Associate for Political and Security Affairs at The National Bureau of Asian Research (NBR). He advises and contributes to NBR research programs on political and security issues in Asia. Mr. Kamphausen previously served as Senior Vice President for Political and Security Affairs and Director of NBR's Washington, D.C., office. Prior to joining NBR, Mr. Kamphausen served as a U.S. Army officer—a career that culminated in an assignment in the Office of the Secretary of Defense as Country Director for China-Taiwan-Mongolia Affairs and included prior postings as an analyst and China policy chief for three Chairmen of the Joint Chiefs, as well as two tours at the Defense Attaché Office of the U.S. embassy in China. Mr. Kamphausen has authored numerous works on China's People's Liberation Army (PLA) and co-edited the five most recent volumes on the PLA produced from the PLA Conference in Carlisle, Pennsylvania. He holds a BA in Political Science from Wheaton College and an MA in International Affairs from Columbia University and has studied Chinese at both the Defense Language Institute and Beijing's Capital Normal University.

Kevin Pollpeter is Deputy Director for the East Asia Program at Defense Group Inc. (DGI), where he specializes in Chinese national security issues with a focus on China's space program. Previously, he served in research positions at the Center for Nonproliferation Studies and the RAND Corporation. Mr. Pollpeter is the author or co-author of numerous works on Asian security issues, including *Entering the Dragon's Lair: Chinese Antiaccess Strategies and Their Implications for the United States* (2007), *The United States and Asia: Toward a New U.S. Strategy and Force Posture* (2001), and "Towards an Integrative C4ISR System: Informationization and Joint Operations in the People's Liberation Army," in *The PLA at Home and Abroad: Assessing the Operational Capabilities of China's Military* (2010). Mr. Pollpeter holds a BA in China Studies from Grinnell College and an MA in International Policy Studies from the Monterey Institute of International Studies, and possesses advanced Chinese language skills.

Arun Sahgal (PhD, University of Allahabad) is Joint Director of Net Assessment, Technology, and Simulation at the Institute of National Security Studies in New Delhi and Founding Director of the Indian Net Assessment Directorate, created to assess long-term strategy. Following a distinguished 36-year career in the Indian Army, he served as Head of the Centre for Strategic Studies and Simulation and Deputy Director of Research at the United Service Institution of India. He has also served as a Senior Fellow at the Institute for Defence Studies and Analyses. Brigadier Sahgal was a member of the National Task Force on Net Assessment and Simulation, under India's National Security Council, and continues to support the council through consultancy assignments. He has written extensively on Indian relations with China and Central Asia and conducted net-assessment studies on Pakistan, Myanmar, Sri Lanka, and the Asia-Pacific region. He recently completed two studies: *Antiaccess and Non Contact War: Doctrinal and Technological Perspectives and Regional Dynamics in the Asia-Pacific Region (2025)* with specific reference to *China's Influence in India's Extended Neighbourhood and Base Line Scenarios in the Time Frame 2027*, to coincide with India's Long-Term Integrated Perspective Plan.

Andrew Shearer is a Deputy Secretary in the Victorian Department of Premier and Cabinet in Australia. He was an adviser for the Center for Strategic and International Studies' independent assessment of U.S. force posture strategy in the Asia-Pacific region, published in August 2012, and was previously Director of Studies at the Lowy Institute for International Policy in Sydney. Mr. Shearer has served as foreign policy adviser to former prime minister John Howard, a senior diplomat in the Australian embassy in Washington, D.C., and strategic policy adviser to former defense minister Robert Hill. He has occupied various positions in Australia's Department of Foreign Affairs and Trade, the Department of the Prime Minister and Cabinet, and the Office of National Assessments. Mr. Shearer holds honors degrees in Arts and Law from the University of Melbourne and has an MPhil in International Relations from the University of Cambridge. He was awarded a Chevening Scholarship by the UK Foreign and Commonwealth Office.

Mark A. Stokes is the Executive Director of the Project 2049 Institute. A twenty-year U.S. Air Force veteran, Mr. Stokes served as Team Chief and Senior Country Director for the People's Republic of China, Taiwan, and Mongolia in the Office of the Assistant Secretary of Defense for International Security Affairs. He also was Assistant Air Attaché at the U.S. embassy in Beijing. Prior to co-founding Project 2049, he was Vice President and Taiwan Country Manager for Raytheon International. He has served as Executive Vice President of Laifu Trading Company, a subsidiary of the Rehfeldt Group; a Senior Associate at the Center for Strategic and International Studies; and a member of the Board of Governors of the American Chamber of Commerce in Taiwan. He holds a BA from Texas A&M University and graduate degrees in International Relations and Asian Studies from Boston University and the Naval Postgraduate School. He has working proficiency in Mandarin.

Travis Tanner is Senior Project Director at The National Bureau of Asian Research (NBR) and Director of NBR's Kenneth B. and Anne H.H. Pyle Center for Northeast Asian Studies. In these roles, Mr. Tanner creates and pursues business opportunities for NBR, determines significant and emerging issues in the field, manages project teams, and is responsible for the success of research initiatives. Prior to joining NBR, he was Deputy Director and Assistant Director of the Chinese Studies Program at the Nixon Center in Washington, D.C. He also worked as a Research Assistant at the Peterson Institute for International Economics. Mr. Tanner's interests and expertise include Northeast Asian regional security, China's economy and foreign affairs, and Taiwanese politics. His publications include *Strategic Asia 2011–12: Asia Responds to Its Rising Powers—China and India* (co-edited with Ashley J. Tellis and Jessica Keough, 2011), *Strategic Asia 2010–11: Asia's Rising Power and America's Continued Purpose* (co-edited with Ashley J. Tellis and Andrew Marble, 2010), *Strategic Asia 2009–10: Economic Meltdown and Geopolitical Stability* (co-edited with Ashley J. Tellis and Andrew Marble, 2009), *The People in the PLA: Recruitment, Training, and Education in China's Military* (co-edited with Roy D. Kamphausen and Andrew Scobell, 2008), and *Taiwan's Elections, Direct Flights, and China's Line in the Sand* (co-authored with David M. Lampton, 2005). Mr. Tanner holds an MA in International Relations from the Paul H. Nitze School of Advanced International Studies at the Johns Hopkins University.

Ashley J. Tellis (PhD, University of Chicago) is a Senior Associate at the Carnegie Endowment for International Peace, specializing in international security, defense, and Asian strategic issues. He is also Research Director of the Strategic Asia Program at The National Bureau of Asian Research (NBR) and co-editor of nine volumes in the annual series. While on assignment to the U.S. Department of State as Senior Adviser to the Undersecretary of State for Political Affairs (2005–8), Dr. Tellis was intimately involved in negotiating the civil nuclear agreement with India. Previously, he was commissioned into the Foreign Service and served as Senior Adviser to the Ambassador at the U.S. embassy in New Delhi. He also served on the National Security Council staff as Special Assistant to the President and Senior Director for Strategic Planning and Southwest Asia. Prior to his government service, Dr. Tellis was a Senior Policy Analyst at the RAND Corporation and Professor of Policy Analysis at the RAND Graduate School. He is the author of *India's Emerging Nuclear Posture* (2001) and co-author of *Interpreting China's Grand Strategy: Past, Present, and Future* (2000). His academic publications have also appeared in many edited volumes and journals.

About Strategic Asia

The **Strategic Asia Program** at The National Bureau of Asian Research (NBR) is a major ongoing research initiative that draws together top Asia studies specialists and international relations experts to assess the changing strategic environment in the Asia-Pacific. The program transcends traditional estimates of military balance by incorporating economic, political, and demographic data and by focusing on the strategies and perceptions that drive policy in the region. The program's integrated set of products and activities includes:

- an annual edited volume written by leading specialists
- an Executive Brief tailored for public- and private-sector decision-makers and strategic planners
- an online database that tracks key strategic indicators
- briefings and presentations for government, business, and academe that are designed to foster in-depth discussions revolving around major, relevant public-policy issues

Special briefings are held for key committees of Congress and the executive branch, other government agencies, and the intelligence community. The principal audiences for the program's research findings are the U.S. policymaking and research communities, the media, the business community, and academe.

The Strategic Asia Program's online database contains strategic indicators—economic, financial, military, technological, energy, political, and demographic—for 37 countries in the Asia-Pacific region.

To order a book or access the database, please visit the Strategic Asia website at http://www.nbr.org/strategicasia.

Previous Strategic Asia Volumes

Over the past twelve years this series has addressed how Asia is increasingly functioning as a zone of strategic interaction and contending with an uncertain balance of power.

Strategic Asia 2001–02: Power and Purpose established a baseline assessment for understanding the strategies and interactions of the major states within the region.

Strategic Asia 2002–03: Asian Aftershocks drew upon this baseline to analyze changes in these states' grand strategies and relationships in the aftermath of the September 11 terrorist attacks.

Strategic Asia 2003–04: Fragility and Crisis examined the fragile balance of power in Asia, drawing out the key domestic political and economic trends in Asian states supporting or undermining this tenuous equilibrium.

Strategic Asia 2004–05: Confronting Terrorism in the Pursuit of Power explored the effect of the U.S.-led war on terrorism on the strategic transformations underway in Asia.

Strategic Asia 2005–06: Military Modernization in an Era of Uncertainty appraised the progress of Asian military modernization programs.

Strategic Asia 2006–07: Trade, Interdependence, and Security addressed how changing trade relationships affect the balance of power and security in the region.

Strategic Asia 2007–08: Domestic Political Change and Grand Strategy examined internal and external drivers of grand strategy on Asian foreign policymaking.

Strategic Asia 2008–09: Challenges and Choices examined the impact of geopolitical developments on Asia's transformation over the previous eight years and assessed the major strategic choices on Asia facing the new U.S. president.

Strategic Asia 2009–10: Economic Meltdown and Geopolitical Stability analyzed the impact of the global economic crisis on key Asian states and explored the strategic implications for the United States.

Strategic Asia 2010–11: Asia's Rising Power and America's Continued Purpose provided a continent-wide net assessment of the core trends and issues affecting the region by examining Asia's performance in nine key functional areas.

Strategic Asia 2011–12: Asia Responds to Its Rising Powers—China and India explored how key Asian states and regions have responded to the rise of China and India, drawing implications for U.S. interests and leadership in the Asia-Pacific.

Research and Management Team

The Strategic Asia research team consists of leading international relations and security specialists from universities and research institutions across the United States and around the world. A new research team is selected each year. The research team for 2012 is led by Ashley J. Tellis (Carnegie Endowment for International Peace). Aaron Friedberg (Princeton University, and Strategic Asia's founding research director) and Richard Ellings (The National Bureau of Asian Research, and Strategic Asia's founding program director) continue to serve as senior advisors.

The Strategic Asia Program depends on a diverse base of funding from foundations, government, and corporations, supplemented by income from publication sales. Major support for the program in 2012 comes from the Lynde and Harry Bradley Foundation, the Smith Richardson Foundation, the General Electric Company, the Chevron Corporation, and the National Nuclear Security Administration at the U.S. Department of Energy.

Attribution

Readers of *Strategic Asia* and visitors to the Strategic Asia website may use data, charts, graphs, and quotes from these sources without requesting permission from NBR on the condition that they cite NBR and the appropriate primary source in any published work. No report, chapter, separate study, extensive text, or any other substantial part of the Strategic Asia Program's products may be reproduced without the written permission of NBR. To request permission, please write to:

NBR Publications
The National Bureau of Asian Research
1414 NE 42nd Street, Suite 300
Seattle, Washington 98105
publications@nbr.org

Index